Stefan Brunnhuber
The Economics of Transformation

Stefan Brunnhuber

The Economics of Transformation

——

A General Theory on Financing our Global Commons, on Money and a Sustainable Development for the 21st Century

DE GRUYTER

ISBN 978-3-11-142143-8
e-ISBN (PDF) 978-3-11-142152-0
e-ISBN (EPUB) 978-3-11-142208-4

Library of Congress Control Number: 2025931791

Bibliographic information published by the Deutsche Nationalbibliothek
The Deutsche Nationalbibliothek lists this publication in the Deutsche Nationalbibliografie;
detailed bibliographic data are available on the internet at http://dnb.dnb.de.

© 2025 Walter de Gruyter GmbH, Berlin/Boston, Genthiner Straße 13, 10785 Berlin
Cover image: MHall6520/iStock/Getty Images Plus
Typesetting: Integra Software Services Pvt. Ltd.

www.degruyter.com
Questions about General Product Safety Regulation:
productsafety@degruyterbrill.com

Author: Stefan Brunnhuber
Language editing: Andrew Godfrey-Collins
Figures and tables: Alistair Bell
References: Erik Fritzche

We cannot move on from old ideas
until we have alternatives
to replace them.
Updating J. M. Keynes for the 21st century
provides a very powerful new idea
that can replace outdated thinking.

I dedicate this book
to Garry Jacobs, President of the
World Academy of Art and Science (WAAS),
who has been extremely encouraging and supportive –
inspiring me not only to write this book,
but also to look for out-of-the-box solutions.

Contents

Preface

Our house is on fire and its foundations are collapsing. The situation requires us to set priorities, make rapid changes and undergo a major transition that will have a profound impact on everyone living in the house. That transition in turn requires a new kind of economics, which we might call an economics of transformation. One that is different from other economic approaches based on the standard condition of cyclical booms and busts, and demands different tools and a different perspective.

Let's imagine that the people living in the cellar of the burning house (standing in figuratively for private households, cooperatives, state agencies, the civil sector) decide to move up to the ground floor due to flooding. While the cellar was powered by fossil energy, the ground floor is meant to be switching to renewables, with more eco-friendly lifestyles and fairer distribution of resources for the people living there. However, at the same time the roof is on fire. To move from the cellar to the ground floor, we have to abandon fossil energy, create a new energy source, stamp out the fire on the roof, stabilise the foundations and avoid further collateral damage, all at the same time. And on top of that, nobody should be left behind. In a conventional, more siloed approach, we would tax the people in the cellar so we could put out the fire on the roof, ask philanthropists to donate money so we could repair the foundations, arrange a restructuring of our loans so we could give up fossil energy and work to attract private investment so we could build the new infrastructure needed for a new, more eco-friendly way of life. However, that approach is flawed, because it would mean simultaneously withdrawing purchasing power, time and resources from the cellar that are urgently needed to extinguish the fire, implementing changes on the ground floor and writing off the revenue of the cellar. We have to do better and recognise that a completely different strategy is needed to tackle the multifarious challenges ahead, under considerable time pressure and conditions of uncertainty. In this book, I explain the most effective and efficient way to do so. The transformation is directed towards an open future where we can never be 100% sure whether we are doing the right thing. But right from the outset we should avoid the common fallacy that economics and finance ought to be driving this transformation. It should be the other way round. It seems clear that we first need to listen to engineers, physicists, environmental scientists and social psychologists about how to address these challenges, prior to any economic decisions. At the same time, it also seems clear that a nursery should be run by an educational specialist, not an accountant, a hospital by the medical director, not the CFO, and a public nature reserve by rangers, not by institutional investors. Meaning sustainability should drive finance and not the other way round, as currently seems to be the case. At the moment, finance is driving sustainability and determining the course of any transformation. I will attempt to show how we can turn this approach around, and how finance can play a crucial, albeit secondary and instrumental role in the overall process.

https://doi.org/10.1515/9783111421520-203

Exploring the contribution of economics and finance to this process of transformation reveals that, until now, we were often looking in the rear-view mirror to explain the future and neglecting biophysical reality. In a general sense, economics and finance are about how to increase welfare, well-being and wealth in the face of scarcity of resources, time pressure and incomplete information. That means we have competing uses and alternatives, which gives rise to opportunity costs. Any decision-making is by and large determined by these costs, trade-offs between alternatives and underlying incentives.[1] Rigorous empirical studies, in-depth historical analysis and mathematical modelling can mainly provide us with information about the past. But we can then apply that information to the future.[2] Most of the information we gather through the framework of various economic schools of thought is valid and important, but cannot account for future risks and fails to understand economics as a complex network. Our native human mind mainly operates in the 'middle dimension' of metres and minutes and can only make linear and short-term decisions. We are simply incapable of grasping complexity and drawing significant conclusions from it. Taking a more comprehensive view of our reality requires a systems-thinking approach, supported by interdisciplinary findings and new emerging technologies that can help us to better understand and explain the economics of transformation, which is the topic of this book. Only by shifting our perspective can we identify the limits of our own (economic) thinking and start looking forward, so that we can discover and create the economic future that we want. Traditionally, economics is far less concerned with change or transformation, and more with allocating goods and services efficiently and profitably. In this sense, traditional economics is extremely efficient but not effective, as it remains agnostic regarding the goals and targets to be achieved.

In contrast, an 'economics of transformation' aspires to combine the efficiency and power of market allocation mechanisms with an effective transformation into a society characterised by sustainability, long-term thinking and fairer distribution. It also seeks to demonstrate that change or transition itself can provide an opportunity to improve the allocation of goods and services and generate revenue. But this well-known difference between effectiveness and efficiency is not enough to explain what makes an economics of transformation different. One of this book's main hypotheses is that the monetary and financial system itself predetermines the effectiveness and efficiency of the real economy of goods and services, across all value chains, trade agreements, investments and consumption patterns. The monetary system has the potential to be a great transformer. This book is therefore less concerned with the find-

---

1 Robbins 1935.

2 This is true of traditional Western schools (mercantilism and physiocrats), traditional Islamic and Chinese economics, (neo-)Marxism, (neo)classical economics, orthodox and heterodox positions, (neo-) Keynesianism, institutionalism, behavioural economics and neuroeconomics, rational choice theory, historical schools and the Austrian School, among others. All of them share the idea that historical data can provide sufficient information on how to assess risks and make rational decisions.

ings of the past, and more with managing the present so we can build a better future. And it is less concerned with single case studies, best practices and historical evidence, and more with attempting to formulate a comprehensive framework for the overall transformation. Any economics of transformation needs to not only describe the challenges but provide solutions to them. It is like in medical school, where we train doctors to understand and cure diseases. The titular 'general theory' is intended to be universal in the sense that it is applicable to most transitional processes. That means it should be agnostic about the goals we want to achieve. Even though the change from fossil to renewable energy is the most prominent goal at the beginning of the 21st century, the theory should also be applicable to other forms of radical transformation, such as the transition from a peace to a war economy or from an agricultural to a data-based one.

And so it is not surprising that most proposals for transforming our society are based on implementing new technologies, investing in R&D and education, advocating new forms of governance and population policies and demanding individual lifestyle changes, rather than directly addressing economics and finance. Each of these proposals has its appeal, but we appear to be constantly leaving out one parameter: the architecture of the international monetary system (IMS). This is crucial because all of the other areas listed above depend in some way or another on the design of the monetary system itself. I would argue that the most important lever for any economics of transformation lies in the financial architecture that underlies all political, social and economic activities. That is true in both democracies and autocracies, in open societies and failed states, in laissez-faire market systems and planned economies. Even terrorist groups, black-market actors and the entire informal sector use or misuse the monetary system in some way or other, or at least depend on it.

Let us delve a little deeper into this topic. Over the centuries, scholarly knowledge has become increasingly specialised. At the time of the Renaissance (1300–1600), there were just a few dozen disciplines. By the 20th century that number had risen to hundreds of disciplines and subdisciplines and now there are thousands. This compartmentalisation has expanded our knowledge tremendously, but at the same time detached it from reality, producing masses of statistically significant yet sometimes irrelevant information ('Do we really need this study?') that is disconnected from knowledge in other disciplines ('Do they actually know what is going on?'). And any further specialisation will risk us losing our perspective on the whole.[3] Each discipline has its own '*differentia specifica*', meaning a quality that cannot be reduced to or explained by any other discipline. This *differentia specifica* typically reflects and legitimates the beauty, truth and goodness the discipline offers us. That is true for fields as diverse as psychoneuroimmunology, quantum information science, multiscale living systems engineering, cognitive science, gender studies and public health. The findings

---

3 See also Karlqvist 1999.

from all these fields are needed for the transformation ahead. And that applies both to economics in general and financial economics in particular. The *differentia specifica* of financial economics is its unique ability to answer the question 'What is the cheapest of all worlds?'[4] under conditions of scarcity, time pressure and incomplete information. If we assume a future of political instability, economic volatility, scarcity, multiple trade-offs, opportunities and uncertainties – all of which affect the overall process of transformation – then by answering that question financial economics can make a distinctive and desperately needed contribution that no other discipline is capable of. That is the topic of this book.

---

4 I am alluding here to the philosophical argument from the 17th and 18th centuries that God can provide conditions for the 'best of all possible worlds' (Leibniz 1710).

Introduction

In response to the global economic crisis of the 1920s and 30s, the economist John Maynard Keynes wrote in his General Theory[5] about how markets are cyclical, unstable and incomplete, have 'sticky-down' wages[6] and tend to produce an equilibrium with intolerably high unemployment rates. In this context, economic actors tend to have a preference of liquidity: whenever an investment becomes too risky or the expected yield too low, the investor will hoard their share and withdraw the necessary liquidity from the market, so that the market equilibrium remains Pareto-inferior.

In essence, Keynes is describing a market failure inherent to the allocation mechanism itself. He calls for a wise external actor, namely the state, to increase its debt load and intervene in market activities in a counter-cyclical manner, hence preventing deflation and high unemployment. These state interventions compensate for market failures or, in some cases, the absence of markets. The 'global steering mechanism' described by Keynes is based on an effective aggregate demand (net income minus savings rate), which in consequence determines the relative prices of goods, the propensity to invest and the utilisation of human capital. Once the deflationary situation has been overcome, the state should clear its debts through increased tax revenue during the next boom period, and the economic cycle will come to an end. I will attempt to show that the postulate of national fiscal deficit spending only applies to a specific case, where nation states have the power and leverage to cope with domestic economic imbalances and shocks and imperfect substitution of production factors. However, it does not apply as a general law that can be used to understand the economics of transformation required in the 21st century. I will show that the challenges of the present require an updated version of this postulate, whereby monetary tools rather than fiscal ones play a dominant role in policymaking.

The situation in the 21st century is however similar in some respects to that of around 100 years ago. The 'stickiness' of wages is linked to the fact that basic human needs are inelastic, while the ecological realities of planetary boundaries, overshoots and backlashes are linked to 'sticky' biophysical laws that economics must adapt to rather than denying or ignoring. The preference of liquidity requires an adjustment,

---

5 Keynes 1936.
6 The idea that our thinking remains incomplete was shared by many thinkers in different disciplines at that time. For example, Gödel in formal logic, Heisenberg in physics and Freud in psychology. Like Keynes, they believed that fully understanding a system always requires variables external to that system. We need either a logical meta-level (Gödel), an alter ego/therapist (Freud), an observer of the experiment (Heisenberg) or a nation state (Keynes) to give us an objective perspective on a system. It may seem paradoxical at first glance, but our understanding of any closed system will remain incomplete unless we can grasp its complexity from an external position. We will explore these ideas later on with a view to better understanding market instability, state interventions and the role of monetary policy. See Brunnhuber 2019, note 66.

https://doi.org/10.1515/9783111421520-001

too: in the face of global asymmetric systemic shocks, private capital, despite its abundant availability, remains short-termist, pro-cyclical and risk-averse. Instead of investing in infrastructure and adaptation mechanisms, corporate money has been used for buybacks of stocks, or remains hoarded in cash accounts. And like in the 1920s and 30s, when liquidity was desperately needed to overcome mass unemployment, the money we need to finance our common future is not available. Though Keynes's core ideas are still valid, we need to update them for the 21st century. We now live in a new age when everything is interconnected with everything else, a world in which we have to live and operate within planetary boundaries, but have caused wide-ranging systemic damage to nature that is now coming back to bite us in many different ways. It is no longer simply a matter of national boom-and-bust cycles that come and go, but rather of systemic, asymmetric damage and shocks that have already occurred and will incur immense global costs in the foreseeable future. Seen through this lens, climate change, asymmetric wars, serial pandemics, biodiversity loss and water stress are not cyclical economic phenomena that nation states can cope with, but rather will remain global challenges for decades until they are solved. In short: what we are confronted with is not cyclical processes confined to national or regional level, but globally disruptive ones that require a different form of economic activity, different players and different fiscal and monetary policies. If we remain trapped in our traditional view of economics, we will end up in a tunnel – and the light at the end of that tunnel will most likely be a train approaching from the opposite direction, not the dawn of a new civilisation. In other words: we need an economics of transformation, where linearity is replaced by complex thinking.[7]

In the past, we could expect that negative spillovers would not cause significant costs or interrupt our day-to-day business, as they would cause damage elsewhere in the world instead. But the situation now is totally different. We will be forced to pay for the damage we have caused. Forced migration, regional droughts, massive plastic waste in the oceans, water stress, state failures and even simple demographic factors such as a growing global middle class with expectations of prosperity and well-being are just a few examples.

In this context, we can say that our human coexistence is undergoing a fundamental change of state – just as water exists in liquid, solid and gaseous forms and its molecules have different relationships with each other depending on the state of matter. Local cyclical processes will take a back seat and global disruptive ones will dictate events instead. New players are becoming more dominant. Nothing can be viewed in isolation any more, things can only be understood from a systemic perspective. Moreover, in this phase of transformation, most events and processes are hybrid in nature. That means they cannot be fully explained or predicted based on past data. Nor do they fully represent the future. Hybrids are always incomplete, fragile, fuzzy

---

7 Žižek 2022.

and transitory. They also lack the aesthetic qualities of proportionality and consistency. Nevertheless, they are important.

I will not attempt to summarise the entire reception of Keynes's work over the last 100 years, but will instead embark on a far more modest undertaking: namely, updating some of his groundbreaking ideas to the realities of the 21st century, in particular those concerning the role of the state, the instability of market activities, the preference of liquidity, the prominent role of aggregate demand and the difference between uncertainty and risk. To paraphrase Keynes himself, 'When the facts change, we should change our mind.'

This book will apply these updated Keynesian principles to the financing of our global common goods, an upgraded understanding of money and the role of sustainable development in general. As is well known, all change involves additional effort, energy and risks, and these in turn always involve economic costs. All change comes at a cost, and that is especially true for the upcoming processes of societal transformation we are facing. However, we should aim to keep that cost as low as possible for all of us. It may sound paradoxical: the economics of transformation does not primarily deal with climate issues, biodiversity loss, water stress, regional economies or reforestation programmes, but rather with the financial and economic conditions that must be in place to overcome all of these challenges. A given financial economist may also have personal opinions about, or proven expertise in, environmental science or social issues, but the academic discipline of financial economics should remain fundamentally agnostic when it comes to such topics. The economics of transformation should not be guided by ideological reasoning, academic schools, conflicting political agendas or mere habit. Our focus should be solely on the type of financial engineering, the shared risk profile, the time horizon and the regions where the liquidity can be spent most effectively and efficiently. No other discipline can provide a satisfactory answer to these questions. Neither philosophy, nor the history of economics, nor resource or environmental economics, nor psychology or any other subdiscipline of orthodox macroeconomics can adequately answer the question 'What is the cheapest of all worlds?'; only financial economics itself can do that.

A theory is *general* if its validity is not confined to single empirical and historical cases, but is more universal in scope. A general theory is characterised by its comprehensive and abstract nature, even if it still makes reference to historical results. A purely inductive approach based on individual cases would run the risk of circularity. Instead, I follow a first-principles approach[8] that is deductive and analytical rather than inductive and experimental, and seeks to develop the best ideas possible based on the inadequate empirical evidence currently available. Such an approach will ac-

---

8 While every empirical approach will remain circular, a first-principles approach will align with the rationale of any market economy. Market allocation will always allow the cheapest and most efficient solutions, and market participants will always choose the best price-to-value ratio. However, it remains to be shown how the market itself should be designed.

cept coherent sets of findings even if individual empirical case studies contradict them. This means we will not simply look at a specific historical case study, such as how to finance a public health system in sub-Saharan Africa or a nature reserve in Brazil, but instead seek to formulate general economic laws of transformation for the 21st century.

I define an *economic transformation* as any process where we introduce new rules of the game rather than optimising the old ones. In this sense, economics is not a historical discipline that analyses past events and identifies common features in order to better understand the present, but one that tries to explain 'how to get from A to B'. It needs to become trans-disciplinary and pragmatic, identifying tools to change the world and looking forward to the future. And only the economics of transformation can unlock the discipline's specific contribution, its '*differentia specifica*': namely, its ability to answer the question of the 'cheapest of all worlds'. Changing the rules of the game means showing the methods and measures needed to shift from one state of affairs to another. Accordingly, any economics of transformation will not simply involve reforming taxation schemes, providing additional funding and subsidies for renewables, increasing charitable donations and philanthropic giving (as noble as those things are), printing money or restructuring loans.

I further define *commons* as those goods and services that a society has agreed to make usable by and accessible to everyone, everywhere and on an equal basis. We can also talk about basic needs and planetary commons, and they can be distinguished economically from positional or luxury goods. This means that the very nature of a global commons is completely different from that of private goods, and so are the ways of adequately financing it. Something's status as a (global) commons is generally speaking not given by nature, but assigned by societies. Air, water, education, healthcare, the Internet, energy and food are not necessarily commons, but they can become commons. The identification and classification of a good or service as a commons is preceded by a society's decision to designate it as such. The opposite is true, too: societies also have the freedom to privatise all these things.

Money is understood in this book as a social mechanism. Besides education, it is probably the most powerful means humanity ever devised to coordinate, hedge, fund and manage our lives, our economy and our common future. The international monetary system (IMS) follows not natural laws but social agreements. It is not a neutral arbiter that simply measures the price of a good or service; rather, its design predetermines our decision-making, for good or ill. It also represents a global public good in its own right, through which ad hoc collaborations are replaced by fair, sustainable and predictable arrangements and incentives that benefit all of us. In this vein, I would like to further define *fiscal policy* as the use of instruments that seek to collect and redistribute money through taxation, fees or subsidies. We will look at how, in a general sense, all fiscal measures have four functions: a funding function to generate liquidity needed to manage public affairs; a steering function to allow a society and its agents to transition from harmful to less harmful ways of acting; a coherence function to correct unacceptable disparities in income and wealth that would threaten the stability of a society; and finally a control function to tackle the price of goods and services, with a particular focus on the consumer price index (CPI) and inflation. All this will be explained in more detail later on. By contrast to fiscal policy, I define *monetary policy* as the use of instruments involving the creation of money, the primary money supply of central banks and regulators (including international institutions such as the World Bank and International Monetary Fund (IMF) and the money creation process of public (and to some extent also commercial) banking systems, which mainly comprises multilateral development banks providing liquidity to the real economy through credit lines, grants and diverse financial assets. Finally, monetary policy has to deal with the different monetary channels through which the generated liquidity enters the real economy of goods and services. In a more general sense, I understand our IMS as a web without a weaver, with no superior agent involved. This further implies that from a statistical perspective, only relative figures and correlations, rather than absolute data, can contribute to a deeper understanding of any economics of transformation. All equations and formulas in this book try to take that into consideration.

I furthermore consider *development to be sustainable* only if it is committed to a long-term perspective and takes sufficient account of social and ecological externalities. Sustainability thus has an inclusive and a temporal component. It integrates and takes into account the entire world population, including both the Global North and Global South, and incorporates a longer time horizon into relevant financial and economic decisions that also considers people who have not yet been born. Sustainable development differs from mere growth in that it is not determined solely by quantitative parameters like GDP, but remains committed to qualitative and semi-quantitative parameters, including subjective well-being, welfare, quality of life, life expectancy, school enrolment rate and the state of the planetary ecosystem. In short: any sustainable development will remain fairly agnostic and undecided regarding quantitative parameters such as GDP unless these (semi-) quantitative and qualitative parameters are met.

In his seminal work, *The Structure of Scientific Revolutions*,[9] Thomas Kuhn argues that there are two phases of scientific activity. Firstly, phases of 'normal science', when experiments provide findings within the framework of existing and approved rules to solve concrete problems. These phases are like playing chess or Monopoly: the rules of the game are not questioned, and we accumulate knowledge and experiences as we move along and adapt within the bounds of those rules. The scientific community simply accepts the given scientific paradigm. Secondly, these phases of 'normal science' are disrupted by 'paradigm shifts', when methodologies, worldviews and the rules of the game are called into question. Paradigm shifts are triggered by new discoveries and findings and repeated anomalies which can no longer be accom-

---

9 See Kuhn 1962.

modated by the old paradigm. A shift in our mindset and *modus operandi* is required to cope with these new challenges and anomalies.[10] The Copernican shift and Darwin's theory of evolution are examples of such shifts. Keynes's theory of market activities is another. With specific regard to the topic of finance, the most prominent challenges and anomalies we are currently facing are the rise of systemic ecological shocks that individual nation states lack the capacity to deal with, new disruptive technologies (AI, synthetic biology, robotics, quantum computing) and unprecedented interdisciplinary empirical findings that fundamentally challenge the concept of '*Homo economicus*'. We need a deeper and revised vision of what should be designated as global commons, a monetary system that transcends conflicting political agendas and a more comprehensive understanding of sustainable development for all. At its core, an economics of transformation involves reconciling economics with ecology through a new and upgraded monetary system. The aim of this book is to demonstrate that an economic paradigm shift in Kuhn's sense is needed to make that possible. And that requires a change both in our way of thinking and in our way of doing things.

Modern, globalised competitive markets with an established, regulated and developed financial sector at their core are characterised by a consistent correlation between the return on capital (r)[11] and the economic growth rate (g). The return on capital is the risk premium or interest rate on invested financial resources, while economic growth is the increase in the value of goods and services during a defined period. The long-term correlation appears to be $r > g$.[12] If r were not greater than g, we would have to manage exorbitant increases in house prices, rents and associated negative social impacts. Savings and reinvestment would ultimately become unattractive, and short-term overconsumption and resource depletion would result in g tending to zero. Accordingly, the correlation $r > g$ represents a general and desirable rule

---

10 However, paradigm shifts do not occur in a linear fashion, with falsification of data or reinterpretation of existing findings determining the course of history. Rather, they are characterised by their non-linear, disruptive, unpredictable nature. A paradigm shift can be defined as a point in a society's development when two events must occur at the same time in order to fundamentally change the 'disciplinary matrix'. First, there must be a change in praxis and methodology – the rules of the game – that provides new information and insights; second, a new perspective on the world must emerge that is better able to integrate these new findings within a new methodology. In short, a paradigm shift forces us to start both acting and thinking differently.

11 r refers to the natural interest rate when an economy is neither contracting nor overheating and is not exposed to unforeseen shocks. See Holston et al. 2017; Waller 2024.

12 For the seminal expression of this idea, see Piketty 2014, 215–218. Piketty argues that the asymmetry of r and g is the root cause of income and wealth inequality, and that progressive taxation is needed to overcome this negative distributional impact. I will explain in the text that $r > g$ is neither necessary nor sufficient to explain inequality. Wage inequality, the consumption patterns of the 'rich' and the declining marginal productivity of capital are just as relevant. On the relevance of $r > g$ for income distribution, see also Piketty 2015; Piketty and Saez 2013.

of modern economics. But it poses us with a dilemma in times of disruptive shocks, when transforming our entire society becomes a priority. If an economy is growing by, let us say, 2% per year and is facing ecological shocks of, let us say, 3% of its GDP per year, the 3% could be offset by an anti-cyclical demand stimulus package. If we further assume that r is 5%, then repayment of these debts to capital owners through increased taxes, austerity cuts or savings would over time ultimately withdraw purchasing power and investment from the real economy in order to keep up with principal payments and the compound interest rate until the next business cycle starts. However, as I will show throughout this book, in the 21st century capitalism is not confronted just with cyclical phenomena but with a transformational process that transcends business cycles – thus creating a need for a new conditioned monetary supply aggregate rather than demand stimulus packages and giving regulators and central banks a key role in funding and hedging systemic risks and uncertainties in ways that go beyond domestic state interventions. In other words: utilising traditional fiscal measures to repay the increasing costs of serial systemic shocks will eventually cannibalise the required transformation process, as that money is desperately needed to fund, manage and hedge the transformation itself on the ground. That is true irrespective of whether the repayments are made directly to private capital owners or indirectly through a public entity that raises taxes. This is where the Keynesian dilemma of the 21st century becomes obvious above and beyond the uneven distributional effect of r on g. That is the dilemma we are all faced with right now, and which I will attempt to address in this book.

The general theory I outline in this book will attempt to take all these factors into account. I will show that this theory has the potential to contribute to the economic schools that influenced Keynes's work, or emerged in response to it, and update them for the 21st century. These include the physiocrats (Quesnay), the classical (Smith, Ricardo) and neoclassical (Walras) schools, the monetarists (Friedman), the Austrian School (Hayek), modern monetary theory (Kelton), historical national schools, neo-Marxism, institutionalism and behavioural (neuro-)economics. I will seek to reconcile these various theories but also to move beyond them. While all these sometimes conflicting economic schools provide an indispensable contribution in and of themselves, one common factor is that they all take the monetary system as a given and do not question its internal design and incentives. That holds them back from achieving the cheapest of all worlds.

While the main body of the text is aimed at a general readership, I also support my ideas with additional empirical and historical findings that are included in the footnotes. There are also boxes in the main text in which I share best practices and examples illustrating my general theory of an economics of transformation.

Finally, I hope readers will not be disappointed that this is not just another textbook on macroeconomics and monetary policy, but instead provides a foundation for multiple policy recommendations that over time will influence all the issues and topics that a traditional textbook would cover.

Part I: **Tomorrow Is Now**

A: The New Normal

The Role of Narrative and the Curse of the Self-Fulfilling Prophecy

What is humans' selection advantage? Walking upright, individual competitiveness, opposable thumbs, sophisticated tool use, emotional granularity and the capacities for compassion and abstract, analytical thinking are all distinctive human traits, but overall they are not specific enough and cannot explain our species' dominance on this planet. Almost all living beings possess some sort of cognition, emotion, memory and consciousness, and are able to adapt successfully to an adverse and changing environment. Many have the capacity to collaborate in large hierarchical cohorts, use tools and engage in labour specialisation.[13]

Humans' selection advantage is far more linked to our capacity to tell each other credible stories that we all believe in.[14] In most cases, these shared stories do not refer to the actual natural world around us, but to a cultural reality that we have created. It is precisely this shared belief in these fictional stories that enables humans to coordinate and collaborate on a large scale. These narratives are mainly about God, death, politics, law and money. Interestingly enough, the more expensive a narrative becomes over time, and hence the more victims it racks up, the more powerful and taboo it becomes too.[15] This apparent paradox is due to the fact that unless an alternative story is available, we are obliged to give all sacrifices and losses, all gains and victories, a sense of ultimate purpose. Human history has shown that it is better to have a false and incomplete story about the world than no story at all. Narratives, even when they are false, serve to stabilise both the individual psyche and our community as a whole. This paradox applies in particular to the stories we tell each other about money and finance. One of the powerful stories we tell each other in financial economics is that we need unlimited and unconditioned economic growth first, after which we can redistribute wealth and common goods. As long as we do not have an alternative story at hand, the mental frames will always prevail over historical facts, scientific evidence and biophysical laws. What, then, is the meta-narrative about finance and money that will give us a selection advantage as we face the challenges of the 21st century and help us to transform our society so we can build a better future?

---

13 See Rueffler et al. 2012.
14 See Harari 2014.
15 A taboo is a collective shadow relating to an event or entity that is not discussed and that a society is therefore not fully conscious of, but that still remains indirectly present and powerful. The four most prominent taboos in modern history are sex, power, death and money. Overcoming a taboo requires a preparedness for rigorous critical thinking, an expanded consciousness and a social agenda that allows us to integrate the shadow. In this book, I focus solely on the taboo of the monetary system.

https://doi.org/10.1515/9783111421520-002

Such a narrative needs to account for the specific human conditions of flawed mental frames, incomplete information, multiple timelines and uncertainties, tolerance for failure and openness to revision, and should be able to balance the opportunities and the obstacles, the problems and the potentials. It also needs to account for the way we manage our commons and offer a deeper understanding of economics under conditions of transformation. We might also hope this new narrative will substantially change investors' and companies' decisions, consumer behaviour and political agendas. It should be able to grasp incompleteness, fuzziness and hybrid states, and to tolerate ambiguities, ambivalences and paradoxes. And it should, finally, be able to make sense of adverse events, disruptive technologies and risks as well as opportunities, possibilities and subtle shifts in our mental baseline.[16] In the early 19th century, 90% of the world's population lived in poverty. By the start of the 21st century that figure had fallen below 10%. Life expectancy was less than 40 some 125 years ago, now it is over 80. Smallpox, which caused over 300 million deaths throughout the 20th century, has been eradicated. The average income of those in the most coveted industrial jobs in the 1950s and 60s was only a little more than the average income of a logistics worker today.[17] And 50 years ago the global illiteracy rate was over 80%; today, it has dropped to less than 20% and continues to fall. Child mortality, one of the most sensitive parameters of a functioning public healthcare sector, was 20% in 1960; by 1990 it had fallen to 10% and by around 2020 it was below 5%. All these positive stories are offset by well-documented negative ones, such as the increase in forced migration, water stress and biodiversity loss, serial pandemics and climate change impacts. If the negative narratives prevail over our consciousness, our storytelling and consequently our decision-making, we risk becoming pessimistic and disruptive, and not giving past achievements the respect they deserve. Conversely, if we allow the positive narrative to dominate, we risk being naive about the challenges and unforeseen events ahead. We seem to need a mix of both. Which of the two future narratives will prevail depends on the meta-narrative we tell ourselves. To sustain both narratives, the good and the ugly, a significant amount of what psychologists call *tolerance for ambiguity* is necessary. And in both cases, there is an untold message about the monetary system in place. If we choose the right story, we might usher in a new, second Enlightenment that enables us to critically rethink the role of finance and money; or a new, second Renaissance that helps us to reposition the

---

16 Our mental baseline has shifted over time: property rights, the ban on child labour, votes for minority groups, trade unions, gender equality, plant-based diets and the conferral of legal status to nature are all examples where we have become more sensitive to social and environmental issues. And this has gradually but steadily shifted the way we do business, allowing us to simultaneously increase wealth and improve health. The growth of a global middle class from 1.4 billion people in 2024 to over 4.9 billion by around 2050 will come with higher expectations of education, housing, mobility, health and public infrastructure. The downside is that we risk adapting to an ecological baseline where biodiversity loss becomes an 'extinction of experience' (Pyle 2003).

17 Norberg 2016.

human species as we face the emergence of new technologies and serial ecological shocks at the same time.[18] If we hold on to the false narrative, we will end up with a self-fulfilling prophecy where a story that has been repeated over and over again finally becomes a social reality in its own right. But the opposite is true, too: if we start applying the right narrative to help us understand the world around us, we will eventually create the social reality we intended to achieve. And we will see that the monetary system is one of the most important and powerful levers for this kind of new narrative, which has the potential to either reinforce or undermine an economics of transformation.[19]

The Anthropocene Era

Historically, we used to live in a large, slow and empty world with low population growth, low levels of energy and resource consumption, short life spans and low levels of public health and education.[20] Now we are living in a fast, full and complex world with high population density and high levels of energy and resource consumption, long life spans and high expectations of healthcare and education. Unlike the past, all economic activities in the 21st century are limited by planetary boundaries, and all economic activities are interconnected in real time. But even if interconnectedness and ecological limits are commonly acknowledged, we are now experiencing all the spillovers and backlashes associated with the economic activities we were engaging in until just recently. 95% of the planet's surface has been altered in some way or another by the human species – affecting the atmosphere, biosphere, lithosphere and hydrosphere. For the first time in history, humans are fundamentally changing the course of the planet through our use of land, global warming, biodiversity degradation, soil loss, nuclear armament, massive plastic waste and water stress. Even if we take human ingenuity to its maximum, there is no breaking free of the biosphere.[21] All economic activities remain embedded in natural life, with all its scarcity and resource constraints, and we as humans are inseparably part of this interplay. Variously invisible (soil), silent (plants) or mobile (animals), the regenerative properties of nature remain the foundation of all human activities. This is true of land use, pollution and waste as well as food production, health and coastal protection. And it fundamentally affects how we should do business and finance. The figure below (Figure 1) illustrates this.

---

18 On Enlightenment as a useful narrative see Pinker 2018, on sustainability and Enlightenment see Weizsäcker and Wijkman 2017.
19 On the mechanisms behind these self-fulfilling prophecy dynamics, when narratives and stories become influential, see Shiller 2019.
20 Rockström and Klum 2016; United Nations 2024.
21 Dasgupta 2021.

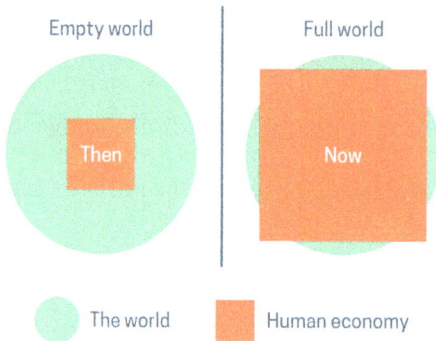

Figure 1: The full and empty worlds.

We call this era the Anthropocene, because it is the human species that needs to respect our planetary boundaries and real-time interconnectedness. It is also we humans who bear full responsibility for those things. And that requires a revised understanding of complexity, systemic uncertainties and risks. We need to rethink the traditional concept of *Homo economicus*[22] and the way we are positioning ourselves as humans in this new era. An autonomous, self-maximising agent will simply lose future opportunities and miss out on wins. Free-rider behaviour is irrational, as ultimately we end up harming ourselves. But we still lack the right financial engineering and the right monetary incentives and design to help us unlock the full potential in each of us[23] Instead, we are confronted with irreversible tipping points and major

---

[22] The traditional notion of *Homo economicus* understands people as autonomous individuals who try to maximise their self-interest, which (it is claimed) will ultimately maximise collective utility overall. Initially formulated by Adam Smith, this notion was further developed in the neoclassical school of economics, which claims that our behaviour is determined by each individual's diminishing marginal utility function. I believe this utility-maximising function still holds true for the 21st century, but operates within a completely different economic framework that makes it possible to simultaneously factor in negative externalities and common goods. I will further elaborate on that topic in the second part of the book.

[23] For as long as we could afford to think in isolated units, the naturalistic fallacy still held: *facts do not generate a moral imperative*. In the Anthropocene, this is no longer the case. We are now forced to reconcile our thinking and decision-making (the ethics) with reality (the facts). Facts imply normative statements. For example, if we observe a rise in global temperatures or a loss of biodiversity, we must make a normative judgement about whether it is good or bad. This point has significant implications for multiple disciplines: legal scholars, for example, need to clarify the liabilities between private and public goods and redefine responsibility for private property. In political science, we need to discuss new forms of local and global governance, their interconnectedness and ways to reconcile short and long-term incentives (this is sometimes referred to as regional biopolitics). In psychology, we need to better understand the things that will help us to transform our behaviour, the impact of irrational framings and how to cooperate more effectively. And economists need to learn to quantify and internalise externalities, to assess the extent to which the free market can be relied on to generate fair prices in light of uneven intra- and intergenerational patterns of distribution and to stratify risks and uncertainties.

feedback loops, and have to cope with unforeseen exponential accelerations and unexpected black swan events that profoundly affect our day-to-day activities.[24] That will also mean ongoing resource depletion, ecosystem degradation and unforeseen asymmetric shocks. And this will all unfold in a multipolar world, with conflicting political agendas and players, including new disruptive technologies that are changing the global terrain of finance and economics. The traditional concept of *Homo economicus* seems to be embedded in the wrong narrative for addressing the situation we find ourselves in. We are now in the driver's seat and do not have any blueprint available to set the course. We literally have to rethink almost everything: the way we do business and grow food; the way we educate our children and make political decisions; the way we eat, build houses and drive cars; the way we go on holiday, do science and organise our power grids. This sort of all-encompassing transformation does not come for free and that is where an economics of transformation comes in. Although this new terrain is challenging all academic disciplines and all facets of life, the main challenges it raises are economic and financial in nature. As we will see, the major cost components are not fixed or variable costs, but opportunity costs (i.e. costs associated with choosing one alternative over another).[25] This whole act of transformation has become a financial liability that we have to pay for and include in our budgets in one way or another. In other words: It is biophysical reality that determines price formation and hence economic decision-making, and not the other way round.[26] The situation is therefore fundamentally different from that in the 20th century.[27] The figure below (Figure 2) summarises the main features of this new era.

---

24 Taleb 2007.

25 Buchanan 2008.

26 Classical economists (Smith, Ricardo, Marx) identified labour as the primary source of value, while for neoclassicists (Walras, Jevons) it is subjective marginal costs. The Cobb–Douglas production function (1928) describes the relative contribution of each of these variables – labour (0.7) and capital (0.3) – to any economic output. Robert Solow (1957) identified an unexplained residuum of 0.875 in this equation. The lesson to learn from this 250-year history is that economics as an academic discipline has failed to consider resources, land and energy as a separate variable that is essential to explain productivity. Only in recent work (Georgescu-Roegen 1971 and 1979; Ayers 2016; Kümmel 2013; Keen et al. 2019) has it been shown that any economic output is primarily determined by the energy input available, discounted by the waste we produce and the resource depletion (land) we generate in order to create the economic output. I will explore this topic in more detail later on.

27 For more detail, see Crutzen 2002. The interconnectedness we are experiencing now in the Anthropocene era is similar to the ecology of mind first described in detail by Gregory Bateson (1972), who argues that it is only context that gives meaning. If there is no context, there can be no real meaning or understanding. Isolation and siloed thinking do not provide a deeper understanding of the world within and around us. That also applies to numbers. Take Robert Costanza's calculation that natural capital had a total value of 33 trillion USD in 1997, equal to global GDP at that point in time. The absolute number means nothing and adds no additional value. Relative changes in that number and its correlation to real GDP, however, make all the difference (Costanza et al. 1997).

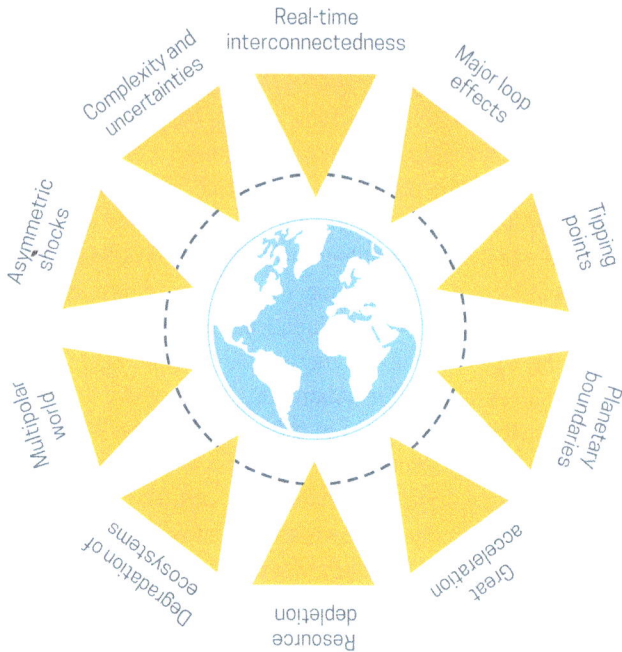

Figure 2: Features of the Anthropocene era.

Efficiency and Resilience Explained

The Anthropocene era began in the 1950s. It was preceded by the Holocene era, which began some 11,000 years ago. During that era, humans settled and began to force nature to adapt to them, contrary to all human history until then: for thousands of years, humans had adapted to nature, and those who were best able to adapt to ecological niches had a selection advantage. At every stage of the Industrial Revolution and beyond, from the invention of the steam engine in 1750 and the Haber–Bosch process in 1908, to Taylorist manufacturing,[28] to lean production, to the breakdown of the Bretton Woods system in 1971, the credo was to bring the idea of efficiency to every corner of this planet. After the fall of the Berlin Wall in 1989, the Washington Consensus of 1992[29] translated this idea into liberalisation, deregulation and privatisation of our entire economy, combined with

---

[28] On Taylorism, see Kanigel 2005.

[29] The Washington Consensus established the principles, procedures and institutions that would dominate the Chicago School-inspired neoliberal world order after the end of the Cold War. In particular, it redefined the roles of the IMF and World Bank. This order has eroded over the past three decades, as US power has declined while that of the BRICS+ and G20 countries has grown. See Williamson 2008.

a general austerity politics intended to cut public spending on public infrastructure, healthcare and education so that governments could meet their debt obligations. The goal was to make allocation of a society's resources more efficient.[30] Austerity policies sought to streamline all components of a system at any cost, to maximise its initial output and to optimise potential throughputs per unit of time. However, efficiency is just one part of the entire equation, not an end in itself. Focusing solely on efficiency will make any system more brittle, volatile and unstable.[31] Making a system both more robust and more sustainable at the same time requires additional resilience measures that precede, or at least run in tandem with, the efficiency ones. Resilience in general describes the capacity of a system to adapt and recover from shocks and to learn from failures.[32] The resilience of a system is measured by the amount of interconnectivity and diversity. It is interesting to note that over millions of years nature itself never selected for maximum efficiency and throughput rate, nor for mere resilience either, but for a sensible balance between the two, where the dominant factor was stability and longevity rather than volatility. Both variables, efficiency and resilience, are intertwined, constantly oscillating and seeking to regain a balance. I call the state that any viable and sustainable system aims for an 'anti-fragile zone' (AFZ).[33] In this zone, any open-flow network system remains in an equilibrium of longevity, stability and sustainability, where it is possible to learn from failure, readjust and adapt after adverse events and maintain the integrity of the overall system. The figure (Figure 3) illustrates this point.

The relation between efficiency and resilience is not a metaphor or analogy, but a kind of general natural law. Systems do not survive unless they factor in this interrelationship. That includes our ecosystem as a whole, which maximises throughput rate while also allowing adequate diversity. The Amazon rainforest is a prominent example. We can observe the same principle in aeroplane safety measures and in functioning

---

30 The IMF's structural adjustment rules (SARs), which call for reduction of fiscal imbalances, privatisation of public goods, trade liberalisation and free capital flows, are also considered elements of austerity policy. See also Williamson 1989.

31 There is a vast body of literature on this topic. Soaring unemployment and additional negative spillovers to the healthcare sector (increase in morbidity and mortality) are the most prominent short-term effects. Lack of public investment in infrastructure (healthcare, education, energy, etc.) and reduced future productivity and competitiveness are less obvious ones, which will leave society unprepared for future challenges over the long term. See Reinhart and Rogoff 2013.

32 Taleb 2012.

33 A system's resilience is enhanced by greater diversity and a higher number of pathways or greater connectivity, because these provide multiple channels of interaction to fall back on in times of crisis. However, these factors have the opposite effect on efficiency: as streamlining increases, connectivity and diversity decrease. Placing too much emphasis on efficiency sacrifices resilience. This sooner or later leads to systemic collapse. The opposite is true as well. If too much emphasis is put on resilience at the cost of efficiency, the system will not be viable either and will become stagnant. These points are of crucial relevance to the monetary field, especially in the face of increasing banking, currency and debt crises. I will explore this topic in more detail in Part II. See Brunnhuber 2023 and Brunnhuber and Lietaer 2005.

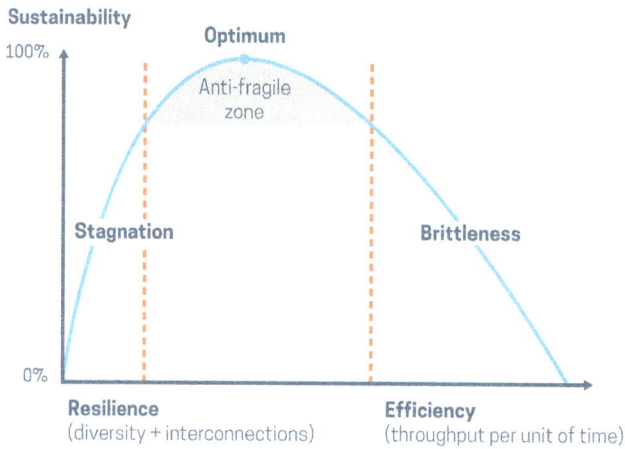

Figure 3: Efficiency and resilience explained.

power grids, and can see the negative effects of neglecting this interrelation in agricultural monoculture and in misguided investment strategies.

We will see in Part II that this also applies to any attempt to redesign and adjust the financial sector in the 21st century. Financial markets are generally considered to be efficient, self-regulating and decentralised systems that allocate goods and services through price signals, where demand and supply spontaneously converge over a defined period. They are regarded as one of the most efficient allocative mechanisms humans ever devised. And they represent probably the largest circular economic process ever invented. Demand on one side of the planet meets supply on the other trillions of times every day, based on a price signal and without much governmental regulation. However, these sorts of efficient markets are incomplete, unstable and volatile and require resilience measures to remain balanced. The shift towards efficiency rather than resilience has had three especially striking consequences. Firstly, an increase in banking, currency and debt crises. Between 1970 and 2019, there were over 150 banking crises, over 400 currency crises and over 200 sovereign crises across 200 or so different countries, including over 75 double and 21 triple crises.[34] The overall output losses and costs include fiscal costs, real economic output losses, growing public debt and non-performing loans reaching an average of 25% of GDP over a two to three-year period.[35] Secondly, the mismatch has become particularly marked in the global currency market, where up to 98% of the 6,000 trillion USD

---

[34] Laeven and Valencia 2023; Nguyen et al. 2022.

[35] Fiscal costs as a proportion of GDP range from 30% (Korea 1997) to 57% (Indonesia 1997), debt growth from 60% (Nigeria 1993) to 100% (Congo 1992), output losses from 98% (Ecuador 1982) to 140% (Congo 1982). The data further reveals that in emerging economies the fiscal costs compared with the overall financial system assets are twice as high as fiscal costs compared with GDP. This trend is reversed in developed countries, showing that a functional financial sector can play an important role in mitigating, adapting to and hedging future shocks (Laeven and Valencia 2012).

(including all assets) of daily currency trading is speculative and only 2% relates to real assets. Thirdly, there is evidence that the entire financial market has become dissociated from real economic activities over the last few decades, to date (2024) surpassing real GDP by a factor of four to five, all in the name of 'efficiency gains'. This inherent instability could be the result either of the inability to tackle and absorb real economic crises and stressors such as systemic pandemics, harvest defaults or mass forced migration, it could be due to a dysfunctional design or it could be a combination of the two. Even if we will never be able to satisfactorily settle this 'chicken and egg' dilemma and definitively say whether it is real economic activities or the financial sector itself that have caused the problems, or whether the latter just exacerbated the instability and losses, we must acknowledge that the financial sector is not acting as a neutral veil that simply reflects real economic activities. Taking a historical perspective, over the last 40 years we have witnessed more financial crises than in the previous 400 years.[36]

Living in a multipolar, highly interconnected world, we are confronted with ongoing, toxic, pro-cyclical chain reactions, which keep on deepening and prolonging crisis after crisis so that it becomes more and more expensive to repair the damage. We are heading towards a monetary non-system, where ad hoc decisions are determining our day-to-day business. This non-system is highly efficient, yet ongoing crises cost on average 25% of GDP in affected countries. So it seems fairly irrational to continue business as usual, where we simply apply and optimise the existing rules of the game and carry on as if there is no tomorrow. And even if we would prefer business-as-usual scenarios to having to make the big changes that are needed, we cannot deny that the existing system has become extraordinarily expensive for all of us. *We are now living in a new era, the Anthropocene. Can we afford to keep the current monetary system?*[37] Only if a monetary system is in an 'anti-fragile zone' will it not merely passively adapt to the environment, but instead perfect a systemic response to ongoing asymmetric shocks and defaults.[38] This means that any economics of transformation in general and any monetary and financial system in particular must be designed to be anti-fragile. As we can see in the figure below, the optimum point of the anti-fragile zone is slightly skewed towards resilience. This asymmetry demonstrates that resilience is more important to maintain the

---

36 Akgiray 2019.

37 Because we are wired to have a strong short-term memory, we quickly forget the pain of a shock. The stock market plummeted by 26 trillion USD between July 2007 and November 2008, equivalent to almost 50% of total world GDP; the rescue package for the banking sector amounted to five trillion USD, and an additional stimulus package of two trillion USD was needed for the same crisis. A decade later, the Covid pandemic caused an overall output loss of 13 trillion USD. This demonstrates that a system that is dissociated from the real world will cause self-induced collateral damage to that real world, incurring an intolerable cost (for the data see Sinn 2009, 86 ff).

38 On this view, social and ecological spillovers, often associated with competitive market activities, are not market failures as such, but rather due to the lack of a properly configured market. If we had an IMS that struck a balance between efficiency and resilience, we would be better able to cope with ecological crises and ongoing externalities. Part II will elaborate further on this topic.

system's integrity than the currently emphasised factors of efficiency and austerity. This has a significant impact on how to redesign any financial system. Remaining in the anti-fragile zone requires both efficiency *and* resilience measures. Any single investment, business project, consumption pattern or policy measure in the Anthropocene era needs to be situated within this zone, with resilience measures outweighing efficiency measures.

Box 1: The anti-fragile zone between efficiency and resilience

$$SS = SS(\varepsilon, \psi)$$

$$\varphi > \varepsilon$$

SS: sustainability, referring to the longevity of a complex system
ε: efficiency measures
ψ: resilience measures

However, there are fundamental flaws in our assessment of efficiency gains and resilience measures that we must remedy right from the outset. Both sides of the equation involve costs equal to income and gains somewhere along the value chain. Efficiency measures are predominant in climate change mitigation efforts, create revenue through increased productivity on the spot and are the domain of the private sector. Resilience measures, meanwhile, can be seen in efforts to adapt to climate change and reduce costs in the event that a hazard materialises. They are the domain of the public sector. The two sides follow a different calculation. If we invest in universal healthcare, there will be lots of jobs for nurses, doctors, administrators and technicians; if we invest in housing, shelter and a basic food supply for all, it will generate millions of jobs for farmers and construction companies; and if we clear up plastic waste in the oceans, it will create jobs and boost industries such as tourism. I will show in the following sections that if we provide the liquidity needed to address negative externalities, to restore planetary commons and public goods and to hedge systemic uncertainties in a different way than we currently do, we can generate additional revenue, social gains and profits through efficiency gains within a more functional competitive market. The return on investment for all of us will then be magnitudes higher than if we solely follow the efficiency pathway. This means that whenever we implement a measure to increase our efficiency, then at the same time we should implement several more to increase our resilience so that we remain within the anti-fragile zone. Both types of measure come at a cost, but can generate jobs and revenue. This mental exercise can help us to see that we humans are not external to nature but part of it, and that the entire economy should follow biophysical laws rather than the other way round. The figure (Figure 4) expands on these points and adapts them to the financial sector.

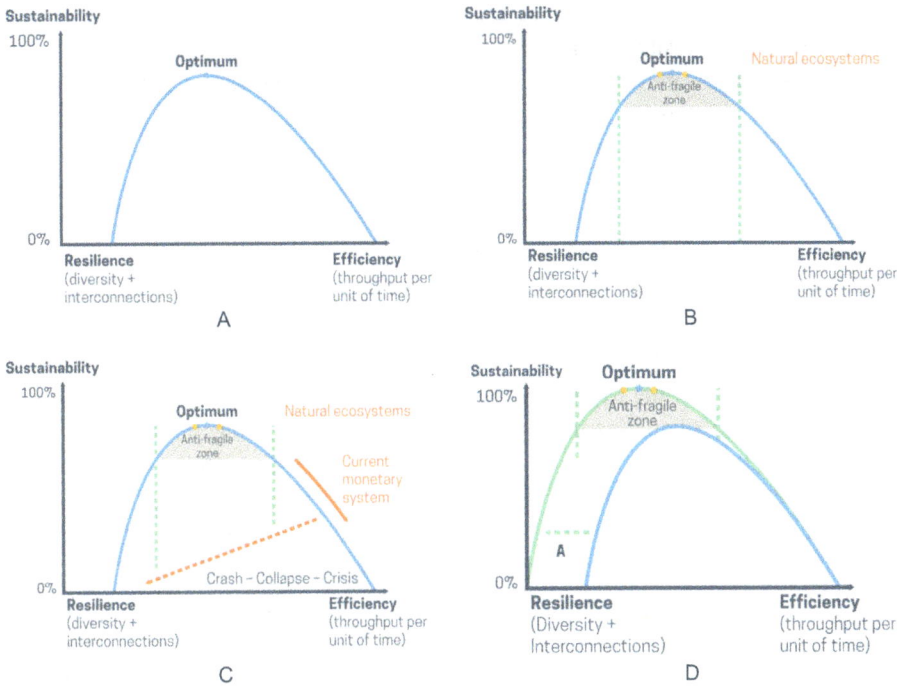

Figure 4: Resilience over efficiency.
The anti-fragile zone of an adjusted monetary system is larger and the level of sustainability (optimum) higher than in the standard scenario.

A: Any sustainable pathway must be charted between two complementary poles of resilience and efficiency. Resilience is accorded more relevance than efficiency and the curve is therefore steeper on that side of the graph, which explains its asymmetry.
B: In the real world, all natural ecosystems oscillate around an optimum within a range I refer to as the 'anti-fragile zone', where sustainability and longevity are maximised and overall costs for the entire system minimised.
C: Currently, our monetary system is on a path towards ever more efficiency. It has already overshot the anti-fragile zone, which will sooner or later lead to more instability, crashes or even collapse. This scenario, though cheaper in the short run, ends up being the most expensive overall.
D: An adjusted monetary system would not only move us towards the anti-fragile zone, but also make it possible to increase the overall longevity and sustainability of the system. That would result in a wider 'anti-fragile zone' and greater resilience at the same time, at the cost of making the financial system slightly less efficient.

We will see in the next sections that any economics of transformation in the 21st century requires more resilience rather than more efficiency. In the age of efficiency, the maximisation of private property claims, the building of hyper-specialised global value chains and the top-down quantification and mechanisation of processes predominate. But these efficiency approaches are blind to their positive self-reinforcement mechanisms, externalities and spillovers.[39] Things are changing as we enter an era of increased resilience,[40] with access and service taking priority over private property (shared economy), and linear global value chains being partly replaced by decentralised and regenerative regional networks (circular economy). In this age of resilience, we need to get used to hybrids between the private and public sectors, between nature and culture, between quantitative parameters (GDP) and qualitative measures of well-being. We will realise that while hyper-specialisation in a single niche increases efficiency, it is just one form of adaptation in an adverse environment. Creating buffer zones, stock surpluses and the ability to diversify and relocate value chains will decrease throughput but increase our resilience. Increasing the capacity to absorb future asymmetric shocks might mean excess healthcare capacities, increased product diversification and new buffers for vaccine allocations and production. It will also require us to adopt new hedging instruments with public–private partnerships, and to minimise transport use, population density, wildlife exposure and environmental burdens such as air pollution. Increased resilience would allow nature to fully heal, incentivise regenerative regional farming, disentangle global value chains and enable localised warehouse inventories. Such resilience strategies will further encourage new rules for the monetary system, providing additional, frontloaded liquidity that enables a better and faster response to future shocks and a reshaping of our individual behaviour: travelling more by public transport, eating less meat, favouring a more minimalist lifestyle. All these things will definitely reduce short-term efficiency and throughput, and they will certainly not come without a cost. But done the right way, resilience measures will generate millions of jobs, reduce spillovers and costly externalities, fund our global commons and unlock

---

39 William Stanley Jevons first described in 1865 the paradox that productivity gains will be counteracted by rebound effects that reduce the impact and benefit of technology-induced resource efficiency. Empirically, such rebound effects vary by up to 80%. Any increase in efficiency will either reduce the price of a good and so enable us to increase consumption of that good (price effect) or provide additional income, which is then spent on other goods or services, resulting in a similar negative rebound effect. The increased efficiency of combustion engines, for example, was used to allow people to either drive more or fly more. Either way, the initial benefits from resource efficiency were dramatically reduced. The opposite is true, too. Any increase in price (taxation) that reduces net income has incremental steering capacity if no alternative is in place. If we want to fly less and drive less while avoiding rebound effects, we need massive investment in public transport in parallel. The combination of technological efficiency gains, rebound effects and taxation needed for any economics of transformation requires an upgrade to the monetary sector, including additional liquidity assistance as described in Part II. On rebound effects see Santarius 2015.
40 Rifkin 2022.

the creativity of billions of people. Any economics of transformation must be able to take all those things into account. But before we start elaborating on the potential gains and opportunities, we first need to get a better understanding of economics in times of transformation by considering different forms of the unknown. That is the topic of the next section.

The Many Forms of the Unknown

Generally speaking, any hazards, risks and uncertainties have the potential to be adverse events that disrupt our daily routine; as such, they represent both potential losses associated with doing or avoiding something, and potential opportunities to do things better.[41] Although there will never be a zero-risk world, if – adopting a purely financial perspective – we were to imagine a world where all risks are (partly) hedged or prevented in the first place and we only invest in a green, inclusive common future, it would be no exaggeration to call that a world of (almost) net zero costs.

Human perception is limited to time and space and operates mainly in the 'middle dimension' of minutes, metres and kilograms. Our ego functions have a limited attention span of several seconds to several minutes. We have finite self-control and self-efficacy, and short, limited memory storage. Our decision-making is determined by linear thinking, which is unable to grasp exponential growth patterns or complexity. We favour short-termism over long-term benefits and prefer conformism – being part of the group – to sticking out. If the whole group is running in a circle we tend to follow, even though we know that we should move forward. Our minds are distorted by multiple cognitive frames that echo, mirror and partly deceive us about the inner and outer worlds. And these perceptions are predetermined by an individual and collective unconscious[42] that might override our day-to-day rational decision-making and make it even more flawed and biased, adaptive and self-deceptive at the same time, prone to constant failures. Even our grasp of probabilities and numbers is biased.[43] As soon as a problem becomes complex, we have to use heuristics to aid our decision-making or rely on educated best guesses, frames and biases, which can potentially distort our perceptions and decisions even more or be simply irrational. These overall cognitive preconditions determine the way we do business and assess associated risks.

---

41 Markowitz 1959; Fama and MacBeth 1973.
42 Jung 1968.
43 It was only in the 16th century that probability measures became available to most people as an aid for their day-to-day decision-making, and we still have a systemic bias that prevents us from fully adapting our rational decision-making using stochastic and statistical measures.

In this context, I would like to distinguish between four forms of the unknown.[44] Firstly, there are *unknown unknowns* – unexpected events we were not even aware of. Sudden terrorist attacks, wars or unforeseen earthquakes are examples.[45] Secondly, there are *uncertainties*. Uncertainties are intrinsic to any complex system. They are not fully tradable, resist having any precise price tag applied and are not fully amenable to statistical analysis and probability measures. Uncertainties never disappear and require an entirely different kind of assessment.[46] Negative collective externalities such as biodiversity loss, water stress, heatwaves, state failures or a sudden onset of mass forced migration are examples.[47] Thirdly, there are *risks*. The main hallmarks of a risk are that it can be quantified, has a specific statistical probability and is typically project-specific. A risk can be clearly defined by multiplying the probability of an expected event occurring by the magnitude of its impact on us. That means that building a hospital in Sweden could involve a different level of risk than building the same hospital in a sub-Saharan country. We are able to put a price tag on a risk and then start trading and hedging it. Once we have identified a risk as a risk, we can try to avoid it or we can choose to either cover or abandon the liabilities and responsibilities associated with it. So far we have been unable to put an adequate price tag on most physical risks affecting the real economy, or on the associated liabilities affecting the banking sector, or on the transition risk of shifting from a fossil-driven to a low-carbon system. The entire monetary system is simply not holistic and data-driven enough to provide a pathway that unlocks the trillions of private-sector liquidity needed to generate revenue, absorb systemic risks and fund and manage global commons, all at the same time. Finally, there are *hedged risks*. Hedged risks not only have a price tag, but are managed and traded on a competitive financial market. The derivative and swap market, with its staggering volume and numerous financial as-

---

44 Fama and MacBeth 1973. Recall also Donald Rumsfeld's words from 12 February 2002: 'There are known knowns; there are things we know we know. We also know there are known unknowns; that is to say we know there are some things we do not know. But there are also unknown unknowns – the ones we don't know we don't know.'

45 See the Global Risks Report by the World Economic Forum (2024).

46 The vast majority of potential events we are facing in the near future have the character of uncertainties rather than risks. Hedging, funding and managing these uncertainties will require a different strategy, emphasising (1) resilience measures over maximising efficiency throughputs; (2) preventive measures over managing damage; (3) collective and public endeavours over individualised, private action; (4) modular and systemic thinking over linear and cause-and-effect processing; (5) simple heuristic rules of thumb over endless checklists and historical data series; (6) the use of new technologies (predictive AI and big data analysis) over Excel spreadsheets that give us an illusory sense of control over such uncertainties.

47 Applying the Lucas argument (Lucas 1976) that no economic intervention can be predicted using historical data from a period when the intervention did not yet exist, we should be careful in our assessment of future shocks. If we take the expected costs of climate change at 5% of global GDP, biodiversity loss at another 1.5 trillion USD and the costs of the last pandemic at over 15 trillion USD, we will get a sense of the magnitude of what we are facing.

sets, is an example. The following table (Table 1) summarises the four forms of the unknown. Only the last of them can be wholly dealt with by the private sector. The first three instead manifest as *negative collective externalities* and require a collective effort involving public–private partnerships.

Table 1: The four forms of the unknown.

	Characteristics	Examples
Unknown unknowns	Unexpected and unforeseen events	War, terror attack, asteroid impact
Uncertainties	Can be labelled and described, but not assigned a probability	Climate change, water stress, forced migration, state failure
Risks	Quantifiable with a price tag and a probability	Currency, interest rate and project risks
Hedged risks	Traded and collateralised on the market	ABSs, CDOs, derivatives, hedging instruments

Note: ABSs: asset-backed securities; CDOs: collateral debt obligations

If we have to live with increasing uncertainties and unhedged risks, we may be forced to realise that we cannot foresee or anticipate our entire future, and will have to come up with prudent, failure-tolerant preventive measures that reduce the potential costs associated with them. And once we have identified and differentiated these different forms of the unknown, we can then decide how to manage them.[48] The more uncertainties we are confronted with, the more we need an altered mindset,[49] new technologies and an upgraded monetary system to enable us to face these new realities. While predictive AI algorithms and big data correlations cannot eliminate unknown unknowns and uncertainties, they can help transform unknown unknowns into uncertainties and uncertainties into risks. This will allow us to put a price tag on identified risks, so that we can start hedging and trading them accordingly and find competitive private market solutions for them. The reverse is true, too. The more unhedged uncertainties we are exposed to, the more we need different financial engineering tools to absorb, hedge, fund and manage them; this can be done by public or

---

48 This creates a vicious circle: inherent uncertainty in the financial sector translates into inherent instability in the political and corporate sector, which further translates into fear and irrational choices that can be measured in rises on volatility indexes in the stock, bond and currency markets. Major signs of this inherent uncertainty include the shadow banking system (worth 200 trillion USD in 2023), the short-term repo market, soaring private debt, high-frequency trading and the multiple and fuzzy reuse of collaterals (rehypothecations). For further data see also Wullweber 2020.

49 One of the most promising approaches is the Inner Development Goals (IDGs) project, which emphasises the need to develop a mindset that goes beyond mere technological or rule fixes.

collective bodies in collaboration with the private sector. And such planetary uncertainties are manifold by their very nature. Some major elements of unhedged uncertainties affecting the financial sector are summarised in the table below (Table 2).

Table 2: General elements of unhedged uncertainties.

Asymmetric	Uncertainties affect us all in an asymmetric manner. Some are hit harder than others
Non-cyclical	Uncertainties manifest in the social and natural realms. They must either be fixed ex post or prevented before they occur
Means to an end	The monetary system and financial sector can provide financial instruments to better hedge uncertainties, but cannot eliminate them. Only the real economy, civil society and political agendas can do so
Beyond private means	Uncertainties cannot be covered solely by private households, companies, commercial banks, private insurers, investors or individual states
Interconnected	Uncertainties are interlinked, causing tipping points, backlashes and overshoots in a non-linear way with fat-tail events
Different timelines	Uncertainties manifest along different timelines. In the short term, they take the form of force majeure (e.g. earthquakes, wars, state failures, social upheavals)
Complex polycrisis	In the long run, uncertainties manifest as a complex polycrisis (global warming, biodiversity loss, serial pandemics, forced migration)
Cumulative	Uncertainties come on top of all the well-known general risks that each society has to cope with (unemployment, health crises, bankruptcies, economic downturns)

These unknowns never disappear, but remain a constitutive factor of any complex system and require an entirely different assessment. They are often the canary in the coalmine, giving the first indication of a looming threat. As we will see in the next sections, outcomes in complex, non-linear systems[50] are unpredictable and not wholly determined by inputs.[51] Attempting to reduce complexity, for example by increasing transparency, introducing a new taxonomy or simplifying processes through extended regulation, is of little use and will be expensive in hindsight. Even after such measures are taken, a system will remain complex and indeterminate. We cannot push the reset button on complex operations and start over, because everything will

---

[50] Whereas reductionism tries to dissect, catalogue and analyse components to explain outcomes, complex systems are sensitive to the history of their own initial conditions. A dynamic characterised by open networking, multiple intermediary hierarchies, feedback loops and self-organising components will move beyond static equilibrium and lead to the emergence of new, unpredictable structures. See Šlaus 2020.

[51] Bifurcations, attractors, critical thresholds and fractals with scale-independent isomorphisms shape and modify the ongoing process. Attempting to reduce complexity, for example by increasing transparency or by simplifying processes through control or coercion, is of little use. See Mandelbrot 1977; Mainzer 1997.

be different the second time round. While most social events and systems may be perceived as merely complicated,[52] they are first and foremost complex. They are multi-factorial and do not allow for any simple cause–effect explanations (causal chains). The intermediate results of any complex system therefore cannot be fully anticipated, as that system will have emergent properties. Applying this insight to the financial sector highlights the need to address systemic uncertainties, which requires a completely different toolset.[53]

Take the derivatives market. Three decades ago, derivatives were the new kids on the block. In an unstable economic environment, it was rational for investors to buy first, second or third-tier derivatives to reduce the risk of failure. This 'hot potato' could simply be handed over to someone else, and at the end someone always paid the bill – usually the taxpayer. As long as a risk remains a local or sectoral phenomenon, it seems to be rational to invest in derivatives in order to hedge microeconomic hazards. This reasoning is fundamentally changing in the Anthropocene era, transforming the entire playing field. The greater our planetary interconnectedness becomes, the more we are operating within biophysical boundaries, and the more that systemic risks and uncertainties are becoming manifest, the less that derivatives are the rational choice to fully leverage and hedge a project. If a well-intentioned investor, let us say the Vatican, tries to switch its fossil assets to green ones, it will simply clear its own balance sheet. The global risks in the real world will not change at all, because the initial fossil investment (e.g. a coalmine using intensive child labour) is still polluting the air and harming children, as the asset is now being managed by a different institution that might be even less ethical and competent than the one previously contracted by the Vatican. This nimbyist approach, where derivatives are 'hot potatoes' that constantly get passed on, has little to no positive ecological and social impact. In an increasingly unstable, non-linear and complex world, we need completely different financial tools. One example is swap lines, which allow us to end unhealthy and unfair practices and exit fossil investments as fast as possible in order to keep the associated costs for all of us as low as possible. I will explore the role of these alternative forms of financial engineering for financing transformational processes in more detail in Part II of this book. In the meantime we can take this argument one step

---

52 'Complicated' refers to a state of affairs where we have to learn, follow and apply a specific protocol in order to achieve a specific goal. Manufacturing a watch, undergoing a neurosurgical procedure or flying a plane are complicated but achievable, rather than complex.

53 Humans have become pretty competent at managing day-to-day risk through increased step-to-step regulation. But risks often build up and create unprecedented amplifiers. In most cases we cannot observe the entire scope of the risk directly and in advance. If markets perceive a risk as too high, they will reduce the capital flow and investment will slow down in the coming years. If they perceive a risk as low, the opposite will happen. This means that markets act pro-cyclically. Besides these endogenous risk amplifiers, there are exogenous risks (wars, state failures), which further increase overall risk. A rational regulator is forced to choose between three forms of regulation: stability, efficiency and uniformity. This is a trilemma, where only two of the three can be picked. See Danielsson 2022.

further by differentiating between six levels of risks and uncertainties, as visualised by the inverse risk pyramid in the figure below (Figure 5).

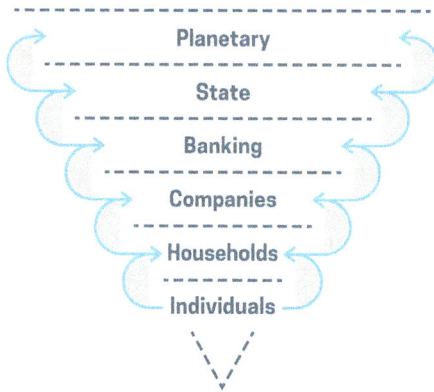

Figure 5: The inverse risk pyramid.

The six levels of the pyramid are as follows. At the bottom, there are individual risks and uncertainties, such as those associated with a sedentary lifestyle, which should be borne (at least to some extent) by individuals themselves. At the next level up there are private households, which might have to pay increased premiums for home insurance because they live in a flood zone. At the third and fourth levels respectively, companies face project risks and regulatory reforms, and banks the risk of potential credit defaults. One level above that, the public sector is confronted with state debts, currency risks, insufficient infrastructure, social upheavals and wars. Finally, at a planetary level we are facing issues such as biodiversity loss, climate change impacts, global pandemics and systemic waste disposal. Each time the risk profile changes, so too does the associated responsibility.

This can further help us to distinguish between private versus public and project versus planetary risks.[54] Though systemic and planetary risks run through the entire inverse pyramid, the higher up we go the more systemic risks manifest and the less able we are to deal with them as individuals. The closer a risk or uncertainty comes to being classified as planetary in scope, the higher the negative collective externalities will be and the more we will need new and different monetary, fiscal and financial tools (securitisation). And, finally, the more systemic a risk is, the more it will become a public asset rather than a private one, and the more that public law will prevail over private law.

---

54 Planetary risks can be calculated using the planetary boundaries approach (see Richardson et al. 2023) or the global catastrophic risk approach (see Bostrom 2008). An integration of both approaches can be found in Baum and Handoh 2014.

The Worm's-Eye and Helicopter Views

Our native human mind is not made to fully grasp complexity and longevity. Humans remain fundamentally risk-averse. Capital mobilisation on the international capital market and the activities of private savers, investors and companies all operate with a 'worm's-eye view' of risks and uncertainties. One common feature is that they all try to avoid perceived risks, even when the associated hazard is objectively small, and prefer a myopic, short-sighted view. Research in social and clinical psychology over the past three decades has found that we frame risks and benefits totally differently. Potential gains are systematically overrated, while potential harms, losses and risks are underrated. However, people prefer relatively safe assets and short-term revenue over riskier, less safe assets with the potential for higher revenue.[55] As none of us know the exact systemic risks we are facing, from our worm's-eye view we tend to underestimate individual risks. Whether we are confronted with currency risks, state failures, legal prosecutions, changes in taxation schemes or even expropriation, each time the investor will know the real risk only ex post. This leaves us as a community with an unsettled systemic uncertainty that society as a whole has to manage. That requires collective effort to shoulder the associated uncertainties using forms of blended finance, where the public sector or institutions of the IMS cover and hedge some of these unknowns. Instead of seeing things from a micro perspective, we therefore need to adopt a macro perspective where we can see the big picture. It is like the relation between water and fish. Fish see water as a given and never question their situation. But we as humans are capable of stepping out of the water, analysing it and deciding to change it, if we wish.

This gap between micro and macro perspectives is a fundamental one that will always persist, but humans have the mental capacity to bridge it.[56] It may sound paradoxical, but from a financial perspective, unhedged or inadequately hedged uncertainties and risks translate into real net costs. Investing in a public good such as a nursery does not create real net costs, as it has a positive return on investment. The real net costs that lie ahead are therefore not investments in a sustainable future, such as installing solar panels on our roofs or building hospitals, sewage systems and nurseries, as these will all generate additional green jobs, profits and revenue in one way or another, but rather the costs associated with getting rid of unhealthy habits and investments, or sim-

---

55 For the *locus classicus*, see Kahneman and Tversky 1979. These patterns can be explained by loss aversion (Schmidt and Zank 2005; see also McDermott et al. 2008) or psychological inertia (Gal 2006).

56 This is the micro–macro fallacy, which is well known in economics. While behavioural finance, rational and public choice theory, experimental findings and game theory are able to explain individual traits and preferences as well as behavioural trends in homogeneous groups and cohorts, this does not apply to the macro level. Modern societies are heterogeneous and do not follow a simple Gaussian distribution. In the section on fractal finance, we will look at how we need completely new tools to grasp the emerging complexity associated with the macro level. See Johnson 2010, Buchanan 2013 and Byrne and Callaghan 2023.

ply avoiding investing in our future. If science tells us that an increase of 1 °C is associated with a sea level rise of 2.1 metres and a 2 °C increase with significant harvest defaults, droughts and mass migration, and epidemiologists tell us that the probability of another pandemic is close to 100% even though we do not know the exact date it will happen, we need to learn to adapt our economy to these biophysical imperatives and change the associated narratives accordingly. In short: today's harmful activities will become tomorrow's risks and then future costs, which in turn will translate into even more risks and costs. To put it another way: real costs arise not from the dams (or other infrastructure) we build, but from the cultural and economic losses of not having built more dams. The real costs for a society arise from not having enough time to adapt to the next pandemic, not from vaccinating the entire global population. Unless we follow the logic of an economics of transformation, everything will be more expensive.

If we further elaborate on this topic from a financial perspective, we will end up with three forms of risks. Firstly, physical risks, which relate to the costs associated with extreme weather, rising temperatures, air pollution and sea levels, biodiversity loss and serial pandemics. Secondly, transitional risks are associated with output losses, the shift towards a low-carbon economy and insurers' and institutional investors' liabilities due to stranded assets. This category also includes currency risks and additional premiums for capital in transitioning economies. Thirdly, political risks, where the transformation translates into asymmetric or civil wars, failed states, electoral gains for extremist parties and extreme income and wealth inequalities that further destabilise nations. This category also includes expropriation, sovereign debt crises that impede public and private investments, massive capital outflows due to underdevelopment of local financial markets and a lack of safe, investable assets. All three forms of risks overlap, reinforce each other and prevent progress towards a risk-adjusted, sustainable long-term future. But they only translate into real net costs if they materialise. Collectively, they can be categorised as transformation risks that we face at each level of the inverse risk pyramid, as illustrated in the figure below (Figure 6).

It is not obvious at first glance, but if we can come up with new and upgraded financial and monetary engineering tools to adequately address physical, political and transitional risks, we would end up in the most efficient and most effective world. And this would eventually affirm the initial claim that any economics of transformation needs to provide an argument for the 'cheapest of all worlds'.

Box 2: Marginal risk premiums and costs

$\delta Tc = \delta py + \delta po + \delta tr$

δTc: costs/risk premium of transformation
δpy: physical costs and associated risks
δpo: political costs and associated risks
δtr: transitional costs and associated risks

Physical risks

- Pandemics
- Loss of biodiversity
- Climate change
- Air pollution
- Soil degradation

Transitional risks

- Output losses
- Disaster management
- Stranded assets
- Shift towards low-carbon economy
- Shift towards regenerative farming

Political risks

- Failed states
- Asymmetric wars
- Destabilised democracies
- Electoral gains for extremist parties

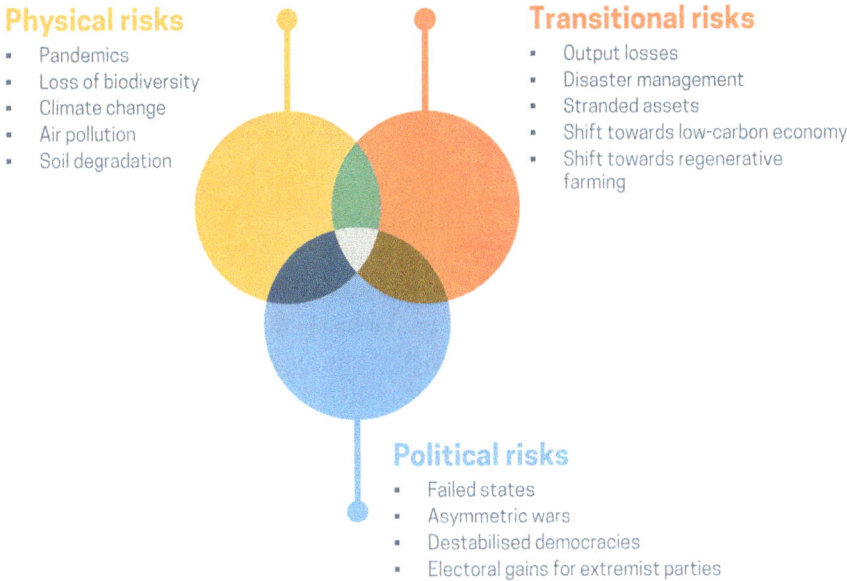

Figure 6: Transformation risks.

The marginal risk premium for expected physical, political and transitional risks, collectively referred to as transformation risks, translate into and manifest as additional costs for present economic activities and output only if they cannot be hedged, managed, avoided or prevented in the first place. Assuming an ideal-typical world, where we aim to minimise risks, uncertainties and externalities, we would end up with an almost zero-cost scenario. That is why investing in a green future does not necessarily incur additional costs, as this green future will generate its own profits, revenue and taxes.

Two Forms of Crisis

As we face a complex, non-linear future, economics allows us to distinguish between two forms of crisis. (A) Traditional boom-and-bust cycles, where investments, interest rates and employment oscillate within an expected growth trajectory towards an optimum equilibrium. This includes short-term anti-cyclical interventions to counteract temporary imbalances as well as systemic instabilities such as market failures, asymmetric information and the emergence of oligopolies and new technologies, which enable 'creative disruption' that creates opportunities for new companies.[57] Even hedging, speculation and hyper-speculation in the financial market could be considered part of this kind of cyclical agenda.[58] Such crises require serial measures; historical longitudinal data can help us to better understand, predict and intervene appropriately in the future. But there is a second form of crisis: (B) external asymmetric shocks, such as wars, state failures, pandemics and natural disasters, add further disruption on top of the first kind of crisis. A long-term 'market fix' requires not just anti-cyclical fiscal and monetary interventions, but a reset of the very rules of the game. Facing up to climate change, biodiversity loss and serial pandemics forces us to realise that there will be shocks ahead that cannot be characterised solely as market failures, but are instead attributable to the lack of any appropriate competitive market in place to address liabilities and negative collective externalities and to hedge and fund associated systemic risks. The unique situation in the Anthropocene era[59] and its associated costs will force us to rethink and realise that there are crises which are not cyclical, but instead disruptive and transformative in terms of speed and scale. This second type of crisis therefore cannot be addressed solely by applying traditional measures in succession and analysing historical data, as these crises involve an exponential, non-linear process that exceeds current growth trajectories, as well as unprecedented spillovers and changes to the entire energy system underlying the real economy. Instead of looking at longitudinal measures, we need to consider proxy data generated by big data correlations, which allows a step-by-step, case-by-case approach.[60] Since we are in this second type of crisis, the monetary and fiscal rules of the game need to change fundamentally, and the IMS has to take that into consideration if it wants to address these challenges. It should be noted that the term 'crisis' is somewhat misleading. It comes from the medical field and refers to a patient in a critical condition, who will either die or else recover and then continue their life as usual. Expecting that sort of getting-back-to-business-as-usual scenario would be an irrational and inadequate response to the asymmetric shocks of the Anthropocene era, if our aim is to build back better. Instead of using the crisis narrative, we need to approach matters from a different angle. At the moment, we are literally shifting

---

57 Academic approaches as varied as marginal value theory, neoclassicism and neo-Keynesianism, Milton Friedman's monetarism, rational choice theory and the theories of Schumpeter and Minsky remain committed in some way or other to the cyclicality of economic activities and do not question the existing monetary architecture itself.

58 *Hedging* (debt repayment is covered by expected yields), *speculation* (expected revenue exceeds repayments under a business-as-usual scenario, including the opposite of full or partial losses) and *hyper-speculation* (where a single event in the future, e.g. an interest rate rise, determines the entire business model; profits are privatised and losses are taken over by the state, creating a moral-hazard scenario) remain within the boom-and-bust cyclicality of any endogenous market activity; see Minsky 1986.

59 See Crutzen and Stoermer 2000 and Zalasiewicz et al. 2010.

60 Brunnhuber 2024, 2023, 2024a.

from one way of organising our society to another. And this new state of societal orga-nisation can represent either an upwards shift towards more freedom, fairness, sus-tainability, resilience and peace or a downwards one towards devolution, war, disas-ter and destruction. Both societal progression and regression are possible and both would involve an adjusted IMS. Within the range of type A crises, changes occur within the given set of conditions. The existing rules of the game are still valid and we can apply, adapt and optimise them. But we are not in a type A crisis, but a type B one. That means traditional approaches have become ineffective, and might lead us down the wrong path with costly results. A type B crisis involves a shift in the state of societal aggregation itself, which requires different tools and new rules to manage.[61] I call this a 'Keynes 2.0 moment':

Box 3: The 'Keynes 2.0 moment'
In the face of multiple ecological crises, competitive markets are not only systemically unstable, short-termist and volatile by their very nature, requiring fiscal interventions, but force us to think outside the box to implement new rules of the game, with the design of the monetary system itself becoming key. In this Keynes 2.0 moment, monetary tools are far more important than fiscal interventions.

Under the current set of rules, we are still trying to anticipate cyclical booms and busts using longitudinal historical data, and failing to see that we are confronted with a fundamental change in our societal state of being. It is rather like the different states that water will assume in different conditions – solid, liquid or gaseous. If we apply this metaphor to our current state of affairs, we will see that the challenge is not so much to reinvent everything from scratch, but rather to upgrade and rearrange the existing components more wisely. It is a little like the shift from wax candles to electric bulbs, from horses to cars or from a peace to a war economy. But shifting towards a war economy seems to be far less radical than the shift we are facing right now. A war economy remains within the existing paradigm: building tanks and train-ing soldiers, instead of building schools and training nurses. The transformation we are witnessing in the 2020s involves the entire value chain, including the ways we produce energy, do business, feed ourselves, build houses, educate our children and manage social ills. Analogously, the use of candles did not really contribute to the de-velopment of an electrical power grid, just as the horse-drawn carriage did not lead to the invention of cars. Both power grids and cars required fundamentally different ways of thinking and acting. And both inventions involved transforming our entire society. This is true now, as we face the shift from a fossil-driven economy towards a low-carbon, low-waste, circular, regenerative and socially inclusive one. We need to change the rules of the game. The figure below (Figure 7) illustrates this general socie-tal shift, where the financial sector takes a prominent role.

---

61 Laszlo 2001.

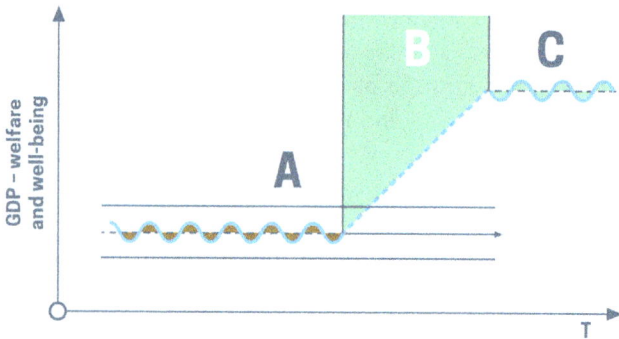

Figure 7: Altered states of societal organization.
The arrow represents a business-as-usual scenario, where we risk ending up in a tunnel rather than a transformational process.

A represents the well-known traditional boom-and-bust cycles. Transfer payment systems like fees and taxes can help us to navigate, balance and steer the economy. Large negative collective externalities are economically insignificant, sectoral risks can be hedged through derivatives, business as usual prevails and the existing rules of the game remain in place.

B is the transition we are in right now, which I refer to as the 'window of opportunity', 'monetary corridor' or 'Keynes 2.0 moment'. I will explain in the next sections how this transition requires us to mobilise about eight to ten times more liquidity than usual, as negative externalities and the funding of global common goods have to be factored in. The entire process remains non-linear and greatly depends on a functioning bio-ecosystem being in place. New hybrids and unorthodox financial engineering instruments are becoming more prominent. Within this transition phase, we require an additional monetary aggregate, which will eventually complement traditional fiscal policy. As a rule of thumb: if an event or market sector generates externalities that far exceed the growth corridor of a given economy, monetary policy needs to take precedence over fiscal policy. We need to recognise that the era of cyclical booms and busts is over. The challenges we are facing in scenario B will not go away until they are solved. And we are in the middle of the S-curve.

C represents the new equilibrium we are heading for once the transition is complete, with a low-carbon economy, a more inclusive social framework, regenerative farming, more circular and regional trading systems and intact nature reserves. From a financial perspective, we will return to business as usual.

The monetary system is not a panacea, and financial economics is at best a marginal academic discipline. But within this 'window of opportunity', they have crucial roles to play. Given that over 50% of our global GDP is very strongly linked to natural resources and another 10–20% is fairly strongly linked, an intact ecosystem is a precondition to enable the transformation. Without phosphorus, there would be no food for eight billion people, without copper no electricity, without wood no paper and without oil no polymers. And without biodiversity there would be no pollination and consequently no ecosystems. We cannot simply expect science to provide us with new elements from outside the periodic table. Which means there is very little scope for technological substitutes that free us from these interdependencies. Nevertheless, the monetary system, which is fully dependent on and embedded in the biophysical reality around us, can represent a powerful leverager and catalyst within this small window of opportunity, for as long as this biophysical reality – biodiversity, climate, water, soil – is still reasonably intact. During this phase of transition, economics and ecology are proving to be not opposites but complements. And it is true that the entire ecosystem does not need the human species to survive. We may be forced to learn that natural resources need to have a price tag and that someone has to cover the bill. If we refuse the price tag, we will just end up having to pay a much higher price in future – while the value of those resources will dwindle to zero. Any economics of transformation will need to move past traditional dichotomies like economy versus ecology, private versus public, consumption versus investment. And the monetary system is key to achieving that. In other words: there can be no functioning competitive market without a healthy planet. And there cannot be an intact planet in the 21st century inhabited by over eight billion people without a functioning market system that allows us to prevent disasters, restore nature and address social externalities. There are two conclusions to draw from the preceding points. Firstly, the longer we wait, the more expensive it will be. Secondly, if we destroy our ecosystem, the opportunity to create a financial system capable of transforming our society will be lost.

On Externalities, Cost and Damage Functions and the Secondary Preventive Approach in Finance

Arthur Cecil Pigou was one of the first economists in modern times to recognise the relevance of externalities and the unaccounted ecological costs of the damage humans are causing to nature. He proposed internalising these costs through a tax.[62] There are several approaches to estimating the environmental costs of human activities.[63] Firstly, the 'willingness to pay' approach. People are asked how much they are prepared to pay for an intact ecosystem.[64] Then there is the 'resource value' approach, which empha-

---

62 Pigou 1932.

63 Bainbridge 2023.

64 Willingness-to-pay analyses are highly sensitive to timelines. Representative studies covering over 90% of the world population found, on a global average, a discount of up to three million USD if a person is prepared to postpone a present benefit to 20 years from now. This is a major reason why cost–benefit analyses of future externalities can be vanishingly small (Falk et al. 2018).

sises natural resources as a form of capital and calculates their past, present and future value for human activities.[65] In a 'damage–cost' approach, we estimate all the costs we are facing now and in the far future that are caused by those externalities, irrespective of any changes in productivity or technological gains. An 'avoidance or replacement cost' approach focuses on the costs necessary to prevent or eliminate a hazard. I would like to elaborate on this last approach, as it can further clarify the role of market allocation in avoiding, triggering and internalising unaccounted costs. It is based on an understanding that market activities are not necessarily the primary cause of externalities. Forced migration, massive ocean waste or soil loss can be attributed not to market failures, but rather to the absence of a proper set of rules for a functioning marketplace. That implies that if we had chosen the right regulatory framework or market design, with the right configuration of ownership responsibilities, risk assessments, guidelines for internal accounting and fiscal and monetary policy incentives, such negative externalities could have been prevented or at least significantly reduced, the power of market allocation for goods and services would not have been diminished and price signals would reflect the actual costs involved. In short, an intrinsic market failure does not always imply the absence of a market. Take child labour: if there were no market in place at all, children would risk being exploited even more. Or take the water supply as a common good. If we refused to put a price tag on it, we would overexploit it more than if we had a price signal in the first place. But unlike the past, externalities in the Anthropocene era no longer come with a free ticket. Acid rain, sulphur emissions, industrial discharges, air pollution, CO_2 emissions, massive plastic waste and food waste are creating backlashes and feedback loops that increase the bill for all of us. And these externalities loop back in an uncontrolled, uneven, random manner. It is like a game of Russian roulette, where we don't know who is going to be unlucky and when it will happen.

From a financial perspective, I would therefore like to further distinguish between five forms of negative social and ecological externalities. *First-order externalities* are spillovers within a given growth trajectory of boom-and-bust cycles. Clear causes and effects are identifiable, and the private sector is meant to internalise these costs and will be penalised if it does not. These spillovers are unintended side effects of market activities. They are supposed to be contained by the market and controlled and compensated for by prices, and will gradually shift income and wealth towards a repair and damage management economy. Planned obsolescence of manufactured goods, side effects of drugs or cars with safety belts are examples. *Second-order externalities* also

---

65 This involves adjusted GDP measures. There are plenty of relevant initiatives, some focusing on specific resources, others with a broader scope. Influential examples of the latter include the Economics of Ecosystems and Biodiversity (TEEB 2010), the System of Environmental Economic Accounting (SEEA; see United Nations 2014) and the ecosystem goods and services approach (Millennium Ecosystem Assessment 2005). For an overview and methodological discussion, see Freeman et al. 2014 and Tietenberg and Lewis 2018.

occur within a given growth trajectory, but the associated costs are too high for the private sector to bear. In this case, public co-transfer payments on a domestic level and additional regulation are required. Ecological spillovers such as damage to the ozone layer caused by CFCs or the effects of an earthquake are examples. Then there are *third-order externalities*, which occur when negative collective externalities reach a scale that goes beyond standard boom-and-bust cycles.[66] Such externalities can take a unidirectional form, where one unaccountable actor harms all of us. The expected hazard for the private sector is too great and domestic public action is needed, such as state guarantees (if the damage has been caused already) or extended regulation. One example is when toxic substances are disposed of in a river, causing multiple harms to the genetic make-up of future generations. Taxation schemes and taxonomies designed to internalise these kinds of systemic shocks would not be efficient enough by themselves. Then there are *fourth-order externalities*, which take a reciprocal but unaccountable form, such that we mutually cause harm to each other – for example, through biodiversity loss or global warming. In these cases, we cannot fully disentangle our respective responsibilities. These kinds of negative collective externalities occur, for instance, if a fossil energy extractor supplies oil to a company, which then produces goods and provides services based on oil derivatives, which are then purchased by consumers worldwide. This creates a 'diffusion of responsibility', where we end up constantly passing on the hot potato to someone else. Taxing and suing each other along the value chain becomes less effective and efficient as the externalities reach a scale that cannot be managed and internalised by conventional fiscal and monetary tools without harming the entire economy. In the present decade of the 21st century, we are also confronted with *fifth-order externalities* or what we might call 'technological externalities'. The dawn of new general-purpose technologies (in particular AI, synthetic biology, robotics and quantum computing) are adding an additional layer of perils and pressures, possibilities and promises to any economic and political process, which will eventually translate into additional unaccountable costs.[67] Such unintended consequences include cyberwars, deep fakes, a breakdown in trust, job losses and global risk cascades. The new general-purpose technologies could therefore potentially amplify the uncertainty and fragility of any complex system, compound and diffuse risks and lower the threshold for a planetary cascade to occur, which would translate into additional costs for all of us. The public and private sectors need to take collective responsibility for the fourth and fifth-order externalities, including regulatory containment and a prioritisation of monetary policy over fiscal policy. In Part II, I will present a more detailed argument for why these externalities require an entirely different financial strategy. The table below (Table 3) summarises the five different forms of externalities.

---

66 If we put a price on the GHG emissions from transport, farming and ecosystem degradation, we would end up with a bill of over 20 to 30 trillion USD annually (Force for Good (F4G) 2022, 105).
67 See Suleyman 2023.

Table 3: The five forms of externalities.

	Forms of externalities	Characteristics	Examples
First order	Spillovers within a given growth trajectory	Clear causes and effects, negative impacts are internalised and penalised	Side effects of an opioid prescription or planned obsolescence
Second order	Spillovers within a given growth trajectory	Public co-transfer payments and additional regulation required	Ozone layer depletion due to CFCs
Third order	Cost and damage functions surpassing the growth trajectory systemic shocks	Private defaults, domestic public action needed	Pandemics, extreme weather, harvest defaults
Fourth order	Cost and damage functions surpassing the growth trajectory, negative collective externalities	Collective public–private responsibility, monetary policy takes precedence over fiscal policy	Biodiversity loss, climate change impacts, plastic waste in oceans
Fifth order	Cost and damage functions surpassing the growth trajectory, technological externalities	Collective global regulatory containment, monetary policy takes precedence over fiscal policy	Cyber wars, deep fakes, misstrust, jobs being replaced, global risk cascades, surveillance

If we do not distinguish between these five forms of externalities and simply follow the existing rules – applying taxes, fees or further regulation to the hazards through extended taxonomies – we might end up in a situation where the private sector avoids making further investments in R&D, and where cherry-picking and a tendency towards oligopolies become the order of the day. In other words: we need a new play-book for the financial sector that adequately recognises these externalities and translates them into a scenario that enables the 'cheapest of all possible worlds'. We can refer here to an argument the philosopher John Rawls formulated some 50 years ago. His 'veil of uncertainty' thought experiment[68] forces us to ask: *what society are we prepared to live in and what set of rules are we prepared to approve if we do not know the final socioeconomic costs and distribution patterns in advance?* If we are rational agents, we will only agree to a set of rules under which the least privileged will also benefit from any general economic developments, social inclusion is guaranteed and the ecological preconditions for everyone to live a decent standard of life are supported. Translating that argument into the 21st century requires a kind of Rawls 2.0: *what set of rules would we agree on if we acknowledge that, firstly, all activities on the planet are interconnected in real time, secondly, that there will be massive negative externalities ahead but, thirdly, we remain ignorant of the extent to which they will affect*

---

68 Rawls 1971.

us? In such a world, there are not only moral and intellectual reasons to address feed-back loops, backlashes and negative collective externalities, but also political and economic ones. Hardly anybody on this planet would agree, behind a veil of ignorance, to a set of rules where negative spillovers can affect us without there being a functioning community we can rely on to appropriately manage, fund and hedge them. It therefore seems irrational, deficient and even lethal to rely solely on a single problem-solving strategy: the utility-maximising function of the individual *Homo economicus* has internalised the entire systemic damage and cost function and incorporated collective efforts to overcome the constraints that individuals operate under. Rawls's *Theory of Justice* (1971) does not explicitly mention the role of finance and money, but it does implicitly force us to consider a new set of rules that will allow the monetary system to face all these challenges.

Systemic Cost and Damage Functions

In the Anthropocene, everything is connected to everything else. We are no longer living in a Newtonian world where we can isolate and externalise our risks and associated costs. The main cost category today is not fixed or overhead costs, variable costs, sunk or irrecoverable costs, marginal costs, operating costs or direct costs, but what are known as opportunity costs:[69] the cost of choosing one alternative rather than another. Opportunity costs reflect the value of what we are prepared to give up in order to gain something else. They represent the unmet needs and unchecked risks of projects we did not carry out because we decided to put our money somewhere else. If we decide to go to war, we might have to stop installing solar panels. Other traditional forms of costs are not entirely irrelevant but they are of subordinate importance, and all businesses and all societies have opportunity costs whether they are aware of it or not. Opportunity costs do not go away, but feed back and rebound onto our balance sheets as additional indirect costs, variable costs or similar. Tracking and managing these opportunity costs becomes key in the age of transformation. They are not only theoretical or hypothetical costs, but real, indirect ones: we pay the price for clean water twice, first at the tap and then second through the additional taxes required to clean up dirty water. And we pay for our lunch first at the restaurant and second through taxes to cover the costs of managing the food waste that results from our failure to properly coordinate the food value chain. There are at least six main potential cost and damage functions we should consider. They are shown in the figure below (Figure 8).

A represents spillovers that remain within the growth trajectory (e.g. a single, isolated harvest default). *B* represents repetitive spike waves with no recovery (e.g. serial global pandemics or ongoing biodiversity losses that necessitate increased damage

---

69 Buchanan 2008.

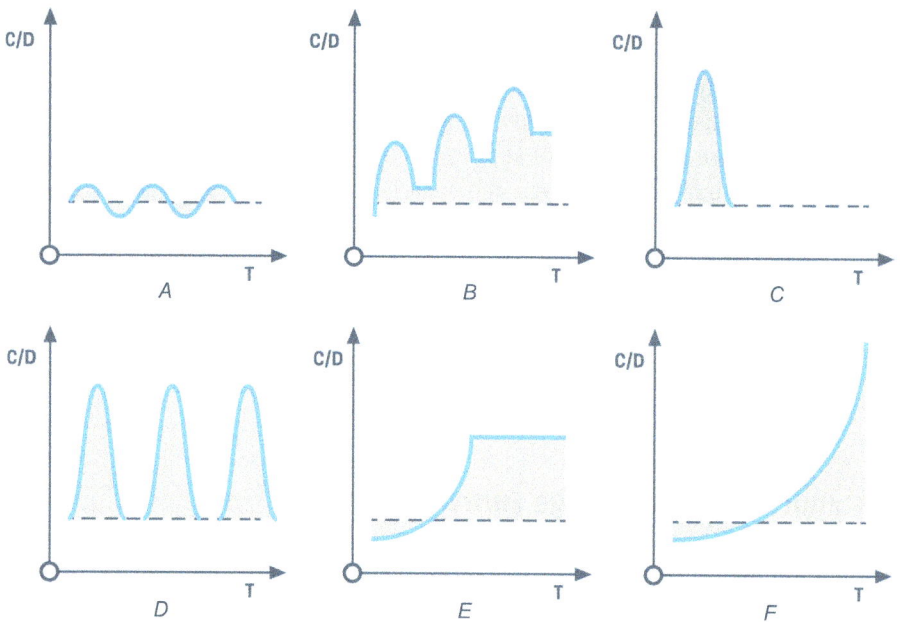

Figure 8: Six main cost and damage functions.
C: costs; D: damage; the dashed line represents an average growth trajectory

control). *C* represents an event with a single spike wave followed by full recovery (e.g. a flood). *D* comprises multiple spike waves followed by full recovery (e.g. heatwaves, multiple harvest defaults). *E* is a 'shock step' with costs over a long time span (e.g. building a dam in response to a sea level rise of five metres). Type *F* cost and damage functions are logarithmic explosions, where we risk losing control of the externality (e.g. massive plastic waste in the oceans). It should be noted that all the cost and damage functions far exceed the current growth trajectory. For any economics of transformation, it is of fundamental significance that we have caused the damage already. Most, if not all, of these externalities are not cyclical phenomena that come and go with the usual booms and busts, but will persist until we have solved them. The cost and damage functions B–F exceed the average growth pathway, meaning (1) that it will be impossible to neglect and ignore the costs ahead and (2) that any business-as-usual scenario will become extremely expensive.

Box 4: Total cost analysis (TCA)
Total cost analysis (TCA): If we broaden our view of all the costs associated with our economic activities, we will see and take account of all expenditures upstream and downstream along the entire value chain. At the petrol station, we pay around 1.50 USD for a litre of petrol to fuel our fossil-powered transport. That price is not accurate because it does not reflect the full costs of road accidents and climate change impacts. These costs are covered by society at large, regardless of whether we drive cars or not. The actual cost of that litre of petrol is more than twice the amount we pay at the pump.

The same goes for the costs of industrial farming, opioid epidemics, plastic use and heavy industry (steel, cement, aluminium). A TCA reveals that we need to transition away from a global value chain and towards more circular and regional value chains that are less expensive and reflect the fact that there are regions on this planet where lower material throughput is vital.[70]

If we look more closely at the associated costs that lie ahead, we can identify a multi-tier cost structure that runs throughout the entire transformation: the costs of the shocks and negative externalities *and* the costs of political and economic measures to prevent or adapt to (potential) shocks. Both add up and are intertwined: the more costs there are on one side, the less there potentially are on the other. In addition, the costs involved occur at different stages along a timeline and are unequally distributed.

Both costs can be further broken down into direct and indirect costs of shocks and externalities on the one side and the costs to the economy for adaptation and mitigation on the other. The indirect costs of shocks and externalities and the costs of adaptation and mitigation far exceed the costs of prevention. From a financial perspective, there will always be a mix of all types of costs. None of them will entirely disappear. However, the total volume of the costs may vary substantially, according to the political measures we take. We can take this argument one step further: externalities and shocks translate into both direct loss and damage costs and more indirect costs, such as opportunity costs from not having invested in other areas like education or healthcare. Adaptation costs relate to additional measures required to cope with expected shocks in the future, like building dams and greywater recycling systems or introducing a public guarantee for harvest defaults. Mitigation costs, finally, are the costs of preventing future damage from occurring. They include investments in positive externalities, such as new technologies, research, education, preventive healthcare measures and nature-based solutions. An ideal world where there are no relevant risks and no shocks, and therefore no adaptation and mitigation costs, would not come for free either. But the only costs we would then have to bear would be the costs of preventing shocks and avoiding future negative externalities. The figures below (Figure 9) illustrate this.

These cost and damage functions cause repetitive, amplified and delayed responses that we all end up having to pay the price for. However, the wiser our choice of assets, and the more quickly we respond, the cheaper the entire bill will be. Instead of internalising the costs ex post and ad hoc and relying on technological substitution only, we should consider taking a more preventive approach. As each of these measures generates jobs and profits, but reallocates resources in a less efficient manner, we need to introduce a 'secondary preventive' approach in finance.

---

70 High-income countries use six times more materials per capita and are responsible for ten times more climate impacts per capita than low-income countries. See UN Environment Programme 2024.

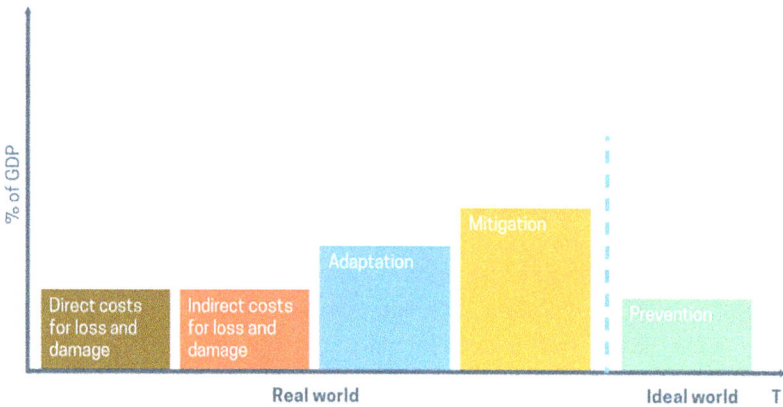

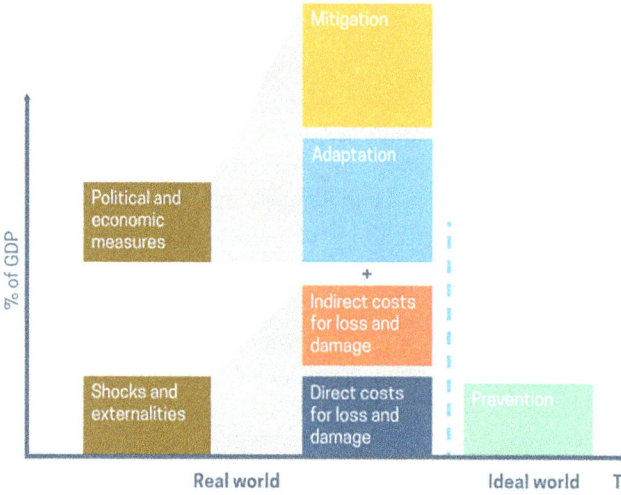

Figure 9: The tragedy of the horizon of scope and time: the multi-tier cost components.
Figure (a) above refers to the costs along a timeline. Figure (b) illustrates that the cost components add up. In an ideal world, only preventive measures would be needed.

The Case of Prevention in Finance

There are endless striking correlations and a vast body of empirical evidence demonstrating that prevention pays off. But while preventive approaches are well established in medicine and public health, they are very rare in the financial sector. A distinction should be drawn between primary, secondary and tertiary prevention.[71] *Primary prevention* is about avoiding future damage, reducing overall expected costs and keeping the entire system in balance. The challenge in mobilising money for primary prevention is the 'no-show' paradox: an adverse event did not occur (because it was prevented), so nobody cares about it and there is less willingness to invest in future prevention programmes. In the case of *secondary prevention*, we recognise the damage we have already caused – to nature, the Global South and future generations – and attempt to keep the expected follow-up costs as low as possible. Any return on investment should be greater than 1. In the case of *tertiary prevention*, the damage we have caused will remain, and we are confronted with additional chronic and systemic ailments, costs and damage. The strategy here is to minimise these costs in the long run. Tertiary prevention is rehabilitative, seeking to avoid or reduce acute and chronic states, follow-up damage and further chronic problems.

> **Box 5:** Climate impacts and the role of secondary prevention in finance
> Take the impact of climate change. The global costs to minimise climate change impacts are estimated to be around 5% of global GDP in 2024. Currently, we are investing about one trillion USD, which is about 1/5 of the amount needed. At the same time, the entire system of global financial flows is flawed, with most of the finance being concentrated in OECD countries rather than in the Global South, where it is most needed. This makes secondary preventive approaches vital. We can either start adapting to climate change now, with measures such as building flood defences, or we can wait until the sea level has risen by several metres and then end up paying even more for the losses and damage (tertiary prevention). Introducing new financial engineering instruments would allow us to shift to a preventive approach in finance (see Part II of this book).

I think about it like this: instead of pretending that each economic data point, figure and trend has a unique and singular cause and diagnosis, we should think in terms of differential diagnostics. Behind the same symptoms are multiple potential diagnoses that we must take into consideration if we want to make the right decisions.

The lesson we can learn is that the more we invest in primary prevention, the less we have to pay for the other two forms of prevention. If we don't invest in prevention at all, the entire bill will be unmanageable. From an economic perspective, primary prevention is by far the cheapest strategy. Any fix-and-repair approach will empirically always be more expensive. If we don't focus enough on preventing the damage, there will be a lot of adaptation and damage costs ahead. Not taking a preventive approach in finance will become extremely costly for our children and indeed for all of us over the next few decades.

---

71 See Kisling and Das 2023.

Conclusion

In this chapter, I have argued that humans' selection advantage is our ability to find the right narrative – especially in the new era we find ourselves in, known as the Anthropocene. Finance and monetary policy should be driven by biophysical realities and interdisciplinary scientific evidence, not the other way round. The better the stories we can tell each other to help us adapt to this new reality, the more successful we will be in creating a positive, self-fulfilling prophecy. Each academic discipline has its own unique *differentia specifica*, something it alone is capable of. For financial economics, that is the indispensable contribution it can make to identifying the *cheapest of all worlds* and turning a challenge into an opportunity for competitive ROI for the private and public sectors and hence for all of us. In short, it is our mindset towards money that can be the game changer. It seems to be a paradox: we can envision the end of the world and the end of our civilisation, but not the end of existing economic and financial incentives, which are all human-made and could be replaced by better ones that counter visions of the end of the world. Instead of allowing traditional and linear economic thinking to rule our decisions, with cyclical booms and busts determining the order of the day, we can acknowledge that we are in the midst of a transformation process that will force us to change almost everything we are used to. Financial economics can allow us to phase out the existing system, accelerate the change, set a new direction and create enabling conditions for the provision and use of the funds that are needed. In the next few sections, we will see how this translates into specific financial engineering tools that can be used, firstly, to fund and manage our planetary commons and public goods and, secondly, to hedge and unlock private capital to enable the transition. It seems that humankind is able to plan a mission to Mars, yet not to manage ongoing, serial economic crises, or to fund and hedge healthcare, education, shelter and food for all. We should stop maximising output at all costs and only afterwards fixing and repairing the damage in a process that is laborious, exhausting and expensive. The new role of efficiency gains and resilience patterns as described in the preceding sections could lead the way, bringing us into the 'anti-fragile zone' where we are able to learn from failure and improve our capacity to adapt to ever-increasing complexity, real-time interconnectedness and multiple unknowns. But this transformational process will not come for free. I have identified several forms of risks (collectively referred to as transformation risks), multiple general cost and damage functions and different forms of externalities, shown the relevance of a TCA and two-tier cost components and introduced the idea of a secondary preventive approach in finance. None of the costs that have been discussed will disappear until we come up with adequate financial engineering responses. Whereas Keynes offered us the economic and political tools to tackle booms and busts and singular shocks, especially unemployment, on a national level, we are now heading towards a *complete transformation of our societal aggregate.* Whereas in a Keynes 1.0 world state deficit spending determines social and economic output, creating domestic windfall revenue but leaving the entire structure of our value chains up- and downstream untouched, we are now in what I have called the 'Keynes 2.0 moment', which is forcing us to think outside the box, beyond national borders, familiar regulations and redistribution measures, all of which are embedded in the biophysical reality of our planet. In the subsequent chapters, I will show that the economics of transformation needs to be completely different from the merely translational approaches of the past, which entail merely adjusting and improving the existing rules, taxonomies and regulatory frameworks. But before we explore the new rules of the monetary game, we have to address the very nature of money and our planetary commons. That will be the topic of the next chapter.

B: Waking the Sleeping Giant

Where It All Began

For millennia, the course of human life on this planet was dictated by Malthusian cycles. Each time the birth rate increased, famines, harvest defaults, wars or pandemics would then reverse the overall growth of our population, well-being and prosperity. There was no real progress, and these cycles repeated themselves over and over again. But between around 1750 and 1820, the situation changed dramatically. With a few exceptions, most of the ingredients for change had already been in place for centuries: by 1820, human societies had invented the wheel and the printing press and knew how to make fire. We had nation states, a banking system, taxation, mathematics, astronomy, religion, music, arts and knowledge of human anatomy, as well as copper, iron, wheat, meat, fruit, vegetables, bread and butter. Most of the elements of daily life as we know it today already existed. Despite that, until 1820 the conditions of human life had barely changed for centuries, if not millennia. Things remained the same from birth to death and societies as a whole, despite all their achievements, evolved solely according to demographic factors. But around 1820, roughly 30 years (just one generation) after the French and American revolutions, something astonishing happened that triggered a whole new process unlike anything seen before in all of human history: the social empowerment of individuals to use their critical minds and creativity and engage in new forms of social cooperation. This human-centred approach[72] changed everything: universal suffrage, minority rights, nurseries and compulsory schooling, a ban on child labour, public health and hygiene measures, new corporate laws, free trade and freedom of establishment and the constitution of a labour market and trade unions fundamentally changed the playing field. It was not increased resource efficiency and capital accumulation but a fundamental shift in our mindset in the first place that changed the course of history. And it was in this era of the Enlightenment that human societies started to apply critical and rational thinking, that new forms of government, liberal democracies and rule of law began to emerge and that modern science, education and technology took off. All these developments came prior to any capital accumulation and resource allocation. It was this fundamental shift in our individual and collective consciousness that enabled us to think, perceive and behave differently, breaking the curse of the Malthusian cycles that had dominated human lives for centuries. A mere technological fix without a change in governance or a mere increase in capital without a shift in our mindset has never been a successful strategy at any point in human history. It has always been the interplay between them that enables the cooperation, coordination and social inclusion necessary to shift our society towards greater wealth and health. We can witness this successful interplay again today in the 21st cen-

---

72 See Nagan 2016.

https://doi.org/10.1515/9783111421520-003

tury. I believe we are at the dawn of a second Enlightenment, when a new mindset, new forms of governance and new technologies and inventions have the potential to transform our societies and economies, just as they did some 250 years ago. This idea is illustrated in the figure below (Figure 10).

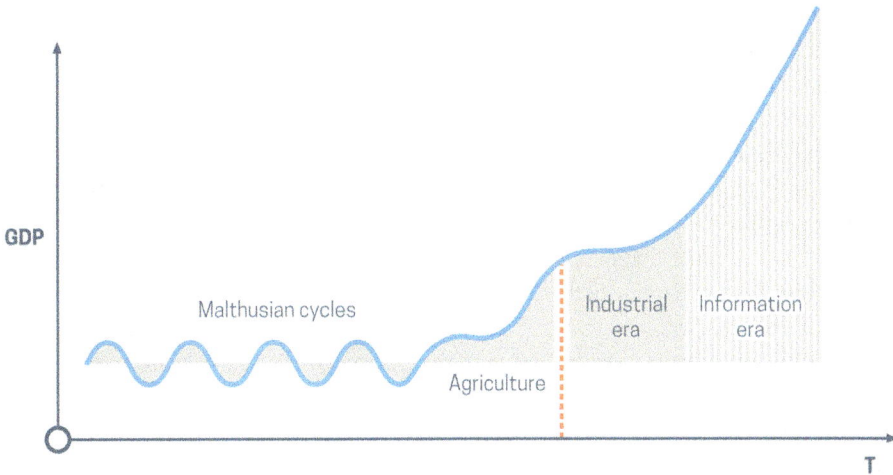

Figure 10: Malthusian cycles – altered mindset and new forms of governance.
The red dotted line marks the beginning of the liberal order that was able to overcome Malthusian cycles

Traditional Ways of Financing

Within the current monetary regime, our opportunities and risks are mainly driven by the financial incentives that are in place. It is the financial system that determines whether or not investments are made and projects completed. If there is no money available, opportunities such as new jobs, technological innovation, universal healthcare, infrastructure programmes and education will simply not be utilised, even if there is a clear need for them. Even if we have the brightest ideas and unambiguous scientific evidence, the existence of the challenges is undisputed and there is universal societal and parliamentary consensus about what has to be done, it is ultimately finance that will determine whether or not all these ideas meet the criteria of the profit floor or are simply abandoned. The same is true of risk assessment. If there is no funding available, companies will not invest in an uncertain environment and will, for instance, reduce their commitment to searching for new drugs to treat cancer or infectious diseases, while governmental bodies will avoid implementing the necessary infrastructure programmes.[73] There are at least six measures that dominate in

---

73 See Verbaanderd et al. 2021, Sattari et al. 2022 and Thelwall et al. 2023.

the current financial regime. They mainly operate redistributively at the end of the value chain ('end of pipe'). I collectively refer to them as TTRAPP:

- Taxation
- Taxonomies
- Restructuring loans and debts
- Austerity measures
- Privatisation
- Philanthropy

Transferring money through fees, tariffs, subsidies and taxation: In a general sense, taxes, tariffs, fees and subsidies represent each citizen's and company's explicit relation to the state as well as the implicit relations between citizens and companies. Both sets of relations together represent a legal agreement on how to redistribute, manage and fund economic activities, wealth and public infrastructure.[74] There are at least four reasons why societies utilise various taxation schemes. The main one is *funding*. We generate money through our general economic activity and redistribute it to alternative assets as required. Another reason is the *steering function*. Tax can influence consumption patterns: for example, a sin tax on nicotine to reduce costs for the healthcare sector, or a tax on fossil fuels to deter investment. A third reason why we need taxes, tariffs, fees and subsidies is to *tackle inflation*. If the CPI becomes intolerably high, taxation schemes can withdraw purchasing power from the market and dampen price increases. Finally, we use taxation schemes to maintain *social cohesion*. If the income and wealth gap becomes unacceptable and the political stability of the community is under threat, we can decide to tax the rich and compensate the less privileged. Funding, steering, tackling inflation and social cohesion are the four most prominent justifications for state interventions in market activities. As we will see, the funding and steering properties that these schemes generate are far too slow, far too low in volume and far too imprecisely targeted to meet all the challenges we are facing in a time of economic transformation.

Total global tax intake represents the money that states collect from economic activities in the private sector through their fiscal policy. In 2024, it was equal to about 14% of global GDP, or roughly 15 trillion USD.[75] Whereas rich OECD countries can take advantage of a broad tax base and a variety of taxation schemes, emerging economies are forced to rely on a tax base that is 80% smaller. That is despite great heterogeneity in global tax structures and a general tendency towards international convergence. Relevant factors include the domestic tax base, income per capita, the openness and composition of a country's economy and its external debt load. The relative amount

---

74 Larsen 2018.
75 See World Bank 2023.

of transfer payments ranges from 10% to 45% of domestic GDP.[76] There are dozens of carefully designed taxation schemes and a vibrant academic and social debate on how to refinance social and ecological goods and services, tackle negative externalities and fund our commons. Progressive income taxation, wealth and inheritance taxes and VAT are the most prominent suggestions. They are all valid options in themselves, but are chronically difficult to realise in a democratic political system. Given that the poorest 10% of Scandinavian citizens are richer than the average Hungarian worker, and that private wealth of about 5,000 USD already qualifies someone as belonging to the upper 50% of the global population, the well-established and conventional way of redistributing money through taxation, fees and subsidies may be one political tool among others, but it does not have the ability, volume or scope to finance our future as a whole. We should therefore discriminate between intake (where the money is coming from) and expenditure (what we spend the money on). The political and academic debate over the last 75 years has demonstrated the intellectual power of such an approach, but also its limits. One inherent paradox of taxation is becoming obvious: in SMEs, over 95% of EBITA is reinvested in the company itself – it is spent on jobs, R&D, new investment and transition measures. Increasing taxes, meaning withdrawing that money from the value chain and then reinvesting it, seems to be a kind of paradox. Such paradoxes are created when we want to do good and avoid harm, but the outcome is precisely the opposite. If, say, a region (such as the Eurozone) that is responsible for 8% of global atmospheric CO_2 emissions decided to exit the fossil age, the corresponding drop in demand for fossil fuel would trigger a decrease in its price, which in turn would very likely increase consumption in other parts of the world. In other words, once a good becomes a globally traded asset, any decrease in demand on one side of the planet will decrease the price of that good and allow it to be bought more cheaply in other places. Only if all countries are prepared to leave fossil fuels in the ground will the overall CO_2 load in the atmosphere decrease. And domestic fossil resources need to be under the control of national jurisdictions in order to ensure they are indeed left in the ground. The Covid pandemic proved that only if the entire global value chain shuts down will CO_2 emissions decrease. Any conventional TTRAPP measures will in one way or another withdraw purchasing power and redirect money into another sector –depriving the economy of the financial resources needed for the transition and hence defeating the purpose the measures were intended to serve. By way of analogy, imagine we decide to build a new hospital. We do not demolish the old one first and then start building a new one,

---

76 If we compare VAT at 20%, compulsory social security at 25%, corporate income tax at 11%, personal income tax at 23% and property tax at 5% of overall tax intake, we will find that each taxation scheme has its own flaws. VAT-based tax intake, for example, requires a cash payback of up to 50% of the revenue to compensate for its regressive nature. A progressive income tax risks people leaving the country. Wealth taxation is confronted with multiple private equity investments, which will slow down future investments without offering substantive alternatives.

but rather wait until the new hospital is up and running before closing down the original site. This process incurs additional costs throughout the process of transformation, which add up. Numerous swap lines would provide the financial engineering and additional liquidity to meet these challenges. This 'green paradox'[77] is a dilemma for any fossil-based product that is tradable globally and produces a negative externality on a global scale (such as CO_2 emissions).[78] Any activity to reduce the dependency on fossil energy is valid only as long as the CO_2 remains in the ground. As long as there are insufficient equivalent alternative investments available, reducing fossil consumption unilaterally is logically counterproductive. What is more, any rational producer of fossil energy will actually be incentivised to over-extract their resources in the short term in order to maximise their portfolio and reinvest the revenue elsewhere. Solely relying on VAT and corporate, capital and inheritance taxes is therefore an ineffective and inefficient way to fund, hedge and manage the transition.[79] It's like pulling on both sides of a tablecloth, and in the end achieving little to nothing. After the government has taxed the rich, it still needs the private sector to do the job of implementing renewables, building hospitals and nursing homes and providing new technologies for the transition. One of the clearest signs that the entire mechanism is systemically flawed is the mismatch between direct and indirect subsidies for activities that are damaging our planet on the one hand and funding measures for conservation and restoration of nature on the other. The former amount to seven trillion USD, the latter to a mere 80 to 150 billion USD.[80] If we continue to invest 500 times more in destroying our natural world than in preserving it, the outcome should be obvious to everybody.

No taxation scheme has yet been devised that would allow us to finance our collective externalities and planetary commons and secure the transformation from a fossil-driven to a low-carbon economy. The amount of money generated through different taxation schemes simply reflects the statistical variance of tax income per year. Meaning the more we generate on one side, the less we generate on the other. The

---

77 Sinn 2012.

78 The 'green paradox' results from a macroeconomic flaw in globally traded goods that causes a global negative externality. There is a microeconomic correlate to this systemic flaw, in which a unilateral wave of adverse behaviours increases disposable income, triggering multiple rebound effects. In both cases, macro and micro, the 'green paradox' eventually defeats the purpose of the measures: externalities and unwanted shocks are increased rather than reduced.

79 Despite all these constraints, potential tax reforms should still include offshore and offsheet taxation, a global flat corporate tax and taxes on high-frequency trading and naked short selling. Especially those engaged in the last two types of trading will need to change their job description. But the goal of these taxation schemes would be less to generate additional volume, and more to create a level playing field, providing more stability and steering the economy towards a greener future.

80 Deutz et al. 2020; OECD 2020.

main reason for this shortfall stems from the multiple Laffer curve effects at play.[81] The tax intake that a state can use to finance alternative projects not funded by the free market initially rises when tax rates are increased, reaches an optimum and then declines. This 'Laffer curve' (illustrated in the figure below (Figure 11) is like a universal law of tax that, economists argue, applies to all taxation schemes.

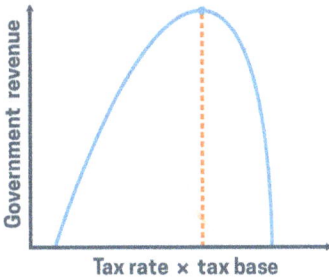

Figure 11: The Laffer curve effect.

This well-known curve shows that for any tax, there are two rates that do not generate any revenue: zero taxation and 100% taxation. The optimum tax yield, the Laffer peak, is somewhere in the middle. Above that rate, government revenue will decline. The empirical question, then, is which side of the peak are we on? The following correlation supposedly holds true for all taxation schemes, regardless of elasticity:

Box 6: Tax revenue, tax rate and tax base

$TR = Tr \times Tb$

TR: tax revenue

Tr: tax rate

Tb: tax base

However, this correlation only applies in a specific theoretical case, where the multiple price equilibriums of a competitive free market reflect the real value of goods and services, where the economy has no relevant negative externalities that feed back into those price equilibriums and where public goods and planetary commons are adequately funded to provide the prerequisites for a functional competitive market. As I remarked in the previous chapter, we are now living in a different era, the Anthropocene, where any economy has to deal with multiple overshoots and backlashes, which are all sensitive to the price levels for goods and services in multiple ways, structural unemployment is rising across the globe and our common goods are systemically underfunded. In this scenario, which is totally different to that underlying the tradi-

---

81 See Gahvari 1989; Mises 1949 ('Every specific tax, as well as a nation's whole tax system, becomes self-defeating above a certain height of the rates'); Bartlett 2012.

tional Laffer curve, any increase in fiscal tax intake would automatically reduce the functionality of the market, as we would be shifting to the right of the Laffer peak and reducing future public revenue. In such a situation, we need additional, conditioned liquidity to fund our commons and tackle negative externalities, and so we should reduce the tax rate to facilitate the private sector funding its own transition towards a greener future. And if we were simply to print money, a process known as orthodox easing, and inject this additional money into the economy, that would simply act like a generalised VAT in a defined currency area: it would increase the overall price level, devaluate income and wages and increase the income and wealth gap. The FIRE sector (finance, insurance and real estate) would reap windfall profits, but overall productivity would be unchanged. This is my point. Most countries are still far too poor and underdeveloped for us to be able to roll out the living standards that we enjoy in the Global North universally. The UN defines extreme poverty using 2,15 USD per day. If we take the scandinavian countries with a low level of inequality (Gini coefficient: 24–26) and a poverty level of about 30 USD per day, the world economy would have to grow by a factor of 5 in order to lift everybody on the planet out of extreme poverty and reduce inequality respectively.[82] For mathematical and political reasons, that cannot be achieved solely using redistributive measures. Rich countries can use their wealth to decouple economic growth and wellbeing from their impact on the planet, (both relatively and absolutely) that addresses energy use, carbon emissions, air pollution, overfishing, plastic waste and all other relevant factors.[83] Throughout this book, I have argued that technological innovations alone cannot bring about the required transformation; the financial system also has a vital role to play. If we want to achieve a global transformation, we need additional, conditioned liquidity to make it happen.

I will explain in more detail in Part II why the solutions that will allow us to square this circle require additional, conditioned liquidity that is generated not through credit lines or fiscal tax intake, but through reforms to regulators' monetary regimes. I call this conditioned liquidity assistance M^{cola}. By contrast with loans and credit lines from the capital market, it would mainly be generated by regulators and central banks. This monetary aggregate supply would have a significant impact on the Laffer curve, government revenue, tax intake and the overall productivity of the private sector. If M^{cola} were primarily used to fund negative collective externalities and planetary commons, which are essential prerequisites for a properly functioning market segment, the effect on the multiple price equilibriums would be different. M^{cola} would only become inflationary, effectively as a form of VAT, if the injected money used to finance externalities and public goods in the first place is higher than the costs of externalities and the negative consequences of underfunded commons on the initial CPI.

---

82 See Roser, 2021.

83 For the relevance of a consumption based approach, that factors in trading activities of rich countries, see already Peters, (2008) and Peters et al. (2012).

This idea can be developed further. I define unmanaged externalities (*Ex*) as costs that feed back into the economy in an unsystematic way. They represent negative collective externalities that we have to cover as a community. The additional cost to fund our public goods (δCo) is defined as the percentage of GDP necessary to adequately fund public goods and allow a competitive market to function properly. The cost per capita of structural unemployment ($\delta \xi$) is defined as the percentage of the workforce in a society that is able and willing to work but is not given opportunities to do so by the current private market, plus the direct and indirect social costs associated with unemployment. The monetary assistance (M^{cola}) required to address these challenges is calculated as shown in the box below:

Box 7: COLA – calculating the additional, conditioned liquidity required

$M^{cola} = \delta Ex + \delta Co + \delta \xi + \delta mpC$

M^{cola}: additional, conditioned liquidity assistance

δEx: marginal cost of unmanaged ecological externalities

δCo: marginal cost to fund our planetary commons

$\delta \xi$: marginal (indirect + direct) cost of structural unemployment (social externalities)

δmpC: marginal costs to mobilise private capital

Let us assume that the public sector represents 30% of a country's GDP but would need to grow to 33% to provide the necessary public funding, and further that the identified externalities that affect the CPI in that currency area amount to 4% of GDP. That additional 7% could not come from additional tax intake, because increasing the tax rate would take us to the right of the Laffer peak and reduce the output that a functional market economy can provide. Injecting more than the 7% through M^{cola} would fuel inflation. The reverse is true, too. Unless we fund our commons and externalities adequately in the first place, we will still have to bear the costs, but our prosperity would be diminished and we would end up with a Pareto-inferior equilibrium.

If we take this argument to the next level, we will end up with an adjusted, green Laffer curve. Whereas in the traditional Laffer curve the government revenue represents public output as a function of the tax rate multiplied by the tax base, a green Laffer curve integrates additional M^{cola} to address externalities and fund common goods. In the green Laffer curve, the peak is defined as adequate output to manage externalities, a functional public sector and close to zero unemployment.[84] If the M^{cola} is too low, overall output and prosperity will be lower, as the costs of externalities and a deficient public

---

[84] The argument still holds if we utilise the same monetary mechanism to fund ODA in regions outside of the designated currency area. The liquidity will generate income and increase the domestic CPI in those regions only if the injected money exceeds the social and ecological externalities, including the collateral costs of an underfunded public sector in the societies in question. If both criteria are met, the monetary aggregate will equal the expected CPI.

sector will not be covered. If and only if the M^{cola} is higher than the costs will we end up with inflationary pressure on the CPI. It should be noted that the M^{cola} will substantially decrease the tax rate, which will in turn unlock the productivity of the economy as a whole, since both externalities and commons would be adequately funded.[85] The figure below (Figure 12) illustrates the adjusted green Laffer curve.

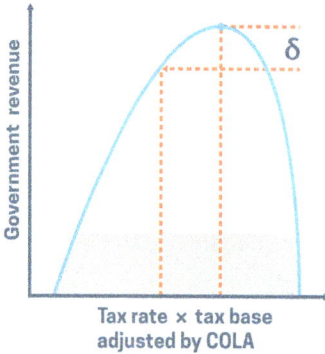

Figure 12: A green Laffer curve.
Under ceteris paribus conditions, the stretched green Laffer curve would add a δ. Adding M^{cola} would increase the potential tax revenue and/or result in lower effective taxation in order to stimulate the economy.

The tax rate that determines government revenue could then shift to the left if the additional liquidity injected into the economy is conditioned, such that it must be used to fund, hedge and manage externalities and commons. The optimum point of a green Laffer curve, all other things being equal, would then be determined by an additional, conditioned monetary aggregate designed to fund and manage our future. One lesson we can draw from the mental exercise of imagining this alternative approach is that fiscal schemes are a substantial part of managing transformation, but the funding aspect is just part of the picture. The delta (δ) in the figures above could be utilised for other government tasks, such as tackling inflation, increasing social cohesion or achieving additional steering effects. We should, moreover, regard this monetary aggregate as complementary to the fiscal one. Both measures will provide us with a higher Pareto optimum, assuming that the costs of future externalities are covered and the social ROI of our commons far exceeds the expected revenue of the private sector. In other words: solely relying on a global taxation scheme, which currently represents about 14% of global GDP, to fund our transformation would require a 50% increase in tax yield. But attempting to achieve that would put us on the far right of the Laffer curve, with lower output and no transformation at all. To conclude:

---

85 Relative changes in tax revenue, referred to as elasticity of taxable income (ETI), depend on two components. The first, more technical one simply comprises linear change relative to the change in tax rate. The second, behavioural one comprises activities to avoid tax increases (e.g. reduced consumption or investment, shadow economy). The net effect of these two components determines relative position along the Laffer curve. If the ETI is less than 1, any tax increase will leave us on the left side of the curve. If the ETI is greater than 1, the expected tax revenue will be lower.

all taxation schemes are end-of-pipe strategies, where we do whatever we want first and then tax the results and try to do good second. No OECD country is yet capable of generating enough liquidity through tax intake to cover the global externalities and fund our future. In short, taxation is part of the solution, but it is not *the* solution.

Taxonomies, or how to put the toothpaste back into the tube: A taxonomy is a scientific practice of classifying and categorising items or events in order to gain a better overview, provide guidelines and make it possible to standardise, compare and harmonise collective action. Across the planet, there are multiple financial taxonomies available that provide new guidelines for investors, regulators and consumers. Each country puts great regulatory effort into outlining and implementing these new standards. One of the most prominent examples is the EU's ESG (environmental, social and governance) standards, known as the European Sustainability Reporting Standards.[86] The term ESG was formally introduced in 2004, but the associated activities date back to the early 1990s.[87] The general idea is to get companies and investors to consider specific sustainability standards in their investment decisions, and adapt their strategies and balance sheets accordingly. Within a competitive market, companies should be accountable for externalities, and associated spillovers should be internalised on their balance sheets, thus helping to steer the entire economy towards a more sustainable future. To date (2024), about one-third of all assets under management (AuM) globally take at least one of the three factors – environmental, social, governance – into account. In Europe, about 6–7% of the real economy considers climate-related issues as part of the environmental (E) component. Over 700 metrics with dozens of categories can be observed, but there is little overlap between them, and greenhouse gas emissions do not appear to be an overarching common denominator.[88] Besides practical implications and limits, which represent a challenge in their own right, there is a general hostility to all ESG-related taxonomies that is more conceptual in nature. Imagine you have three children. How do you decide which to favour over the others? Emile (E), Samuel (S) or Georgina (G)? Should military spending (tanks, munitions) be considered part of ESG because it helps to defend our free world? Would it be better or worse to invest in a fossil fuel company or one that produces landmines?

---

86 The ESRS is published by the European Financial Reporting Advisory Group (EFRAG). See EFRAG 2024.

87 See Pollman 2022. There are significant similarities to the introduction of new macroprudential metrics and measures in parallel to GDP, including the Human Development Index (HDI), the Genuine Progress Indicator (GPI) (see Kubiszewski et al. 2013), the Thriving Places Index (TPI) (see Centre for Thriving Places 2024) and Wealth Accounting and the Valuation of Ecosystem Services (WAVES) (see World Bank 2021). They all share a recognition that our current measures of prosperity and well-being do not adequately consider negative impacts on our ecosystem.

88 For example, ESG templates in Africa do not necessarily match those used in Europe, Asia or the US. See Barman 2018 and Cort and Esty 2020; for an analysis of the different stages of countries' ESG disclosures, see Singhania and Saini 2021; for an international comparison see Singhania and Saini 2023.

Would it be better to push for a green transition at a polluting company's next executive board meeting or to exclude investment in that company from your portfolio? And, finally, who is accountable for all the associated negative externalities we are generating? The fuel extractors, the car industry, the drivers, the politicians or even the public transport system (trains and buses, for instance, often use petrol)? Or should we all be accountable? And if so, what kind of regulatory frameworks and financial budgets are needed to address all the dilemmas? All the currently existing taxonomies are like a mixed salad bowl: full of appealing ingredients that don't go together. They are torn between inconsistent directives, which attempt to insert more transparency into the system and further internalise and re-privatise externalities that we all generated collectively. It is commonly said that we can only manage what we can measure, but anything we can measure we can also manipulate, avoid and neglect.[89] The entire ESG accounting system appears to produce a lot of noise but little measurable impact and no robust economic signals that would help steer our society towards a better future. It is true that any ESG template expresses the non-financial risks of a company and represents a kind of shadow tax reflecting all the negative collective externalities associated with its economic activity. But factoring in all these costs on a corporate and individual level is simply too expensive and/or too imprecise and the benefits too low to meet all the goals of the sustainability agenda. Instead of blaming the private sector, we should instead aim for an adjusted collective political agenda that sets new rules.[90] One example is the goal of banning child labour, where companies can make a real difference by ensuring children are sent to school. In doing so, they not only document a hazard, but provide an incentive for change. However, the additional costs required to send a child to school, which is a collective and not a private responsibility, should be covered by additional liquidity assistance from the public sector. The same principle should be applied to ecological and govern-

---

[89] The inter-rater reliability is over 99% in the conventional credit ranking but drops to less than 50% for ESG templates, which greatly reduces their validity. In addition, it has not been clarified statistically whether this is due to causation or mere correlation: do ESG standards make a firm more successful or is it that only firms that are already performing strongly are able to adopt ESG standards? ESG funds in general require higher management fees (more than 50% higher on average), which translate into higher regulatory efforts and costs. See Berg et al. 2022.

[90] Take the Scope 3 directives, which require companies to include and document all costs along their entire value chain. The Sustainable Finance Disclosures Regulation (SFDR) offers a preliminary framework. Article 6 qualifies investments as conventional and mainstream, Article 8 classifies those that support ESG standards in principle and Article 9 defines those that actively apply the standards and provide specific tailored KPIs. Only 3% of all investments comply with Article 9. At the time of writing (2024), the entire disclosure process is a statistical artefact with little to no real economic impact. In addition, Article 2 (17) SFDR only describes the disclosures of corporate activities, but does not impose any obligation to become green. In order to simplify this inefficient and opaque process, we should require investors to comply with Article 2 (17), add DNSH (do no significant harm) and PAIs (principles of adverse impact) and then forget the rest. This would also significantly increase comparability with other ESG templates. See CDP 2023.

mental standards, too. Under the current rules of the game, it is as if we are trying to put toothpaste back in the tube. An almost impossible and certainly very expensive endeavour. As a rule of thumb, investors do not invest in assets that don't correspond to their risk profile. Whereas specific project risks can be hedged, managed and internalised on the market, systemic risks cannot. Systemic risks are *negative collective externalities*, representing an overuse of our planetary commons; they primarily follow biophysical laws rather than market rules. As long as we are unable to properly quantify such uncertainties, we will need a different, more complex monetary system to cope with them. Financial disclosure directives alone are of little help to deal with the magnitude of all the crises ahead. In other words, ESG standards reflect in a general sense any social, environmental and governance trade-offs we are collectively accountable for, and providing a new ESG-related taxonomy is definitely a powerful tool to address future problems. But it is not a stand-alone solution. If we take economics as a transformative process seriously, we should instead advocate a multi-tier *inventory approach*. ESG standards allow us to better document our economic activities in the first place, put a price tag on unaccounted spillovers, adjust our balance sheets and redirect investor behaviour. Having no transparency about expenditures and therefore neglecting any inventorisation is not an option. That would make things even more expensive and uncontrollable, and just as random and unfair as ever, meaning the damage we have caused will not disappear and will remain unmanageable. Once we recognise the need for inventorisation, we will then have to agree who is paying the bill. That requires us to undergo the mental exercise of distinguishing between disclosure, documentation and billing. For the latter, we have two options. Firstly, we could re-privatise the identified costs: that is, once companies have documented and disclosed their activities, we legally oblige them to internalise those costs. However, we would then have to expect multiple leakages, avoidance strategies and exception policies, with increasing regulatory costs, greenwashing and bankruptcies. The time horizon left to exit the fossil industry is too short to rely solely on this policy measure. The entire process risks becoming atactic. The second strategy, once an inventory has been mapped out, is to designate the damage we have caused as a negative collective externality that we are all accountable for. We should take into consideration that we have already caused the damage and incurred the associated costs. Dissecting the individual liabilities and reversing the entire engineering process seems to be an impossible task. So instead we will need to devise new hedging and funding instruments that involve (partial) interventions by international financial institutions and regulators.[91] In the next sections I will make

---

91 To be more precise: investors first apply Article 2 (17) SFDR (as explained above) and are then encouraged to invest in G-funds (which focus on (mis)management of human rights issues), E-funds (which provide expertise on climate change and nature restoration) and S-funds (which focus on human capital and basic social needs). Finally, the public sector steps in with state guarantees and hedging instruments to complement the rest of the ESG template. The reader might not fully agree with this approach politically, but it is the cheapest way to finance our transition. On the current debate, see also Finance Watch 2024.

several proposals for how to overcome the constraints of the existing ESG agendas. All this requires new rules, a new polity for the monetary sector and a more proactive role for international financial institutions.[92] The figure below (Figure 13) illustrates the inventory approach.

A No inventory

↓

B Inventory approach

C Billing
      → **D** Re-privatising

      → **E** Public-sector involvement

F
      → Complementing ESG investment
      → Hedging systemic risks
      → Funding and managing planetary commons

Figure 13: The inventory approach: a multi-tier process.

A represents the business-as-usual approach, which is the most expensive variant. Externalities won't disappear, but rather increase over time and hit us in an unexpected and unequal manner.

B is the inventory approach, where we start documenting and reporting losses and damage on a macro- and microprudential level.

C represents the process of putting a price tag on those externalities.

D is the current state of affairs, where we aim to internalise and re-privatise negative collective externalities.

E is the option of hedging and funding part of the ESG agenda through additional, conditioned liquidity assistance from the public sector. From a regulatory, policy and financial perspective, option E seems to be the fastest, cheapest and most rational way to address the trade-offs we are faced with.

F is the public spending needed to make additional ESG investments, hedge systemic risks and fund and manage our planetary commons. In short, public spending is

---

92 The objection is that we will face moral hazards and free-rider effects. However, on this proposal moral hazard is substantially reduced as the investor is committed to at least one of the three ESG components and the complementary commitment of the public sector is conditioned. So, for example, if a company favours S, enabling minimum social standards along the value chain, the associated E and G should be covered by a public entity. I will discuss the key role of this kind of conditioned liquidity assistance in Part II.

cheaper than re-privatisation, and any upstream regulation is faster than downstream approaches.

> **Box 8:** Four steps to get out of the maze
> Four steps to get out of the maze: firstly, monitoring a selection of approved biophysical parameters (water quality, biodiversity, minimum wage), with on-spot screening upstream in line with a 'do no significant harm' (DNSH) approach and 'principles of adverse impact' (PAIs). Secondly, providing objectives for investors and companies downstream in line with Section 2 (17) of the Sustainable Finance Disclosures Regulation (SFDR). Thirdly, encouraging inventorisation of total Scope 3 emissions and associated costs. Fourthly, providing the necessary funding and hedging through new financial engineering instruments and a new set of monetary rules.

Restructuring debts and loans: For reasons of simplicity, I shall assume all financial assets to be either equity or debt (along with the associated securitisation). Equity comes from the Latin *aequitas*, meaning fair and just, and refers to risks and profits being shared equally. Debt, meanwhile, is not capital but a form of borrowed money (with a risk premium) which has to be paid back. Over the last two decades, the equity-to-debt ratio has been shifting towards more debt, and the nature of corporate debt has shifted from traditional banking credit to corporate bonds.[93] Debt servicing has become a double-edged sword. James Tobin described as capitalism's Achilles heel.[94] On the one hand, if investment is done properly, it can provide future opportunities, while loans and a balanced share of risks and burdens between the generations are vital for any development and a transition towards a more sustainable future; on the other hand, debt can be a curse, especially if the investment was a mismatch, the repayment schemes undermine investments in key sectors such as healthcare, education or infrastructure and/or the growth rate of the debt outpaces GDP.[95] Servicing the debt load or serving the people has become an unresolved dilemma for countries representing almost half the world population, with a greater proportion of government spending going on servicing external debts than on domestic education and healthcare. Taking the interest rate–growth differential (r–g) as a general bench-

---

93 To go into a little more detail: whereas the equity-to-GDP ratio remained stable between 0.7 and 1% over the last two decades, the debt-to-GDP ratio increased to 300%. The amount of new corporate bonds issued is four times higher than new equity shares. Instead of 'going private and public', the corporate world has become more indebted, further masked by the shadow sector and now prefers mergers and acquisitions to initial or secondary public offers. Again, this development was triggered by regulatory arbitrage. Especially in OECD countries, tax codes and disclosure agreements favour debt over equity. In numbers: tax rates are up to 10% higher for equity shares than for debt obligations, which represents an indirect and hidden public subsidy for corporate bonds. For further detail, see also Akgiray 2019.

94 Tobin 1989.

95 UN Global Crisis Response Group 2023.

mark[96] reveals that in most Global South countries the interest rate (r) exceeds the expected growth rate (g), which increases susceptibility to future shocks, crowds out domestic investments and locks the economy into a low future growth trajectory.[97] Under conditions of uncertainty, debt increases inequality and instability within a society. The private sector is affected first, requiring additional credit lines that are offered by the rich (rich glut), and the public sector ultimately has to cover the additional costs by taking on further debt.[98]

We are confronted with a global debt burden of almost 1000 trillion USD, made up of borrowing by governments (2/5) and borrowing by businesses and households (3/5). 80% of that total has been generated by rich OECD countries. However, it is the countries of the Global South,[99] especially developing nations, that suffer the most from their debt curse, due to uneven access to additional liquidity and private capital as well as higher borrowing costs. Currently, over 100 countries have been forced to cut their spending on education, social protection and healthcare because of increased interest rates and repayments. Low-income households are most affected by the lack of public services and risk falling back into poverty.[100] However, the devil is in the detail.[101] We can identify six major sources of loans for developing countries: private lenders; China; other bilateral agencies; the Paris Club; multilateral development banks; and the World Bank's international development assistance (IDA). Private creditors (commercial banks, bond holders and institutional investors) account for two-thirds of total external public debt in developing countries, which makes restructuring of different maturities, grace periods and interest rate and risk spreads more complicated and expensive.[102] In general, developing countries pay substantially more for debt relief relative to GDP than rich OECD countries, which further exacerbates the asymmetry between the Global North and Global South. The main lesson we

---

96 Blanchard 2019.

97 Aguiar et al. 2009; Lorenzoni and Werning 2019.

98 Schularik 2022.

99 The loss and damage funds, for which 700 million USD has been pledged so far, are an example. With good intentions, we will end up with a 'too low, too slow' scenario. On top of that, the loss and damage funds rely on the functionality of the existing system that we are trying to move away from, which defeats the purpose.

100 Volz et al. 2020; Vasic-Lalovic et al. 2023; Zucker-Marques et al. 2023.

101 This involves at least four aspects: (1) a legalistic rather than an economic approach. Any haircut would disadvantage concessional debt, indirectly subsidising other creditors (Lazard 2022); (2) a shift from collective action clauses (CACs), which require a hyper-majority to restructure loans, towards single-limb CACs, which allow restructuring throughout all bond series (Megliani 2021); (3) the harmonisation of soft debt relief measures, including interest rate reductions or maturities (Reinhart et al. 2016); and (4) adjusting the interest rate for special drawing rights (SDRs) to finance debt restructuring (Paduano and Setser 2023).

102 External debt servicing as a share of exports has risen from 3.9% to 7.4%. Post-WW2 agreements (such as the 1953 London Agreement) limited external debt servicing to 5% to avoid undermining domestic recovery.

can learn from history here[103] is that in order to return to a path of economic and sustainable growth for all, which would substantially contribute to a positive sum game for all, the minimum required to fairly share the burden would be 0.7% of GDP for ODA, equivalent to 5.7 trillion USD,[104] plus 200–300 billion USD annually as a back-stop mechanism to cover and compensate for additional costs for loss and damage due to climate change.[105] The way debt nominated in foreign currencies is currently structured generates an ongoing trade-off between haircuts, additional lending, grants and concessional contracts. Whereas additional grants and loans will keep debt vulnerability and risk indicators high and fail to attract private investments, debt relief will reduce nominal debt burden and create more fiscal space to fund public goods, improve risk assessment and allow further private investment to be mobilised.[106] Despite all these limitations, the general argument still holds: the system as a whole is flawed, so that an unmanageable debt burden crowds out public commons; massive liquidity outflows to the Global North cause systemic fiscal tightening; the lack of proper reimbursements for loss and damage leaves billions uncovered and unprotected; and fraud, corruption and tax evasion counteract any attempts to bring about a 'fresh start' and level playing field as we progress towards a common future.[107] Taken together, these factors create a vicious circle that whole countries, regions and even continents cannot escape. The trap is systemic in nature, not a matter of individual failure. Only if we are prepared to change systemic incentives might we end up with sounder future development. In order to make our financial system more inclusive and provide additional liquidity, a debt workout mechanism is required that allows upfront loading, long-term maturities and public guarantees to hedge, fund and manage public interests and to scale up and mobilise private capital investment in volatile and risky environments. Simply borrowing money from the capital market will further increase the wealth gap, because that money is being borrowed from

---

103 The World Bank's Heavily Indebted Poor Countries (HIPC) Initiative, the G20's Multilateral Debt Relief Initiative, the Debt Service Suspension Initiative (DSSI) and the IMF's Catastrophe Containment and Relief Trust (CCRT) all share the common narrative that debt burden remains an unmanageable vicious circle for poor countries, who find themselves caught on a treadmill with no end in sight.
104 Seery 2020.
105 The current commitment of the international community is 700 million USD, which equals about 0.2% of the loss and damage. See The Guardian 2023.
106 For example, a 15% haircut would translate to a ten-year debt repayment period (Yan and Qian 2022). Each dollar provided by an MDB for debt relief would translate into 7 USD of additional fiscal space, which has a higher leverage than additional lending itself (Zucker-Marques et al. 2023).
107 One prominent proposal is debt-to-nature swaps, where creditors swap their old debts with a haircut for new but conditioned bonds with an additional public guarantee (Brady bonds). See Griffith-Jones et al. 2021.

those who already have enough. It will put an additional constraint on the next generation to pay back these debts, and we risk further privatising our common future.

> **Box 9:** The USD treasury trap
> US treasury bonds (T-bonds) are a benchmark for the global credit market. Demand for these bonds is
> currently decreasing in countries like China and Japan, which reduces their face value. Whenever the
> value of treasury bonds drops, the associated interest rate (yield) increases. This interest rate itself
> serves as a benchmark for commercial credit lines. If the interest rate goes up, companies and states
> will find it harder to replace existing investments, which in turn will drive up unemployment. For the
> public sector, a higher interest rate translates into a higher net debt load, which will further crowd out
> new, green public investments. This treasury trap, reinforced by the US central bank purchasing pro-
> grammes, can further accelerate this vicious circle, causing a toxic cascade effect especially in the pe-
> riphery of the global financial system.

To summarise: measures to address the global debt load, such as debt relief, haircuts, flat
rates, fair shares, swaps, suspensions, negotiating different lending conditions or credit
enhancement, are important components of any successful transformation,[108] but they
remain within the confines of the existing monetary system and leave its architecture
untouched. Operating solely within that system would result in a too little, too late, too
slow rat race scenario that would ultimately be too expensive for all of us.

Austerity measures: Austerity refers to policy measures that seek to cut public spending
in order to meet governmental debt obligations and allocate a society's resources more
efficiently. Historically, this translated into liberalising, deregulating and privatising our
economy.[109] Such efficiency measures are best described as streamlining a system's components and better managing potential throughput per unit. Outsourcing, private investments in R&D, educational programmes, preventing fraud and corruption and implementing new technologies will indeed help us to deploy our resources more effectively
and efficiently.[110] And for as long as we waste about a third of our food production, equal
to the amount necessary to feed Canada and India combined, there is still a long way to
go to make our supply system more efficient.[111] Supporters of austerity argue that reduced (external) debt loads and deficit spending can help further increase future
productivity and output. However, austerity is just one half of the equation and not
an end in itself. Focusing solely on efficiency makes a system more fragile, volatile and

---

108 Zucker-Marques et al. 2023.
109 The IMF's structural adjustment rules (SARs), which call for reduction of fiscal imbalances, privatisation of public goods, trade liberalisation and free capital flows, are also considered elements of
austerity policy. See Williamson 1990.
110 Increasing public-sector finance will primarily involve more outcome-oriented measures and decentralised administration (see Alfonso et al. 2006). But even a fully efficient administration would
not be more robust and resilient to external shocks.
111 See Food and Agriculture Organization of the United Nations 2019.

unstable.[112] In order to make a system more robust and sustainable, resilience factors first need to be in place. Resilience is defined as the ability to recover from a shock and is measured by a system's interconnectedness and the diversity of its mechanisms. A systems-thinking approach can demonstrate that the most efficient system is simultaneously the most fragile and volatile. Nature never selects for efficiency, but rather for a sensible balance between throughput (efficiency) and interconnectedness (resilience), with stability rather than volatility as the dominant factor. This is true for airport security, power grids, agricultural monocultures and every ecosystem, and should be true for the monetary system, too. And as shown earlier the two variables, efficiency and resilience, are intertwined. We need to find sensible financial measures that strike the right balance between them, placing us in an optimal 'anti-fragile' zone where the system can learn from failure and maintain its overall integrity. Anything outside this zone is either too unstable (too efficient) or too stagnant (too resilient). Figure 3 above illustrates this general point, which can be adapted to most austerity policies.

The native human mind is characterised by short-term decisions and flawed mental frames, and operates in the 'middle dimension' of metres and minutes. We are not wired to deal with complexity. This is why humans require cultural achievements like new technologies and an adjusted monetary system to fill the gap. Such considerations should also apply to austerity measures and the international financial system in general, especially when we are facing increasing volatility and banking, currency, government and debt crises. Financial markets are generally considered to be efficient, self-regulating and decentralised systems for allocating goods and services through price signals, where demand and supply spontaneously converge over a defined maturity. They are seen as one of the most efficient allocative mechanisms humans ever devised. And they represent probably the largest circular economic process ever invented. Demand on one side of the planet meets supply on the other trillions of times every day, based on price signals and without much governmental regulation. However, these sorts of highly efficient markets are incomplete and unstable and require resilience measures to remain balanced. Only when a system is in an 'anti-fragile' zone will it not merely passively adapt to the environment but instead perfect a systemic response to asymmetric shocks and failures.[113] This means that any anti-fragile features will improve the overall performance of a financial system. I will further outline some measures that meet the criteria of increased resilience and the 'anti-fragile zone', and go beyond mere fiscal austerity.

---

112 Soaring unemployment and additional negative spillovers to the healthcare sector (increase in morbidity and mortality) are the most prominent short-term effects. Loss of future productivity and competitiveness due to a lack of public investment in infrastructure (healthcare, education, energy, etc.) is a less obvious one that will leave society unprepared for future challenges. See Reinhart and Rogoff 2013; Johnson 2017.

113 On this view, social and ecological spillovers, often associated with competitive market activities, are not market failures as such, but rather due to the lack of a properly configured market. If we had an international monetary system that struck a balance between efficiency and resilience, we would be better able to cope with ecological crises and ongoing externalities.

Privatising our future: Currently, 85% of all global assets are privatised, while 15% are public. The same percentage, 85%, of all investments are private too, which means the private sector dominates. However, private cash deposits of over 12 trillion USD remain unproductive, stock repurchasing programmes surpass R&D budgets and institutional investors are sitting on a carbon bubble exceeding 40 trillion USD, forcing them to write off substantial parts of their assets in the near future. These stranded assets do not yet include the challenges of other systemic shocks like biodiversity loss and harvest defaults, serial pandemics, air pollution and mass forced migration.[114] On top of that, a significant portion of private credit creation has become decoupled from the real economy, lowering economic productivity and inflating the FIRE sector instead. In the face of massive collective externalities and spillovers, unprecedented asymmetric shocks and an ever-growing complexity and interconnectedness, where profits are privatised and losses are socialised, there are limits to further privatising the system. The private sector should still lead the way in the overall economic transformation, but we should avoid privatising the remaining 15% of our public goods. And we should note that private capital will always be pro-cyclical, myopic and risk-averse. That means a monetary mechanism is needed that allows us to mobilise trillions of dollars of private investment in long-term, anti-cyclical measures in a risky environment without destroying the very nature of our global commons.

Philanthropy and the force of doing good: Worldwide, philanthropy and charity account for about 2.4 trillion USD of assets annually being put towards good ends. That is equivalent to charitable foundations spending an annual average of 10% of their assets. There are over 260,000 such foundations in almost 40 countries, with a high concentration in North America (60%) and Europe (30%). If we adopt a wider definition of pledged giving, which includes donating money, volunteering time or direct and informal aid, then Asian countries lead the field. Most foundations are independent NGOs, corporate funds, family offices or governmental bodies. However, organisations with new legal forms are emerging, such as limited-liability corporations and donor-advised funds that act like savings accounts. The main goals of these foundations are education, social welfare and addressing specific UN SDGs. However, the devil is in the detail. First, tax deduction programmes to support charity throughout the world are covered in all countries by the taxpayer, and investments and grants depend on the functionality of the existing system. If there is a bust or expectations are too unrealistic, the philanthropic funding phases out, causing a 'non-profit starvation cycle'.[115] Empirically, charity payments per capita are highest in the lowest-income segments, which further increases the wealth gap and defeats the purpose of charitable giving. In sum, philanthropy is enabled by an indirect subsidy from society, which allows rich individuals and foundations to provide money to whichever social and envi-

---

114 Aigner 2019; Damgaard et al. 2019.
115 See The Economist 2024, 4 ff.

ronmental projects the donor finds most attractive. Giving grants or gifts and supporting others have always been important aspects of our social coexistence. But the idea that we can build an entire transformation process on a gift economy and leave the monetary architecture untouched seems counterintuitive.[116] This system is obviously unstable, fragile, volatile and unprepared to manage future shocks, finance the green transition or cope with the new reality of a multipolar world.[117]

However, we can reverse the perspective. Instead of finance driving our future, with all the constraints associated with it, we should start looking for a monetary regime that allows the opposite: one where our future drives finance. The traditional model is locked in a trap where we either tax the current value chain, borrow money from the capital market, solicit private investment from companies, rely on philanthropic donations or simply tighten our fiscal efforts in order to finance a greener and fairer future. None of these traditional approaches, which I collectively refer to as TTRAPP, are wrong per se; they simply lack the speed and scale that our common agenda demands. The conversion rate from a fossil economy to a more circular, decarbonised one is simply too low and the risks and uncertainty too high for the private sector to fully come on board with that agenda.[118] We are simply overconfident that the existing IMS will fix things. However, irreversible ecological and social tipping points, stranded assets with massive write-offs, the breakdown of entire global value chains, forced migration and political instability will bring with them additional costs that the international financial system and domestic private and public budgets will somehow have to manage. In short, the transition we are all going through right now is not a cyclical phenomenon, but a non-linear, disruptive one. It doesn't come for free, but has a price tag attached. Again, the longer we wait, the more expensive that price tag will be.[119] And if we refuse to put a

---

116 The same is true for individual behavioural changes. As important as they are, they cannot provide the leverage necessary to shift our society in the necessary direction. Each time we give up something sinful (e.g. flying or eating meat), demand for the associated products will decrease and prices will fall for those who continue consuming them. In addition, isolated behavioural changes generate multiple rebound effects that further undermine the purpose of those changes. In order to be more effective, behavioural changes need to be embedded in an upgraded monetary framework, such as my proposal for a Bretton Woods 2.0. For further details on these behavioural biases see Brunnhuber 2023.

117 75% of all climate finance circulates within Europe, the USA, East Asia and China. Emerging markets lack the finance to cover the impact of this global negative collective externality, as they face additional currency, project and political risks. The gap will be between 15 and 30 trillion USD by 2040. In order to cope with this flawed system of financial flows, we need an IMS that provides the liquidity necessary to overcome the constraints. See Climate Policy Initiative 2023.

118 Schroeder 2006.

119 According to Swiss Re and Climate Policy Initiative, catastrophic natural events and associated financial losses increased fourfold between 1970 and 2020. The estimated flow of global climate finance (one trillion USD in 2020) is less than a tenth of the 11 trillion USD required each year over the next 25 years to limit warming to 1.5 °C. See Alberti 2024.

price tag on our future and the natural world, we effectively set the price at zero and discount our common future.[120]

Box 10: Climate finance

Take climate change as a case study. Most financial experts and academics agree that a carbon tax is the best steering measure to shift companies, consumers and states away from the fossil age and towards a low-carbon economy. The required carbon pricing should come to around 200 USD/t of CO_2 emissions. Currently (based on figures for 2024), we are able to cover about 25% globally with cap-and-trade and taxation schemes at a much lower price (80 USD/t).[121] A global carbon price would immediately affect all bonds, treasuries, securities, firms and any capital allocation. It should run in shadow form for one to two years and then become real. Minimising the damage associated with climate change will cost up to 5% of global GDP. We can either invest in preventing the damage (primary prevention), adapt to the spillovers (secondary prevention) or repair the damage later on (tertiary prevention) through loss and damage funds. We should be aware that tertiary prevention is by far the most expensive option.[122] The fact of the matter is that the more we are prepared to pay upfront for primary preventive measures, the less we will have to pay for the two other categories. We currently invest about one trillion USD in climate change measures. But the figure that is needed is around five to seven times greater, which means there will be far higher adaptation and damage costs ahead than ever before. So far, investing in climate mitigation has simply not been sufficiently profitable for the private sector, while governments are constrained in how much funding they can provide and institutional investors have obligations to their constituents (in particular pensions for the baby boomer generation, who number 70 million in the US alone).

A rising CO_2 concentration in the atmosphere due to emissions from fossil fuels is a negative collective externality, jointly caused by producers, manufacturers and consumers. Privatising this collective externality through taxonomies and taxation, waiting until the profit floor for companies is suitable and leaving the public sector and regulators out of the equation will be extremely expensive and ineffective. CO_2 emissions are not the result of a global market failure, but rather due to the lack of a suitable competitive market able to provide efficient price signalling and market allocation.

These co-financing strategies are a kind of end-of-pipe approach, something that is common in engineering. We first implement certain technologies, lifestyles, rules and

---

120 We should differentiate between commodifying and pricing our future on the one hand and the question of 'Who is going to fund, hedge and manage that price tag?' on the other. The more we are confronted with collective externalities and global public common goods, the more the active state and an active regulator should lean in to fund and hedge the price tag. See Sukhdev 2012; Brunnhuber 2023.

121 The global carbon budget if we are to meet the 2 °C target is about 40 billion tonnes, which would give countries an average of seven years to exit fossil energy completely. But we still have fossil resources available for decades: coal for 138 years, oil for 54 years and gas for 49 years. That means the vast majority of these resources have to stay in the ground, and we must come up with sensible financial mechanisms that respect private property and its expected revenue while also tackling the negative externalities associated with them. Instead of regulating the price, we could start limiting the volume (cap) and then start trading within these new biophysical boundaries. The relative price of goods and services would adjust more efficiently than if we regulated the price in the first place.

122 There is a vast body of literature on this topic, demonstrating over and over again that preventing damage is far cheaper than fixing it. One example is 'hysteresis': the restoration of an ecosystem once it has been destroyed. See Dasgupta 2021.

economic activities that cause damage to our environment (e.g. air pollution), then add a filter at the end of that process to prevent excessive harm. The co-financing strategy follows the same logic.[123] Traditional finance likewise represents a kind of end-of-pipe strategy, where money is redistributed as required but the current system is kept in place. In short: the economy grows first, then we take a certain amount of money (through taxes or fees) from the value chain and distribute it to social and ecological projects. The figure below (Figure 14) illustrates this:

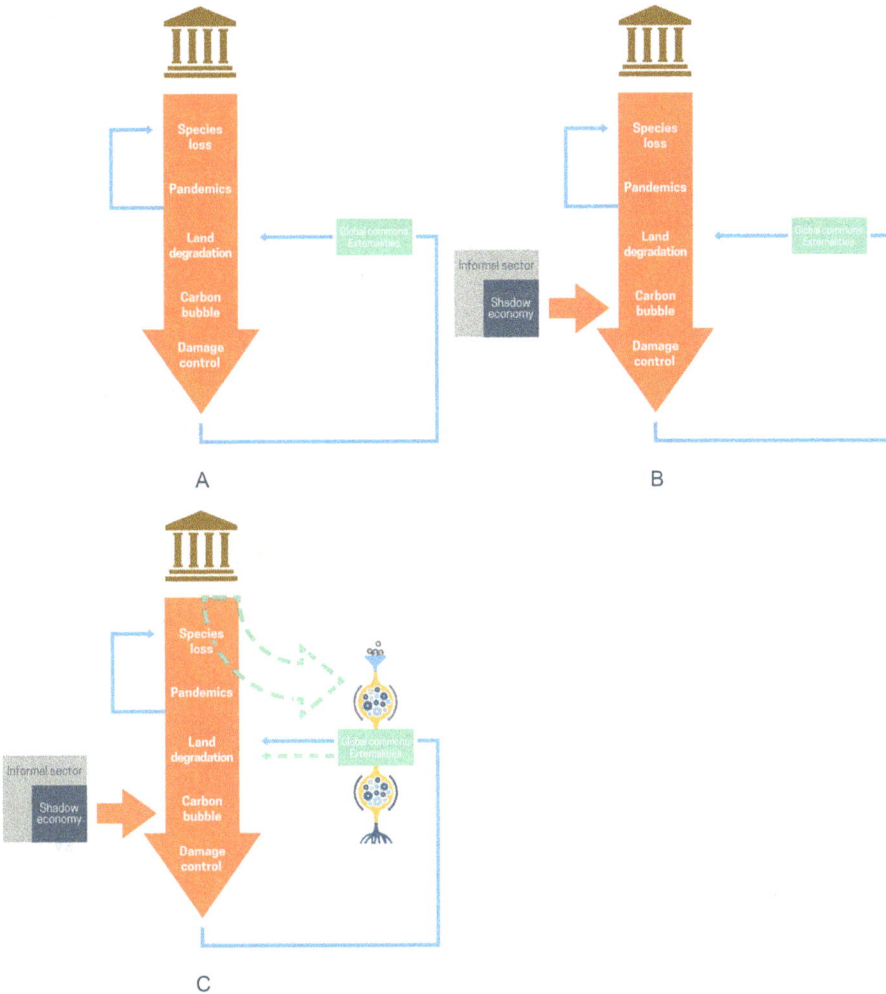

Figure 14: Traditional financing: end of pipe and beyond.

123 African Development Bank Group 2022.

A shows the traditional approach to finance (large arrow), characterised as an end-of-pipe strategy. We maximise the output first, redistribute second and fund our externalities and common goods third. In this manner, we distribute about one-third at a domestic level, leaving a small portion to fund, hedge and manage our planetary commons and externalities (box on the right). *B* includes the black market and the informal sector, which push the economy in the wrong direction (boxes on the left). *C* shows the shift in the financial system that will be needed to create additional, conditioned international liquidity (curved green arrow), to manage and fund global commons, to hedge and mobilise private capital and to enable investment in new technologies so that they can be scaled up and made accessible for everybody. It would seem that we are busy repairing and stabilising the existing financial system, which is inherently unstable, operates pro-cyclically and is prone to generating serial crises, and that we rely solely on that system to generate subsidies, taxes, tariffs, charity, loans and grants to fund and manage our future. That has an air of paradox.

The Evolutionary Perspective

It seems be obvious that orthodox finance has not been able to build change, development or evolution into its theoretical framework. In order to incorporate the concept of development into finance itself, we must refer to the vast body of interdisciplinary literature on this topic. One major finding is that human consciousness (including all its emotional, perceptual and cognitive components), behaviours and social interactions are characterised by stages and levels.[124] None of the components are a given, but rather develop subtly over time. If we apply this interdisciplinary finding to finance and our monetary system, we can distinguish three major levels of development: pre-conventional, conventional and post-conventional (see Table 4).[125]

The core argument is that each later stage can critiize the limits, incorporate the strengths and achievements of the previous one(s), while at the same time transcending them and moving towards a greater whole. Each shift from one level to the next involves not just a shift in our mindset, but also in our practices and ways of interacting with the world. This is true of any successful development in human consciousness, but also of the monetary system. Any successful evolutionary step in our monetary system will therefore have the structure of an inverse spiral or pyramid (see figure below (Figure 15)) that moves towards a more inclusive, resilient, integral whole (A) and involves

---

124 Wilber 2000; Brunnhuber 2023.
125 Other authors use different terms and different forms of granularity, which then allows them to distinguish four, six or eight levels instead. See Brunnhuber and Lietaer 2005. But the core argument still holds: our financial system is evolving and the current stage is not the last one in history.

Table 4: The logic of development.

Evolutionary stages	Economic system	Currency system	Examples	Characteristics
Post-conventional	Knowledge-based age	Electronic complementary currencies	Multicultural human rights Universal fairness Sustainability Priorities Complex open networks Complementarities AI, synthetic biology and robotics	Openness Self-transcendence Integral praxis Synchronicity Multiple time perception Conscious choice Reciprocal tolerance
Conventional	Industrial age Competitive markets	Paper-based currencies Gold standard Bretton Woods Treaty	Nation-state jurisdiction Functional specialisation Technocratic development Experimental praxis	Ego-based individualistic Socio- and ethnocentric Causal and analytical Linear and short-term procyclical timeframe
Pre-conventional	Agrarian societies Bilateral barter	Commodity-based currencies	Regional mythologies Belonging Magical/mythological Worldview Magical/mythological determinism Ritualised praxis	Pre-personal Symbiotic Archaic Collectively determined role identity Cyclical timeframe

a shift in practices and procedures (B).[126] This means that each level or step represents a coherent set of mindsets, behaviours or approved social standards. The later stages should always honour and integrate the earlier ones, while also transcending them and attaining greater explanatory power. The conventional level, which represents the status quo, is not the end of evolutionary history. I shall show in Part II that this shift in the evolution of our monetary system is underway and is having a significant impact on how we finance our commons and tackle systemic externalities (I shall also provide a comprehensive framework to explain economics in a state of trans-

---

126 To be more precise: any successful development stage requires, firstly, an increase in *differentiation*, where the status quo is critically assessed; secondly, *integration*, where opposites and challenges are integrated; and, thirdly, *transcendence*, where past achievements are respected but refined and expanded so that we can do more, see more and perform better. If these internal components of any successful development fail, we end up with fusion instead of differentiation, dissociation instead of integration, chaos and regression instead of transcendence. See Wilber 2000.

formation). This kind of evolutionary approach is supported by the sociologist Georg Simmel, who said over 120 years ago that 'the debate on the future of money is not about inflation or deflation, fixed or flexible exchange rates, gold or paper standards, but about the kind of society in which money is to operate'.[127]

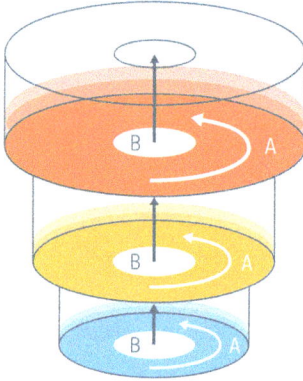

Figure 15: Monetary evolution explained: the inverse pyramid.

A represents the different narratives we use to explain economic activities within the existing rules (translation); *B* represents the narratives we use to explain economic activities that apply new rules of the game (transformation).

The Non-Neutrality Axiom: Not Like Fish in the Water

I define monetary regulators as the institutions and public agencies that are entitled to set the rules of the game in the monetary domain. That includes, despite overlapping responsibilities, central banks, the Bank for International Settlements, national treasuries and parliaments and international financial institutions such as the World Bank Group, the IMF, the WTO and multilateral public development banks. These public bodies hold the political mandate to make the relevant decisions upstream and allow other (international) public entities such as the WHO, the ILO and the FAO and private stakeholders such as institutional investors, transnational corporations and hedge funds to act accordingly downstream. Setting the rules of the game refers here to polity measures, whereas all other actors pursue policies and practices within the framework of these rules.[128] This distinction is crucial to better understand the design of the monetary system and its implications. The figure below (Figure 16) illustrates the general idea.

---

127 Simmel 2004 (originally published 1900).
128 One of the most striking challenges we are facing here is best described in terms of a 'diffusion of responsibility'. As long as the different levels of regulatory responsibility are not clear, causal attribu-

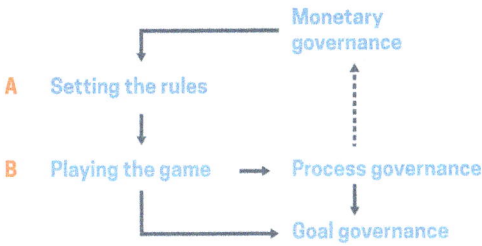

Figure 16: A multi-tier approach: monetary governance – setting the rules and playing the game.

This multi-tier process is best described as monetary policy governance.

A represents the regulators who set the monetary rules of the game: for instance, the fact that money is interest-bearing and created by central banks, that the commercial banking system is organised around a fractional reserve system and that the IMF has special drawing rights for its members.

B represents the level where we have to apply these rules of the game. *Process governance* involves national laws and constitutions (anti-trust legislation, taxation schemes, fees and tariffs) and the rules of a market economy (liabilities and property rights), but both are supposed to remain largely agnostic regarding the results of the game itself. *Goal governance* involves the targets that investors, producers and consumers set for themselves to achieve outcomes, such as specific economic output (electric cars, pharmaceutical products), social standards or environmental projects (restoring a nature reserve or protecting an endangered species) or third-sector activities (investigative journalism, cultural activities or research). Instead of aiming for an ideal-typical, academic greenfield approach for the overarching monetary sector (which will be impossible to apply in reality) or advocating for ad hoc, business-as-usual procedures so we can muddle through with the existing monetary system (which will be too expensive), we should instead support a practical, intermediary, best next step that respects existing institutions but dares to move beyond them and upgrade their potential in terms of speed, scale and volume, providing new financial engineering tools and clarifying certain aspects that are essential for any monetary system in order to meet present and future requirements. Such a multi-tier approach is fundamental in order to recognise the prime actor role of the monetary system itself. The conventional approaches, which are all valid in their own right, will remain defective unless we provide additional, conditioned liquidity to enable them. Measures such as taxation schemes that redirect purchasing power, suspensions of interest and principal repayments for a couple of years so that re-

---

tion will fail. Consumers, investors, states and monetary regulators have shared but distinct responsibilities, which should be aligned.

sources can be diverted to respond to a systemic shock and assorted new technologies, taxonomies and transition plans are all subordinate to the primary role of a functioning monetary system.

In general, we would be better off taking a systems-thinking approach that seeks to integrate findings from other disciplines, rather than following the recommendations of a single, specific school of economic thought. Systems thinking has the potential to overcome the multiple lock-ins of a *siloed systems dilemma*: we know that everything is interconnected and that every silo requires updates that affect the overall system. Moreover, we fail to see the dynamics of that system, because we are trapped in the mandate imposed by the silo we are in right now. [129] Before this multi-tier monetary governance approach can succeed, we first need to clarify the very nature of money itself.

Money as a Social Contract

Our financial market is one of the few, if not the only international institutions that most, if not all, actors operate within. Despite different political agendas, every country – whether it is a Western-style democracy or an autocratic regime, a developing economy or a failed state – operates within the existing monetary system. Neither international religious institutions like the Catholic Church nor globally active NGOs like the WWF, the Red Cross, the Club of Rome or the World Academy of Art and Science have the reach and acceptance of the IMS, and their values and regulations are not shared by everyone equally. Even terrorists, the black market, fraud, illicit transactions and corruption as well as the entire informal sector depend in some way or another on a functional global financial market. In this general sense, the international global capital market, its associated institutions (IMF, WB, central banks) and its monetary policies determine the rules of the game for fiscal policy, real economic activities, investors' decisions, non-profit commitments and household spending. The IMS acts like a systemic attractor, for better or for worse. Its design determines whether money is a road to freedom or to serfdom.[130] If we overlook the crucial role of the design of the monetary system itself, we will fail to

---

129 For example: credit rating agencies amplify a pro-cyclical tendency on the market and are trapped in a conflict of interest between issuers and borrowers; the WTO is facing multiple ecological crises that affect multilateral trade agreements intended to safeguard global value chains, but it does not have the mandate to address climate issues itself; the IMF has a voting quota where the largest CO_2 emitters are the biggest donors and hence have the most voting powers, while the V20 are exposed to the greatest impacts from climate change but have the least borrowing powers for special drawing rights.

130 Like power, sex and death, the monetary system is taboo. It goes unquestioned, its overall dynamic never filters into our consciousness and we remain unaware of all its meanings and impacts. The world would be completely different if we made the overall dynamics of our monetary system fully conscious. That is particularly important given that the monetary system shapes not just eco-

understand its relevance and potential integrating function. We will then act like a fish in water, taking the monetary system as a natural law and responding accordingly. But we could instead step out of the water and critically analyse its components.

> **Box 11:** How money comes into our world
> About 97% of the money in circulation globally is generated by the commercial banking system via fractional reserve credit creation. About 3% is created by central banks themselves. This 3% (which is also called base money or M0, and includes cash) acts as a loan to the commercial banking system. When central banks generate base money to purchase treasuries or corporate bonds as collateral, they increase their balance sheets accordingly. Any sovereign state authorised to print money can utilise this method and there are theoretically no limits to the maximum possible loans.

However, traditional perspectives have consistently excluded money from the equation. A less developed view sees our economic activities as opposed to the environment and the earth system in general. Nature is simply regarded as a free, exploitable resource (see A in the figure below (Figure 17). A more sophisticated view then distinguishes between the real economy, the social world and the environment, and we find ourselves caught between the three; all sustainable development and planetary commons are located in their smallest common denominator (B). These two perspectives entirely overlook the importance of the monetary system itself. Doing so paints a misleading picture: the monetary system has always been there at the core of our society, acting like an attractor (C), or a funnel (D), affecting all human activities in one way or another. The design of the monetary funnel determines outcomes for our social reality, real economic activities and the environment. The figure below (Figure 17) illustrates this.

This blind spot prevents us from looking at the entire process from a systemic perspective. The money system can act like a systemic attractor, facilitator or integrator, or like a distractor and destroyer, depending on its design. The money system is the elephant in the room that nobody talks about. Money is not a thing or a natural law, but rather a convention, a social mechanism, a club rule and a set of legal codes that we can change as we see fit. However, its current architecture runs counter to the goal of a sustainable future and prevents us from integrating the market system of the real economy and its systemic social and ecological externalities. In addition, the current IMS chronically underfunds our global commons, mismatches systemic risks and uncertainties and overlooks the pro-cyclical and short-term dynamics of the financial market. There are at least seven key ways in which the current configuration of the monetary system is flawed. They are outlined in the table below (Table 5).

If we had an upgraded and adjusted monetary system that respects the achievements of the existing financial architecture but remedies its flaws, unchecked spillovers

---

nomic transactions but also our interpersonal relationships (psychological context), matters of war and peace (geopolitical context) and even spiritual aspects (Lietaer 2000).

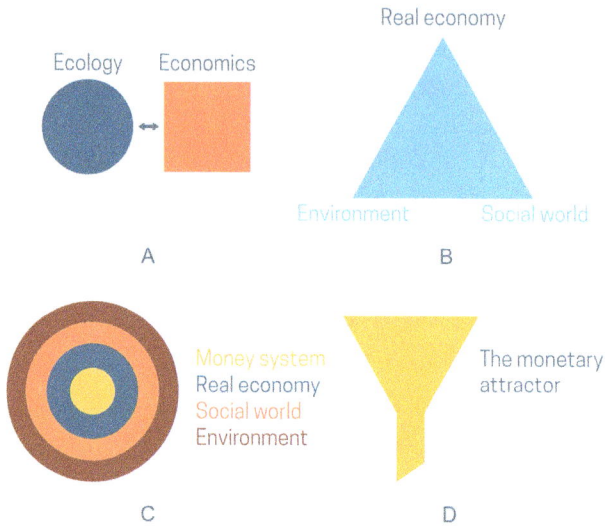

Figure 17: The money system as a systemic attractor.

Table 5: Money is not neutral – seven elements of the current system that are damaging our future.

The non-neutrality of our monetary system	Examples and further explanation
Pro-cyclical amplification of boom-and-bust cycles	Banks provide and withhold credit lines according to the requirements of the real economy and amplify cycles, instead of counteracting them
Short-term perspective and aversion to risk	A discounted cash flow enforces short-term decision-making and tries to avoid risks rather than hedging them
Compulsory growth	A compound interest rate forces states, companies and households to grow to pay back their debts
Destruction of social capital	Instead of encouraging trust, solidarity and cooperation, fear, greed and parasitic competitiveness are cultivated
Widening income/wealth inequalities	Current incentives support financial assets rather than real economic needs, further increasing the income and wealth gap
Multiple rebounds	Efficiency gains are cancelled out by increased consumption that further hinders progress towards a sustainable pathway
Inherent instability	Increasing volatility in the financial system, with banking, currency and debt crises further exacerbating risks in the real economy

and pro-cyclical constraints, we might have a powerful tool to create a healthier and wealthier planet.[131]

The Four Forms of Capital

Taking this argument one step further, we can distinguish between several forms of capital. Partha Dasgupta defines three forms: *human capital*, which encompasses our education and skills, our state of health and our mindset; *natural capital*, which refers to our ecosystem, from pollinators to plants, from climate to water; and *produced capital*, which includes machines, buildings, roads and property rights such as patents.[132] The three forms of capital are interlinked, with human capital providing labour and innovation for produced capital, which in turn generates goods, services and income for human capital. Produced capital deposits waste and pollution in our natural capital and natural capital provides natural resources and regulatory services for produced capital. Natural capital provides food, health and shelter for human capital, which uses land and pollutes natural capital. Each of them has their own characteristics and agendas. Natural capital requires some sort of stock and capacity to regenerate, and cannot be fully substituted by the other two. Human capital relates to well-being, prosperity, self-efficacy, a feeling of freedom, mutual trust and social inclusion. Produced capital needs to be written off and can to some degree serve as a substitute for human capital, but it depends on both the other types of capital. The figure below (Figure 18) illustrates these interrelationships.

We can build further on these points. Paul Ehrlich[133] showed that the impact (I) of human activities on our environment depends on the size of the population (N) multiplied by affluence (y) and divided by an efficiency coefficient (β).

Box 12: Ehrlich equation

$$I = \frac{N \times y}{\beta}$$

I: impact of human activities
N: population
y: income per capita
β: efficiency coefficient

---

131 'Effective altruism' is a prominent example (see MacAskill 2017), where 'earning in order to give' becomes the overarching goal. The argument goes as follows: a hedge fund manager could pledge their income to a deworming campaign and do far more good than if they quit their job and became an organic farmer (cf. Strom 2007). But this approach operates within the existing financial system and assumes that it functions properly, when the reality is that it is flawed from the ground up. In short, we need to upgrade the system to meet the requirements of the 21st century, instead of merely working with or around the existing one.
132 Dasgupta 2021.
133 Ehrlich and Holdren 1971.

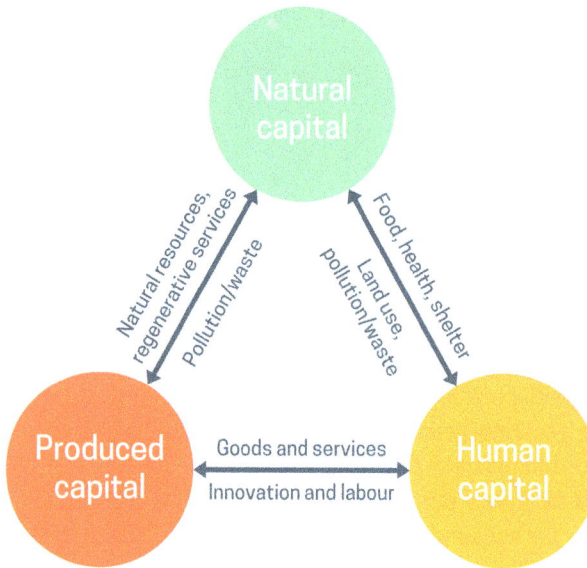

Figure 18: Three forms of capital.

Dasgupta developed a more complex version of the Ehrlich equation (see box 13 below):

Box 13: Dasgupta formula

$$I = \frac{N \times y}{\beta(e, t)} \geq G(S)$$

I: impact of human activities
N: population
y: income per capita
β: efficiency coefficient
e: education
t: technology
G: regenerative capacity of nature
S: stock of natural capital (biodiversity)

This formula means that any human impact on our ecosystem (I) depends on the size of the population, multiplied by income per capita and divided by an efficiency coefficient (β), which in turn depends on the level of education and technology. The larger this efficiency coefficient, the lower the impact on the ecosystem. This impact reflects our footprint on nature, which is currently greater than the regenerative capacity of nature (G). G itself is a function of its stock (S), in particular the level of biodiversity: humanity's current impact on the environment would require about 1.6 planets to be sustainable. In order to balance out this inequality, we must either reduce the size of the population and/or levels of consumption, invest in conservation and restoration (*G* and *S*) or increase our investment in education, technology and R&D in order to increase the resource efficiency of the overall system. From a practical perspective, we might have to consider a mix of all these measures.[134] However, increasing natural capital and its regenerative properties (*G* and *S*) would require not just additional *efficiency* measures (throughput per unit of time), as that would leave us with an even more brittle and volatile system, but also additional *resilience* strategies (diversity and interconnectedness). As explained earlier, a balance between both these first-order principles, efficiency and resilience, is necessary for a complex open network system to remain within an 'anti-fragile zone' and so attain maximum sustainability. While investing in R&D, education and technology has the potential to increase productivity and resource efficiency, it would leave the overall system's capacity untouched. On the other side, investing only in natural capital would increase the resilience of the overall ecosystem, but leave population growth and education untouched. A fourth form of capital, *monetary capital*, can play a key role in achieving that balance. The traditional three-way distinction overlooks the role of the IMS and finance as an additional and separate form of capital. Monetary capital involves different forms of risk assessment, discount rates, expected returns and adequate supply than the first three types. It follows its own logic and should not be subordinated to or subsumed under one of the other forms of capital. By doing so, we would miss out on one of the key levers for building a greener common future. All four forms of capital are interwoven and interlinked in specific ways. Whereas natural capital is the overall foundation of the others, human capital enables produced capital in the form of machines and buildings, and both in turn are enabled by monetary capital. Monetary capital itself is generated by human capital, which further loops back. Collectively, the four forms of capital are structured not like a circle but rather like a funnel, with monetary capital playing the role of a systemic attractor that pulls all the other forms of capital in one direction – for good or ill, depending on its design. Monetary capital thus determines human and produced capital, and also how and where we invest natural capital. Similar to the architecture of a house or the constitutional laws of a country, the architecture or grammar of monetary capital is the main determinant of the other three forms of capital's outcomes, states, characteristics, resources and capacity for regeneration. From a systemic perspective, monetary capital acts like *a scale-*

---

134 In numbers: population growth of 1.1% and income growth of 2.3% would result in a 3.4% increase in resource depletion. Any technology efficiency increase would therefore need to be at least 3.4% per year to maintain the status quo. Given a footprint of 1.6, a 10% increase of efficiency per year would be needed. That would translate into a 67% increase over the status quo within a decade. As such a number is completely unrealistic, we would instead need to reduce population growth, reduce consumption, increase investment in education and/or invest in restoring nature. These considerations show that we need additional liquidity in the system to rebalance the two sides of the equation.

independent isomorphic fractal (a topic we will explore in more depth in the next section). It allows us to either protect nature, humans and technology – or destroy them. Given the instability and multiple flaws of the current monetary system, in which banking and currency crises, imported energy and food inflation and a toxic pro-cyclical mix of adverse, misdirected institutional incentives systemically generate backlashes to all efforts towards a greener, more inclusive and more sustainable future, it is clear that properly designing monetary capital is crucial in order to fund, manage and hedge the three other forms of capital. Or to put it the other way round: neglecting this fourth form of capital will leave us permanently behind the curve as we attempt to achieve a better future. If we take monetary capital as an additional, distinct form of capital, this would strengthen Ehrlich's and Dasgupta's arguments. The figure below (Figure 19) illustrates its role.

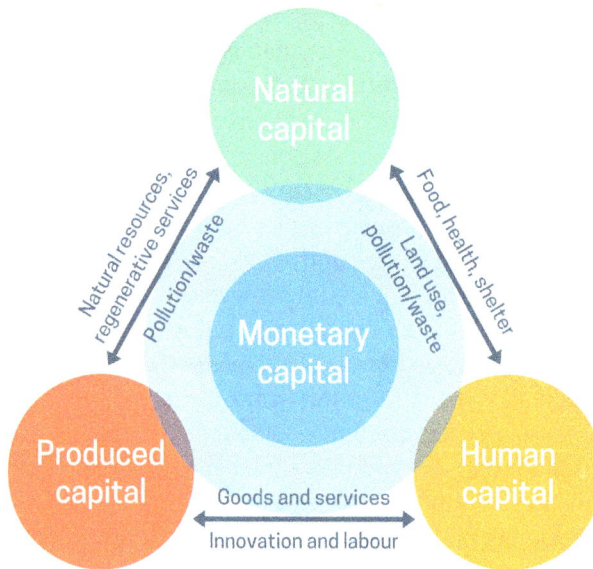

Figure 19: Monetary capital: the fourth form of capital.

What I shall call the 'integral capital formula' updates the Dasgupta formula to incorporate this fourth form of capital (see box 14 below).

Box 14: Integral capital formula

$$I = \frac{N \times y}{\beta(e,\,t) \times \left(1 + M^{cola-ef}\right)} \lessgtr G(S) \times \left(1 + M^{cola-re}\right)$$

$$\Rightarrow \frac{N \times y}{\beta\left(1 + M^{cola}\right)} \lessgtr G(S)$$

I: impact of human activities

N: population
y: income per capita
β: efficiency coefficient
e: education
t: technology
$M^{cola-re}$: additional, conditioned monetary aggregate to increase resilience
$M^{cola-ef}$: additional, conditioned monetary aggregate to increase efficiency

$$M^{cola-ef} < M^{cola-re}$$
$$M^{cola-re} + M^{cola-ef} = M^{cola}$$

This formula shows that if we provide an additional monetary aggregate (M^{cola}) that can only be used to invest in education and technology, we would increase the efficiency coefficient of any resource exploitation and so decrease the impact on G and S. This would also decrease population growth while increasing income per capita. The relative amount of additional money $(M^{cola-re})$ we have to invest in G and/or S needs to be higher than additional liquidity used to increase resource efficiency $(M^{cola-ef})$. Assuming a high ROI for investments in education and technology (see next sections) and the huge opportunity costs of not investing in nature, this conditioned liquidity assistance would pay for itself. It would restore our stock of natural resources and the regenerative power of our ecosystems. There is a potential downside, however: simply injecting additional money into the system would act like a general VAT that increases the CPI and widens the income gap. We should also avoid additional redistributive measures based on taxes and fees, as they would redirect purchasing power instead of increasing it. Regulators would play a key role in providing this additional, conditioned liquidity assistance (M^{cola}), as explained in more detail in Part II. If done in the right way, it would not increase inflationary pressure on price signals, but rather dampen and reduce potential costs that we have already incurred. If we had an adequate M^{cola}, it would also generate more human and produced capital and increase the resilience of natural capital.

Fractal Finance: From Silos to Systems

In 1610, Galileo complained in a letter to Copernicus that the local authorities refused to simply look through the telescope and acknowledge that the earth is rotating around the sun and not the other way round. Galileo argued that whenever we want to advance into new domains of knowledge and possibility, whether through inventions or discoveries, humans need to apply a new mindset, new thinking and new technologies to gain a deeper understanding of the world around and within us – conquering new territories that were always there but had not previously been explored. If we had refused to look through Galileo's telescope, we would still think that the earth is the centre of the universe and that the sun rotates around it. The situation today in the 21st century could not be more similar to the one Galileo complained of. Just imagine if we ignored the findings that have emerged out of deep learning, datafication or AI. Just imagine if we refused to consider the numerous interdisciplinary findings from earth system science that show we are living in a complex, fully interconnected world. No political party, religion or ideology can grasp such complexities, but only science, our creativity and our critical minds. Complexity is not visible to the naked eye. Complexity and uncertainty have always been there and will never go away, but in the 21st century we are now confronted with them in a spatially and temporally condensed form. Just like 500 years ago, we once again need a new mindset and new technologies to cope with new realities. Applying this idea to the topic of the present book, we can speak of a Galileo-effect for economics. Instead of following the recommendations of specific schools of economic thought, we should adopt a systems-thinking approach. Instead of using traditional statistical tools, we should apply new technologies and methods such as AI and big data analytics to grasp this complexity and deepen our understanding of money, ways of financing our commons and sustainable development for the 21st century. In short, for any economics of transformation we will need the right tools and the right mindset.

Beyond Fractured Economics: The Systems-Thinking Approach

We can only evaluate something and act on that evaluation if we have a methodology for doing so. Traditional economics does not provide us with methods and tools that enable us to see networks and their effects, or to evaluate associated risks and backlashes. When we take stock of the dozens of economic theories currently available to us, the first step should be to appreciate their wisdom, while also recognising their flaws. None of them are 100% wrong; all of them provide relevant but fragmented knowledge which they claim can be generalised to economic activity as a whole. Traditional economics uses longitudinal measures, such as GDP, unemployment or inflation, to understand the present, empirical field studies to identify correlations and experimental or historical data to look into the future. This holds true for the physiocrats, Marxists and neoclassicists, for the traditional Keynesian approach, for the Austrian School and assorted historical schools, for institutional economics and behavioural finance. None of them question the design of the monetary system itself or are able to describe the financial system and the associated risks as a complex system. Rather, all these theories depend in some way or another on the monetary system itself. And all of them use historical data to predict the future. However, finance remains a complex network, not an equilibrium-based model. That means it doesn't follow the logic of game theory or align precisely and exclusively with the findings of behavioural finance.

> **Box 15:** High-frequency trading: pro-cyclical self-organised criticality
> One prominent example is high-frequency trading (HFT) on the stock and currency markets. HFT can be carried out by AI in a matter of nanoseconds, at a rate of one billion transactions per second. HFT operates with a pro-cyclical self-reinforcement mechanism: in contrast to the general economic assumption that reduced demand or increased supply drives down the price of a good, demand for a good increases as its price does. In these anomalous cases, price formation does not tend towards an equilibrium, but rather towards self-organised criticality. Thorstein Veblen[135] described such goods as Veblen goods. This phenomenon is well known in relation to natural disasters and nuclear chain reactions, but has now entered the financial market too. We either need to abandon HFT completely or link it to the 'middle dimension', so that trading is forced to remain within the range of seconds rather than nanoseconds.

There is no doubt that all these schools of thought generate significant and valid results, but they are simply unable to grasp the network effects and associated risks intrinsic to complex systems. And none of them question the design of the monetary system itself, which means they leave it untouched and treat it as a given. In a more general sense, traditional economics fails to answer the non-trivial question: *how can we finance our common future in the face of uncertainties and future shocks in a multipolar, fully connected world?* If we rely on traditional economics to try and understand transformation, we will find ourselves using linear and analogue results premised on the belief that we can extend and prolong the present into the future. We will then end up unable to deal with the future. The figure below (Figure 20) illustrates this point. Extending the present (A) into the future leads us to pretend that the future will look like D, whereas actually this course would lead to a scenario of collapse (E) and eventually a Pareto-inferior equilibrium (F). The alternative is to aim for a new, greener and wealthier state (C), which requires transitional measures (B) to be taken first.

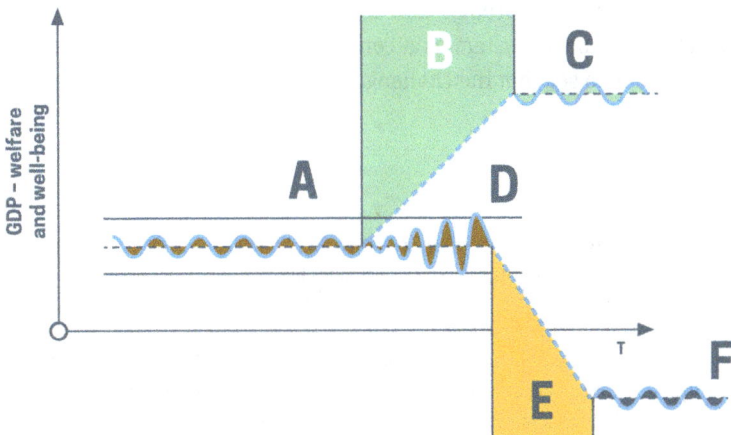

Figure 20: A systems-thinking approach to economic transformation.

---

135 Veblen 1899; see also Banuri and Ha 2020.

A represents traditional anti-cyclical supply and demand policy (Keynes 1.0), where repairing, compensating and deficit spending remain within a given growth trajectory.

B represents the transformational shift that is required (Keynes 2.0), in which monetary tools take precedence over fiscal ones.

C represents a new equilibrium where regenerative, circular or steady-state economics prevails.

D represents the conventional tunnel view, where we use historical data and project it into the future. Our analysis remains linear and expensive. There will be a critical slowdown of the entire system, with the speed and frequency of traditional interventions apparently indirectly proportional to the stability of the system itself. The biophysical environment will have further degraded. We will then have lost the 'window of opportunity' to correct and transform our society.

E is a deflection point, where we are operating outside the 'window of opportunity'. Ecosystems have passed multiple, non-linear tipping points, causing massive backlashes and negative externalities that we can no longer internalise. Regardless of their political agendas, societies will be faced with numerous state failures, waves of forced migration and social upheavals. In this scenario, additional ongoing political and economic costs will come on top of a massive downturn in well-being and wealth, which will ultimately end in a new equilibrium.

F represents this new equilibrium that nobody wanted in the first place. It will very likely not be the end of the world, but it will be the end of the world as we know it today. And we will have missed the opportunities of the Keynes 2.0 moment and the timeline it could have opened up,[136] instead ending up in a net negative equilibrium.

Instead of extending the past and applying conventional economic thinking, we should take a systems-thinking approach that incorporates interdisciplinary evidence[137] and looks at the financial system as a complex open-flow and network system.[138] We will then be able to see that the challenges ahead are not cyclical in nature,

---

136 There is a vast body of literature on each of the six scenarios described above. However, most studies do not sufficiently distinguish the role of the monetary system within a 'window of opportunity'.

137 Interdisciplinarity in this context does not refer to the smallest common denominator, but to the specific contribution each discipline can make towards addressing a shared topic of concern. In the present context, finance and economics can make a specific contribution regarding the optimal allocation of resources, building liquidity to achieve a specific goal and setting prices under conditions of risk, uncertainty and scarcity. This is something no other academic discipline can yet do. In short, finance and the design of the monetary system can, as described throughout this book, make it possible to achieve the 'cheapest of all worlds'.

138 See the World Academy of Art and Science's (WAAS) Tao of Finance working group and the Club of Rome's Rethinking Finance, which both apply systems-thinking approaches to finance and the IMS. In particular, see Brunnhuber 2020 and 2023 and Club of Rome 2024.

but non-linear and disruptive, following multiple S-curves, and that we are confronted with massive collective externalities and future cost and damage functions that go far beyond the traditional growth trajectory of 2–3% globally.

> **Box 16:** Historical transitions in numbers
> In numbers: the post-WW2 European recovery plan known as the Marshall Plan[139] represented roughly 5% of US GDP, the EU eastern enlargement about 0.1–0.2% of EU GDP, the Rio Declaration of 1992 to fund the Global South 0.8% of global GDP and German reunification about 0.1% of German GDP.[140] When the Comecon and Eastern Europe's planned economy collapsed, ushering in a competitive market economy, the familiar rules of the game that were already in place needed to be adapted. Even the decades-long transition from an agricultural to an industrial society involved a lower transfer of money per year than that demanded by the challenges we are currently facing. The amount of money required for the systems change needed in the 21st century is about eight to ten times higher than any historical precedent.

We have to transform an entire energy system – and we have to do so while 80% of our economic activities still depend on fossil energy, while the entire global economy is still growing by 2–3% per year, while we are facing unprecedented social and ecological externalities that we can no longer ignore and while operating in an opaque political environment where the line between allies and enemies is constantly shifting. Rather than simply applying the existing monetary rules to a new historical situation, the challenge seems to be the opposite: the Anthropocene era forces us to re-evaluate the existing rules and come up with new ones that allow us to reframe the entire global energy system, create circular and regenerative economies instead of extractive ones, fund our global commons, scale up emerging new technologies and make them accessible to all and provide the tools needed to mobilise trillions of private-sector funding for our common future. There is no real historical blueprint we can draw on. And this time the change has to be applied to ourselves, to our political agendas, to our business activities and to our day-to-day private lives. It is like a marathon runner performing surgery on their own heart in the middle of a race using a new and not yet fully proven method. The paradigm shift from a fossil to a renewable era will require at least 7–10% of GDP each year, surpassing all growth trajectories of the past. In other words: we must admit that we caused the damage in the first place and need to adopt a secondary preventive approach and new rules of the game in order to lower future costs. This systems-thinking approach will encourage us to move beyond well-known academic rituals, economic schools and activism, and to dance with this complex open network system instead of pretending to control it. Traditional economics operates inductively, taking individual behaviour as its starting point in order to derive a general law, or the other way round, deductively, using general assumptions as a theoretical framework to predict individual behaviours.

---

139 See German Marshall Plan 2024.
140 Calculated based on German GDP in 1991.

This approach is supported by the idea that the native human mind, armed with a pencil or Excel sheet and a capacity for critical thinking, is able to grasp complex systems. But that idea is mistaken. Humans are a deficient species, which is not fully adapted to nature, causing multiple unintended consequences originating from intended and conscious actions. The gap between reality and human understanding can only be bridged by narratives we all believe in, cultural achievements we all rely on and technological inventions and scientific discoveries that act like prostheses. Humans operate in this 'middle dimension' of metres and minutes, hammers and nails, wheels and fire. Our window of perception is small and everything outside that window requires a support system to make up for all our deficits. Non-linear tipping points, black swan events and exponential backlashes cannot be perceived through mere mental effort, equilibrium models and rational choice theories. Understanding and evaluating risks under complex conditions falls outside the repertoire of conventional economics. It is like driving a car at night and not putting the lights on, but instead looking through the rear mirror and hoping that will give us the information we need to navigate the road ahead. However, new technologies and methods, in particular AI and big data analytics, can provide that information. If we want to better understand the intimate link between a systems-thinking approach and finance, the relevance of that approach to an economics of transformation and the role that the monetary and financial system can play in building a sustainable future, the systemic elements discussed in the following section will be of particular interest. They are all grouped around the concept of ordered complexity.

Towards Ordered Complexity

Complex does not mean the same as complicated, correlated or causally related. Complexity means that we are not able to separate thought from action, an object from the tool used to measure it, input from output or a system from its context. This is particularly relevant to the present topic. The financial system is a complex system in the specific sense that we cannot disentangle it from its context and the actors that operate within it. That means we cannot fully control it, as we are part of it. However, we could try to dance with the system instead.[141] There are several elements that are of particular relevance for the monetary system: the *fractal architecture* of our financial system; the concept of *emergence*; the power *of non-linear leverage points* to shift our economy from one state to another; the role of *complementary pairs*; and the *dawn of new digital technologies*. These elements provide a better theoretical framework that allows us to grasp

---

141 This refers to the concept of fuzzy logic: if clear-cut quantitative data does not provide robust information about the dynamics of a system, humans make decisions based on vague, incomplete, sometimes inaccurate information and the overall system lacks certainty and transparency, then ambiguity, qualitative parameters, relevance and coherence will be more important than quantitative data analysis. See Zadeh 1965; Ragin 2000; Tsoukalas 2023.

the monetary system as a network and identify the built-in risks, uncertainties and flaws and the impacts they have on any economy undergoing transformation. Systems thinking seeks to overcome the 'micro–macro fallacy' that conventional economics is confronted with. Findings at a micro level do not necessarily provide a valid basis for statements and conclusions at a macro level. Behavioural finance and rational/public choice and game theory can explain individual propensity to utility maximisation and other behavioural patterns of small, homogeneous groups and cohorts, but they cannot scale up their findings to macro and societal level. Modern societies are heterogeneous and do not follow a Gaussian distribution. The best way to describe the link between the micro and macro levels within a complex system is in terms of its fractal architecture. Meaning that regardless of whether we look into the nano or the macro world, we will be able to identify similar features – known as fractals.[142] A fractal (from the Latin *fractus*, 'broken') is a figure that remains the same no matter how far we zoom in or out. Fractals represent similarities rather than equalities. Examples can be found in river basins, songs and paintings, lungs and blood vessels, galaxies and clouds, crystals and snowflakes – and in the stock, currency and credit markets. In 'Mandelbrot fractals', we can see that the macro (snowflake) contains the micro (triangle) and the macro level depends on *isomorphic, scale-independent* variables. If we want to understand and intervene at a macro level, which is far more complex than the micro level, we will need new tools, above and beyond Excel sheets and pencils, and must identify financial fractals. In the figure below (Figure 21), the triangle is replicated and recombined to create new shapes, leading finally to a snowflake mandala. The underlying figure, however, remains the same.

A   B   C   D

Figure 21: Towards fractal finance.
The triangle remains the same from (A) to (D), even as complexity increases.

Treating finance as a complex system recognises that the input and initial conditions do not fully determine the output. All variables in a complex open-flow network are interconnected. Historical data can therefore not account for the dynamics and magnitude of future outcomes and the associated risks. The intermediate results of any complex financial system cannot be fully anticipated, as that system will have emergent properties.

---

142 See Mandelbrot and Hudson 2008; Schubert 2023.

Complex systems[143] are non-linear, meaning the outcomes are not 100% determined and so remain unpredictable. Bifurcations, attractors, critical thresholds and fractals with scale-independent isomorphisms shape and modify the ongoing process.[144] While many social phenomena may be perceived as complicated, they are first and foremost complex and chaotic.[145] They are multifactorial and do not allow for any simple cause–effect explanations. In particular, finance as an intermediary between savers and investors has become a complex, self-serving black box. Whereas in the 1980s over 80% of corporate shares were managed by private households, around that same proportion is now managed by pension funds, investment banks, mutual funds, insurance companies and sovereign wealth funds, backed up by multiple credit rating agencies, consultancies and accounting firms. If we look at the balance sheets of these firms, we will find that most of the financial liabilities relate to trade within the financial sector itself.[146] This development has made the financial sector an almost unmanageable black box, with many serious unintended consequences. The initial idea of 'shareholder value' has been supplanted by myopic, pro-cyclical herd manoeuvres.

The difference between complementarity and causality is key, and grasping it represents a foundational shift in our mindset. Complementarity is a relationship between two components that are incompatible yet mutually necessary. These opposing components do not cancel each other out, but are both needed to better describe phenomena.[147] This also applies to the monetary system, where two components remain intertwined with each other, leading to multiple feedback loops and operating in a complementary manner. Causal links in a complex, non-linear world are very rare, if they occur at all. Causalities in the social realm represent singular, historical events, rather than a general economic law. Instead of searching for the invisible, we should aim to identify complementary pairs. On the view advocated here, complementarities are not metaphors or analogies, but rather co-constitutive of a general economic law – independently of the pairs' flow or content that we choose or discover. An obstacle in one place could be-

---

143 See Gribbin 2005. On social sciences and economics, see Johnson 2010, Buchanan 2013, Byrne and Callaghan 2023 and Šlaus 2020.

144 Mandelbrot 1977; Mainzer 1997.

145 A chaotic system is defined by two components: A system is in constant motion and the outcome and output of that system is sensitive towards subtle changes in its initial state. The proposal made in the book, considers the economic system being chaotic and introducing a new monetary supply aggregate refers to a subtle change in its initial state which will eventually change the outcome of the system. See Farmer 2024

146 See Akgiray 2019 for an informative study. Over the past 50 years, the revenues and profits of this industry have risen from about 2–3% of GDP to over 8%. There is no economy of scale whatsoever, despite an absolute increase in volume. When the financial sector is dealing with other people's money, the principles of an economy of scale do not seem to apply.

147 General examples include energy and time, wave and particle, determinism and chance, structure and function, substance and process, autonomy and interconnectedness, physical and mental. See Bohr 2008; Meyer-Abich 1965; Walach 2010.

come a catalyst or attractor in another, and then elsewhere a challenge or a goal. This complementarity can help us find a new equilibrium for finance and for the future. Table 6 below illustrates some prominent examples relevant to the financial sector, which are further explained in the text:

Table 6: Examples of complementary pairs in economics.

Fiscal and monetary policy	Resilience and efficiency
State and private sector	Free market and state interventions
Commons and positional goods	Development and stagnation
Society and individual	Investment and consumption
Ecology and economy	Local and global
Pre- and redistributive measures	Freedom and responsibility

Both components are needed and depend on each other. The challenge is to identify the right pairs and their internal relationship, instead of abandoning them in favour of mere correlations or causal links. Finally, complex systems develop in a non-linear fashion. The *emergence* of a new systemic state is described as a property, with interactions between local and decentralised agents ultimately changing the state of the entire system. Emergence is more than the sum of its initial, isolated parts; instead, these parts are transformed through their interactions. The probability of such emergence arises out of alternating, asymmetric interactions between the components in the network, which cause multiple feedback loops. It's like placing one brick next to another over and over again until we reach a point where the bricks' morphology forces us to classify what we have built as a Renaissance building.[148] In this sense, complex systems remain non-determined and non-predictable. Accordingly, every complex network has its own *tipping points*. If we look at the intersection between finance and sustainability from a systemic perspective, emergence translates into multiple leverage or tipping points. It has the potential to irreversibly shift the state of the system. Four of these points are of particular relevance. (a) Linear interventions involve well-known stress tests or regulatory adjustments; (b) dynamic interventions additionally take feedback loops, delayed responses and uncertainties into account; (c) complex measures involve changing the rules of the game and implementing new technologies; and finally (d) paradigm shifts reset the values and purpose of the entire monetary system. The higher the leverage point, the more we need to invest in changing our mindset and the more we will end up changing the financial architecture rather than simply providing means to finance the change. Conversely, the lower the leverage point, the more effort we have to exert to finance the change, but the less affected the monetary architecture will be. If we decide to leverage the entire financial system using stress tests, green taxonomies and taxation schemes, we will need to put a lot of effort into optimising the existing rules of the game. If we dare to fundamentally question

---

148 Parisi 1999.

the design itself, we will end up with a new system that operates on the basis of new values and provides new forms of financial engineering. The following figure (Figure 22) summarises some of the main interventions.

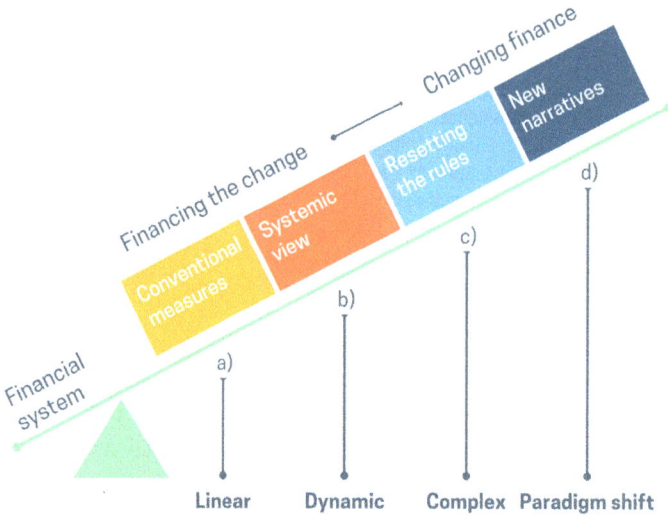

Figure 22: Tipping points for the financial sector to enable transformation.
Conventional measures: stress tests, taxation, subsidies, taxonomies, regulatory adjustments; systemic view: taking account of feedback loops, delays, risks and uncertainties, double materiality; resetting the rules: central bank mandates, private goods and commons; new narratives: goals of the system, values, new financial engineering tools, new monetary channels.

The figure (Figure 23) and table (Table 7) below summarise the characteristics of ordered complexity.

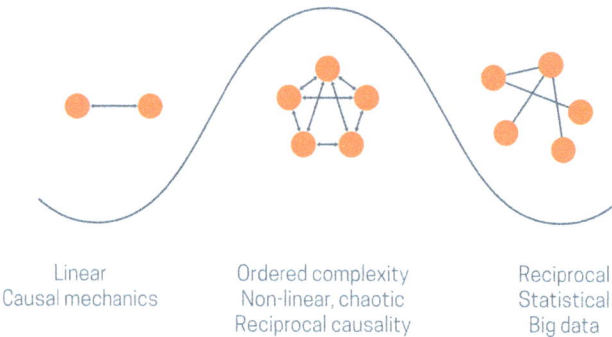

Linear	Ordered complexity	Reciprocal
Causal mechanics	Non-linear, chaotic	Statistical
	Reciprocal causality	Big data

Figure 23: Beyond causality and correlations: ordered complexity.

At one end of the spectrum lies simple linear causality, which represents a mechanistic view of the world. At the other end are systems that interact based on correlations and probabilities. Entities are weakly coupled and there is no linear causality involved. Here, the world is seen through the lens of statistics. Between these two extremes lies the domain of complexity, where mutual causalities and feedback loops create an ordered complexity. Between singular causal events and mere random collisions lies the realm of complex self-organisation, which encompasses the vast majority of real-life systems, including ecosystems and our financial system.

Table 7: Main characteristics: linear causality, ordered complexity, correlations.

Linear causality	Ordered complexity	Correlations
Mechanistic perspective	Complementarity	Technology (AI, synthetic biology and robotics)
Historical evidence for a single case	Fuzzy logic	Doubling and mirroring the world
Historical data	Fractals	Transcending the middle dimension in speed and scale
Stress tests	Emergence	Predictive
Taxonomies	Non-linear tipping points	Disclosing the network effects, with all their interdependencies and interrelatedness
Linear, proportional interventions	Reciprocal, circular causality	Self-learning and self-improving

Fintech and the Token Economy: The Great Facilitator and Integrator

Technology has always been the result of human ingenuity, creativity and reasoning. And it has always evolved alongside human societies and shaped human behaviours and the environment by driving further specialisation, research and development. That was true for the wheel and the plough, the book press, electricity and the Internet. And it is true today for AI, robotics, synthetic biology and quantum computing. Each time it has been a human idea, which materialised in the society humans were living in, that translated into economic activities and new challenges for the financial sector.[149] At the same time, every technology has been a double-edged sword. From

---

149 From physical matter (fire, the wheel, the printing press) to genetic codes (synthetic biology) to information (data analysis), *Homo technologicus* has always manipulated its environment, seeking to control, contain and utilise it to build a better world. But none of these endeavours are economically neutral; they always affect the creation of wealth, income distribution and political power structures. This means that the return on creativity and human intelligence has helped to determine the course of history.

breadknives to chatbots, the regulatory framework and practical applications have al-ways been the determinants of whether a technology succeeds or fails. But a compre-hensive political framework is needed to enable scalability, accessibility and afford-ability for all. As with the shift from the agricultural to the industrial era, there is an interplay between the emergence of new technologies (in that case: the steam engine, the lightbulb and many others) and a new polity (in that case: the liberal order). Over the course of 200 years, the emergence of the liberal order made it possible to double life expectancy, reduce poverty by 90% and child mortality by even more, increase the number of democracies from just one to over 50% of countries and increase the rate of people completing primary education from 17% to 86%, and enrolment rates to up to 95%. Traditionally, general-purpose technologies operate intersectionally, affect-ing not just a single economic segment but the whole of society. The plough, the wheel, the steam engine, the railway and the electric bulb are examples of such foun-dational innovations.

Box 17: On cognitive capitalism

There is a vast literature on 'cognitive capitalism', which looks at the relationship between a society's cognitive abilities and its economic success. The level of spending on education relative to GDP corre-lates empirically with a society's growth rate and international competitiveness. According to these studies, Asia has a higher collective IQ than Europe or the USA. However, AI will sooner or later replace most cognitive abilities, and collective creativity will be the game changer for international competi-tiveness instead. Creativity can be defined as tolerance of individual differences and variance. Societies and economies that are able to unlock, support and foster individual creativity instead of mere cogni-tive abilities will then have a competitive advantage over those that do not or cannot. The data, infor-mation and knowledge generated through creativity is further enhanced in societies and economies that critically assess, review and continually adjust this process through an established third sector (comprising, in particular, scientific bodies and NGOs, as well as a free, critical press) and ultimately feed back into economic and political decisions. Both creativity and critical feedback will in the future be key to any competitive advantage between different political systems. Societies that ignore the fact that free and trustworthy information leads to more reliable price signals and ultimately permits better political and economic decisions quickly become uninvestable. That is why open, human-centric socie-ties will outperform autocratic, collectivist ones. In short: the outcome of the systems clash between open and closed societies has been decided already.[150]

There are at least five features that distinguish the new general-purpose technologies of the 21st century (in particular, AI, synthetic biology, robotics and quantum computing) from their predecessors. Firstly, they transcend the conventional boundaries between the social and biological worlds. In the information age, general-purpose technologies not only operate cross-sectionally but add another layer of complexity: they blur the natural boundaries between biological, physical and societal reality. Brain–chip interfa-ces will bridge the gap between physiological process and technology in a way that a

---

150 On cognitive capitalism, see Rindermann 2018, Heinsohn 2019 and Brunnhuber 2023a.

hammer, wheel or steam engine cannot. Take the advances of the Internet of Things (IoT), which is becoming a global digital neural network in which sensors provide real-time information about the state of the earth and help us react accordingly.[151] AI, big data analytics, quantum computing, robotics, the IoT, drones, smart grids, renewables, energy storage, next-generation nuclear, e-mobility, blockchains, 3D printing, nanotechnology, materials science and gene editing[152] all in one way or another cut across the dualisms of private and public, science and humanities,[153] biological and psychological, and have become critical components of the transformation process – all orchestrated by the financial system. Secondly, these new technologies are able to make the interconnectedness and interdependency visible and measurable, thus freeing us from silos and showing us that we live in a system and that every impact we generate and every result we achieve is the result of a net effect. We are living literally in a web without a weaver. Thirdly, these new technologies can mirror the world in real time. Instead of relying on isolated experimental data, field studies and surveys, all of which are dependent on the past, to draw conclusions about the future, complex AI and big data correlations can double the world in real time, simulating potential interventions and changes and allowing us to adapt our real world accordingly. Fourthly, these technologies have an in-built capacity for rigorous self-improvement entirely unlike any previous general-purpose technology. No microscope, plane, wheel or printing press has the intrinsic technological capacity for ongoing self-maximisation and self-learning. A plane, once produced, remains a plane, a wheel a wheel and a printing press a printing press. AI, in contrast, undergoes a constant process of self-improvement and adaptation. Fifthly, the new technologies can reach out into the macro and nano worlds with unprecedented speed and on an unprecedented scale, exploring spheres we did not even know existed and far surpassing the potential of the native human mind. These five properties – blurring the boundaries, visualising the world as a network, mirroring in real time, self-improving and reaching out into dimensions inaccessible to the human mind – together represent the *differentia specifica* that no other past general-purpose technology has been able to provide, and mark a major technological shift that we are now going through in the 21st century. This is having an unprecedented, foundational impact on how we analyse economic data and financial transactions and derive political recommendations from them,[154] as summarised in table below (Table 8).

---

151 See World Economic Forum 2024.

152 Almost 50% of future success in implementing the UN SDGs will depend on these new technologies. Similar to the industrial era, these new technologies can increase productivity by 1.5% per year and scale up our GDP by over 25%. See Force for Good 2024.

153 Brunnhuber 2024.

154 The impact of these new technologies transcends the 'two cultures' of science and the humanities. A third culture is emerging that is able to integrate traditional forms of understanding and explanation. See Brunnhuber 2024a.

Table 8: The differentia specifica of the new technologies of the 21st century.

Differentia specifica	Examples
Blurring boundaries	Transcending the differences between the physical and mental spheres
Visualising interconnectedness in real time	Proof of concept that we are in a web without a weaver
Doubling the world	Mirroring the real world, enabling simulation of alternatives
Built-in self-improvement	Automation, ongoing optimisation of learning and adapting to a complex world
Enhancing our knowledge and consciousness	Transcending the native mind and reaching out into unknown territories (nano and macro) onmi use

Unlike in the past, when the role of technology in finance was limited to cash machines and digital bank accounts, we now need new technologies (or new applications of existing technologies) to deal with the increasing complexity. Technology has become a major building block and agent of change. The rise of a token economy reflects the change in finance. Any transferable assets can potentially be tokenised.[155] That includes non-financial transactions, such as those involving securities, media and art, currency-based transactions, such as those involving CBDCs and cryptocurrencies, and tokenised access to platforms, shared ownerships, certifications and new incentives. Each time a digital token is utilised, it reflects new forms of value creation, meets unmet needs and creates a kind of digital barter system that runs in parallel to, though is still intertwined with, the conventional financial system. The disruptive and transformative nature of any token economy, including all its technological, legal, ethical, economic and cultural dimensions, becomes obvious when business models allow decentralised transactions using a P2P e-wallet without intermediaries such as banks. To be more precise: a token, created for instance by an initial coin offering and linked to a blockchain-based smart contract, is able to provide the additional liquidity and purchasing power needed for a given transaction.[156] What is missing is

---

[155] This further translates into a shift from client servers and a cloud-based system (Web 2.0) to a collective, decentralised blockchain-based system (Web 3.0); see Voshmgir 2023 and 2024. There are at least eight interconnected fields or technologies – some new, others upgraded – that are opening up new opportunities and risks: cryptocurrencies, AI, cloud computing, blockchains, 'new space', synthetic biology, solar fusion and quantum computing (personal communication with Philipp Schöller, 4 September 2024).

[156] At present, these 'decentralised finance' (DeFi) business models have a volume of almost 50 billion TVL (total value locked) and remain a niche product. Fully decentralised finance is a myth. Creating and maintaining any DeFi model will always require some sort of hierarchy. All DeFi models to date have failed because they (often surreptitiously) involved some sort of centralised finance

the governance and adequate funding to make it all happen. There are three aspects of particular importance for the monetary and financial sector. Firstly, digital distributed ledger technologies (blockchains) to ensure the transparency of financial transactions and combat illicit activities. Secondly, generative AI algorithms to provide additional information on complex networks, predictive coding and a doubling of the world in digital form, so that we can simulate transactions in real time and manage the complexities associated with common goods, such as traffic infrastructure, healthcare systems and power grids. Thirdly, integrated digital financial platforms that allow institutions to provide integrated financial services, from accounting to credit lines to B2B and B2P services. The open banking model, based on a data-in-motion principle that allows local banks direct access to balance sheets, can reduce costs, increase trust and accountability, generate massive quantities of bottom-up alternative data and allow secondary debt market scaling (mortgage-backed securities).[157]

I am aware that these preliminary findings on ordered complexity and the new technologies associated with it are still rather abstract and theoretical. What, then, are these technologies' practical implications for an economics of transformation? If we agree that fractals and fuzzy logic, emergent structures, non-linear tipping points and complementary pairs not only better describe the nature of networks and their intrinsic uncertainties, and offer an improvement over the equilibrium models that prevail in traditional economics, then it makes sense to also apply them to finance. In the next sections, I will show that the finance of the future needs features of ordered complexity to provide a comprehensive solution to the challenges facing us. New digital technologies enable an economics of transformation that operates in networks with multiple risks and uncertainties. AI, deep learning and big data correlations do not eliminate complexity, but can provide preventive tools that allow us to better visualise, simulate and then deal with the challenges of complexity that we are confronted with in the 21st century. Scale-independent fractals, attractors and a helicopter view enable a better understanding of the system's dynamics than any linear thinking; for those dynamics cannot be grasped by the naked eye, Excel sheets, educated best guesses, longitudinal historical data or equilibrium models. If we start looking at our financial system from a systems perspective, we will realise that it is an open, complex network, with a tendency towards self-organisation, unforeseen butterfly effects and fuzzy and hybrid logics dominating over clarity and precise quantitative prognoses, in which irreversible tipping points, fatality events, non-causal

---

(CeFi). The defaults of the crypto stock exchange FTX, the stablecoin TerraUSD and the crypto bank Celsius are recent examples. See Meyer et al. 2022; EUBOF 2022. Instead of further decentralising the financial and monetary system, we should start by upgrading it.

157 1.3 billion people have no bank account and 160 million MSMEs are facing a funding gap of over five trillion USD. Three-quarters of these MSMEs do not even have access to bank loans. This is a sign of capital market inefficiency. High interest rates, complex administrative procedures and a lack of collateral mean millions of firms cannot access adequate liquidity. See People-Centered Internet 2023.

emergent structures and multicausality are becoming the new normal. If we finally admit that none of us know enough about our future, we can then turn our attention to the concept of ordered complexity and the power of new technologies. But before we consider some specific examples in Part II, we have to get clear about the tragedy of our commons, which is intimately bound up with the issues under discussion here. That is the topic of the next section.

Waking the Giant: The Real Tragedy of Our Planetary Commons

A son once asked his father, 'What do I have in common with a bird? I can't fly, I don't have feathers, I can't crawl, I can't lay eggs.' The father replied, 'You're giving the wrong answer to the right question. You should be thinking about what you and the bird *do* have in common. You share over 95% of your DNA coding, you both experience hunger, desire, fear, excitement, you can both form social bonds. Though not obvious at first glance, these commonalities are much greater than the differences. If you acknowledge the common features first, you can much more easily appreciate and welcome the differences.' Historically, we used to live in a large, slow and empty world with a small population and low levels of individual energy and resource consumption, where a functioning commons predominated.[158] Private equity, ownership and wealth played a subordinate role. In the 21st century, we are living in a fast, full and complex world with a high population density and a high level of individual energy and resource consumption, where private property and wealth creation dominate over public goods.[159] In numbers, as mentioned earlier: About 80% of all liquid and illiquid assets on this planet are private assets, 20% are common assets. If we only consider liquid assets, the proportion that are privately owned increases to 90%.[160] This is due in part to the Washington Consensus of 1992,[161] when we decided to privatise, liberalise and deregulate the planet, expecting more wealth and prosperity on the one hand and more democracy on the other. But both those expectations have largely proved to be wishful thinking.[162] It seems that the monetary mechanisms we have been using to install, manage and fund our commons only worked well within a framework of low or negligible negative externalities, minimal interconnectedness, high economic growth and low unemployment.

---

158 Rockström and Klum 2016.
159 See Club of Rome 2018.
160 The world is largely privatised in an uneven manner. See the Credit Suisse 2021 Global Wealth Report.
161 Williamson 2008.
162 In fact, autocracies are on the rise and numerous ecological backlashes are challenging the liberal order that enabled large parts of the world population to achieve higher levels of well-being and wealth. See Brunnhuber 2023a.

But we are now living in a new era,[163] and the playing field has fundamentally changed when it comes to funding, managing and securing our (global) commons. However, there are several reasons why we should not abandon the principle of commons, but rather expand it. In a general sense, commons help us to pool private risks, hedge systemic uncertainties and ensure political stability. Properly installed, funded and managed, commons such as national security, public sanitation, healthcare, universal primary education and nature reserves can provide an indispensable precondition for more private wealth, profits and prosperity.[164] However, in a full world where everything is interdependent and interconnected in real time and where we have been overshooting planetary boundaries, private wealth depends on healthy, functional commons. A full world without functioning commons would therefore be a poorer world in all respects. This forces us to reconsider what should be a private good and what should be a common good. We might then need to challenge outdated thinking to finance the necessary changes.[165] There are several reasons why it has become difficult to fund our commons. 1. The current monetary system is unstable, generating a series of currency, banking and state crises. Each time there is a financial crisis, we end up busy repairing the system and trying to build back better, but the commons are always last on the list. 2. Multiple lock-in effects prevent us from unleashing the potential of our commons, so that they remain chronically underfunded. This includes the high debt burden, conflicting subsidies and taxation schemes and the defence and military complex. 3. If we use conventional financial measures that are mainly based on redistributing money, it will take over three generations to secure our commons globally.[166] 4. Privatising our commons will create additional negative social and ecological externalities that the public sector will have to manage. 5. Funding requires additional, conditioned liquidity that no taxation scheme has ever been able to deliver. 6. The informal sector (illicit transactions) is pulling the financial system in the wrong direction. Any future proposal to finance our commons has to take these constraints into account. This affects private property and associated liabilities as well as common goods and their potential overuse. From an evolutionary perspective, cooperative behaviours that go beyond maximising yields for individuals are relatively unstable and expensive. So that they do not collapse, specific rules, sanctions and universally shared narratives are needed.[167] If commons are not properly funded and regulated, they will be systematically cannibalised by pri-

---

163 See Crutzen 2002. Although the term Anthropocene in a geological sense was recently (April 2024) rejected by the International Commission on Stratigraphy, I am using it here in a social and economic sense.

164 In a survey of almost 20,000 people across the G20, 58% were very worried about global commons and over 74% supported the idea that economics should prioritise human well-being and ecological protection over profit. See Gaffney et al. 2021.

165 Von Weizsäcker and Wijkman 2017.

166 Woodward 2015; Winthrop and McGivney 2015.

167 Mazzucato 2023.

vate actors and moral hazards will prevail. An adapted financial system that is able to fund, hedge and manage our global commons upfront would avoid such parasitic behaviours and help to unleash their full potential.[168] It looks like we are using the wrong financial mechanism to address the right problems. Financing our commons requires a new, out-of-the-box approach, where the private, public and third sectors complement each other rather than competing on the marketplace. Private market solutions alone would leave us as a global community with uncovered negative externalities, short-term windfall profits and risk-averse, pro-cyclical behaviour. That would eventually be more expensive, as companies would need to add an additional risk premium to meet their rent-seeking targets. On the other side, state interventions are traditionally slow and subject to political constraints and administrative overload. Moreover, the public sector alone cannot always provide the expertise and knowledge needed to manage commons. The third sector, with over ten million NGOs, can provide the expertise but is chronically underfunded. These NGOs mainly operate where there is no state capacity or market mechanism in place.[169] In Part II, I will explore the new monetary and financial coalitions that are being formed between the private and public sectors (public–private partnerships) and between the public and third sectors (P3Ss) in order to properly fund and manage our commons. The relation between private and common is like an asymmetric iceberg paradox. Although the commons only make up 10–20% of all assets, they represent the basis for all private wealth accumulation. If we use the iceberg as a metaphor to better understand the link between private and public goods, we will reject the traditional binary view in which private and public are seen as mutually exclusive opposites. In truth, the larger, private sector cannot exist without the smaller, public one. More generally speaking, commons do not need to generate revenue, but private revenue creation is reliant on commons. Instead of favouring a binary approach, we should instead take a complementary one, and understand that commons are a precondition for private goods, not the other way round. That means the private sector can unlock its full potential only if the required commons are in place. If we acknowledge that commons are a precondition for any private initiative, then we will need to look more closely and seriously at how to finance them. Leaving this sleeping giant to slumber means we are not tapping into the full potential of either our commons or our private sector (see figure 24). Economically speaking, we remain in a Pareto-inferior equilibrium with lower wealth, productivity and efficiency and higher social and ecological costs. The pearl of wisdom here is that if we want to properly finance and regulate the 10%, we need far more financialisation than today, but we need it to be designed differently. The benefits will eventually outweigh the costs. In short: we *can* patent the sun,

---

168 Based on game theory and evolutionary biology, Robert Axelrod demonstrated across several tournament experiments the requirements for stable reciprocal cooperation. See Axelrod 2006.
169 Examples include Médecins Sans Frontières (MSF), World Central Kitchen (WCK) and the many local initiatives trying to restore or protect regional nature reserves. In most cases, public and corporate initiatives fail to provide the necessary services.

fresh water, access to preschooling or healthcare, but we *shouldn't*. As Keynes put it on a BBC radio interview in 1942: 'Anything we can actually do, we can afford.'[170]

Private wealth
and income

Planetary
commons

Figure 24: The iceberg paradox.

So rather than further privatising the world by exploiting commons even more, we should aim for a sensible interplay between the private, public and third sectors. In order to better understand this interplay, the monetary and financial sector will be key. Traditionally, we define commons as goods and services which are non-excludable, meaning it is impossible to prevent people from using them. Moreover, they are semi-rivalrous, meaning one person's using a good or service diminishes another's ability to do so.[171] In this sense, commons are easily neglected, congested and overused, due to multiple free-rider effects that ultimately deteriorate our common assets. From a financial perspective, a common good is not a thing, but a convention, like the rules of a club, a marriage contract or a legal code governing our use of or access to a good or service. It is therefore not a matter of natural law, but depends on us as a community to determine whether a good or service ultimately becomes common or private, which will come down to the nature of that good or service. I define *commons* in a general sense as *goods, services or rights accessible by everyone and regulated by their (local, regional and/or global) stakeholders.* Examples include fresh air, species conservation and access to healthcare, preschooling or water. In short: our commons are not a given, but rather reflect the *sensus communis*, meaning they represent what we all want to happen for all of us. Just think of the Grand Canal, which the Chinese started building in 485 CE and completed in 1290. More than 1,782 kilometres in length, it is still in use as a water supply system. Societies depend on these sorts of physical resources, which follow a completely different logic to private goods and services.

In 1968, Garrett Hardin published a seminal paper on the 'tragedy of the commons'.[172] His main argument was that commons are either underserved, neglected or

---

170 See Keynes 2012 [1942], 270.
171 Standing 2019.
172 See Hardin 1968.

overused, due to free-rider and moral-hazard effects, and so the provision of commons will always be deficient.[173] This triggered several decades of academic debate, culminating in the Nobel Prize in Economics being awarded to Elinor Ostrom.[174] Today, the discussion is far from over. The UN SDGs[175] and recurrent external ecological shocks are raising the issue again, since most, if not all, of the resulting challenges affect our commons in one way or another. There are several characteristics that can help us to better discriminate between the nature of private and common goods or services. They include:

Covering basic needs for all: Commons should exclusively cover basic needs, such as education, health, shelter or security, not luxury (positional) goods and services, such as a swimming pool, SUV or a private gardener.[176] Positional goods' intrinsic value is determined by access, use and ownership relative to another person. In contrast, public goods and services are meant to be collective entitlements that are incommensurable and an end in themselves.[177]

Non-tradability: Private goods and services allow unlimited maximisation of profits and rent-seeking. Public goods, in contrast, require maintenance and regenerative measures once they are in place. In this sense, they represent a circular kind of economics, rather than the linear or exponential yield curve associated with profit-seeking companies. Private goods should meet the criteria of tradable and commercialised goods, whereas public goods do not necessarily have to be traded: they usually remain stationary and represent a positive collective externality for the private sector. Everybody should have access to roads, a sewage system and nurseries; we need to put a price tag on them, but then decide how to finance them.

The ceiling effect: One of the most striking differences from private goods is that commons typically have a 'ceiling'. Whereas private market activities grow without limit, commons by their nature are different. Once everybody is provided with or has access to a common good, the mission is accomplished. For example: if there is a need for 1,000 preschooling places, we need to provide and finance them. The same is true for

---

173 However, the distinguishing features of commons are not their non-rivalry or moral-hazard effects, as both those apply to some private goods as well. If everyone has a toothbrush, it does not mean that the good becomes rivalrous, as it remains a private good. Moreover, free-rider and moral-hazard effects are not confined to commons, but also extend to certain private goods, creating multiple negative externalities.

174 See Ostrom 1990.

175 See United Nations 2024.

176 See Veblen 1899; Schneider 2007.

177 We can refer here to Maslow's famous pyramid: at the bottom of the pyramid are more common and collective needs, such as shelter, food and bonding; the higher we climb up the pyramid, the more individual the needs become. In this psychological theory, common basic needs likewise take precedence over private achievements. See Maslow 1943.

fresh air, public parks, access to healthcare and restoration of nature reserves. In economic terms: the marginal cost curve for commons becomes close to zero once the job is done.

Regenerative nature: Once commons have been put in place and everybody has access to them, they require mechanisms to repair, recycle, maintain, refurbish, replace and reuse them over and over again. Meanwhile, private goods by their very nature can be stored, replaced, traded and collected without limit. Common goods are circular and regenerative by their very nature; they are means to an end and do not force communities to grow in order to maintain their status. In contrast, private goods involve a continuous, accumulative process of linear, exponential and unlimited growth and insatiable demand. In other words: we could collect private goods such as SUVs, pools, paintings or jewellery ad infinitum, but once we have provided access to nurseries or collective healthcare, higher education, security and shelter, and restored our nature reserves, there is no need for further growth. Once we all have fresh and clean air and all children have access to preschooling, these commons have been attained.

New financial engineering instruments: Three options have traditionally dominated the economic discussion on how to best fund our commons. The first is privatising them, and thus removing any public liabilities associated with them by turning them into private goods. The second is to manage common goods by restricting access to them to defined communities. They are thus turned into club or cooperative goods. This form of limited membership reduces one of the biases that commons are subject to, namely overuse. The third option is allowing public or state authorities to regulate the usage of commons through laws and entitlements, with the commons being financed by taxes, fees, charity or philanthropy. In the following sections, I will describe a fourth option, which uses new, unconventional monetary channels to finance common goods.

Social return on investment: Another prominent feature is that commons have an impressive social ROI. Compared with the annual ROI for S&P stocks (10%) and treasury bills (3–5%),[178] the arithmetical average for investment in UN SDGs is 10–100 times higher. Investing 100 billion USD in commons can generate a social benefit of 1.5 trillion USD equivalent in social and ecological goods.[179]

---

178 Damodaran 2019.
179 Bjørn Lomborg and his team undertook an ROI analysis of unspectacular but highly efficient and highly preventive measures that could be used to meet the targets of the UN Agenda for Sustainable Development. Such measures include investing in education (ROI 1:30), maternity and postnatal health (ROI 1:87), anti-malaria campaigns (ROI 1:48), improved nutrition (ROI 1:33), child vaccination (ROI 1:48) and skilled migration (ROI 1:20); stimulating trade and specialisation (ROI 1:7 for OECD countries and 1:99 for LDCs); and introducing a sin tax on nicotine, sugar and/or alcohol (ROI 1:23). They could save up to 4.2 million lives per year and an investment of 35 billion USD/year would have a social

Public legal coding: Public goods are collective liabilities: not an act of charity by the private sector, but legal entitlements shared by all of us and regulated by public law. Private goods, on the other hand, have limited liability regulated by private law. Any overuse and moral-hazard effects of common goods create additional costs for the public sector. Free-rider effects of private goods instead cause negative externalities, which are paid for either by the taxpayer, future generations or a third party. The associated risk assessment, liabilities and accountability should therefore be governed by a public legal code.[180]

If we take these characteristics together, we could define *public or common goods* in a general sense as ones that *meet basic needs for all, are not necessarily commercialised and tradable, have a ceiling effect, require regenerative activities, are governed by public law and are funded and hedged using sources other than private international capital, domestic private savings, taxes or fees.* The following table (Table 9) summarises these characteristics.

Table 9: Major characteristics of our commons.

Non-tradable	Commons should have a price tag, but in general should not be tradable
Basic needs	Commons should cover basic needs (education, health, shelter, security), not luxury (positional) goods and services
Ceiling effect	In contrast to private goods and services, commons have a ceiling once all basic needs are met
Regenerative	At the ceiling repair, rebuild, maintain and restore represents a circular, regenerative aspect of the economics of commons
Public finance	Funding, hedging and financing should not primarily depend on private resources (philanthropy, taxation, fees, loans or private equity)
Public laws	Risk assessment, liabilities and accountability should follow a public legal code, not a private one
Prerequisite	Commons are prerequisites for private-sector activities
Sleeping giant	Commons have a staggering ROI for the community involved, far exceeding competitive revenues from private goods

Common resource pools, public goods and club goods: We can take this argument further by distinguishing between common resource pools, public goods and club

---

benefit of 1.7 trillion USD. We can do more good in this way than by simply providing 175 billion USD in ODA per year. See Lomborg 2023.

180 Pistor 2019; see also chapter 5 of Brunnhuber 2023.

goods. *Common resource pools* are non-excludable but rivalrous. Greenhouse gas emissions, unrestricted grazing, which drives desertification, overfishing, which depletes global fisheries, pollution from industrial activities, traffic congestion, coral reef destruction due to expanded tourism, ocean pollution due to plastic waste and unregulated groundwater extraction are well-known examples of common resource pools being put under strain by our economic activities. Common to all of them is the unregulated access to the goods and the competitive, rivalrous situation they create around a scarce resource. Then there are *public goods*, which are non-excludable but non-rivalrous. That means that one person's use of them does not diminish another's, despite the unrestricted access to those goods. Examples include fresh air, flood protection systems, fire and weather services, public beaches, national constitutions, lending libraries, motorways, lighthouses, police forces, universal healthcare, the Internet and the sun. *Club goods* or *cooperative goods* are non-rivalrous within certain limits and excludable for non-members.[181] Membership determines use of and access to these goods, whose marginal cost tends towards zero. Examples include membership of a golf club, the EU or NATO. The size of the club and the membership fees determine the extent (if any) of congestion and overuse, and hence the marginal benefits for each member.

Towards our planetary commons: There are several ways to further classify our commons. The table below (Table 10) sets out some basic geographical classifications for different types of commons.

Table 10: Commons broken down by type and geographic scope.

	Biological commons	Cultural/social commons
Global	Oceans, sky, Antarctica, human genome, ecosystems, blood banks, seeds	Internet, AI, basic necessities, human rights, scientific knowledge
Regional	Mineral deposits, Great Lakes, mountains, regional flora and fauna, groundwater resources, forests, fisheries	Recipes, traditional medicines, public housing, universal healthcare, social inclusion, free elections, street lighting, national defence
Local	Bike paths, natural springs, harbours, community gardens, public parks, community farmers markets, public pools and gyms	Lending libraries, complementary currency systems, local customs, music and art

Traditionally, global ecological commons include outer space, the atmosphere, Antarctica, non-coastal seas and the deep seabed. These global commons fall under international jurisdiction, which is meant to ensure equitable use by all states. In the Anthropocene era, however, this concept needs amending, as the viability of the entire earth

---

181 Buchanan 1965.

system is under threat, with humanity having already surpassed six of the nine bio-physical boundaries identified by scientists.[182] This puts the entire world community in a hazard zone, with unprecedented domino cascades and tipping points that translate into additional costs. From a financial perspective, I have characterised this non-analogue trajectory as a 'window of opportunity' or 'Keynes 2.0 moment', in which the monetary system will become a key player for as long as the earth system as a whole is still reasonably intact. I propose to expand the concept of *planetary commons* introduced by Rockström et al.[183] to include the social and human spheres, so that it falls within the purview of the financial sector. By contrast with regulating the equal use and exploitation of common resource pools, public goods and club goods, planetary commons require a different governance and financial framework to regulate the resilience, safeguards and longevity of commons that we all collectively depend on. Most of these planetary commons are located within the sovereign territory and legal jurisdiction of nation states: for instance, the Amazon, wetlands, mangroves, coral reefs, fossil resources. That necessitates an entirely different governance and financial approach.[184] Extending this concept of planetary ecological commons to the social and human sphere requires us to accept that we as a world community must apply the standards of safeguarding, security, resilience and sustainability not only top-down to the earth system dynamics but also bottom-up to each individual, so that basic human needs are protected in a way that transcends the self-determination and sovereignty of individual nations (as is done, for instance, by the Human Rights Declaration). Both follow a similar logic. If a threshold is not met (human rights, dignity) or is surpassed (ecological tipping points), it will undermine the viability of that commons. The table below (Table 11) gives some examples.

Table 11: Examples of ecological and social planetary commons.

Ecological planetary commons	Social planetary commons
Atmosphere	Universal healthcare
Hydrosphere	Education
Biosphere	Food and shelter
Lithosphere	Security
Cryosphere	Information

Both types of commons claim a legal status that transcends state sovereignty, are based on principles of equitable use and access and require financial support and compensation mechanisms to enable the states, communities and indigenous groups

---

182 Richardson et al. 2023.
183 Rockström et al. 2024.
184 See for example the Montreal Protocol on Substances That Deplete the Ozone Layer (originally agreed September 1987, subsequently amended four times): UN Environment Programme 1987.

that host or represent these planetary commons to meet their primary responsibility. That requires a nested, embedded approach that allows scalability upstream and downstream as well as subsidiary responsibility. I am aware that all taxonomies that attempt to classify commons are incomplete, flawed and overlapping. I will illustrate this using the Amazon rainforest as an example of a planetary commons, fisheries as an example of a common resource pool, healthcare and nurseries as examples of club goods and a communal park as an example of a public good to emphasise that they all, despite different regulations and jurisdictions, require similar financial mechanisms that are entirely different from past approaches to financing commons.

The Amazon as a planetary commons: Although the Amazon is a planetary commons, it falls under national jurisdiction. Alternative uses of the rainforest would incur opportunity costs at national level, while there will be a global economic impact if it is not protected sufficiently. The marginal costs of protecting the rainforest need to be made equal to the marginal costs of an alternative use. For example, to incentivise them to stop burning down the rainforest and creating farmland for cattle to produce meat for the European market, the nations in which the Amazon is located need alternative revenue opportunities for the local workforce and indigenous communities. One possibility is eco-tourism, another is funding for forest ranger jobs.

Fisheries as a common resource pool: Avoiding overfishing in unregulated open seas requires adequate protection. If the marginal costs of protecting these areas are funded at a level equal to the expected revenue from fishing, overfishing will be prevented. This would require adequate funding of marine monitoring, helicopters and GPS software and compensation for the fishers to incentivise them to look for another job and/or fish somewhere else.

Healthcare or nurseries as club goods: If we treat healthcare or a place at a local nursery as a common rather than a private good, it will be financed by members of that community as a whole, excluding those who do not belong to it. In this sense, accessing healthcare or having a preschool place would become a club good. The marginal costs of becoming a member of that club would be determined by additional costs for overuse or congestion, which would need to be less than the costs of building another nursery or hospital.

Communal park as a public good: Similar to club goods, the marginal benefits of accessing and enjoying a communal park should be less than or at least equal to the marginal costs of congestion and overuse, which should then in turn be less than or at least equal to the cost of building another communal park.

All four examples share the main characteristics of a commons, as explained above: they meet a basic need, are not tradable and have a ceiling that means they need maintenance rather than continuing to grow without limit. Once the investment materialises, the marginal costs will tend to zero. These commons have a high social return on investment and should be regulated by public law. Moreover, all these examples demonstrate that investing in commons is an essential prerequisite for successful private and commercial activities. Hence, not investing in them would expose our community to additional negative externalities and costs that we would have to cover in some way or another, and would leave us in a Pareto-inferior equilibrium. From a financial perspective, we must therefore distinguish the costs and benefits of investment in commons, including the costs and benefits of protecting nature reserves, of alternative uses and of congestion or overuse. Finally, we would need to consider the costs of associated negative collective externalities. This is summed up in the following equation (see box 18):

Box 18: Costs, benefits and externalities

$Co = Oc - Ex$

Co: net costs/benefits of planetary commons

Oc: benefits of protecting a nature reserve, of alternative uses and of congestion or overuse

Ex: costs of associated negative collective externalities

The examples demonstrate that, *ceteris paribus,* any regulatory and political efforts to secure our commons require adequate funding. Opportunity costs or benefits can be defined as relative losses or gains when we are forced to choose one option and forego the next best alternative. Benefits (Oc) and the costs of externalities (Ex) stand in a complementary relationship. The more we invest in Ex, the higher Oc will be. The costs of our commons (Co) can be funded using a mix of conventional measures, including taxation, green taxonomies, restructuring of loans, austerity, philanthropy and privatisation (TTRAPP) and additional liquidity assistance $\left(M^{cola}\right)$. Let's consider the following example. The roof of a house is on fire and we are facing additional costs due to water damage in the lower floors caused by flooding. The opportunity costs of investing in education or healthcare are substantially increased, as the money has to be invested in constantly repairing the roof and the water damage. The opportunity costs are linked to foregoing opportunities to get a university degree, earn more money (and hence increase the productivity of the economy) and receive better healthcare, which would in turn mean less sick leave, higher productivity and greater capacity to cope with the damage. Assuming there is enough human capital available, M^{cola} can partly mitigate this dilemma. Since the opportunity costs reflect financial compensation for alternative uses, which require high initial investment that will then phase out over time once the measures are implemented, the overall marginal costs of government investment in commons tend to decline over time. In an ideal world, where there are no externalities and where all commons are funded, a society is exposed only to low variable running costs to maintain its commons. The following table (Table 12) attempts to systematically classify our planetary commons.

Table 12: A preliminary comprehensive taxonomy for our planetary commons.

Commons	Characteristics	Opportunities + externalities	Examples
Planetary commons	Rivalrous and non-excludable	Marginal costs of protection = marginal costs of an alternative use + externalities	Amazon, coral reefs, wetlands
Common-pool resources	Rivalrous and non-excludable	Marginal costs of protection = funding of expected losses/revenue + externalities	Fisheries, groundwater extraction, plastic waste, unrestricted grazing
Public goods	Non-rivalrous and excludable	Marginal costs of memberships = marginal costs of overuse/congestion + externalities	Healthcare, nurseries, lending libraries, motorways
Club goods	Non-rivalrous and excludable	Marginal costs of access or use = marginal costs of overuse = marginal costs of an alternative investment + involved externalities	Communal parks, EU membership

The Logic of Collective Action

The outcome of collective and collaborative action is determined by the relative size of the groups involved.[185] The larger the group, the greater the marginal costs to organise collective action, since the gains for each member decrease with the size of the group. Smaller groups have lower marginal costs to organise collective action and higher benefits per capita, which puts them at an advantage over larger groups. This logic adds an additional layer of complexity to our planetary commons. The group of stakeholders for planetary commons comprises eight billion people across the globe, which makes the costs of collective action extremely high and the relative benefits per capita extremely low. At the same time, in future we will face unexpected asymmetric shocks and increased costs for externalities, which will translate into extremely high costs for the community and intolerable costs per capita. In situations where individuals are confronted with uncontrollable systemic uncertainties, collective action becomes a more rational choice than individual action when it comes to funding our planetary commons, and collaborative incentives preferable to competitive ones. Therefore, a rational actor would support a small group that is able to achieve the desired collective outcome with low marginal costs, instead of advocating for endless global campaigns to raise awareness about the challenges we are facing. We will see in the next sections that monetary regulators and international financial institutions are among the potential candidates the rational actor could choose. That is especially true in situations where the international financial market is acting pro-cyclically, is unable to factor in long-term trends, but instead operates within a short-term horizon of days and months, and

---

185 Olson 1971.

is risk-averse with regard to systemic uncertainties. The well-documented tragedy of the commons arises if individuals or companies start prioritising their pro-cyclical, risk-averse, short-term self-interest over public common goods. But this view is incomplete and somewhat misleading. The above-mentioned causes of moral hazards only apply to scenarios where an overcapitalised, pro-cyclical, short-termist, risk-averse and under-regulated private market is competing with an unregulated and underfunded commons, causing massive spillovers and unintended externalities. It is only under such circumstances that we would either colonise, neglect or overuse our planetary commons. If our commons and public goods instead enjoyed adequate funding and generated alternative jobs and income, free-rider effects would become largely irrelevant. However, that would require us not to rely solely on traditional redistributive measures, such as taxation, fees, tariffs and donations, but instead to use pre-distributive measures, in particular monetary facilities that would allow us to frontload the required funding for our commons.

From a financial perspective, the real tragedy of our planetary commons therefore is not their overuse or neglect, nor any moral-hazard or free-rider effects, but the underlying financial incentives that prevent an adequate supply to preserve and manage these commons in the first place.

I shall show throughout the next few sections that if we had a different monetary design, we would be able to preserve our planetary commons, provide adequate financial opportunities, open up alternative jobs and revenue streams and diminish the costs of negative externalities. We would then be able to create better market solutions and more functional commons at the same time. The main questions are: what makes a common good a common good? And if a right, a good or a service causes moral hazards, what kind of economic or financial mechanisms are required to ensure a maximum of wealth, both for the private and public sectors and for society as a whole?[186] It may sound paradoxical, but we know how to treat malaria, educate preschool children, set up a sewage system and prevent water-borne infectious diseases, how to build hospitals and schools and how to train teachers and doctors, but we are unable to awaken this sleeping giant within the existing monetary system. It looks like what we need above all is not technical and vocational skills, but the right financial engineering. Our commons should not only correct market failures ad hoc, fix negative spillovers and clean up the mess ex post, but become market makers and market shapers themselves, so that risks are better pooled, market solutions perform better and the future is made more predictable. Awakening the sleeping giant – that is to say, unlocking the potential of our commons – requires not so much technical skills as it does sufficient liquidity and purchasing power. And we will see in the next sections that this would in turn require a shift from austerity to an augmented and adjusted monetary policy. Dealing with and managing planetary commons is like playing a Bruckner symphony. Perform-

---

186 Coase 1960; Holcombe 2001.

ing a Bruckner symphony requires 18 or so musicians and instruments, a conductor and a great deal of training, discipline, talent, expertise, knowledge and effort. And it requires the preparedness to collaborate over 4 minutes and 15 seconds. This was true some 200 years ago, when Bruckner composed his first symphony, and it is true now and will be in the future too. A symphony is complete if all those things are in place. It cannot be made infinitely more effective or productive, and we would be ill advised to play it faster, louder, with fewer musicians or with no conductor to improve the efficiency. The symphony will always take 4 minutes and 15 seconds to play. Once all the criteria are met, the job is done and we can all enjoy this piece of art.

Conclusion

It is easier to enable new thinking than to get rid of outdated practices. New thinking occurs when we leave the familiar behind and engage in new practices. Or as Einstein said, 'It is the theory which decides what we can observe.' It is high time to change our theory of how to fund and manage our commons and to move past outdated and expensive practices that still dominate our thinking. In this second chapter, I have tried to demonstrate that we need to awaken the sleeping giant, namely our planetary commons. To make that happen, we have to change our mindset. We are currently still holding on to a narrative that has turned out to be extremely expensive and inefficient. Traditionally, we have relied on linear thinking and adopted an end-of-pipe strategy, where we redistribute money through taxation schemes, adjusted green taxonomies, restructuring of loans, austerity policies, privatisation and philanthropy. None of these approaches are wrong, but they all yield uninspiring, underwhelming results when it comes to the question of how to finance our common future over the next two decades. These measures are either too low in volume, too slow in speed and/or too imprecise to meet the targets we have set. Seen from an evolutionary and systemic perspective, our monetary system is not equipped to face these challenges, leaving us with an unprecedented and unpaid bill. That bill will translate into increasing political and economic costs and mounting losses of wealth and well-being in the years ahead. The monetary system seems to be the elephant in the room that nobody talks about. It is not a neutral veil that simply measures price signals, like a thermometer we stick into the water to measure the temperature. Rather, our monetary system is a human-made social contract that we can change and adapt to the requirements of the 21st century. At present, it acts like a systemic attractor that is pulling our economy in the wrong direction. If we start considering finance as a fourth form of capital alongside natural capital, human capital and produced capital, we can start upgrading and adjusting its mandate. What is required is additional, conditioned liquidity, above and beyond traditional credit lines, so that we can hedge and mobilise the trillions of private-sector investment that is needed to fund and manage our planetary commons. An economics of transformation in the 21st century requires six to eight times more liquidity and funding than any previous transformation. And that in turn requires a shift in our mindset. Traditional economics cannot provide the theoretical framework for this transformation that we all desperately need, but systems thinking can do so. Conventional economics, regardless of school, uses linear historical datasets, field studies and reviews, randomised control studies and experimental designs to identify singular causal links. None of these approaches are completely without merit, but they all share three limitations. Firstly, they do not consider the monetary system as an independent variable. Secondly, conventional economics cannot grasp the complex dynamics of the financial system. Moreover, thirdly, it cannot properly integrate and consider risks and uncertainties. But a systems-thinking approach can do so: it can equip us with the tools necessary to understand that ordered complexity is the new game in town. We need to move beyond mere causality and statistical correlations and utilise emerging new technologies in order to bring this shift about. We need to move past cyclical booms and busts and linear projections, and instead embrace fractals and fuzzy logic, complementary pairs and complexity, non-linear cascades and contagion effects, emergence and leverage points. Together, these will shed an entirely different light on how to make this transition happen. We will then start shifting our mindset away from finance driving sustainability and towards sustainability driving finance. At the moment, we are psychologically trapped by the idea that there can only be one monetary system that provides a single form of liquidity for all purposes, and that allocative distribution through that monetary monoculture is the most efficient and effective approach. The aim is not to formulate an ideal-typical financial architecture, in the manner of a greenfield experiment, but rather to set out an evidence-based best next step to finance our common future as economics transforms over the next 15–20 years. In Part II, I will show that if we take these preliminary considerations seriously, we will end up with a Pareto-superior equilibrium, where our commons are adequately funded, negative collective social and environmental externalities are addressed and managed and a new green alternative marketplace can lead us into the future. It will further stabilise international financial markets in an anti-cyclical way, strengthen monetary regulation, reduce negative externalities and help to increase social welfare and well-being and stabilise democracies. Instead of further privatising our future, we can start identifying (almost) unlimited new, innovative financial instruments and forms of financial engineering, including blended finance, derivatives and swaps, direct digital cash transfers and new state guarantees, among many other options. And that will tell us what we ought to do if we want to live in a world of possibilities, opportunities and choices rather than being consigned to an inevitable tragic fate. This will culminate in a multi-stakeholder, non-regret approach for everyone involved. I will flesh out all these points in more detail in the remainder of this book.

Part II: **New Territory**

C: Economics of Transformation

The Art of Transformation: Adaptation Is Key

Some 900,000 years ago, the population of *Homo heidelbergensis*, a species that later evolved into *Homo sapiens*, declined by 99%. With about 1,300 members left on the planet, it came close to extinction.[187] This decline was due to an ice age and lasted about 100,000 years. It was only the ability to tame fire that enabled our ancestors to survive. Without this capacity to adapt, we, *Homo sapiens*, would not even exist. Some 50,000 years ago, *Homo sapiens* invented the needle – and something amazing happened once again. Humans started sewing furs that allowed them to explore new territories and survive in colder climate zones. This complex adaptation process involved not just simple tool use and the evolution of the executive functions needed to make needles. It also involved new ways of allocating our resources and organising our communities. Devoting time to making needles meant spending less time on other activities, and so a division of labour was collectively agreed on: some members of the group would make needles, others would hunt buffalo or build huts. Humans started to prioritise. Perhaps they could not collect as many berries as before, and their children now received a different education. Ultimately, the decision to make needles came with opportunity costs. But those costs were worth it, because needle-making would prove to be a valuable skill for the future.[188] The need to constantly adapt seems to be a general characteristic of humans,[189] and has fundamental implications for how to do an economics of transformation. Unlike the 1930s, when mass unemployment was the major challenge facing society, in the 2020s we are in the midst of a transformational process that cuts across all areas of society and so requires a far more comprehensive response than was needed a century ago. But a successful economic transformation isn't automatic. It won't be brought about by an inevitable social evolution, or by reforming, adapting and optimising the existing rules, or by a revolution that destroys the existing order, or by furious protests where we yell at each other, break things and then go home again. Transformation is not just a matter of figures and data, nor is it a chaotic play-dead reflex in response to a shock or exponential development. It doesn't follow an algorithm with an open linear decision tree or result solely from the use of a new technology. Even the common metaphor of a circle to describe economic processes is incomplete, as it excludes the possibility of genuine creativity and novelty: the circle metaphor suggests that we keep going round and round again without changing. Transformation implies something completely different.

---

187 See Hu et al. 2023.
188 Hare and Woods 2020.
189 See Diamond 1991 and Harari 2014.

https://doi.org/10.1515/9783111421520-004

The Staircase

We should be very careful to choose the right narrative, as it fundamentally determines how we see the world and take economic decisions within it.[190] Transformation is an intentional and conscious process, and hence a choice. I will call a process transformative if it respects how things are and what has already been achieved, but also critically points out problems, identifies contradictions and incorporates ambivalences, while at the same time transcending them and moving towards a greater whole.[191] If we apply this general idea to the present case – that is, an economics of transformation – and avoid the conventional view of cyclical booms and busts and linear thinking, we will favour a different picture. Properly understood, economic transformation is best described as a spiral staircase. As we ascend the staircase, we can see more; we become better, more inclusive, more comprehensive; we start to integrate contradictions and opposites. Conversely, if we go down the stairs, we will regress instead – or we could decide not to move at all and stop transforming. And if we ignore the limits of the staircase, we risk falling over the railings.[192] This means that transformation always involves a possibility of failing, of causing death, disease and suffering, of creating losers and winners. It simultaneously brings with it massive limitations and massive opportunities. It demands a failure-tolerant attitude that allows us to face the risks that have to be borne, to correct wrong decisions and to try out new things under conditions of uncertainty and time pressure, while holding on to the hope that the whole system will not collapse. Edison is said to have carried out over 6,000 failed experiments before finally getting the lightbulb to shine. It was rigorous scientific findings and unorthodox 'out-of-the-box' proposals that overcame 'business as usual' and the prevalent 'less is more' mindset. Our species and its ances-

---

190 See Harari 2018.

191 It seems we are more anxious about the change itself than about the negative consequences of all the crises and uncertainties we are facing. A vast body of research on stress from the last 50 years has shown that it is not objective stressors like pandemics, climate change and biodiversity loss that increase stress and irrational behaviours, but rather the perceived loss of control at individual and societal level that eventually leads to tunnel vision as a way to avoid cognitive dissonance. We then overlook the opportunities and focus only on the risks. In short: in opaque, complex situations characterised by recurrent shocks, we need the right mindset and narrative to help us regain a sense of control and self-efficacy. See Brunnhuber 2024.

192 The notion of a 'Lyapunov exponent' provides a theoretical explanation for the need to respect limits. In a limited space, each event is bounded. That results in unlimited foldings, which then increases the diversity and variability of further refractions. The difference (delta) between two unbounded variables or events will lead to exponential development and ultimately to system collapse. Applying these findings to the social world prompts the question: where should we set boundaries and limits? What social developments do we want to avoid? What goals and outputs do we need to clearly define? Areas where we need to set boundaries include ocean waste, pandemics, climate change and biodiversity loss. The pathway to achieve the desired goals will remain undetermined. On the Lyapunov exponent see Dynamic Math 2024; see also Levermann 2023.

tors have successfully transformed over the last almost one million years. And we should be able to repeat the success story of taming fire and inventing the needle today – with a transformation that allows a sustainable common future in the 21st century.

The metaphor of transformation as a staircase allows us to further differentiate between interpreting the world at each step (translation) and moving forwards ourselves (transformation): when we not only start interpreting the world differently but also change our practices. The staircase provides us with the direction to go. At the top, it brings us to a *terra incognita*, an unknown land where uncertainties, further contradictions and potential disruptions await. With each step we take, our perceptual baseline shifts towards a better way of life and higher standards of living: bans on child labour, minority rights, trade unions, higher living standards, reduced poverty, technological innovations, scientific discoveries.

All these transformational steps occur only when jurisdictions are reconciled with ethics and changes in individual mindsets lead to new institutional arrangements. As we head up the staircase, we may come to recognise that things have never been better, yet have never felt worse.[193] We can decide to progress up the staircase, or to regress and go down. The staircase also has fixed inner and outer boundaries that we should not overstep, else we risk falling; and as we head up, it will open up and become wider.[194] With every step we take and each level we climb, our consciousness, our thinking, our perceptions, our behaviours and our decision-making change. The process is largely determined by how fast we go and how the staircase itself is designed. In this sense, transformation has a vertical rather than a horizontal vector. As we progress upwards, we will gradually open up ever-wider vistas. Our economy, our agriculture, our social lives, nature as a whole must progress in this spiral fashion to flourish. Regional economic cycles, regenerative agriculture and all the cultural achievements that are handed down from one generation to the next likewise follow the same principle. Each time, something is added and something is removed or left out. It is never just a circle that spins on the spot, but always a spiral movement up or down. The fact that we keep turning transformation into a narrative of linear progress is probably one of the major systemic flaws in our thinking, rather than something amiss in the world itself. Over thousands of years of human history, this process of adaptation led to Malthusian cycles. Crop failures, catastrophes and crises reduced the population, only for it then to increase again further down the line. These cycles alternated over centuries, with only a small, privileged minority benefiting from advances. For many centuries, life was indeed a circle. However, in the 19th century things changed abruptly. For the first time in human history, large swathes of the pop-

---

193 Acemoglu and Johnson 2023.
194 We need to distinguish between two general forms of limitations: external limitations (e.g. planetary boundaries) and internal limitations (e.g. our mental frames and biases). Both constrain our possible options in the transformation that lies ahead. See Byers 2014; Brunnhuber 2024.

ulation began to enjoy greater life expectancy, prosperity and well-being. Liberal rule-of-law mechanisms guaranteed the protection of minorities, child labour was banned and social security systems, access to education and a public health system were provided to the population at large. Unprecedented capital accumulation enabled more wealth for more people. Humanity didn't need to worry as much any more, because food, housing, technological advances, education and healthcare were available. The loss of adaptability to nature primarily affects the 20% of the world's population who have benefited directly from the massive accumulation of capital and increase in prosperity since around 1820. Now, in the 21st century, the 'social quest' to redistribute goods and services along a rigorous growth trajectory, which was so vigorously pursued in the 19th and 20th centuries, is being overshadowed and challenged by an 'ecological quest', as we witness backlashes from all the negative externalities. We will have to learn to adapt again, as we cannot negotiate with nature: it follows biological and physical laws, not the social laws of labour disputes, strikes and changing ownership and liabilities, nor the adapted mechanisms of rule of law. We must be careful to ensure the upcoming transformation process doesn't fall back into the cycles we knew for centuries of human history. And, as we will see, the money system has a key role to play here. The figure below (Figure 25) illustrates this point. What it shows is that economic transformation is not a circle or cyclical process, in which we meet ourselves over and over again, but an open enterprise, where with every step we take, upwards or downwards, everything is at stake. What fire and the needle were thousands of years ago, the sustainability agenda is today. In both cases, a complex process of adjustment is associated with opportunities and sacrifices, with curiosity, courage and risk. And in both cases, the process becomes transformative and involves some sort of adjusted economics to succeed. And because this process of change and adjustment will happen anyway, whether we want it or not, the only question is then whether or not we will succeed in mastering an 'art of transformation' or instead become 'masters of disaster', stumbling from one panic-and-neglect or delay-and-denial reaction to the next.

The staircase metaphor helps us to see that the transformational process we are heading for is not a two-dimensional, cyclical one, but rather three to four-dimensional. That poses even more challenges for our mindset. All these preliminary factors turn the process of transformation into an art. The term 'art' is meant here in the sense of the ancient Greek *techne* (τέχνη), that is to say, a learned, practical, rule-guided craft of creating something new. Before we attempt to translate all that into the field of economics and finance, we need to get clear about the role of humans, as the primary agent in the Anthropocene era (for further discussion, see also excursus 1).

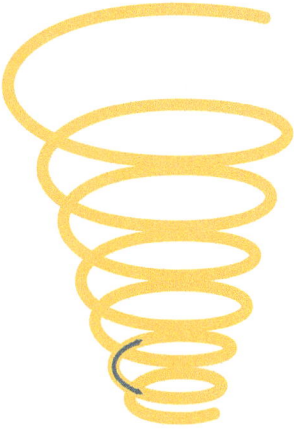

Figure 25: Transformation as a spiral staircase.

The Curse of the Circle

Circularity is a hallmark of most if not all biological systems. Nature does not produce any waste, but regenerates itself. From crystals, to cells, to microbes, to higher-order living beings, to whole ecosystems with millions of interacting species, the principle of repair, reuse and recycle dominates.[195] But the free competitive market system also has a built-in circular component. Indeed, it is the largest and most perfect circle humans have ever created. Trillions of times per day around the globe, supply meets demand, mediated by price signals. The free market represents a decentralised, self-regulating system that no other mechanism can replicate.[196] Through price signals, this quasi-circular market provides information that is not available from any other source and allows people to make rational decisions.[197] But any competitive economy is at the same time also unstable and imperfect. Asymmetric information, spillovers and negative social and ecological externalities, the tendency towards oligopolies and

---

[195] From a biological perspective, the three criteria for a sustainable system are reproducibility, longevity and resilience. Accordingly, circularity is governed by three fundamental laws: (1) the rate of regeneration of renewables must exceed the exploitation rate; (2) the substitution rate of non-renewables must exceed the exploitation rate; (3) toxic input into the environment must not exceed the relevant biophysical absorption rate. See Daly 1977 and Reheis 2022.

[196] A sustainable transformation will never occur without a functioning, rules-based market system. Price formation is one of the most accurate allocation mechanisms for redistributing goods and services – better than warfare, administrative measures, public debates, majority votes, autocratic decrees or diplomacy. See Brunnhuber 2023.

[197] New carbon capture, utilisation and storage (CCUS) technologies are circular in the sense that they relocate the carbon dioxide in the atmosphere back to where it was hundreds of millions of years ago. The fossil age can be seen as a kind of 'starter battery' for human civilisation (Fuller 2022), which will ultimately be replaced by renewables and other forms of energy. See Radermacher and Beyers 2024.

increasing income and wealth disparities are the most prominent flaws.[198] But rather than abandoning this allocation mechanism, we should instead upgrade and adjust it to the requirements of the 21st century. It is similar to the discovery of antibiotics or the manufacturing of cars. When humans discovered antibiotics, we soon realised they generate side effects such as antimicrobial resistance or accidents. Instead of abandoning antibiotics, we invested in R&D and new technologies, and introduced new guidelines to tackle these spillovers. The same is true for cars or planes: to tackle the problems they cause, we increased safety measures, introduced speed limits and installed filters. Each time, we created new market segments with additional capital to face these challenges – and each time, the initial idea of the market's circularity was affirmed rather than abandoned, and the market became fairer and more inclusive, with a more skilled workforce and more advanced technologies.[199] Viewed through this lens, there are two elements to any global market economy: a horizontal one, where supply and demand are settled through a price signal in a circular way, and a vertical one, where additional liquidity, skills, regulatory efforts and technologies continually improve the circular process. It is this circularity of the global market system that enables all agents to reuse, repair and recycle goods and services along a global value chain. Similar to the initial process of transformation, which likewise involves a vertical and a horizontal component, each time we step up the staircase, the final results of a functioning competitive market economy follow the model of a spiral staircase rather than a mere circular loop. Each step up we take, we can do and see more and better. This is a circularity involving repetition of the similar, not of the same. Human societies in general and an economics of transformation in particular should adapt to this cyclical process while simultaneously enhancing it, shifting baselines and expectations, spiralling upwards towards a greater, more inclusive whole. Mere circularity, by contrast, would mean constantly retreading the same paths, without ever improving or adapting to our ever-changing environment. There would be no progress, growth or development. If we aim for a more circular economy in order to cope with social and ecological externalities, such as biodiversity loss, climate change, ocean waste and serial pandemics, we therefore need more, not less, of a competitive market. Our knowledge of this cyclical process is a kind of metacognition that transcends mere cyclicality and which only humans can provide. In my view, the move towards a more regional, circular economy represents not a general law but a special case – one that requires specific vocational skills to repair, reuse or recycle goods.

---

198 See Mayer 2024.

199 Our perceptual baseline is thus shifting towards higher standards and a better quality of life. Whereas 200 years ago 90% of the total population was poor, today in the 21st century we now consider a 10% poverty level unacceptable. In short, things have never been better, even if they have never felt worse.

Maximising Utility in the Middle Dimension and the Pincer Grip

Economics provides one of the most powerful tools to shape the political narrative that governs our world. As a discipline, it is concerned with how people behave, make choices and express their preferences. Every theory has to make simplifying assumptions in order to better explain parts of the world. One of the basic assumptions in economics is that people have rational preferences which are independent of other people's preferences and which they will try to maximise. The orthodox economic understanding of people is encapsulated in the figure of the *Homo economicus*:[200] a rational agent who pursues their self-interest and maximises their utility according to an order of preference. What makes this idea compelling is that, from an individual inner perspective, humans seem to constantly maximise their utility in one way or another in order to successfully adapt. The downside is that it easily becomes tautological, and hence non-falsifiable and useless. In reality, economic actors operate with forms of rationality that are partly bounded and determined to a great degree by exogenous factors like education, cultural habits/beliefs or neurobiological make-up.[201] What seems to be a rational choice at first glance is in fact caused by sociological and biochemical factors. Rather than our decisions being rational in the first place, we engage in a mental exercise of rationalising them. This idea is further supported by empirical evidence from behavioural economics showing how a combination of incomplete, asymmetric information and irrational choices leads to systemic market failures.[202] Agents' orderings of preferences can be mutually reinforcing, leading to pro-cyclical cascades and contagion effects that create unintended systemic risks that governmental bodies then have to deal with. This is becoming even more relevant in the Anthropocene era, where the challenges that rational agents are faced with are fundamentally different from in the past.

Humans are confronted with two overlapping developments that differ from anything witnessed in the past: serial ecological crises, with multiple feedback loops and cascades, and the dawn of new technologies, with unpredictable impacts on us. Both are challenging the role and position of humans in the 21st century and having a significant impact on how we perceive the world and do business. The rise of new technologies and the serial ecological crises are trapping us in a pincer grip.[203] Both devel-

---

200 See Pareto 1906; Smith 1986.

201 Dahrendorf 1973.

202 Ormerod 2005.

203 Over the course of history, there have been five major affronts to humans' sense of our own importance and centrality. Firstly, Galileo's discovery that the earth rotates around the sun rather than vice versa; secondly, Darwin's finding that humans are descended from apes; thirdly, Freud's theory that human consciousness is mainly the result of unconscious processes; fourthly, the ongoing, self-inflicted ecological crises that threaten all life on earth and that we seem powerless to stop; fifthly, the dawn of AI and synthetic biology, which show that, sooner or later, it will be possible to replace human cognitive capacities with a machine or algorithm and to rewrite and modify the code of life.

opments force us to answer the question: what is it to be human in the 21st century? What is the *differentia specifica* of humans, in the face of disruptive technologies that transcend most of our cognitive and analytical capacities and an increasingly entropic world order where an ecological polycrisis is becoming the new normal? Whether we are reaching down into the nano world, where distances are measured in nanometres (a billionth of a metre) or out into the vastness of space, where interstellar distances are measured in light years, all the knowledge we gather from these parallel worlds will still remain bound to the 'middle dimension'.[204] The world humans inhabit is one of minutes and metres, hammers and nails, keyboards and steering wheels. Everything we learn from the nano and macro worlds is mediated through this middle dimension. And within this middle dimension, we are constantly confronted by all our constraints and limitations. We cannot hold our breath for an hour, cannot run very fast, are not very strong, cannot live without food. In contrast, elephants communicate with their ears and trunks, bats orient themselves by echolocation and also have better vision and memory than humans, chimpanzees have a better short-term memory, rats and dogs have a stronger sense of smell, eagles have vastly superior vision, catfish can taste with their entire body.[205] Similar observations can also be made for trees and plants. Findings in chronobiology show that trees interact with and mimic their environment and are able to learn.[206] Each species has its own specific environment or *Umwelt*,[207] as the biologist Thure von Uexküll termed it. Each species' *Umwelt* is shaped by its own senses and differs significantly from the human *Umwelt*, meaning that each living being perceives the world in a completely different way, with senses that are at once incomplete and perfect. *Incomplete*, because they represent only a tiny subset of potential ways to perceive the world. And *perfect*, because each of these distinctive senses is a perfect fit for the organism's environment in terms of helping it to survive. This perfect fit comes at the cost that the organism will struggle to cope outside its own *Umwelt*. That goes for turtles and rattlesnakes, for beetles and hummingbirds, and even for trees. All these beings are subtly interconnected with millions of other species on this planet. There will always be a gap between their worlds and the human understanding of those worlds, which can never be more than an educated guess or analogy. We will therefore never truly understand how a bat perceives ultrasound or how a seal perceives changes on the water surface, since human senses, the human mind and the human *Umwelt* are different from those of

There are three lessons to learn. Firstly, humans are becoming more and more marginal. Secondly, science and technology can fundamentally change the course and position of humans on this planet. Thirdly, each time we successfully adapt to these discoveries, we increase our understanding of the world and the depth and breadth of our consciousness.

204 Schumacher 1973; Tomasello 2019.
205 See for further examples Yong 2022.
206 Mancuso 2022.
207 See Uexküll 1949, 11.

other species. Our senses of smell, touch and taste are restricted to certain domains, our senses of hearing and sight to specific wavelengths. We have a base set of six to ten innate primary affects that we share with other animals, but then refine them over our life cycle. Our cognitive capacity for critical analytical reasoning is determined more by frames, unconscious expectations and implicit norms than by objective facts, data or probabilities. And our decision-making and behaviours are more strongly guided by convincing narratives that we all share and believe in, even if they are factually incorrect, than by statistically supported risk assessments, historical data or utility calculi. And even if we uncover previously unknown correlations using big data algorithms, or learn how to treat Parkinson's disease with a brain–chip interface and cancer or viruses by modifying genetic codes, such achievements are only really comprehensible to us once they are materialised in the 'middle dimension'.[208] Unless we can grasp this new knowledge within the middle dimension, our distinctively human ability to adapt will be lost and the art of transformation will fail.

There are several lessons to learn here: our perceptions of the world are limited, we act less rationally than we think and we are adapted to a small but significant segment of our world, where we fit (imperfectly and incompletely) into a niche.

The Gap, the Crutch and the String Player

Humans are simultaneously the most adaptable, the most vulnerable and the least genetically determined species.[209] We can't help but constantly adapt, correct and optimise ourselves, solve problems and then start all over again. We can live as hermits or in large cohorts, become meat eaters or vegetarians, fly to the moon or stay grounded, eat or fast, speak or be silent. An animal like a wolf will never become vegan. Nor can it really be held responsible for its actions. Cooking, gardening and playing music are three special forms of adaptation unique to humans. The ability to adapt sometimes goes so far that we even adapt to practices or conditions that are unhealthy or irrational, inefficient or addictive.

How does the human species fit into the complex world we live in today? Unlike other animals, which are fully adapted to their niche, humans remain a deficient species and require a crutch to bridge the gap between us and our environment. This gap is filled

---

208 From a physics perspective, all these dimensions (from nano to cosmic) are unlimited and do not set any boundaries. It is the human species that is subject to planetary boundaries (outside) and mental frames (inside), which set the limits of our lives on this planet.

209 The genetic difference between individual humans is less than 0.1%, we share about 60% of our genome with a banana and we have the same number of genes as a roundworm. The DNA sequences of our stress axis (HPA axis) have remained the same over the last 300 million years. Genetic make-up therefore seems far too unspecific to explain the cultural variety and individual differences that we can witness across the world.

by scientific findings and technological inventions, by law and order, by cultural habits, educational curricula and language. These crutches are all human-made, and hence transitory and incomplete, but provide the tools we need to organise ourselves in a complex and entropic world. In this ongoing process of adaptation and readaptation, we have become more fragile and vulnerable, more prone to interference and deception, but at the same time friendlier and more cooperative. It sounds paradoxical. This 'survival of the friendliest'[210] has become a selection advantage due to our lack of adaptation to nature. Long ago, we started to tell ourselves fictional stories that we all believe in and that can be used to coordinate the behaviour of large cohorts. Narratives about God, the legal system and money are the most prominent examples; these things only 'exist' because we all believe in them. This isn't how things are for other species. In short: we need drones, drugs and dams to survive, but other living beings do not. And this gap will never go away, and has only widened as we have evolved.[211] We can observe tool use, systems of social ranking, cognition, emotions, self-perception, greetings, rituals, communication, language, expressions of suffering and even humour and dignity among various animal species. But these capacities serve a different purpose than they do for humans: namely, to maximise adaptation to a given biological niche. Humans not only adapt to their niche but create new ones, which they then transcend and destroy over and over again. The development of our consciousness actually widens this gap and forces us to rely on ever more elaborate crutches to compensate. It is this free choice, and the freedom to either increase or decrease the adaptability and responsibility that comes with it, that makes humans human. The figure below illustrates the difference between humans and other organisms (both plants and animals) and the evolutionary aspect of the widening gap that humans have to bridge.

In the figure (Figure 26) below (a) represents animals that are fully adapted to their ecological niche but have little flexibility to survive outside it. Meanwhile, (b) represents humans. The yellow wedge stands for the fact that we are never fully adapted to nature and need a crutch to make up for the gap. That gives us an adaptability that other species lack. (c) shows how this gap is widening over time as our consciousness evolves, meaning we need an ever-bigger crutch to cope.[212] There are two dominant frames used to explain the role and position of humans on this planet. The Renaissance frame, which puts humans at the centre of the universe, and the Darwinian frame, which places us at the top of an evolutionary ladder. Both are misconceptions that are responsible for the ecological crisis we are heading into. Humans in the 21st century are neither at the top of a ladder looking down at evolution, nor at

---

210 Hare and Woods 2020.
211 Tegmark 2019; Tomasello 2019.
212 Blumenberg 2014; Bowlby 1995 [1950]; Gehlen 2014 [1940]; Plessner 1975; Plessner 1983; Scheler 2007.

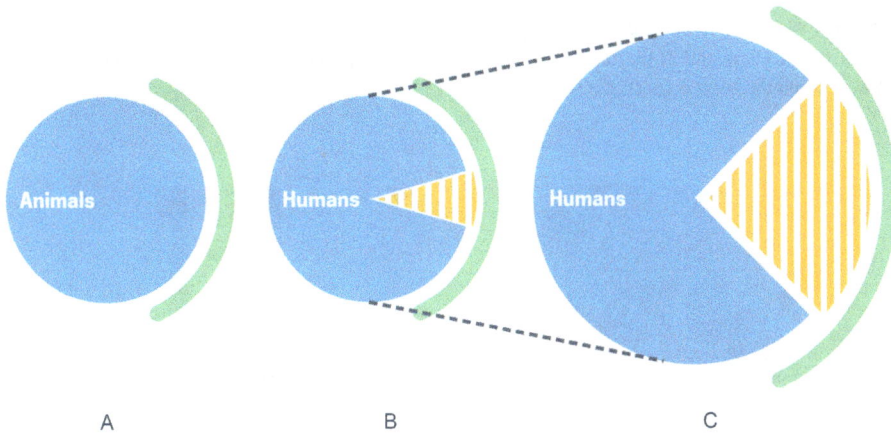

A   B   C

Figure 26: The gap and the crutch.
(a) animals are fully adapted; (b) humans are not and have to adapt to their niche; (c) the gap widens as humans continue along our evolutionary path.

the centre of the universe.[213] Rather, we are marginal yet important string players within the great orchestra of life, able to participate in the countless parallel worlds of other living beings,[214] to explore those worlds, to resonate and communicate with those worlds and their inhabitants, without fully controlling or understanding them.[215] See Figure 27 below.

> **Box 19:** Homo economicus in the Anthropocene era
> In the Anthropocene era, *Homo economicus* is becoming a utility-maximising agent 2.0, who knows that their rational choice is bounded and limited and that they are operating under conditions of uncertainty and time pressure and with incomplete, asymmetric information. They are aware that they are risk-averse, are subject to all sorts of biases and frames and tend to make irrational choices and short-term decisions. That they are never fully adapted to their environment and need a crutch, which in turn depends on cultural achievements, technologies, research findings and other people's habits. That they are operating in the middle dimension and require tools. In short: they can reflect on the fact that their maximising behaviours depend on exogenous factors and require collaborative skills more than competitive ones, and can acknowledge that they know very little to nothing about complexity and that the better they can adapt the greater the selection advantage will be. Within these frames, humans have a distinctive order of rational preferences that they will seek to maximise. In doing so, they will reach out to the infinite parallel worlds (both nano and macro) around them as far as they can and with all the tools available to them. This meta-cognitive position or helicopter view is

---

213 In contrast to polytheistic and pantheistic religions, monotheistic religions favour a vertical frame, which supports humans' exploitation of nature and the associated ecological crisis.
214 The paradox is that the orchestra or web of life is complex and we humans cannot fully understand and control it. But we do constantly strive to reduce that complexity, which in turn adds another layer of complexity. We might call it hyper-complexity.
215 Brunnhuber 2024; Prigogine and Stengers 1984.

shifting their understanding of themselves away from being an isolated, autonomous agent at the centre of the universe and at the top of the evolutionary ladder, and towards being a marginal string player within the great orchestra of life.

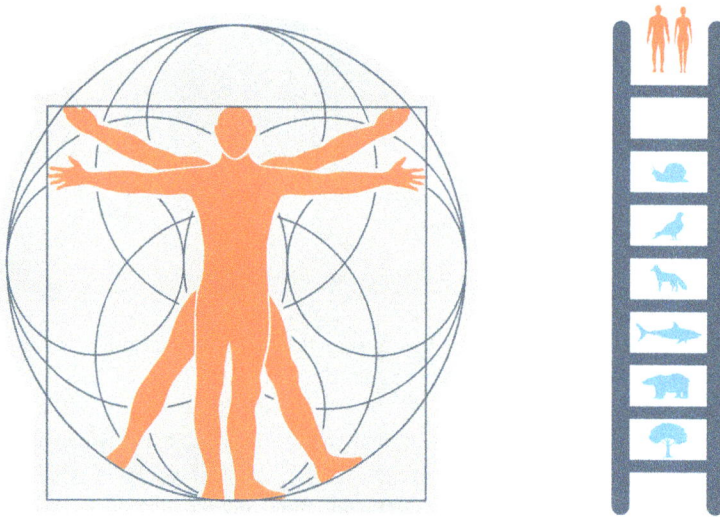

Figure 27: Two main frames used to understand humans' position.
Left: at the centre of the universe; right: at the top of the evolutionary ladder

As a string player (see figure 28 below), we are better equipped to see more and do better. Our mindset or consciousness will determine the course we take up the staircase[216] – and a new kind of economic thinking and an out-of-the-box approach to finance will be a great enabler on that journey. This new consciousness will be one that is constantly evolving, never fully adapted, always confronted with unresolved contradictions and opposites.[217] Transformation is therefore a vertical process rather than a horizontal one, a matter of choice rather than a well-practised technique. It is not a linear process, but a spiral going up and down within fixed boundaries, widening and opening up

---

216 Aurobindo 1997; Maturana and Varela 1987; Wilber 1998.

217 On an individual level, there are complements like pride and humility, frugality and generosity, caution and boldness, planning and impulse, knowledge and instinct, while on a societal level, there are ones like state and free market, private and common goods, the environment and the economy. The great traditions of Western and Eastern wisdom can help us to understand that these apparent opposites are actually complements: the principle of 'both-and' rather than 'either-or' should determine our way up the staircase. It's like the poles of a battery: we always need both to achieve the correct voltage. In psychology, this is referred to as 'tension and ambivalence tolerance'. It is considered one of the key cognitive capacities for successful development.

as it approaches the top. In terms of the staircase metaphor, we are currently caught between two steps, existing in a state of limbo. The familiar common ground is coming to an end, yet the new, open space is not yet within reach. There is no fundamental difference between the needle example discussed above and the imperative to create a sustainable way of life today. As *Homo technologicus*, we today need drones, dams, drugs and data to successfully adapt to a new, even more complex and entropic environment. If we are string players operating in this complex open network system, never fully adapted, acting with bounded rationality under conditions of uncertainty, how does all that translate into economics and finance? The common assertion that we are interconnected in real time and have to operate within biophysical planetary boundaries leaves us with the challenge of how to translate this into our everyday lives, into the way we reason, evaluate economics, engage in politics, do business. Since no transition comes for free or automatically, we need a vehicle or extra lubrication to enable that shift. The economic and financial implications of that shift will be the topic of the rest of the book.

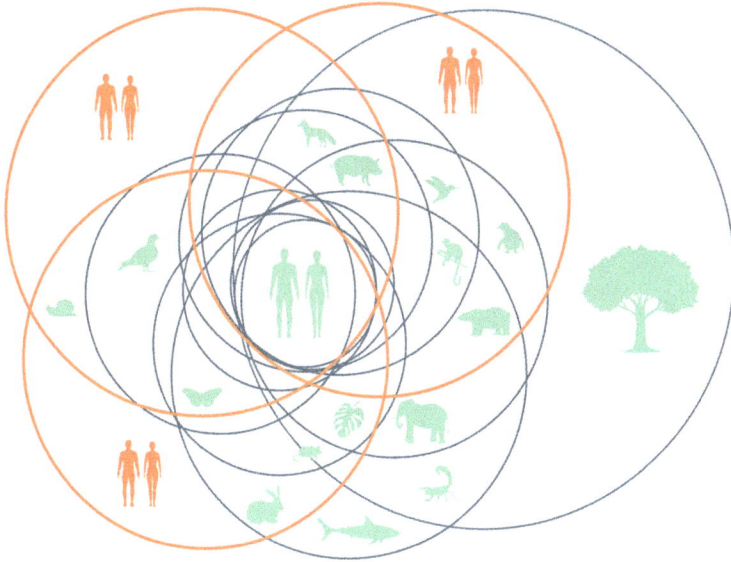

Figure 28: The parallel frame: humans as string players, interacting with each other and with nature.

The New Game in Town

Which factor more strongly determines the course of a ship on a stormy sea: the captain or the ship itself? Even the most experienced captain is heavily reliant on the design of the ship. I would estimate that about 80% of a ship's course is determined by its design, while just 20% of successful navigation is down to the captain's training and experience.

This metaphor can also be applied to the monetary system. Even the best-intentioned actors working in the financial sector are confronted with the incentives (both good and bad) provided by that system. If we had an upgraded monetary system that respects the achievements of the existing financial architecture but remedies its flaws and constraints, we might then have a powerful tool to integrate our disconnected financial markets and create a healthier, wealthier planet. *Traditionally*, we mainly redistribute money from the private sector in order to fund, manage and hedge public goods and global commons. However, as we have seen in the previous chapters, this 'end-of-pipe' approach is slow, administratively demanding, small in scale and insufficiently targeted to meet the challenges we are facing in the Anthropocene era. Following this traditional pathway would leave us with a 'too little, too late, too expensive' scenario. The figure below (Figure 29) illustrates this again:

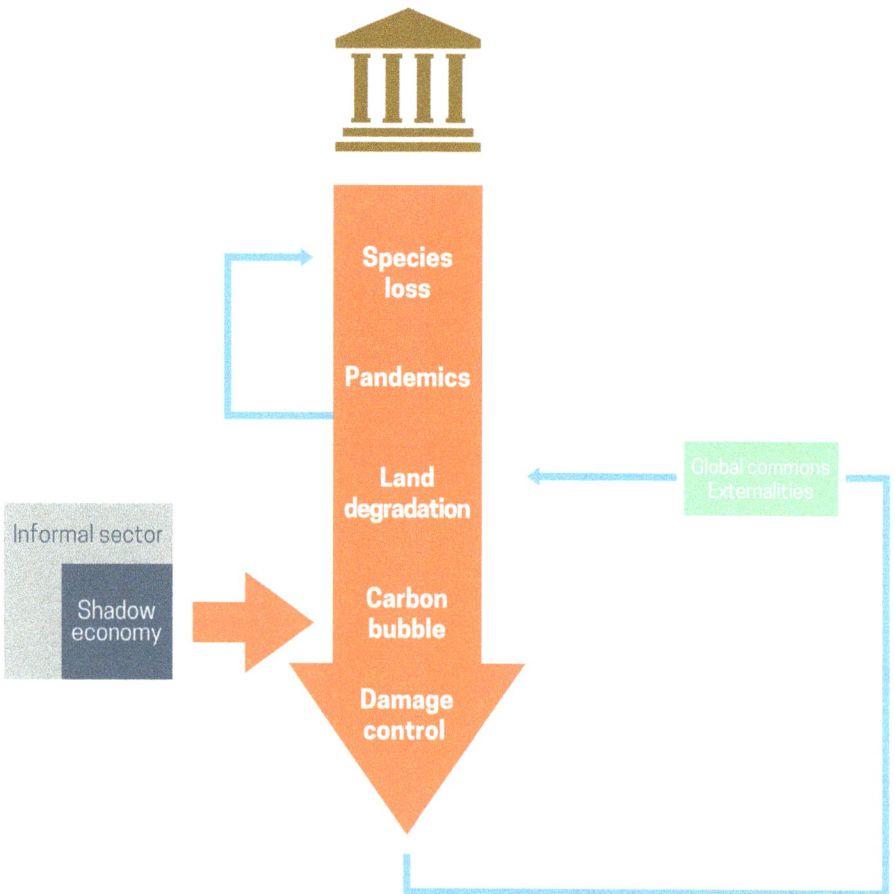

Figure 29: The traditional way to do it – end-of-pipe, redistributive approach.

The large arrow represents the entire global value chain. Any time we produce a good or provide a service, we are contributing to species loss, climate change and land degradation, which in turn create multiple negative collective social and ecological externalities that will eventually feed back and incur additional costs, as we must manage the resulting damage. In this end-of-pipe scenario, common and public goods take second place to private profits and so are chronically underfunded. At present (2024), 80% of the global value chain is still dependent on fossil energy. At the same time, the entire economy is affected by the shadow economy (dark grey box) and informal sector (light grey box), which pull all economic activities in the wrong direction. The small blue arrow on the left represents redistributive measures at a domestic level (e.g. taxation and fees), the blue arrow on the right represents transfer payments (philanthropy, taxation, official development aid or green impact investment). In this standard approach, we first generate wealth and income, which create multiple social and ecological externalities which loop back. We then create a compensation mechanism and fund global commons. Assuming a 3% global growth rate, the total annual rate of conversion from fossil to green energy needs to be much higher to override the existing growth dynamic within a timeframe of 20 years. That would mean switching a substantial portion of the global value chain, including all income, profits and revenue, to a non-fossil energy source each year. It would provide regenerative farming, build circular regional economies and protect the environment. The problem right now is that any time we build a solar panel or buy an electric car, we still generate income and revenue upstream and downstream that depend on an economy that is 80% powered by fossil energy and is growing by 3% annually. This is one major reason why we need to upgrade the currency system to incentivise and consolidate green investments and generate multiple positive second-round effects, so that we can pave the way to a sustainable future. At a global level, we are entering a Keynes 2.0 scenario. Planetary boundaries, global interconnectedness and backlashes from negative externalities are driving a shift towards closed economies, where spillovers can no longer be ignored and are affecting global value chains in myriad ways; massive under- and unemployment, forced displacement and underfunded planetary commons are fuelling deflation and underinvestment, with systemic risks vastly exceeding corporate risk adjustments and conventional measures like volatility indexes, stress tests and credit default swaps becoming poor proxies for the damage and losses we are facing.[218] There will be regions that might stagnate or even fall into recession, due to an ageing population, lack of innovation, low resilience and poor institutional capacity-building, though we may hope the overall net effect at a global level will still be positive. The next sections will elaborate on this Keynes 2.0 scenario from a financial and monetary perspective and explore potential challenges that must be overcome.

---

218 Diem et al. 2022.

The Change of Course

If we start digging deeper into the logic of any economics of transformation, we will realise that we not only have to abandon linear thinking, which has accustomed us to extending measures from the past into the future, but also to specify the change of course that is needed for the financial sector – and then make it happen. Two aspects seem to be of particular relevance: a conditioned multiplier effect and a conversion rate for the economy.

A Conditioned Multiplier Effect

The well-known 'multiplier effect' refers to the relative increase or decrease in final economic outcome that results from investing a certain amount of money in, or withdrawing it from, an economy. The marginal propensity to any additional economic activity – relative consumption versus investment, spending versus saving, supply versus demand – will reflect the expected additional activity of the relevant kind. A multiplier greater than 1 indicates that the net effect far exceeds the initial spending, as each unit of injected money triggers additional revenue, wages, consumption or investment capacity, demand or supply in that economy. The marginal propensity to any additional economic activity triggered by additional liquidity injected into an economy is:

Box 20: The multiplier effect

$$M = \frac{1}{1 - MPE}$$

M: multiplier
MPE: marginal propensity to any economic activity (consumption versus investment; demand versus supply; spending versus saving)

If a consumer saves 40% of their additional income and spends 60% of it, every additional unit of account injected into an economy will generate 2.5 units of additional spending throughout the economy. The multiplier is therefore 2.5. If a government decides to favour a supply-driven policy over a demand-driven one and inject an additional 5% on the supply side, then (assuming the same savings rate of 40%) this additional 5% would ultimately increase spending by 8.3%.

The way the multiplier effect is used in traditional economics is flawed in certain respects and subject to a number of criticisms. There are three main reasons to upgrade and adjust it. *Firstly*, the policy of public deficit spending to create additional income and revenue raises the question of how to finance that spending. If the money is borrowed from the capital market, the credit line (including the principal and compound interest) has to be paid back at some point, which will offset the additional public revenue. If the public spending is counterbalanced by increased taxation, the initial increase in effective aggregate demand will be reduced by that same amount. And if the additional public spending is financed by printing additional money, that money will, *ceteris paribus*, increase the CPI or decrease the value of the money accordingly and hence defeat the purpose. The *second* flaw of the traditional multiplier mechanism is that the additional public spending does not discriminate between whether the status quo of the real economy requires a demand-driven or supply-driven policy. Simply digging a hole and then refilling that same hole generates additional jobs and reduces unemployment, but adds little value to the overall economy. A supply-driven policy prioritises investments over consumption, encourages competitiveness and market efficiency through free trade, lower taxes and privatisation and favours investment in education, healthcare and R&D that will eventually increase the market output. A demand-driven policy, meanwhile, focuses on marginal wage increases, with a multiplier increasing overall aggregate demand.[219] On the traditional view, a demand or supply-driven economy will correct, compensate for, replace and repair a deficit or imbalance in an anti-cyclical manner within a given growth trajectory. This traditional view reflects the general assumption that economic activities can be broken down into either consumption or investment. Consumption refers to wages and short-term day-to-day needs such as food, transport, rent, clothing and energy. Investment refers to long-term economic activities, such as building a sewage system, motorway or hospital or simply buying land. However, as valid as this distinction is, it remains arbitrary, since any investment strategy once initiated will immediately generate wages and income that fuel increased consumption, and any marginal increase in consumption will mean additional investment strategies in the near future. And at the end of the value chain, there will hopefully always be someone who is willing to buy a veggie burger, a bike or a solar panel. If we decide to use our scarce monetary resources to build a dam, manufacture a drone or investigate a new drug, the very same day the money we invest will create revenue and wages and hence additional consumption. If we consider the quality of human capital and its connection to nature to be key to the success and sustainability of any future business and politics, the more relevant economic performance indicator is the relative social return on the money injected into the real economy. Consumption and investment are a complementary pair rather than opposites. When Keynes introduced an anti-cyclical demand-driven policy to overcome mass unemployment in a deflationary situation, that was a response to specific historical circumstances. When we apply Keynes to the 21st century, we need to transcend the demand versus supply and consumption versus investment dilemma and offer a rational position that goes beyond these oppositions. In this new approach, monetary and fiscal policy will precede any main street activities in order to enable or prevent a demand-driven or supply-driven policy. There also

---

219 See Bénassy-Quéré et al. 2018, 574 ff.

seems to be a *third* constraint on the traditional multiplier mechanism: the multiplier induced by public spending is intended as an anti-cyclical repair mechanism to bring an unbalanced economy back on track. The mechanism is meant to repair a misbalance between aggregate demand and supply in one domain, but leave the overall value chain untouched. That is to say, it is a reparative rather than a transformative measure. In the case of a transformational process, like that described in this book, spending, investment and consumption practices collectively require a deliberate and predictable shift from one state of affairs to another. This transformation is affecting the entire global value chain, the underlying energy sources, our impacts on the environment and the role of planetary commons. If we take these three limitations of the traditional multiplier mechanism – namely, the payback dilemma, the lack of discrimination between demand and supply-driven policy and the mechanism's anti-cyclical nature – into account and admit that an economics of transformation requires additional liquidity, then we will be forced to recognise the need for an upgraded, adjusted and conditioned multiplier that satisfies these limitations and provides an intrinsic monetary steering tool to help create a greener future.

We can take this argument one step further. An additional monetary aggregate that leaves economic activities untouched but provides conditioned liquidity to prevent or cover the cost of systemic shocks would drastically change the playing field. Instead of withdrawing purchasing power through taxation, fees or credit lines, this aggregate would eventually increase welfare by the same multiplier directly while also adding a social benefit indirectly. In that case, 5% additional spending on systemic shocks would multiply to 8.3% while at the same time preventing indirect costs for social upheavals, foreclosures, unemployment and future disaster management. Empirically, the return on investment would be increased by a factor of 2 to 3, meaning that instead of the initial 5% we would end up with 8.3% plus 2–3 × 5%, equal to a social welfare effect of around 20%. The entire financial system would also be stabilised. I will describe the benefits in more detail in the section on the monetary inflation brake. The box below (Box 21) illustrates the general point.

Box 21: The conditioned multiplier as a mechanism to prevent or cover the cost of systemic shocks

$$cM = \frac{1}{1 - MPE} + SB$$

cM: conditioned multiplier
MPE: marginal propensity to any economic activity (consumption versus investment; demand versus supply; spending versus saving)
SB: social benefits

The overall benefit occurs only if we avoid redistributive measures and instead provide additional, conditioned liquidity. This mechanism would not only mean that any additional liquidity injected into the economy would magnify demand or supply, consumption or investment in some way or another; these measures would also be redirected to address unemployment, our planetary commons and the costs of negative spillovers at the same time. In an ideal world where we have funded and managed all our commons and overcome, internalised and financed all our spillovers, a functional competitive global market would allocate goods and services at next to zero cost. Each cost on one side of the planet would then generate revenue, wages and gains on the other. And each instance of public deficit spending on one side would be equal to private assets, investments or consumption on the other. A conditioned multiplier of this kind would ultimately generate multiple positive second-round effects, which would further amplify the successful and sustainable transition. While the conventional multiplier would amplify spillovers and systemic risks, a conditioned multiplier would finally do the opposite: it would generate multiple positive feedback loops and drive progress towards a green transition (see box 22 below).

Box 22: The conditioned multiplier effect in more detail

$M^{cola} \times cM \approx \delta Ex + \delta Oc$

M^{cola}: monetary supply aggregate for conditioned liquidity assistance

cM: conditioned multiplier

δEx: marginal reduction of costs of externalities

δOc: marginal costs of protecting a nature reserve, of alternative uses and of congestion or overuse

---

A conditioned multiplier would generate multiple positive externalities or, conversely, reduce the marginal costs of negative externalities and so unlock a return on investment in public goods. In a fully connected world, every economy becomes a closed economy, where externalities materialise as costs and revenue at some point. Set at the right level, additional, conditioned liquidity would therefore cover the initial expenditures for commons and externalities. In a finite but ideal world, we would then ultimately end up with next-to-zero costs, with the only expenditures we face being systemic uncertainties that every complex system inherits. In a general sense these ideas can be incorporated into a Keynes 2.0 wealth multiplier (see box 23 below):

Box 23: The Keynes 2.0 wealth multiplier

$W = W\left(M^{cola}, Roi, cM, v, \delta r\right) \times (1 - \delta f)$

W: additional wealth generated in a society

M^{cola}: monetary supply aggregate for conditioned liquidity assistance

Roi: return on investment

cM: conditioned multiplier

v: velocity of money circulation

δr: interest rate differential relative to conventional currency

δf: failed projects due to unforeseen events

This equation can be explained as follows: increasing levels of wealth and welfare in an economy depend on the amount of additional liquidity $\left(M^{cola}\right)$ injected into the economy per year, multiplied by the expected return on investment (Roi), a conditioned multiplier (cM), the velocity of the money in circulation (v) and an interest rate differential (δr)[220] (the difference between investing in harmful and beneficial projects), adjusted by projects that failed due to unforeseen systemic risks. This conditioned multiplier should not take the form of a traditional credit line to the private sector, nor merely printing money through the conventional monetary channels, nor simply compensating for losses through taxation in an anti-cyclical manner. Rather, it should provide additional, conditioned liquidity assistance for the entire transformation process. And it should be applied in three domains only: funding planetary commons; hedging and unlocking private capital; and addressing social and environmental externalities and systemic risks.

We should therefore distinguish between three ways to provide additional liquidity to an economy through a monetary supply aggregate. Each has its benefits, but also comes with challenges. Firstly, an *abundant supply* would potentially lead to misuse, moral hazard and inflation and ultimately to the destruction of productivity and wealth. There is a risk of simply printing money and utilising existing monetary channels, but leaving total factor productivity untouched. Secondly, *paucity of supply*, where economic agents are competing for a scarce resource, would increase the price of capital and potentially increase the wealth gap and lead to a war-prone economy. Thirdly, a *proportional supply*, where the amount of liquidity is qualified based on a risk-adjusted ROI analysis that considers the opportunity costs of not investing in an asset, would require us to also factor in the direct costs that lie ahead and the costs of any preventive measures. To be more precise: rather than competing for liquidity or having too much of it, we calculate the exact amount necessary to tackle the problems we are facing. If a region identifies the need to build a new sewage system, ten nature reserves, 100 hospitals, 1,000 schools, and 10,000 nurseries, the necessary money should not be withdrawn from the value chain via taxation and redistributed. Rather, a significant part of the required liquidity should come in the form of an effective, qualified monetary supply aggregate.[221] We would then be able to benefit from multiple positive externalities, a rise in employment and additional tax revenue in these sectors. A proportional monetary supply is politically more demanding, but generates a Pareto-superior equilibrium with higher wealth and well-being for all of us. As long as we are not concerned about an increase in the relative price formation

---

220 The interest rate differential (δr) between green, beneficial projects and brown, adverse ones should be > 0.

221 M0 (base money) has massively increased worldwide over the last 30 years. But while this increase was cyclical and exponential in nature, M1 and M2 increased only linearly. These two other monetary aggregates represent the volume of money that did not enter the real economy but was instead stored in bank accounts or entered the FIRE sector, and so did not improve overall productivity but rather increased the API (asset price index). There is no empirical evidence of a causal or correlative relationship between M0 and the CPI, nor between M0 and the face value and exchange rate of any of the major convertible currencies. See Marouani 2018.

that results from raising money through private charity, ODA, debt relief programmes or taxing offshore havens, we should not be too concerned about raising a similar amount of money through an effective monetary supply aggregate of this kind. We might instead expect the additional monetary aggregate to decrease the overall price level (CPI), as it will decrease the dependency on fossil energy, create multiple positive second-round effects, reduce negative spillovers and increase investments in regenerative farming, greater resilience and preventive measures. The figure below (Figure 30), illustrates the three forms of money supply.

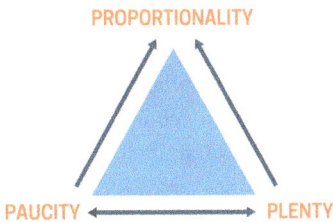

Figure 30: Three forms of money supply.
Paucity will either lead to more competition (wars, conflicts and an increasing wealth gap) or unfair redistribution ex post; a plentiful monetary supply will either increase misuse or generate additional inflationary pressure; whereas a proportional supply will instead only match the direct and opportunity costs and factor in the costs of prevention.

If all our commons were funded and externalities managed and hedged, we would live in a next-to-zero-cost world, as the revenue generated by the market system would in turn enable healthy wages and green, sustainable investment and consumption. The only remaining costs would be potential systemic risks, which are inherent to any complex system and will prevail regardless of any economic activity. In general: printing money depends on three fundamental conditions to enable a successful transformation. Firstly, the biophysical environment must still be reasonably intact; secondly, political bodies must still function; thirdly, a global marketplace must permit free price formation under fair competitive conditions. More specifically: as long as states have a broad and diverse fiscal base which is interlinked with monetary expansion, the more effective the additional liquidity will be; if a competitive market allows free flow of resources and the environment still serves a reasonable buffer function, we can apply this conditioned monetary multiplier. And to be even more specific: the faster and sooner we apply this conditioned monetary facility, the cheaper it will be. But the reverse is true too: under conditions of failure, where the international market system is fractured, political bodies become dysfunctional and the ecosystem is close to collapse, our common future will be more expensive. In the next section, we will further quantify the necessary measures and introduce a conversion rate so that we can better grasp the impact necessary for any economics of transformation.

The Conversion Rate

An economics of transformation is no longer a cyclical process, where we apply traditional credit lines, portfolio diversification, debt-to-equity ratios and stress tests only
to hedge systemic risks, compensate and repair for losses and damage along an expected growth trajectory and fund our public goods by redirecting taxpayers' money.
Rather, it requires additional, out-of-the-box approaches to financial engineering,
asset management and collective risk assessment, and must tackle chaotic, disruptive
and entropic asymmetric shocks that far exceed the worst expectations of our conventional, linear thinking. In order to better quantify the impact involved, I would like to
introduce the notion of a conversion or replacement rate, which describes the level of
economic activity necessary per annum to shift from a harmful to a beneficial state:
whether that be a shift from fossil energy to renewables, from an economic activity
that destroys natural habitats to one that preserves them or from an economic state
of exponentially increasing waste to one that substantially reduces waste. Each time
we create income and revenue along the existing value chain, we unintentionally increase the absolute size of the 80% share of the global economy that depends on fossil
energy – whether we build renewable energy sources like wind turbines or solar panels, invest in nurseries or hospitals, incentivise regenerative farming or implement
measures to protect a nature reserve. That is because whenever income, wages and
revenue are generated through these beneficial projects, they feed back into a value
chain that is still growing by 3% annually and is 80% fuelled by fossil energy, augmented by a multiplier greater than 1. It should be noted that the conversion rate is
not identical to the rate at which renewables themselves grow annually. Even if renewables grow by 10% per year, the requirements of a successful transformation will
not yet have been met. The conversion rate needed to get us to a state where no more
fossil energy is being used at all must greatly exceed the 3% growth rate of global output across the entire global value chain, both upstream and downstream. Otherwise,
overall economic activity will remain a perpetual rat race, with fossil fuels remaining
dominant for ever. We would then end up constantly behind the curve, with costs
endlessly mounting up. A conversion rate to renewables of 3% or less would create a
situation where fossil energy as a proportion of world GDP would never disappear,
causing unending damage to the planet and creating negative externalities for nature
and human communities. The conversion rate would look as follows (see box 24):

Box 24: The conversion rate

$$g(t+1) = g(t) + c \times g(t) \times (1 + \kappa^t - g(t))$$

g: required growth rate of renewable energy

t: timeline

c: marginal growth rate of renewable energy

κ^t: growth rate of the global economy

　　This translates into an average annual conversion rate:

$$Cr = (1+\kappa) \times \sqrt[n]{\frac{1}{q}} - 1$$

Cr: conversion rate
κ: economic growth rate equal to general growth rate
n: time span in years
q: proportion of existing renewables

This equation translates as follows: assuming a 20% proportion of renewables along the entire global value chain and a general growth rate of 3% annually, in order to meet a next-to-zero emission target in 10, 20 or 30 years' time, an economy would need an annual conversion rate (*Cr*) of 21%, 12% or 7% of GDP respectively. Taking a more realistic view, the conversion rate should actually be a logistic function, where the initial rate is far higher than 7% and then decreases substantially over time. In other words: in order to convert or replace the 80% of energy supply from fossil sources (including all wages and revenue upstream and downstream) into renewables so as to achieve the net zero agenda, the conversion or replacement rate would have to be above 7% until 2050. However, the current financial regime does not support this ambitious strategy. To elaborate further on these figures: if we assume a 7% conversion rate is required, that translates into several trillion USD annually. However, five to seven trillion USD is currently still invested in fossil-related products and services in some way or another. We therefore need additional financial engineering tools to achieve that conversion rate. The rate of conversion to a low-carbon economy simply reflects a linear and proportional component within an overall non-linear process. If we include the costs of addressing any future pandemics,[222] which includes costs to reduce disease transmission and improve early detection and monitoring, we would require another 30 billion USD annually. That figure is roughly 1/500th of the overall cost of the Covid pandemic, 15 trillion USD. Finally, we need to add the indirect and direct costs of nature services to the bill.[223] Measures such as cross-pollination, water purification, flood prevention and carbon sequestration have a value of 100 trillion USD annually. Currently, we lose about 10 to 20 trillion USD of these ecosystem services annually, mainly due to soil degradation, desertification and the conversion of forests to farmlands. Viewed in financial terms, restoring ecosystem services would cost about 160 billion USD annually. But in fact those investments would not be costs but common assets, which would provide over 500,000 additional jobs and generate an ROI of between 1:8 and 1:38. As explained earlier, the amount of fixed costs to maintain our planetary biodiversity, prevent future pandemics and cope with climate change, while high to begin with, will tend to zero once these challenges are met. Simply put: not investing in these common assets could lead to a substantial output loss

---

222 Dobson et al. 2020; Williams et al. 2023.
223 Bromley 2023; Brink et al. 2016; WWF 2020 and 2023.

for any sustainable growth trajectory. But such a conversion can only be achieved if there are attractive alternatives in place or in sight. That was true when we shifted from telegrams to telephone and then to video calls, from horses to petrol-driven cars and then to electric vehicles, from pencils to Excel sheets to big data. Each time, the alternative was simply better and more competitive. As the required conversion rate for the transition to renewable energy far exceeds the existing growth trajectory, we cannot expect that simply redistributing that amount of money via taxation would serve our purpose. That would lead to the paradoxical situation where the private sector loses part of the purchasing power needed to create a green marketplace. Such an intervention, even if done in a gradual manner, would cause a massive global recession, creating additional social and ecological externalities which would defeat the whole purpose of the economic transition. We can take this argument one step further: if we keep the baseline ratio of fossil fuels to renewables at 80:20 and assume a growth rate of 3% globally, but posit that technological efficiency will increase over time, add a conditioned multiplier that enforces positive second-round effects, apply an interest rate differential that allows us to discriminate between green and adverse investments and provide additional, conditioned liquidity, then the initial conversion rate would benefit.

Box 25: Factors determining the conversion rate

$$Cr = Cr\left(\alpha, \beta, \delta r, cM, Re, M^{cola}\right)$$

Cr: conversion rate
α: resilience coefficient (regulatory and containment measures)
β: efficiency coefficient (technology and education)
δr: interest rate differential
cM: conditioned multiplier
Re: rebound effects
M^{cola}: monetary supply aggregate for conditioned liquidity assistance

The extended conversion rate is to be understood as follows: if an economy is undergoing transformation, the required conversion rate to enable a shift from an adverse to a positive state would be determined by the costs of increasing R&D and education investment, introducing a risk premium that distinguishes between brown and green investments and consumer behaviour, applying a conditioned multiplier that ensures positive green second-round effects on an ongoing basis, correcting potential rebound effects and injecting additional qualified liquidity to mobilise private capital and fund our commons. In sum, the conversion rate depends upon general and necessary mechanisms for cases where economic activities have to shift from one state of affairs to another and operate within spatial and temporal limits. That could be a shift from a war to a peace economy or from fossil to green, or a shift towards protecting scarce resources or nature reserves. Each time, political will and/or scientific evidence, including a future costs analysis, forces an economy to transform. Beyond well-known regulatory efforts (taxonomies and disclosure agreements) and taxation schemes (carbon tax), subsidies, charity and free-market activities, the conversion rate determines the proportion of economic activity that must transform per annum in order to remain within the limits. What is needed is a rearrangement or disentanglement of the financial allocation of private and public assets. We have to distinguish between, on the one hand, financial instruments that allow us to mobilise private-sector investment while tackling systemic risks (this can be achieved by three measures: by additional tax cuts, by fiscal depreciations or write-offs and by certain types of state guarantees and hedging instruments) and, on the other, additional funding instruments to manage planetary and public goods as well as negative externalities. (I elaborate on these issues in more detail later in the section on transition finance.) Not using the disentanglement effect means that we reduce the global competitiveness of the market participants, create less wealth and prosperity, force industry to exit the existing trading zone and prevent the transition towards a green future from happening. It appears that the single most important agent of any economic transformation is not technology, education or mere economic growth, but rather new rules of the game for the financial sector that enable new disruptive technologies, new forms of education, R&D and a different form of economic growth that will make it possible to achieve a more sustainable future. Accordingly, an additional monetary aggregate will be a key factor to enable economic transformation, functioning like grease for the transformation engine or a buffer against systemic risks. But before we further elaborate on this additional monetary aggregate, we must first consider how monetary and fiscal measures are interlinked; the ideal relationship between them is known as the Pareto ratio.

An Applied 80:20 Pareto Ratio and Monetary Triangulation

The Pareto principle: Again, what determines how successfully a ship can navigate stormy waters: the experience of the captain or the design of the ship itself? Statistically speaking, I would estimate it is about 80% down to design, 20% down to experience. A system's design matters more than who operates it. Applied to the present topic, this means that real economic transformation requires a change in system dynamics and institutional incentives rather than a behavioural shift within the existing system. While things like stress tests, ESG rankings and bank equity shares are all important, they will repeatedly fail to achieve their goals unless they are embedded in a new monetary design. The figure (Figure 31) below illustrates this.

Throughout this book, I have argued for an adjusted monetary policy to face the challenges of the Anthropocene era. Conventional fiscal policy uses redistributive measures, where we either introduce multiple taxation schemes to reimburse expenses or create a credit line that means future taxpayers will have to fund the additional debt load. In either case, fiscal policy is used as a tool to correct consumer be-

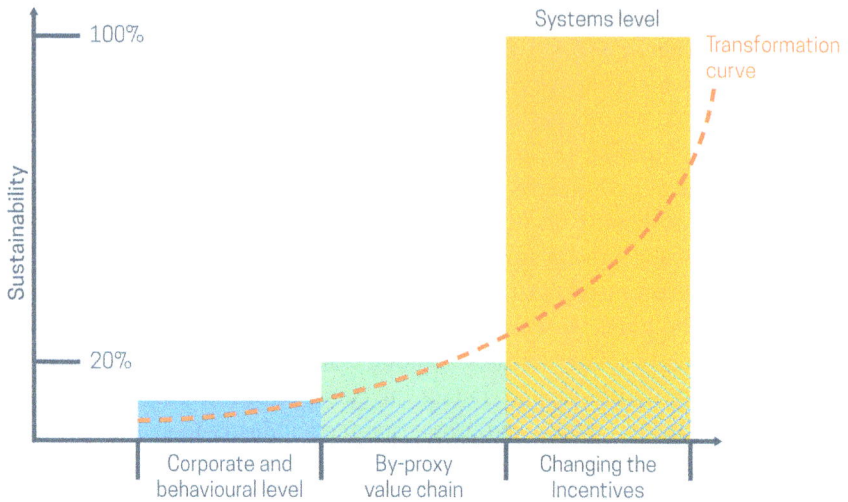

Figure 31: The captain and the ship: The applied Pareto ratio.

haviour (through a sin tax or moral hazard), fund public services, address income and wealth gaps (through capital, corporate and inheritance taxes) and withdraw purchasing power in the event of inflationary pressure. Monetary policy, meanwhile, is a pre-distributive measure. It provides the grease to run the engine, the buffer to protect against systemic risks and ensure the economy has adequate liquidity. But monetary and fiscal policy are not independent but interlinked, depending on the project in question.

In order to better quantify the relation between the two, I shall elaborate on the findings of the Italian economist Vilfredo Pareto (1848–1923) on this topic. In 1897, Pareto identified the ratio 80:20 as a rearrangement or cluster formation that occurs spontaneously in many cases. The 80:20 ratio often creates an efficient optimum between an input and its output. The proportionality between the two remains an unbalanced, asymmetric relationship, representing a kind of complementary pair. This 80:20 principle is like a predictable, built-in imbalance between effort and reward, cause and effect. In business, 20% of the services and products often account for 80% of the sales value or profit. Wealth and income distribution, stress and stressors, traffic congestion and roads follow the same principle. In terms of energy consumption and output, 20% of the planning is responsible for 80% of project success; 20% of farmers produce 80% of the world's food; 20% of the world population produces 80% of the world's problems – each time, the Pareto principle applies. This empirically based rule of thumb can help us to better understand the asymmetric workings of complex, non-linear systems and how best to increase their efficiency and effectiveness. The Pareto ratio can help us to prioritise decision-making and reduce complexity.[224] If we take these empirical observations, consider findings from fractal finance and apply them to the relation between monetary and fiscal policy, we can further conceptualise and adapt the 80:20 Pareto rule to the economics of transformation. In order to finance, hedge, manage and fund our commons (*Co*) and negative collective externalities (*Ex*) and mobilise private capital (*mPC*), the Pareto ratio between fiscal tools (*Ft*) and monetary tools (*Mt*) can be applied as a rough rule of thumb as follows (see box 26):

Box 26: The Pareto ratio applied: monetary and fiscal measures intertwined
lo = local; pla = planetary

$$Co^{lo}:\frac{Ft}{Mt} = \frac{80}{20} \qquad Co^{pla}:\frac{Ft}{Mt} = \frac{20}{80}$$

$$Ex^{lo}:\frac{Ft}{Mt} = \frac{80}{20} \qquad Ex^{pla}:\frac{Ft}{Mt} = \frac{20}{80}$$

$$mpC^{lo}:\frac{Ft}{Mt} = \frac{80}{20} \quad mpC^{pla}:\frac{Ft}{Mt} = \frac{20}{80}$$

Commons (*Co*) require a different Pareto ratio between the monetary and fiscal component depending on their geographic location, range and impact (local versus planetary). If a commons, negative externality or project involving private capital is local or regional in scale, the fiscal aspect will dominate the monetary one. If it is planetary in scale, the order is reversed. The more global a project is, the more international monetary institutions need to lean in to provide adequate funding and hedging instruments. Take the Amazon rainforest and a local nursery as examples of best practice. The Amazon rainforest is a planetary commons and a tipping point for climate-related environmental spillovers. International monetary institutions, like the World Bank, IMF and multilateral public development banks, therefore need to provide 80% of the required funding through a monetary facility, while 20% should come from fiscal sources. In the case of the local nursery, the ratio is reversed: 80% fiscal, 20% monetary. Properly applied, the Pareto principle avoids or reduces free-rider effects, as each investment involves a steering and a funding component. A reliable investment in these commons, whether they are local or global, will further increase the credit rating of the state involved and further decrease the capital costs for additional funding. It will overcome the diffusion of responsibility and, in the case of negative externalities, the moral hazards involved, and further increase overall prosperity and well-being. The chart and table below (Figure 32) illustrate this point and provide some examples.

We can take this argument one step further and add findings from complexity finance to the picture. One major characteristic of complex systems is their non-linearity and fractal structure. That means their architecture is isomorphic and scale-independent. Applying these findings to the question of how to practically fund and manage our commons and externalities and how to mobilise private capital reveals that we need to further distinguish between fixed and variable costs: the baseline

---

224 Koch 2022.

	Location	Examples
A	Local	Communal pre schooling, libraries
B	State	Universities, hospitals
C	Country	Sewage and energy systems
D	Continental	Nature reserves, maritime waste
E	Global	Global warming

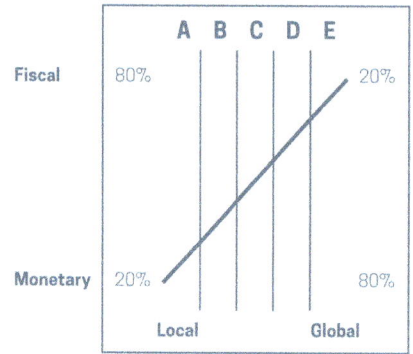

Figure 32: Applied Pareto ratio for commons and externalities.
A to E represent different projects from a local to a global scale (left). The ratio between monetary and fiscal measures ranges between two inverse Pareto ratios (right).

project funding for commons should be provided by a monetary facility (fixed costs), funding for maintenance and repair (variable costs) by a fiscal component. The fiscal aspect will permit the local community to take full responsibility for the project and prevent misuse and moral hazard. The same holds true for global commons. The funding of a hedging instrument, such as a currency or interest swap, should comprise an 80% monetary component, which is covered by public entities, and a 20% private or fiscal component. The following figure (Figure 33) visualises this ratio:

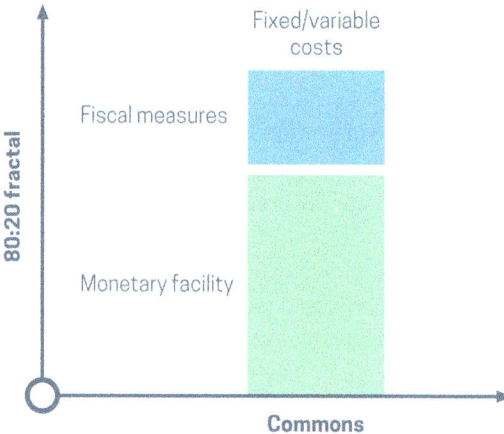

Figure 33: The 80:20 fractal.

The Pareto ratio provides a first rule of thumb for how fiscal and monetary measures should interact and be applied in order to facilitate an economics of transformation. It can help reduce moral hazard, provide adequate funding and steering tools and 'nudge' and facilitate local and global, public and private actors to get involved. In the next section, I will further clarify how to introduce this additional monetary aggregate by a process I call monetary triangulation.

Monetary triangulation: In traditional economic models, we are locked in between polarities like state and market, economy and ecology, private and public. But instead of looking for the lowest common denominator between these polarities without eliminating the fundamental dichotomy, we should start recognising the differences between the two, acknowledging their limitations and overcoming them by introducing a third party, namely the regulators and central banks. Rather than following one specific economic school of thought, adopting a systems-thinking approach allows us to devise out-of-the-box solutions to generate the funds needed to finance global common goods *and* to de-risk and mobilise trillions of private-sector liquidity at the same time. The current situation is like a man who has lost his keys at night but is looking for them only in the areas illuminated by the streetlights, without considering that they might be lying hidden in the darkness. In the traditional view, central banks and regulators remain passive, act indirectly and reactively and are agnostic regarding the results of competitive markets and state interventions. In order to overcome this siloed approach, central banks need to become proactive and preventive, orchestrating and facilitating private market activities and national state interventions at the same time. This makes monetary triangulation a forceful integrator, enabling us to deal with collective externalities and fund common goods all together. Such a triangulation would allow us to shift towards a Pareto-superior equilibrium, so that we will end up with more, not less, competitive markets and a stronger, more resilient public sector.[225] The current situation resembles a Nash equilibrium or the prisoner's dilemma, where, given a certain set of rules, two agents have reached a position in which they are no longer willing to further collaborate for fear of harming their own position. We are in a Nash equilibrium on a global scale: North versus South, state versus market, economy versus environment. For the financial sector, this further translates into the opposites of demand-driven versus supply-driven policy, consumption versus investment, private versus commons. The most obvious way to escape these multiple lock-in effects is to introduce a third party accepted by both sides and adopt new rules that optimise outcomes for all involved.[226] Regulators and central

225 For Nash's original account of the eponymous equilibrium, see Nash 1950 or Brunnhuber 2021b. Snidal provides a theoretical explanation of how to coordinate cooperative behaviours in global political institutions.
226 The functionality of the market and its price signals is associated with the size of companies. The size of a company, meanwhile, is determined by the relative costs of transactions within that company, compared with the price of those same transactions on the market. The better the market mechanism is, the cheaper the transactions will be and the smaller companies will become, as more companies will outsource certain transactions. The opposite is true, too. The larger companies are on average, the higher the probability of an oligopoly or cartel, the higher the prices will be and the less

banks could play that role. The figure below (Figure 34) illustrates this proposal. The left half of the figure shows the dilemma, where the dichotomies remain in place, while the right half shows them being overcome by a green monetary facility. The green rings around the circles on the right represent additional, conditioned liquidity assistance (M^{cola}), which transcends and reconciles the opposites of demand versus supply, investment versus consumption, state versus market, real economy versus ecology. M^{cola} is the grease for change, the buffer against systemic risks, the enabler of an economics of transformation.

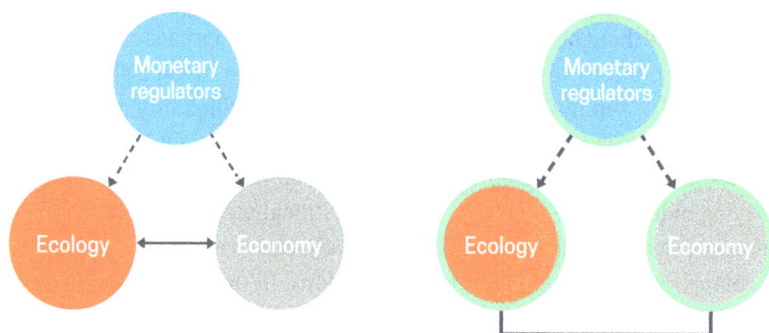

Figure 34: Overcoming polarities: triangulating the system.
The green circles represent the additional and conditioned liquidity needed to build a green future and overcome the dichotomy of ecology versus economy.

These traditional differences and oppositions only hold true if the magnitude of the mismatch between demand and supply, consumption and investment remains within a growth trajectory of, say, 2–3% annually and spillovers and negative externalities do not fundamentally affect our balance sheets. However, if we have identified a seismic shock, systemic risk or instance of damage which entails additional real costs that exceed the expected growth corridor, it seems to be rational to advocate for additional financial and monetary instruments. The expected costs of climate change, soaring healthcare demand, biodiversity loss and the next pandemic are examples.[227] In all these cases, we have caused the losses, damage and disasters already, which will entail huge costs in the near and far future. The question then is not how to avoid the costs altogether, but rather how to mitigate and reduce them as far as possible. In all such cases, we are not confronted with a cyclical readjustment of booms and busts,

---

flexible a given company will be in dealing with unprecedented challenges. So the size of companies indirectly reflects the functionality of the market. The monetary triangulation proposed in this text will increase the functionality of market-driven price formation and in consequence decrease the size of companies in the future. This will also maximise wealth, both for the private and public sectors and for society as a whole. See Coase 1960; Holcombe 2001.

227 The estimates of these costs reflect a society at war with itself. See Bilal and Känzig 2024.

but, as outlined in the previous sections, with a disruptive process that fundamentally changes the playing field for all parties. To put it the other way round: while the losses and damage remain low (both absolutely and as a proportion of GDP), it makes sense to apply conventional fiscal instruments, such as credit lines, and rely solely on charity, transfer payments and anti-cyclical stimulus programmes. It is like prescribing medicine to counteract the side effects of a drug, or an additional safety measure like a car seatbelt. But if the expected costs far exceed the growth corridor, we should not rely solely on regulatory efforts to internalise these costs, either by increasing tax revenue or temporarily postponing the bill to the next generation using private credit lines. That would be tantamount to cannibalising the present – or like shooting yourself in the knee and expecting to be able to run faster and longer.

> **Box 27:** The curse of crowding-in and crowding-out effects
> Crowding-out effects are linked to the state's steering function. If the state decides to increase its activity in one field (security), it can crowd out the private sector in another (sustainability), but the net effect (measured by change in GDP) for the economy as a whole may remain the same. The private sector will then build tanks and bullets instead of solar panels, while interest rates, capital costs and private-sector activities as a whole will be unaffected. The situation is different for crowding-in effects. In that case, an expanded and augmented fiscal and monetary policy creates additional opportunities for the private sector to be involved, and interest rates and capital costs will tend to decline.

We need to dare to think outside the box and consider a risk-adjusted, augmented monetary policy that overrides conventional fiscal policy in order to prevent a massive increase in the CPI, mainly due to food and energy price pressure, the loss of productivity and the costs of political instability (e.g. social upheaval, rise of extremism). A secondary preventive approach in monetary policy will still be expensive, but if wisely administered will cost far less than any 'fix-and-repair', 'business-as-usual' or 'wait-and-see' scenario. It is like a smoke detector or rescue boat, which are there in case of events (specifically, fires or heavy storms) that only occur very rarely but cause devastating damage when they do.[228] Such events cannot be predicted or prevented entirely, so a smoke detector or rescue boat is a wise, vital investment.

Equipped with the notions of a conversion rate, a conditioned multiplier effect, a Pareto ratio between monetary and fiscal measures and monetary triangulation, I will now further explore the role of central banks and regulators in bringing about a successful transformation.

---

228 In these cases, moral hazard only becomes relevant if the agent still has the choice to avoid or take advantage of an event in the near future. In the case of uncontrollable but probable events associated with a harvest default where the damage or hazard has been caused already, such as extreme weather, free-rider effects become almost negligible.

New Channels and a New Monetary Supply Aggregate

Central bank digital currencies (CBDCs) and central bank currency swaps (CBCSs): Despite being exempted from democratic control and governmental accountability, central banks remain connected to national governments. They have never been neutral or independent, nor have they ever operated in a sterile, laboratory-like environment, and even their aspirations to autonomy, transparency and accountability were bounded by specific national jurisdictions. To describe the new role of regulators in the Anthropocene era, we must distinguish between (a) their objectives, (b) their functions and (c) their legal empowerment.[229]

(a) Objectives. Central banks are specialised public bodies that secure public goods such as price stability (inflation targets) and financial stability (resilience against systemic risks) and provide support for government policy (employment and economic growth).[230]

(b) Functions. In order to meet these objectives, central banks are equipped with a set of monetary tools. Their functions include collecting statistical data, reviewing socially responsible investment criteria, supervisory functions, acting as a lender of last resort and managing OFRs (official foreign reserves) of gold, IMF SDRs, foreign currencies, etc.[231] A small number of central banks[232] are able to provide additional monetary facilities to mitigate and adapt in the event of emergencies arising from systemic risks.

(c) Empowerment. This refers to legal regulations and measures that enable regulators to pursue their objectives and serve their functions: for instance, regulations on collateral loans, repurchasing agreements, quantitative easing and tightening, outright securities and the provision of advice and support for national governmental policy and development. Over two-thirds of current central bank laws promote this agenda.[233]

In summary, central banks should be able to independently choose which monetary instruments they use, rather than which objectives they pursue.[234] This seems to be particularly relevant in the case of systemic, far-reaching risks that exceed national jurisdictions.

---

229 See Tamez et al. 2024.

230 Bolton et al. 2020; Barro 1996; Elderson 2022.

231 Dilip and Kundu 2020; Bossu and Weenink 2021.

232 In numbers: 8% of the 169 legal frameworks for central banks analysed by IMF staff (Tamez et al. 2024).

233 In numbers: 73% of the 169 legal frameworks analysed by IMF staff (Tamez et al. 2024) permit central banks to promote their country's development.

234 See Debelle and Fischer 1994.

At present, around 110 out of 131 countries are developing or experimenting with CBDCs.[235] The design is clear, but the full scope of their relevance and impact remains to be seen. The idea is that central banks create a new form of money. Viewed historically, this new monetary aggregate is the fifth step in the progression from coins to paper notes to the monopoly of national central bank money to the fractional reserves of the commercial banking system. Each step enlarged the monetary base, providing liquidity to the real economy, and partially replaced the previous monetary aggregate. The replacement of cash money by fractional reserve bank money peaked in the late 20th century at 97%. CBDCs are a digital form of money running in parallel to cash, coins and the credit money of the commercial banking sector. They will be backed 100% by the central banks and circulate both on the traditional monetary channels of the conventional commercial banking sector (open-market repos and regular refinancing facilities) and on new, alternative channels. CBDCs will complement rather than replace the existing monetary aggregates, functioning like an official legal tender, similar to cash and bank money, that can be used without limit by private and public entities.[236] They are also fully convertible and (like cash) not interest-bearing. As lenders of last resort, central banks are now starting to extend their liquidity guarantee to these new digital currencies, while gradually reducing their guarantees for the conventional banking system, including state guarantees. Citizens will soon have access to this new digital monetary aggregate through an e-wallet, currently with a limited volume of 3,000 euros.[237] The anonymity and privacy when using CBDCs is comparable to that offered by bank money, cash or a prepaid card.[238] With the e-wallet, CBDC users will be able to make payments online or offline using near-field communication (NFC) technology, similar to a cash credit card. CBDCs will be underpinned by a smart digital contract that makes it possible to tailor them to specific targets and projects. CBDCs and CBCSs seem to be perfect candidates not only to provide new monetary channels for the real economy, but to implement and deliver the additional liquidity necessary to fund our future. IMF SDRs, green QE, outright securities, additional purchasing programmes and OFRs could then be facilitated and managed through this new monetary channel.

Despite the rather dry, technical introduction I have given to this new form of money, this next step in the evolution of our monetary system has some radically dis-

---

235 Atlantic Council 2024.

236 Comparing transactions per second shows one competitive advantage of CBDCs: Bitcoin (5–7/sec), Libra/Diem (1,000/sec), Mastercard/Visa (5,000/sec), TARGET2 (10,000/sec), the digital yuan (10,000/sec) and the digital euro blockchain (up to 300,000/sec).

237 A waterfall effect will automatically convert any additional digital euros into conventional banking money. This design will protect the commercial banking system in its fractional use of credit lines and primarily limits high-volume use of CBDCs. China, the UK and Sweden have implemented similar technical restrictions in the design of their first-generation CBDCs. The EU CBDC is due to be launched in 2026/27. See European Central Bank 2024.

238 Huber 2024; Kumhof and Noone 2021.

ruptive potential, which is essential for the design of any future international financial architecture. Two aspects are of particular relevance. Firstly, CBDCs are a candidate to stabilise the monetary system itself, reducing the risks of bank runs and the pro-cyclical tendency of the traditional commercial banking system and its intrinsic bias towards the FIRE sector, which can cause it to exacerbate volatility and neglect the needs of the real economy.[239] This anti-cyclical mechanism for easing and tightening the money supply is of particular interest in times of increasing volatility, contagion effects and cascading domino risks for capital funds, private equity and insurers. It will further support the role of central banks in securing price stability. Secondly, CBDCs provide an additional public steering and funding tool for common goods and the management of negative externalities and future shocks, in cases where private market activities alone fail to provide adequate resources.[240] CBDCs have the potential to provide and withdraw liquidity to and from the economy in a more direct manner. We could apply the Friedman rule to CBDCs:[241] the opportunity costs of covering the means of payment for economic transactions and holding reserves in a country's own currency are next to zero. Central banks should provide as much liquidity as necessary to meet the demand from the commercial and public banking sectors, allowing better and faster liquidity and adjustment of interest rates in the event of shocks. If it is implemented the right way, we can expect that this monetary supply aggregate will not exert any inflationary pressure, as demand and supply will match the needs of the real economy.

Box 28: The evolution of an additional monetary aggregate
Two bottom-up developments occurring in parallel support the relevance of an additional monetary aggregate. Firstly, the emergence of cryptocurrencies. There are currently over 2,300 different types of cryptocurrencies in use, including Bitcoin, Libra, Ethereum and Solana. They all operate in a digital-only format, use distributed ledger technology, are underpinned by a digital social contract and are issued and created by private 'miners'. Cryptocurrencies are highly capitalised (2.4 trillion USD in 2024), highly volatile (> 5% in 24 hours) and speculative. The crypto community sees money as a private good, with limited liability, and favours decentralisation and denationalisation of the monetary domain. Secondly, complementary non-profit community currency systems: there are over 3,400 regional currency systems operating in 23 countries across six continents. They include Time Dollar systems, local exchange trading systems, local complementary currencies like the Bristol Pound in Bristol, UK, the WIR in Switzerland and RegioMoney in Bavaria, Germany, and multilateral barter systems. The overall market capitalisation is low and their macroeconomic impact next to irrelevant. Yet these thousands of real-time community currencies act like sandbox experiments to prove the potential of an additional monetary aggregate. They clearly facilitate transactions that might otherwise not have hap-

---

239 While conventional monetary easing has been too slow and too ineffective in times of crisis, a monetary regime that uses CBDCs would make the ambiguous role of interest adjustments less relevant and provide a more effective mechanism for public funding, all in line with Article 104 of the Maastricht Treaty. See Egmond and de Vries 2024.
240 Desan 2022; Jackson and Dyson 2012.
241 See Friedman 1969 and Smith 1998.

pened. This whole field of evolving parallel currencies today is like the moment when the Wright brothers took off in their first plane: small in scale, imperfect in execution, its import unclear. What mattered was not that, by some miracle, the Wrights' contraption flew at all, but rather that it showed that flying was possible. If we translate this point into the monetary domain, recent developments demonstrate the need for an additional monetary aggregate that acts counter-cyclically, like the metaphorical rescue boat, meeting previously unaddressed needs. Whether we use a top-down, public approach (CBDCs, CBCSs), or a bottom-up, private one (crypto- or community currencies), we as humans decide how much use we make of each discovery and invention so that we can create the society we want to live in.

No more passing the 'hot potato': from derivatives to multiple swap lines. Over the last three decades, derivatives have been one of the major financial assets used to hedge and manage risks. They should play a contingent claim on financial assets, like stocks or bonds.[242] However, this partly unregulated, over-the-counter market with a nominal value of over 300 trillion USD annually has been offering first, second or even third-tier derivative assets to reduce the risk of failure and pass the hot potato on to someone else. Once the risk materialises, someone else always has to pay the bill, and eventually that cost will be passed to the taxpayer. As long as perceived risks remain local or sectoral, a derivative is a rational choice to hedge microeconomic risks and leverage diverging expectations. The Anthropocene era, however, has unmasked systemic risks and uncertainties, which can no longer be hedged solely with derivatives. Expectations of the future impact of global warming, pandemics and biodiversity loss are more likely to converge than diverge, leaving the total risk uncovered. This explains the nature of the serial shocks we are all facing. Even if a rational investor can sincerely say they did 'everything right', they will still be hit by the unexpected consequences of negative feedback loops and fat-tail events with unprece-

---

242 Technically speaking, derivatives markets are composed of options, futures and swaps. Over 80% of derivatives are related to interest rate securities, 10% to currency risks and about 10% to the commodities market. At present, over 90% of trade in derivatives takes place within the financial sector. This is mainly the result of regulatory arbitrage. The Glass–Steagall Act (1933), followed later by the Gramm–Leach–Bliley Act (also known as the Financial Services Modernization Act, 1999) and the Commodity Futures Modernization Act (2000), triggered an avalanche in the trading of derivatives. That trade is backed up by rigorous mathematical equations: in particular, the Merton Modigliani model, Eugene Fama's efficient market hypothesis and Harry Markovitz's capital asset pricing model. Security spot prices serve to summarise all available information. The empirical result of this joint regulatory and scholarly work has been a massive increase in spot prices, volatility and trading volume. Trading volume has increased to 10 to 15 times the volume of commodities (e.g. oil or wheat) that actually exist, meaning that spot prices now follow future trading and not the other way round. The entire process is like a twofold, pro-cyclical feedback loop: the real price of a commodity is now the result of bad financialisation or, in the case of CDSs, irrational herd behaviour: educated people doing stupid things. The risks have remained the same, but they are eventually covered by the taxpayer. See also Akgiray 2019.

dented cascade effects.[243] Instead of reducing risks, we are generating further systemic risks, which in turn create additional costs. The greater the planetary interconnectedness and volatility become, the more rational it will be to abandon derivatives.[244] If, for example, the noble investor decides to switch from brown to green investments, it can clear its balance sheet, but in the real world the biophysical reality will not have changed at all. The brown investment will now be managed by another organisation that the noble investor has no control over and that might be less competent than the old one. The 'hot potato' is still there and the ecological and social impacts remain unchanged. This explains why we need a financial mechanism that overcomes these constraints. Let us further elaborate on this complex issue to better understand the argument. Instead of handing over the hot potato to someone else, we should aim for a financial derivative that allows us to contain, prevent and neutralise the associated systemic risks. Multiple tailored swap lines could serve that purpose.[245] Currently existing examples include interest, currency, debt-to-equity, debt-to-nature, credit default and commodity swap lines. Swap lines allow the parties to exchange and offset risks, increase their cash flow (which otherwise would not happen) and continue business under a different but adjusted regime. We can apply this lopsided model to the polycrisis we are facing. Take the seven trillion USD of subsidies for the fossil industry globally, comprising two trillion USD of direct subsidies and five trillion USD of indirect subsidies – mainly additional healthcare expenditures and degradation of natural resources. The entire fossil industry has an expected EBITA of one trillion USD globally. This further translates into multiple ownerships and contractual obligations to stakeholders. At the same time this seven trillion USD bill translates into wages and jobs with a total value equal to seven trillion dollars. These subsidies are a perfect example of a negative collective externality that comes with 'ending fossil fuels'.[246] The question is twofold. Firstly: who is responsible for these externalities? The owner of the fossil site, the producer of fossil derivative products, the investor, the state or the consumer? The answer: we are all responsible for them. Seen from this angle, it makes next to no sense to reverse-engineer the process and merely identify single ownerships and responsibilities. The toothpaste is out of the tube and we all have to deal with the situation together. Secondly: who is paying the bill for these negative collective externalities, with all their

---

243 Risks then not only multiply but transfer to other less obvious sectors, such as food supply, health, public infrastructure and non-climate drivers of change. See European Environment Agency 2024.

244 Pichler et al. 2021; Tabachova et al 2023.

245 See the US Securities and Exchange Commission's regular reports on swap lines. The 2024 report can be found at https://www.sec.gov/about/divisions-offices/division-trading-markets/security-based-swap-markets.

246 For example, as long as over 50% of the world population is still reliant on synthetic fertiliser, which depends almost entirely on fossil energy, to produce their daily food, ending fossil fuels would push millions of people into famine and poverty with devastating consequences. We need an entirely different perspective on how to phase out fossil fuels than the one we currently operate with.

collaterals and spillovers? The same answer: we all are, albeit with distinct responsibilities. The Global North, G7 and OECD countries need to pay a bigger share than the V20 and Global South. If we all want to phase out fossil fuels and pay this seven trillion USD bill, we need a monetary mechanism in place that enables us to distinguish countries' collective and individual responsibilities, multiple ownerships and obligations. Instead of creating additional hedging instruments, we will need multiple swap agreements. In the case of the seven trillion USD of fossil subsidies, the oil should stay in the ground, but the multiple ownerships, obligations and revenue expectations also need to be respected. We need some kind of mega-scale swap line geared towards keeping fossil fuels in the ground and expediting the reduction of CO_2 emissions to zero. The additional liquidity and compensation required to swap from fossil to green assets would be earmarked, so that instead of drilling for oil, a portion of the money would have to be used to build hospitals and nurseries or to plant trees. These swap lines would reflect the obligation to abandon revenue from fossil energy and generate future revenue through green assets alone.[247] The public sector would lean in and provide additional liquidity to compensate for the private sector's lost future revenue. In addition, swap lines would need to meet the criteria of systemic fractals and should be scalable. Altogether, that would be difficult but doable, given the complexity of the derivatives market, which was where we first started to hedge systemic risks. In order to make this the real deal, we need the regulators to lean in. That is the topic of the next section. But let us first look at how these ideas apply to the Amazon rainforest (see box 29 below).

Box 29: A case study – rescuing the Amazon with a conditioned CBCS
Brazil owns the majority of the Amazon rainforest, a well-known critical tipping point for the global climate, which is considered a planetary commons. At the same time, Brazil has a debt load in foreign currencies (mainly USD) equal to 30% of its GDP, or over 600 billion USD annually, and an inflation rate of over 8%. Currently, Brazil is deforesting the Amazon at a rate equivalent to 2,000 football pitches per day. The land is used for further resource extraction, palm oil/soya production and crop and cattle farming. This creates thousands of domestic jobs and meets the demand of the Global North. However, deforesting the Amazon comes at the cost of enormous negative spillovers that harm all humanity. It has been calculated that the Amazon has a face value of about 250 billion USD.[248] Economically speaking, Brazil cannot afford *not* to burn down the Amazon. However, a CBCS line could fundamentally alter the playing field. If the IMF, the World Bank, the Fed, the People's Bank of China and the ECB were to provide Brazil with a *conditioned currency swap line* that allowed it to convert a portion of its own currency (the real) into USD, renminbi or euros, Brazil would be able to pay back its external debts, reduce imported inflation and convert the deforestation industry into a green industry in which rangers and indigenous peoples are paid to preserve the Amazon instead of burning it down. It reflects a result based approach. For each hectare saved per year, the money is transferred. This would further create a positive externality for the Global North, as the global temperature would be stabi-

---

247 To be more precise: because approximately 100 companies account for 71% of the global carbon footprint, the CEOs of these companies should be incentivised to phase out and shut down as fast as possible and to build up alternative investments for their shareholders instead.
248 Banerjee et al. 2022; Brouwer et al. 2022.

lised, the tipping point would be avoided or postponed and the costs of disaster management due to wildfires, floods, heatwaves, etc., equal to about 5 to 7% of GDP in OECD countries, would be reduced over time. A monetary agreement along those lines would be a non-regret approach for all parties involved. The central banks' balance sheets would grow,[249] our palm oil would become more expensive to reflect the social and ecological externalities until eventually being replaced by an alternative product and we would end up eating more veggie burgers rather than beef.

The figure below (Figure 35) summarises the argument.

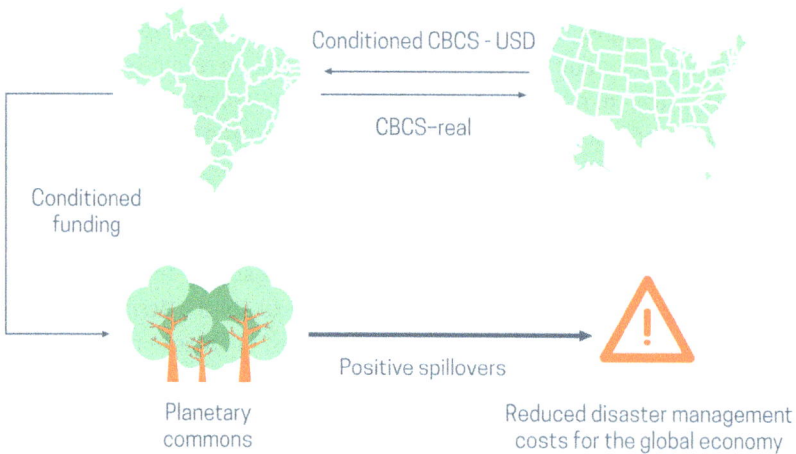

Conditioned CBCS - USD

CBCS–real

Conditioned funding

Positive spillovers

Planetary commons

Reduced disaster management costs for the global economy

Figure 35: Saving the Amazon rainforest.

The ultimate step: central bank currency swaps (CBCSs): Central bank currency swap lines are one of the hidden monetary and financial champions that could allow us to meet the funding and hedging needs of our global commons.[250] Technically speaking, a currency swap line is a political agreement between two countries' central banks to exchange their domestic currencies with each other. It represents an inter-regulator exchange of a highly convertible currency (USD, euro) with a weak currency. Most swap lines are capped and bilateral, and can help to prevent fire sales and tackle unprecedented shocks. At present, a total of two trillion USD equivalent is eligible for settlement between central banks through these currency swap lines, of

---

249 To be more precise: the global currency market is the largest and most liquid capital market, with around seven trillion USD equivalent in turnover per day (!), including all assets and facilities. Injecting an additional 250 billion USD equivalent to manage and finance the Amazon over one to two years will not have an impact on the face value of any major currency.

250 For a historical reference on central swap lines see the KIndleberger argument (1978): Lenders of last resort should provide unlimited liquidity to stabilize the international monetary system. see also Bernanke (1982), Mehrling (2022).

which only 300 billion USD equivalent is reserved for developing countries.[251] For example, the Eurozone has established a swap line with the US dollar amounting to 290 billion USD equivalent in 2023, making it possible to settle the face value of currencies, while the Canadian dollar has a capped 240 million CAD swap line with Mexico and the USA a 15 billion USD one.[252] Theoretically, any country with the sovereignty to print its own money can do so without limit. If a country is indebted in a foreign currency and is facing imported inflation, bilateral or multilateral currency swap lines could technically be used to tackle these challenges.[253] Take the V20, the most vulnerable countries on this planet and the ones most affected by climate change. It would be more than rational to increase the swap lines with these countries by a factor of 2 to 3, equivalent to 600–900 billion USD. That would represent the fastest, most inexpensive solution and require the least regulatory effort to provide additional liquidity for concrete measures. The following case study (see box 30) demonstrates this.

Box 30: Swap lines for the V20 in the face of massive climate change impacts

The V20:[254] the most vulnerable countries are facing disproportionate hazards, with rising floods, wildfires, unreliable rainfall, droughts, water stress and biodiversity loss; further food insecurity and health impacts (heat-related deaths, increased dengue and vibrio transmission, malaria outbreaks); overall decrease in GDP per capita; loss of labour hours; acceleration of imported inflation and interest rate rises; and higher costs of capital for sovereign credit lines. The striking part of this story is that the Global North is overwhelmingly responsible for these challenges and we have all the solutions at hand. CBCS lines would be a fast and precise monetary tool to alleviate the problems. The final result for the central banks of the Global North would be that their balance sheets would increase by the volume of USD equivalent required, while the V20 countries would finally have the drugs, drones and dams that they need, as well as enough money to offset all the losses and damage they are exposed to.

As long as central banks and regulators continue with their current monetary policy, which facilitates the fossil-driven economy at a large scale, they should extend their mandate to factor in the scientific findings on planetary boundaries, resource depletion, biodiversity loss and climate-related issues in order to stabilise the CPI in the future. A green CBDC and the associated swap lines are candidates to play this role, which would help to create a level playing field. The figure below (Figure 36), summarises this argument.

---

[251] At present, there are no swap lines between the US or EU and African countries, but there are (mostly undisclosed) swap lines between China and over 32 countries. See Steil et al. 2024.

[252] The IMF's special drawing rights (SDRs) are a special case. Over 95% of the 450 billion SDRs (as of 2023) are used by OECD countries and MICs.

[253] Access to bilateral swap lines is mainly restricted to OECD countries. 99% of least developed countries (LDCs), 95% of landlocked developing countries (LLDCs) and small island developing states (SIDSs) and 70% of middle-income countries (MICs) have no access to such agreements. See Perks et al. 2021.

[254] Established in 2015 at the annual meeting of the World Bank and the IMF, the V20 comprises the world's 68 most vulnerable states, which are especially susceptible to the impacts of climate change. It represents a total of 1.7 billion people, a GDP of 3.8 trillion USD and 5% of emissions. See Vulnerable Twenty group 2024.

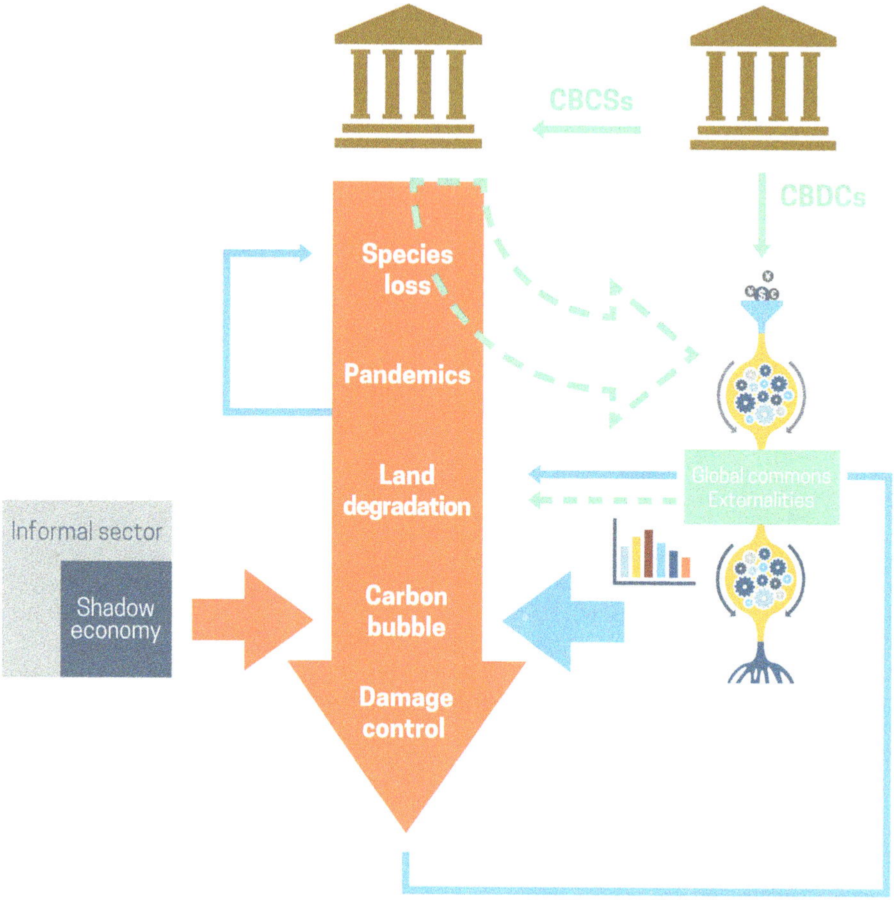

Figure 36: Rethinking finance: CBDCs and CBCSs can provide the additional liquidity required to fund, manage and hedge our commons.

The process is still incomplete, but this parallelisation of the monetary system has already begun. Developments include a bifurcation of the interest rate to differentiate between brown and green investments, central bank purchasing programmes that favour green investments, the implementation of CBDCs and CBCSs with smart contracts that can target and condition financial transactions, taxation schemes and a cap-and-trade system that facilitates the co-existence of a conventional and a green economy. That will ultimately lead to a green marketplace in which green taxation and the additional revenue that is unlocked generate numerous positive second-round effects.

This figure above (Figure 36) is an upgraded version of the ones from earlier in the book, where CBDCs and CBCSs directly or indirectly provide the liquidity required to overcome the cost avalanche and risk cascades associated with negative systemic and collective externalities. One final issue we need to deal with before we conclude our argument is the polity paradox or open economy trilemma. That is the subject of the next section.

Overcoming the open economy trilemma: The 'open economy trilemma'[255] consists in the fact that countries cannot simultaneously maintain independent monetary policies, fixed exchange rates and uncontrolled capital flows. To use some extreme cases as examples: if a government opts for an agenda of free capital flows with no tariffs, controls or monetary independence, which mainly refers to the capacity to raise or lower interest rates as it chooses, it will end up with a floating currency regime and have to abandon fixed exchange rates. If a government instead opts for fixed exchange rates and an autonomous monetary policy, it will end up with a Bretton Woods scenario, with no or restricted capital mobility. And if a government chooses fixed exchange rates and free capital flows, it will have to give up monetary autonomy, as experienced in the age of the gold standard. This trilemma was further explored in Dani Rodrik's seminal papers, which argue that nation states, democratic politics and greater global economic integration lead to an inescapable 'global paradox'.[256] According to Rodrik, if a government chooses national sovereignty and democratic politics, it has to renounce further global integration, culminating in some sort of Bretton Woods-style agreement. If the government embraces greater global integration and democratic politics, it will end up with increased global federalism and less national sovereignty. And if a government chooses to strengthen global integration and national sovereignty, it will end up with a golden straitjacket and restricted democratic rights. It is possible to have any two of the elements, but never all three. The figure below, (Figure 37) illustrates this idea.

In the face of global challenges and the need to fund and finance planetary commons and negative collective externalities and unlock private capital, we are fundamentally trapped in this global paradox. National sovereignty and democratic voting in open societies simply risk falling short of what is needed to address global challenges. On the other side, over 50% of the global population does not live in an open society. The free world cannot simultaneously maintain national sovereignty, address global challenges and support democratic rights without impossible trade-offs. What monetary tools are needed to give us a realistic way to escape, or at least mitigate the costs of, this trilemma? I will attempt to show one way out of this trilemma that enables pegged exchange rates, an independent monetary policy and free capital flows within the context of democracy and deepening global economic integration, while at the same time maintaining the sovereignty of nation states. The trilemma, irrespective of the form it takes and how the different elements relate to each other, is based on the unquestioned assumption of the global monetary system existing in its current form. This global monetary monoculture, through which all capital flows and all

---

255 First introduced by Oxelheim 1990 and Obstfeld and Taylor 1998.
256 Rodrik 2011.

Enabling conditioned
capital and a Bretton
Woods compromise

National
sovereignty

Democratic
politics

Ensuring independent
monetary policy and
reducing the golden
straitjacket

Reconciling global
federalism and
national identity

Global
integration

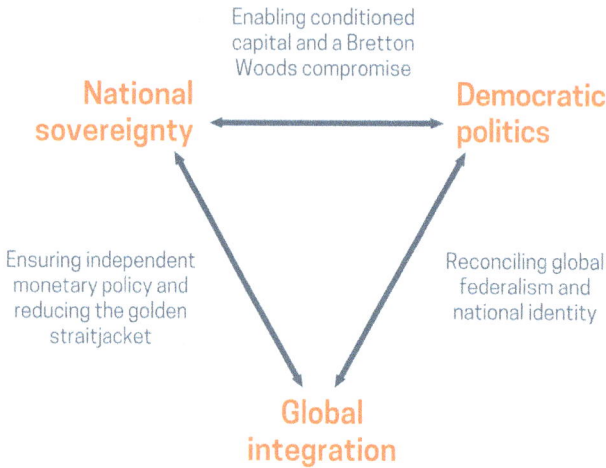

Figure 37: The global open economy trilemma.

goods and services are traded, places a golden straitjacket around national sovereignty and monetary policy. It also imposes constraints on our democratic voting and diminishes the full potential for the future wealth of nations. Despite the fact that over 150 currencies are available globally, they all follow the same intrinsic design and use the same monetary channels to provide the liquidity required for their economies. However, if we had an additional monetary system designed in a different way and utilising different monetary channels and different technologies, we would then be able to overcome or at least mitigate the trilemma described above.[257] If it is designed and regulated the right way, injecting this additional liquidity into the market would then have the potential to meet requirements and reduce the golden straitjacket imposed on nation states that follows from further economic integration. This adjusted monetary design would be able to reconcile global market rules on the one hand and regional sovereignty and democracy on the other. An additional, quasi-parallel monetary system like the one described in this book would finally allow partial capital controls in a Bretton Woods-style compromise, as the electronic money would be distributed to specific sectors or regions based on a smart contract.

Throughout the book, I have advocated a pre-distributive mechanism, whereby the existing monetary system provides additional but conditioned liquidity upfront in order to finance the transformation of our economy. It could be implemented either top-down, through an additional mandate for monetary regulators and central banks (CBDCs/CBCSs), through an extended internal money creation mechanism for public banks, multilateral banks and the World Bank or through IMF special drawing rights. All these options would differ from a conventional credit line via the capital market.

---

257 Lietaer et al. 2012.

Alternatively, the additional liquidity could be generated bottom-up through corporations or regional/national public bodies (regional complementary currencies or cryptocurrencies). In either case, or in a hybrid of both, the required liquidity to finance business, social and ecological projects would not be generated via the redistributive mechanism we currently use, which primarily comprises taxation, fees and philanthropy. This conclusion is not obvious at first glance, but has significant implications for how to implement unconventional monetary policies in the Anthropocene era, when geophysical planetary boundaries and growing interconnectedness are leading to asymmetric shocks, non-linear tipping points, feedback loops and fat-tail events – even in cases where nation states have done everything 'right'. While this conclusion is not immediately obvious, it becomes inescapable with a little further reflection. To be more specific: as long as we fail to question the design of the financial and monetary system in the first place and do not adjust it to the new requirements in the Anthropocene era, the trilemma will remain unresolved. Let us focus again on extreme cases for the purpose of illustration: with this additional and conditioned liquidity in place, a nation, or a region such as the EU, could overcome the limitations of the trilemma. Removing or at least limiting the ability to independently issue liquidity at a national, regional or corporate level to finance local, regional or global commons and/or provide adequate hedging instruments to unlock private capital would effect a Bretton Woods-type compromise by establishing a form of conditioned capital and a pegged currency between the regular currency and the 'green' currency. The design of the additional electronic 'coins', governed by a smart social contract, would exclusively channel the flow of free capital towards the desired goals. This additional M^{cola} would also have the potential to enhance global federalism where needed and politically agreed upon, as in the Sustainable Development Goals (SDGs) that were endorsed by the world community in 2015.[258] It would deepen economic integration by providing the additional purchasing power required to mobilise the two-thirds of the global population currently unable to participate in globalisation. Overall, it would provide governments with the required financial leverage and political sovereignty, including additional 'green' tax revenue to tackle the numerous environmental, social and political challenges we face as a world community. If we take this concept one step further, M^{cola} eligible for the payment of taxes and wages and running in parallel to the conventional currency system would trigger a significant steering effect on business and public affairs, providing a stabilising, anti-cyclical counterbalance to monetary policy's pro-cyclical tendency and reducing illicit transactions. Additional positive externalities would be generated by direct investments in mitigating the negative externalities in the Anthropocene era. For example, each 'green' dollar or euro spent on the desired goals – the eradication of poverty, infrastructure development, improving access to healthcare or educational programmes, tackling

---

258 See United Nations 2024.

global warming and biodiversity loss, preparing for the next pandemic – would reduce short-term and long-term negative externalities and spillovers. This is visualised in the figure below (Figure 38):

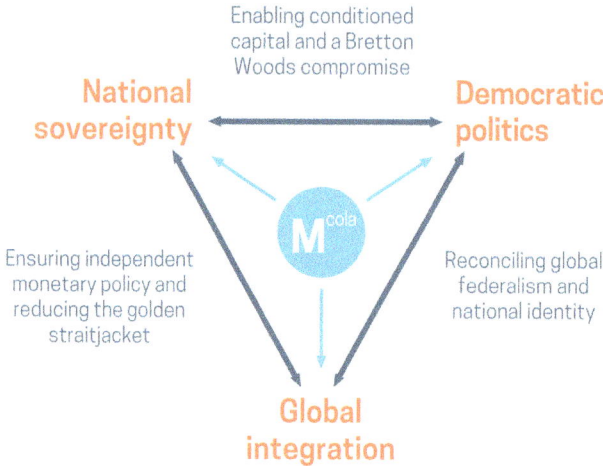

Figure 38: Overcoming the global trilemma.

Again: money is not a natural law; rather, it is one of the most powerful human inventions for promoting welfare and wealth. It can be changed and adjusted, just like club rules or a marriage contract. It is not a panacea, but it can provide a powerful tool to mitigate self-imposed political constraints and soften or even overcome the limits of the global trilemma we are currently caught in – ultimately leading us to the monetary ecosystem discussed in the next section.

Towards a Monetary Ecosystem

The conclusions of the preceding sections can be encapsulated in the idea of a monetary ecosystem. US dollar supremacy is considered the single most important factor behind global financial instability, yet is also an anchor for monetary stability. It causes debt traps, inflationary pressure and a lack of adequate liquidity in the periphery of the global economy on the one hand while providing a safe haven and a benchmark for investments on the other.[259] There are several caveats to address before we take this argument further. If we note the expected growth rate of BRICS+ countries,

---

259 It has been argued that a currency basket with multiple currencies would be a source of instability too, as the volatility of the exchange rate would be amplified and it will take decades before most currencies can be traded without any capital controls. See Gallagher and Kozul-Wright 2022.

which is twice that of the G7, and further note that the Global South requires twice as much investment as the Global North (4–8% of GDP vs 2–4%) over the next few decades, and further agree that we need additional, conditioned liquidity to finance our future, the best next step for a greener currency regime would be for regulators and central banks – during a 'window of opportunity' over the next two decades, while the ecosystem is still fairly intact, the global market is not fully fragmented and global war has not broken out – to use their sovereign right to create money to provide the additional liquidity that is needed. This additional monetary supply aggregate would come in a digital format underpinned by blockchain technology and a smart contract that means it can only be spent on the UN SDGs, thus creating a competitive green future marketplace. This would add green CBDCs or CBCSs to the basket of major currencies currently in place.[260] Globally, this would represent a several trillion USD bill. The relative future weight and relevance of any currency involved would be determined by the amount of this additional green liquidity. This would represent a first sign that the currency area involved is committed to a more sustainable future.[261] It would further avoid the debate over USD supremacy or a multicurrency basket and make the entire IMS more stable and reliable. And last but not least, it seems to be relatively easy to implement. The result would be a green, long-term, risk-hedged, anti-cyclical, built-in stabiliser that better reflects the overall costs and opportunities. The overarching argument still holds that this green monetary ecosystem would transcend and avoid the conflicting political agendas that exist in a multipolar world. That might not be obvious at a first glance, but we would call it unhealthy or even insane to keep repeating business as usual over and over again and expect that things will change and results will be different. 'Out of the box' and the 'best next step' seem to be the order of the day. The figure below (Figure 39) illustrates these points with reference to the international SWIFT payment system. The green parts represent the additional, conditioned liquidity that can only be used to build a greener and more inclusive future. This monetary aggregate would provide a steering, funding and stabilising mechanism that is desperately needed.

The green circles represent the required additional and conditioned liquidity provided by central banks through CBDCs or swap lines to finance loss and damage funds and global commons, to cope with future ecological shocks and to provide liquidity for

---

260 Gresham's law, which states that bad money drives out good, would become invalid: a green euro or green dollar would be more stable and represent a more realistic price signal than the conventional one. We may expect that the inverse to Gresham's law (Thiers's law) will then hold: good money drives out bad. The introduction of a green digital currency would stabilise the currency value overall. See Rolnick and Weber 1986; Bernholz and Gersbach 1992.

261 Technically speaking, this would require a bifurcation of the interest rate (brown versus green). The spread would then reflect the added risk–return premium. Currency carry traders (CCTs) would hedge between the two spreads and bear the risks during their transactions, which could help to dampen volatility in the currency market. See Hsu et al. 2024.

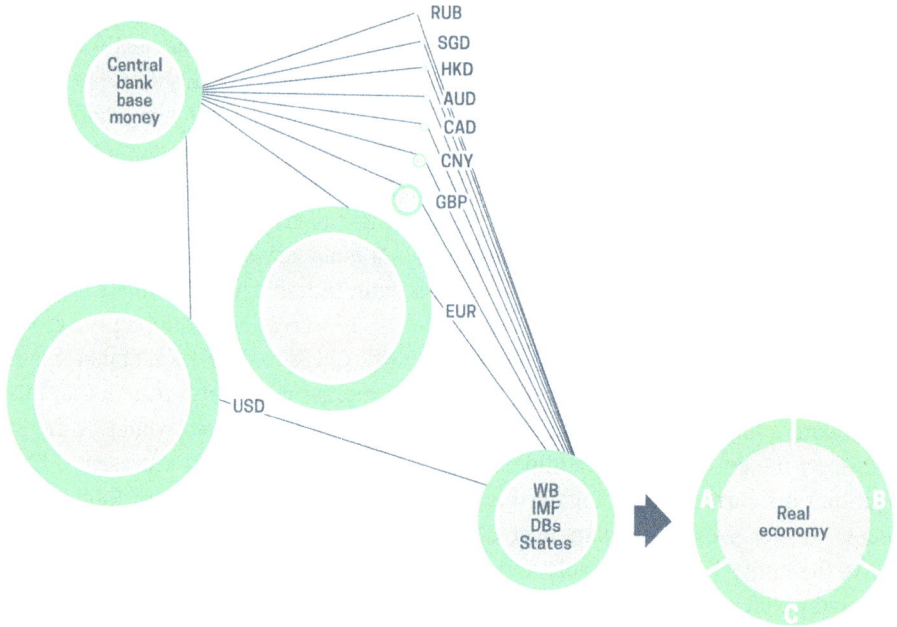

Figure 39: Towards a monetary ecosystem: a dual green digital currency system within a multipolar currency world.
A: managing collective negative externalities; B: funding planetary commons; C: mobilizing private capital
The circles represent a selection of the most active currencies for international transactions in 2024 as a proportion of SWIFT payment values. RUB = Russian rouble; SGD = Singapore dollar; HKD = Hong Kong dollar; AUD = Australian dollar; CAD = Canadian dollar; CNY = Chinese yuan; GBP = British pound; EUR = euro.

additional financial instruments (hedging, guarantees, etc.) to further mobilise private capital.[262] What would be the effects of this additional, green, conditioned liquidity line on the conventional economy? It would not harm that economy. Quite the contrary: corporate and state planning, production and price levels would become more resilient and reliable with a longer-term vision. Furthermore, it would stabilise the economic cycle of booms and busts in an anti-cyclical manner. A green monetary ecosystem would stabilise the multiple currency regimes in place, reducing the volatility of weaker currencies and the threat of further depreciation and increased interest rates, while facilitating the use of additional green liquidity to foster a green economy. Despite arguments to the contrary, we need much more financialisation (finance/GDP). However, that financialisation must be designed in a more democratic and humane manner, so as to protect the planet while increasing wealth for two-thirds of the global population. If there is a single most important variable besides technology, governance, behavioural

---

262 This is partly in line with the proposal of Hiebert and Monnin 2023, which calls for a systemic risk buffer to cover the potential future costs.

change and demographic factors when it comes to enabling transformation, it is new, digital financial engineering instruments within a new monetary design. That would be a real game changer, and could be set in motion in less than a year, if the six largest central banks agreed to create this optional, complementary, green currency line. These funds would be earmarked and used exclusively to finance SDG-related projects or the like. This electronic liquidity would run through different monetary channels from those of the conventional system. We would then have a supplementary currency effectively operating in parallel to the conventional monetary system and generating the liquidity needed for the next decades. For example, this new technology could be used to create targeted financial liquidity and channel it to millions of people in Africa through their mobile phone network. In India, the existing microcredit banking system could be used to transfer additional liquidity to millions of its citizens or to provide tailored harvest catastrophe bonds (CAT bonds) in the event of a drought. Any dollar spent and invested through these green, parallel channels would have the potential to reduce absolute poverty globally. The electronic format would further prevent or at least reduce corruption and fraud, as each transaction would be transparent and public. As the currency could be used to pay taxes, government agencies could expect additional liquidity to rebuild public infrastructure such as nurseries, parks, hospitals and libraries. And the millions of NGOs globally would finally receive the funding they need to do their jobs properly. This targeted additional liquidity would improve education and provide access to universal healthcare that would otherwise never materialise. It would reduce resource depletion and clean up the air, preventing negative effects on our planet and on public health. Implementing green CBDCs and CBCSs would help to transform our entire society, which is still 80% fossil-powered, into a green marketplace. And we would eventually unlock the untapped potential of millions of unemployed people by creating new jobs, which would in turn unlock the creativity of billions more people.[263] Designed in the right way, CBDCs can make financial transactions cheaper, fairer, faster and more sustainable. Central banks and the public banking sector would be able to extend their balance sheets and operate anti-cyclically, helping to prevent bank runs. These currencies would operate solely in digital form, and the acquired data from the transaction could be used in some cases as a substitute for tangible collaterals and to reverse the information asymmetry where the lender knows more about the transac-

---

263 Complementary, parallel currencies have been used for local and international trade throughout the last 1,000 years of monetary history. The German 'MEFO' bonds (1930–1935), for example, provided proof of concept, albeit one that was terribly misused. Over 3,500 complementary regional currency systems operate globally, providing sandbox approval for social and ecological purposes, while the dawn of privately issued cryptocurrencies, which are speculative and unregulated by their nature, and public CBDCs with a smart digital contract demonstrate that the future of money will be organised as a monetary ecosystem rather than a monetary monoculture. See Rössner 2018.

tion than the borrower.[264] Finally, CBDC providers are not only lenders of last resort, but purpose-driven, mission-based market makers – as opposed to plumbers that come in to clean up the mess afterwards. Redesigning the financial system would not solve all our problems, but it would make them easier to address. This, or some similar mechanism, is the missing link needed to achieve better outcomes in terms of people, prosperity, peace, planet and partnerships. If we want to think outside the box and consider an alternative approach, our financial system will be pivotal.[265]

Sustainability should drive finance: If we took up that suggestion, we would then enter an era where finance no longer drives our common future but the other way round. An era where nurseries are not run by accountants but by trained educational specialists, and hospital chains not by the CFO but by the medical director. Where money is seen not as a natural law, but as a convention we can change, where regulators develop the next stage in the evolution of money, CBDCs, and where an additional monetary facility provides funding tools to hedge and manage public goods and public guarantees to mobilise private capital. Where it is not scarcity or abundance but an adequate monetary supply that provides the liquidity necessary to shift from fossil fuels to renewables and to fund our planetary commons and negative collective externalities. Where new technologies, in particular AI, big data and distributed ledger technology, will reveal their potential as a 'force for good' and provide a built-in stabiliser for our monetary regime. The figure below, (Figure 40) summarises the different options we have in the Anthropocene era, as economics undergoes a transformation.

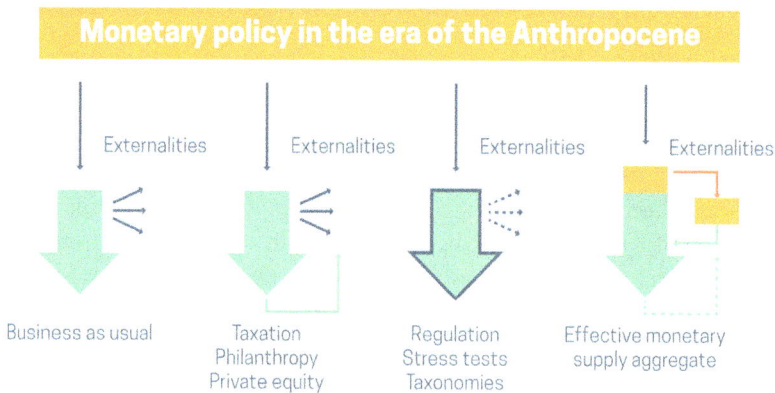

Monetary policy in the era of the Anthropocene

| Externalities | Externalities | Externalities | Externalities |

| Business as usual | Taxation Philanthropy Private equity | Regulation Stress tests Taxonomies | Effective monetary supply aggregate |

Figure 40: Monetary policy in the Anthropocene era: an effective monetary supply aggregate.

---

264 The well-known net effect, which causes monopoly yields and windfall profits, can then be utilised for the common good. See Brunnermeier et al. 2019.
265 For further details, see the WAAS initiative 'The Tao of Finance': https://new.worldacademy.org/tao-of-finance/.

Conclusion

In the original ancient Greek, 'politics' (πολιτικά) referred to the process of making decisions for the good of the community as a whole. The modern concept of monetary policy continues this idea: it is the process of making decisions in the financial domain for the good of the community as a whole. This definition still holds true in the era of transformation. It is our commons and the environment that will determine whether we are able to achieve more wealth and lower negative externalities – what is known as a Pareto-superior equilibrium – since human rights to things such as preschooling, universal healthcare and fresh air will stay the same regardless of which economic regime is in place. It is the (mis)alignment of the monetary system that has prevented us from funding our commons. The monetary system acts like a catalyst, enabling infinite transactions and steering societies as a whole towards good or bad outcomes. Every monetary system has a quantitative aspect, measured in terms of the volume of money injected into and circulating within the economy, and a qualitative one, measured in terms of where money goes and what it does.[266] If we synthesise the ideas set out in this book and try to specify the role of the monetary system, we can conclude that a conditioned multiplier would help us drive the transition in the right direction. A conversion rate substantially higher than the growth rate would help support this change. Aiming for an 80:20 Pareto ratio can provide a first rule of thumb, with monetary and fiscal policy running in tandem to provide steering and funding tools. It would be like a combination of carrot and stick.

Monetary triangulation will widen the scope beyond existing polarities like state and market, demand and supply; the next step in the evolution of money will be characterised by new forms of money, namely CBDCs and CBCSs. They have the potential to provide the liquidity we need in the face of the asymmetric shocks that will come in the near future. We will then be able to mitigate, and perhaps even overcome, the constraints of the open economy trilemma and end up with a monetary ecosystem where sustainability will finally drive finance and not the other way round. The current situation is like having racehorses cooped up in a rabbit pen, unable to unleash their full potential. Rather than repairing the rabbit pen, we should put the racehorses on a suitable racetrack.

This *effective monetary supply aggregate* (M^{cola}) should precede the effective supply and demand aggregate in the real economy in times of transformation. And the alternative monetary channels we use and the resources we have available would then determine the relative prices of goods and services in the economy as a whole. Any sovereign state that has the ability to print money and does not have to rely on debts nominated in a foreign currency therefore has the following options, which I

---

266 Brunnhuber 2024a.

refer to as *reverse monetary engineering*: if the economy is operating at its limits and lacks skilled workers, the additional monetary supply aggregate can be used to invest in educational programmes, encouraging the migration of qualified workers or demographic policies. If sufficient land, energy or resources are not available, the additional liquidity should be used to import energy, scarce resources and additional R&D. But the monetary mechanism remains the same: funding our planetary commons, unlocking and de-risking private capital and investing in a common mission. A defective system cannot transform on its own; there needs to be a reasonable alternative at hand. As long as we rely on an unstable, volatile, short-termist, pro-cyclical system to fund our common future, we risk betting on the wrong horse and creating endless trade-offs and additional costs. Keynes 2.0 will not be a mere extension of the past, but capable of overcoming its own constraints. Adequate risk adjustments, management of externalities and common goods and resetting the overall framework will become key. Or as Keynes apocryphally put it: *When the facts change, I change my mind. What do you do?* Intellectual courage, scientific clarity, an attentiveness to empirical evidence and bold political decisions will be needed in order to confront challenges and adapt the existing system for the good of humankind in times of transformation. An effective monetary supply aggregate would have the potential to reconcile different schools of economic thought: neoclassicism, the Austrian School, monetarism and the vast body of empirical experimental research from the fields of behavioural finance and institutional economics. All of these different approaches are powerful and relevant, yet they are unable to replicate the *differentia specifica* of financial economics and the unique contribution it can make to achieving the 'cheapest of all worlds'. In the next and final chapter, I will be more specific. I will address the role of the informal sector and the growing relevance of transparency and data-driven decisions, and further elaborate on the concrete impact of an additional monetary aggregate on inflation. I will also introduce the notion of a monetary inflation brake and explore the best next steps in terms of concrete green transition plans. A section on geopolitics outlines the links between money and power politics. The petrodollar system and the Belt and Road Initiative provide examples of best practice. In the section on a Bretton Woods 2.0 agenda, I describe the institutional conditions required to reset the monetary framework, including a new global supply chain act, a changed role for rating agencies and an investor dispute settlement mechanism – all embedded in the new paradigm of an additional monetary aggregate. Finally, I will summarise my argument for a general theory of money, the financing of our global commons and sustainable development for the 21st century. One major factor affecting all these various aspects is the interplay between the law of entropy and an economics of transformation. That will be the first topic of the final chapter.

D: Getting Real

The Law of Entropy and an Economics of Transformation

We live in a finite world and every economic activity is embedded in nature. That means we have to respect biological and physical laws, which precede and precondition economic ones. The leading proponent of this 'bio-economics' is the Romanian mathematician and economist Nicholas Georgescu-Roegen (1906–1994).[267] His major contribution to any economics of transformation is the recognition that economics is subject to the second law of thermodynamics: energy and matter have an irreversible tendency to move from a low-energy, disposable state to a high-energy, chaotic, non-disposable one.[268] In short: time discounts the world in one way or another, progressively leading to more disorganisation, complexity, noise and chaos.

Box 31: The law of entropy
$t[1] < t[2] \Rightarrow En[t1] < En[t2]$

$t+$

$t+$: *irreversible time axis*
$t[1]$: *time 1*
$t[2]$: *time 2*
$En[t1]$: *state of entropy at time 1*
$En[t2]$: *state of entropy at time 2*

Along an irreversible time axis ($t+$), for any given time, $t[1]$, preceding another, $t[2]$, the amount of entropy at the latter, $En[t2]$, is always greater than that at the former, $En[t1]$. Thermodynamics describes the degree of disorder, depreciation, use, decay, noise, dissipation and loss of energy along an irreversible timeline (entropy), which further converts into increasing complexity. This foundational principle can be applied to human activities in general and to any particular economic activity. In order to make sense of the increasing complexity, the web of life creates an inner order of complexity and reflects the degree of organisational structure along an evolutionary path, running from cells to plants to animals to humans. This nested and dynamic complexity evolves against the tide of the second law of thermodynamics (negentropy),[269] which seems to push in the opposite direction. This apparent paradox between laws of physics and obvious evolutionary patterns of biology is further complicated by human activities. The anthropogenic factor, expressed in cultural achievements, governmental organisations, legal rights and technological innovations, adds a third layer to the physical and biologi-

---

267 Georgescu-Roegen 1971 and 1993; Ulgiati et al. 2004.
268 Clausius 1865; Boltzmann 1974.
269 Schrödinger 1944; Eigen 1987; Prigogine and Stengers 1984.

https://doi.org/10.1515/9783111421520-005

cal realms. Any higher degree of ordered complexity is generated in living systems through organised and available information content, which can be assimilated, used and internalised. And this seems to be true for both biological systems and human activities. If living systems fail to make this information available, they will not contribute to a higher degree of ordered complexity.[270] The figure below (Figure 41) illustrates how evolutionary biological and human activities are able to incorporate information and create a structured complexity within the overall process of entropy (see also excursus 2).

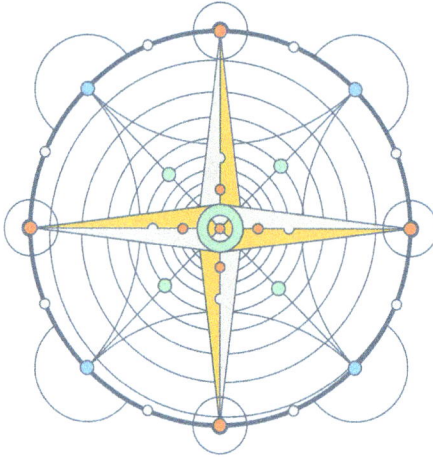

Figure 41: The web of life: ordered complexity. (adapted version of Dr Anneloes Smitsman's EARTHwise Compass ©)

The mechanistic worldview that originated in the agricultural revolution has a built-in tendency to neglect feedback loops, spillovers and externalities and is based on the idea that human activities could be reversed over and over again. The law of entropy describes a process of increasing informational content, progressing from simplicity to complexity over time.[271] Human activities are then superimposed over this physical law.[272] We have attempted throughout history to incorporate and embody the ever-growing informational complexity by means of new rules, institutions and forms of governance. In other words: the adaptability, creativity, ingenuity and self-regulation of economic processes enable second-order forms of complexity above and beyond

---

270 Shannon 1948.

271 It is not matter, cells or atoms that determine the process of life and its associated complexity, but *information*. Access to shared information – whether it be myth or scientific fact, whether it be stories about gods, laws, money or a nation – is humans' selection advantage. See Shannon 1948; Smitsman and Currivan 2019; Harari 2024.

272 The second law of thermodynamics operates on a different time scale (millions of years) from human economic activities (years and decades).

the biological web of life.[273] It seems that any economic activities will increase the complexity of the overall system, which in turn irreversibly increases overall expenditures, potential costs but also revenue at any given point in time. Any economic activity therefore contributes to greater disarray and non-disposable entropy via waste and negative externalities at every moment along an irreversible timeline. This also holds true when we invest in renewable energy, restore nature, apply new technologies to fight cancer or reduce waste or implement new regulatory frameworks to tackle poverty, low wages or future pandemics. With each economic intervention, we automatically increase the overall complexity of the system and increase the potential risks, costs, revenue and opportunities at the same time.[274]

Box 32: The law of entropy and economic activities

(t+)

$t[1] < t[2] \Rightarrow Cx[t1] < Cx[t2]$

$t[1] < t[2] \Rightarrow R[t1] < R[t2]$

t+: irreversible time axis
t[1]: time 1
t[2]: time 2

Cx[t1]: state of ordered complexity at time 1
Cx[t2]: state of ordered complexity at time 2
R[t1]: risks, opportunities, costs and revenue at time 1
R[t2]: risks, opportunities, costs and revenue at time 2

However, from a financial perspective rooted in the human middle dimension of space-time (t^h), the relative impact of the law of entropy on any economic activity will remain negligible, as long as the relative impact of costs, expenditures, gains and profits (δR), reflected in the multiple price formations and the relative increase of ordered complexity (δCx) on negentropy, is higher than the marginal increase of entropy.

Box 33: Negentropy and economic activities

$\delta NEn\left(t^h\right) = \delta Cx + \delta R$

$\delta NEn\left(t^h\right) > \delta En$

---

273 These *ordered forms of the complexity of life* possess an evolutionary coherence, with the increase and diversification of information providing a deeper understanding of nature, human activities and their reciprocal relationships, interdependencies, boundaries and barriers. See Laszlo 2009; Laszlo 2016; Bateson 2016.

274 This refers to technological discoveries (Promethean technologies) that provide a higher output per unit of input. Fire, agricultural farming, breeding techniques and the steam engine are some examples. As long as nuclear or hydrogen energy's input remains higher than its output, the promise to overcome entropy is parasitic on the overall expected ROI. See Montesi 2023.

δNEn: marginal increase of negentropy
t^h: space-time of human activities
δEn: marginal increase of entropy
δCx: marginal increase of ordered complexity
δR: marginal increase of risks, opportunities, costs and revenue

Only when the noise, chaos, waste and loss of energy, which are expressed in economic terms as externalities, translate into additional inevitable costs and potential benefits for human activities along t^h will the second law of thermodynamics substantially impact on the financial sector. Along an irreversible time axis, any economic activities will still irreversibly contribute to an increase of entropy, and hence to an increase in the complexity of the system. For the human domain (t^h), this further translates into increased potential contagion effects, which in turn translate into costs, revenue, opportunities and risks. In short: any wind turbine built today reduces the potential opportunities of any newborn in the future, but the potential opportunities of any newborn are affected only if the impact on additional entropy from investing in the turbine exceeds the impact of that investment on negentropic ordered complexity. This fact deserves our full attention, because it can reveal the *differentia specifica* of economics and finance. The main purpose of economic rules should not be to violate physical and biological laws, but rather to provide the means for a meaningful and enjoyable life within these limits. Although any human endeavour – whether it be the building of a wind turbine or nursery, or the manufacture of a tank or bullet – will increase the entropy in a system, economic rules in general and financial incentives in particular can provide the metrics, measures and means to create an intermediary space and temporary stability within the human 'middle dimension'.[275]

One of the major reasons why economics in general and financial economics in particular remain insensitive to biophysical reality is that academic economics has been resistant to providing a comprehensive marginal productivity function that includes energy and money as independent factors.[276] Classical theories[277] saw labour as the main source of wealth, while neoclassical ones[278] also included land. The Cobb–Douglas marginal production function[279] came up with a coefficient of 0.3 for capital and 0.7 for labour, and Robert Solow[280] further identified an unexplained residuum of 0.875. Energy (resources, land, raw materials) and the impact of money

275 Prigogine and Stenger 1984; Weizsäcker 1974.
276 See Keen et al. 2019; Keen 2021.
277 See Kolb 2017, 29 ff; Blum 2004, 43 ff.
278 See Kolb 2017, 63 ff; Blum 2004, 55 ff.
279 Cobb and Douglas 1928; Douglas 1976.
280 See Solow 1957; Bachmann et al. 2022.

(money creation, financial engineering and the IMS) have not played any crucial role in previous mainstream theories.

Box 34: Conventional production function

$Y = C^a \times L^{1-a}$

Y: output
L: labour
C: capital
a: elasticity of production

It would seem that over the last 150 years we have tolerated a discipline of economics that refuses to factor in energy and money as independent factors. More recently, biophysically informed economic theories have tried to overcome these constraints. The entire picture of output, marginal productivity, aggregate GDP and price formation is starting to shift. According to these new theories, output is roughly equal to energy input minus the waste we produce in order to generate it. If we then discount 'energy' from the production function accordingly, we can easily end up with negative net value added.[281] The box below shows an energy-adjusted production function:

Box 35: Energy-adjusted production function

$Y = C^a \times L^b \times p^c$

Y: output
C: capital
L: labour
p: energy
a, b, c: elasticities of production
$a + b + c = 1$

If we apply this general idea to the monetary system, the general production function would benefit. At any point in time along an irreversible time axis, the monetary supply aggregate can play a crucial role in mitigating, adapting, absorbing, funding and managing ever-increasing complexity and entropy. If the monetary supply is scarce, meaning economic actors are forced to compete with each other for limited resources and the supply remains below the expected funding of negative externalities (i.e. global commons) and undermines the ability to mobilise private capital, the overall costs will be higher and the marginal contribution to dissipated energy and entropy will rise. If the monetary supply aggregate is too high or inadequately qualified, the overall costs will exceed a social optimum and the marginal impact on additional entropy will rise as well. We have to conclude that in both cases – scarce supply and

---

281 See Ayers 2016; Kümmel 2013; Keen et al. 2019.

inflation – there would be a negative impact on entropic disarray. That is why an economics of transformation is not a circle, but an irreversible vector, with the laws of physics providing the irreversible timeline as the horizontal axis. Adding the human factor does not negate the law of entropy, but verticalises it. Both then represent the overall progression up a spiral staircase that I explored in the previous chapters. Any marginal share of additional entropy (δEn) that humans create needs to be less than any business-as-usual (BAU) scenario. It therefore seems to be rational to end war, stabilise the world population, help the Global South to leapfrog forwards, avoid luxury goods, advocate for a regulatory framework that supports repair and recycle strategies, encourage new and more efficient technologies and research methodologies and implement educational programmes in order to reduce the marginal increase of complexity and entropy in the system. I argue that unlimited quantitative growth, where scarce resources are treated as if they could be endlessly replaced, is not just an artificial construct, but an intellectual exercise that creates the illusion that we can overcome the law of entropy through economic rules.[282] If we deny this illusion, we will have to reject the idea that humans can partially reverse the timeline through new technologies, behavioural changes and regulatory efforts. Rather, any input (resources, land, labour, energy) and output (goods, services, waste and externalities) are sensitive to price signals, which should determine the design of the monetary system. If the injected liquidity is conditioned and qualified enough, the law of entropy is not violated.

Box 36: Marginal increase of entropy and the monetary system

$$\delta En \left(M^{cola} \right) < \delta En$$

$\delta En \left(M^{cola} \right)$: marginal increase of entropy with additional qualified monetary instruments
δEn: marginal increase of entropy without additional qualified monetary instruments

Living in a Near-Zero-Cost World

In the Anthropocene era, everything is interconnected in real time, planetary boundaries are beginning to assert themselves and human activities are pressing towards a 'big acceleration', with exponential impacts on our planet. In the economic domain, these characteristics translate into a closed planetary economy, with high un- or un-

---

282 See, for instance, Herman Daly's (1977) concept of a 'steady-state economy' or Robert Costanza's (1980) theory of 'embedded energy', according to which economic value expressed in monetary terms equals the energy embedded in the relevant economic activities. Even Kenneth E. Boulding's (1966) spaceship argument, according to which any waste will be reactivated and reused at some point in time through new technologies, must remain consistent with the second law of thermodynamics.

deremployment, significant output losses, low productivity, systemically underfunded planetary commons and massive associated costs, including ongoing negative social and environmental externalities. Scholars sometimes refer to this as a deflationary state of economic affairs. Negative collective externalities and asymmetric shocks on one side of the planet will affect someone, somewhere and somehow on the other. And unlike in the past, such externalities and asymmetric shocks translate into additional expenditures and costs. In short: there are no more free lunches and there is no such thing as dry water. We have identified a 'window of opportunity' over the next two decades when states and their associated public bodies will still be functional, our ecosystem will still be fairly intact and our global economy will not be fractured and fragmented, which will provide competitive advantages, labour specialisation and location advantages that we as a global community can all benefit from. Utilising this window of opportunity, however, requires an out-of-the-box approach to financial economics so that we can fund, manage and hedge systemic risks and uncertainties, provide adequate liquidity to fund our public goods, manage the rising costs of externalities and build a financial framework to mobilise the trillions of private-sector investment needed for our common future. The major cost components in a closed planetary economy are not variable, fixed or operational costs, but opportunity costs. Opportunity costs represent the loss of alternatives if we are forced to manage damage and lack of productivity instead of using the same amount of money to invest in education, fund research or simply reduce our workload. Within a closed economy, opportunity costs (Oc) are equal to the costs of expected but unmanaged externalities (Ex), underfunded commons (Co) and missed opportunities to unlock private capital (mpC) due to systemic uncertainties. At the same time, these opportunity costs are negatively correlated with the volume of efficiency measures (β), such as technology and education, and resilience measures (α), such as regulation and legal containment. The primary source of funding for these challenges could be additional conventional credit lines, debts and loans, a raft of taxation schemes and/or conditioned liquidity assistance provided by central banks (M^{cola}). The box below shows the formula if M^{cola} were the primary source of funding.

Box 37: Financing opportunities in a closed planetary economy

$$Oc = \frac{Ex + Co + mpC}{(\alpha + \beta) \times M^{cola}}$$

Oc: opportunity costs
Ex: costs of unmanaged negative externalities
Co: costs of underfunded global commons
mpC: costs to mobilise private capital under conditions of uncertainty[283]

---

283 Mobilising private capital primarily involves state guarantees, transition plans, innovative public–private partnerships and regulatory containment measures.

α: *resilience measures (regulation, safety, legal containment[284])*
β: *efficiency measures (technology, education, healthcare[285])*
M^{cola}: *monetary supply aggregate for conditioned liquidity assistance*

This means that Oc without M^{cola} will always be higher than Oc with M^{cola}. Given that the additional expenditures that arise in the near future will far exceed any feasible growth trajectory of our global economy, and that credit lines and taxation will further constrain our ability to deal with the overall transformation, additional liquidity facilities will become key. Since the opportunity costs of not investing equal the costs of externalities, M^{cola} would provide the necessary liquidity to (partly) offset these costs. And since the opportunity costs of not investing are equal to the costs of defective commons and the costs of not mobilising private capital, we can conclude: if we could fund and manage all global negative collective externalities, and all our commons and all necessary private capital were mobilised, we would end up in a near-zero-cost world. This conclusion is not obvious at first glance. If the scenario described were to come about, a global decentralised market would generate green income and revenue on one side of the planet, which would equal income and revenue somewhere else. And this fully decentralised market allocation of goods and services, operating in an economic environment where externalities are eliminated over time and all our commons are funded, would provide the preconditions for a functional global marketplace. If we are prepared to provide additional, conditioned liquidity to fund Co and Ex, their associated costs would tend to zero. And if we are able to provide additional hedging instruments to mobilise private capital, the associated costs would, likewise, ultimately tend to zero. Only two uncertainties would remain. Firstly, what Joseph Schumpeter (1883–1950) called the 'creative destruction' of the entrepreneur, where new companies provide new and innovative ideas that replace old ones; secondly, the systemic uncertainties inherent to any complex system.

Box 38: A near-zero-cost world

$$Oc = \frac{Ex + Co + mpC}{(\alpha + \beta) \times M^{cola}} \longrightarrow 0$$

$$\delta Ex + \delta Co + \delta mpC \longrightarrow 0$$

$$M^{cola} \longrightarrow 0$$

---

284 Legal containment includes licensing costs, audits, active bans, law enforcement and international treaties.
285 Healthcare should take an integral approach that honours each individual's bio-psycho-social and spiritual dimensions and recognises the importance of a healthy environment and living conditions. This approach is known as OneHealth.

In other words: if the marginal costs of additional externalities (δEx), additional funding for commons (δCo) and mobilising private capital (δmpC) are properly funded (M^{cola}), the overall costs of any planetary closed economy will over the long run tend to zero. That would create a new economic equilibrium where M^{cola} would also tend to zero and the remaining costs to finance our future would be preventive measures to avoid unexpected future shocks. It would not be a Marxist planned economy nor the fully privatised world of the Austrian School that would provide a social optimum. Rather, an adjusted, conditioned monetary supply aggregate would deliver the preconditions for a Pareto-superior equilibrium. I admit that we are not (yet) living in a near-zero-cost world, but any attempt to move in that direction would reduce the expenditures ahead and be in line with our first-principles approach, expressed in the first chapter, of aiming for the 'cheapest of all possible worlds'.

We could take this argument one step further. The concept of double materiality is deeply embedded in the financial sector.[286] The real economy is not only affected by deteriorating ecosystem services that generate asymmetric shocks such as heatwaves, harvest losses and forced migration, but also generates numerous negative externalities itself. From a financial perspective, the shocks and the externalities are two sides of the same coin, but they are interlinked in a complex, non-linear manner. Causing serial externalities can lead to unprecedented ecological tipping points and social trigger points that backlash onto the real economy as shocks. And both externalities and shocks are associated with additional expenditures that affect the real economy along different timelines. This includes credit risks, the depreciation of collateral, business defaults, underwriting risks (such as increased insurance losses), operational risks (forced closures and disrupted supply chains) and liquidity risks (such as a growing need for refinancing and liquidity facilities).[287] The figure below (Figure 42) illustrates all this. The green circle represents the planet earth and the orange square economic activities, while the dotted grey circle represents society, which mitigates the impacts of our economy on a finite planet, and serves to adapt and potentially transform that economy.

I see the monetary system as a complex web without a weaver, a multiplex network, not merely an equilibrium or a set of statistical correlations. Complex webs create systemic risks, which reflect a potential negative externality that incurs additional costs for all economies involved. Instead of looking for isolated causes, it seems more important to identify the components within the web that have the highest impact. On the one hand, real economic risks, like pandemics, geopolitical tensions, disruption of the global supply chain, extreme weather and harvest defaults, increase financial instability. And it looks like a two-way hazard: the financial system is unstable and volatile itself, and the real economic risks amplify and translate into further fragility

---

286 European Commission 2019; Oman and Svartzman 2021.
287 NGFS 2020.

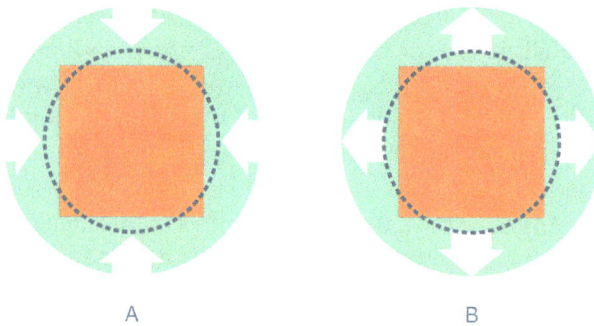

A   B

Figure 42: Double materiality explained.
(a) External shocks are hitting our society (dotted grey circle) and economy (orange square). (b) Negative collective spillovers from our economy and society are impacting on the environment. Both these processes occur asymmetrically, and the associated costs add up.

of the financial system. If we start increasing the efficiency of that financial web, we risk increasing volatility and instability. On the other hand, if we increase its interconnectedness, we are confronted with contagion effects. Such systemic risks then manifest in the form of pro-cyclical herding, fire sales, interbank loans, derivatives, cross-holdings, overlapping portfolios and investment diversification.[288] We would then be 'too interconnected to fail'.[289] Standard risk assessments, including stress tests, volatility indexes, increasing bank equity shares and credit default swap markets, are poor proxies for these uncertainties. Even value-at-risk models, calculated shortfalls and expected losses underestimate the risk exposure.[290] They are inadequate measures to evaluate and recognise the risks. The combined total of all the risks we are aware of seems to be smaller than the total systemic risks, which are at least 100 times greater than standard corporate credit risks. This means that over 90% of these systemic risks appear to be underestimated on a micro, corporate and balance-sheet level.[291] In order for this complex web to redirect, reorganise and restructure itself, public 'nodes' or 'agents' are needed that are prepared to cover and negate a portion of the systemic risks that might occur.[292]

---

288 Diem et al. 2020.

289 Pichler et al. 2021; Armanious 2024.

290 Credit default risks diminish as the density of a network increases, which can potentially secure against and compensate for losses. Systemic risks, in contrast, increase the probability of a collapse when the density of the network increases, due to domino cascades and contagion effects. Complexity finance has shown that a leverage of > 5 increases the risk of systemic default significantly, but a value below that level does not. See also Tabachová et al. 2023.

291 See Battiston et al. 2012.

292 The dilemma is that the Basel III capital requirements do not necessarily increase the stability of the banking sector, as the equity requirements would need to be three to four times higher to avoid contagion effects. At the same time, increased capital requirements would make the system inefficient

Let us imagine an economy under transformative pressure that has no monetary aggregate available at all and has to rely on multilateral barter. The net effect would be next to zero. Economic agents would simply exchange their goods and services. If money is regarded merely as a means of payment and storing value (with no compound interest rate), the net effect over time would be similar. The only resource such an economics of transformation could then rely on is human ingenuity. If, however, we regard a monetary aggregate as a means of payment and storing value, and then add the capacity for time and risk transformation and the endogenous property of creating money, the financial sector would suddenly become a powerhouse – for the good or ill of humankind. If we add the monetary system as an additional variable to this production function, as explained above, it will look as follows (see box 39 below):

Box 39: Qualified money-adjusted production function

$$Y = \left(\left(1 + \delta M^1\right) \times C\right)^a \times \left(\left(1 + \delta M^2\right) \times L\right)^b \times \left(\left(1 + \delta M^3\right) \times F\right)^c$$

$\delta M^3 = M^{cola}$

Y: output
δM^1: capital as a function of money
δM^2: labour/wages as a function of money
δM^3: additional monetary aggregate
F: financial sector
$a + b + c$ = elasticities of production = 1
M^{cola}: additional, conditioned liquidity assistance to fund externalities and underfunded commons

---

This equation means that the output of an economy depends on the relative share of capital, labour and the monetary sector. Assuming $a = 0.3$, $b = 0.6$ and $c = 0.1$, a 20% depreciation of the financial sector due to a banking or currency crisis would not only lead to a 2% decline in output but, *ceteris paribus*, to a much greater decline in overall output, since capital and labour depend on money. This means that the financial sector is both a dependent and an independent variable of the overall production function. M^{cola} to provide additional, conditioned liquidity would therefore potentially stabilise the output. Within a window of opportunity, the argument for a near-zero-cost world still holds in the face of the second law of thermodynamics. Money and energy seem to be the two blind spots that prevent us from successfully transforming our economy to a less entropic, less costly state. If a successful transformation were achieved, where all commons are implemented, managed and funded, all externalities are either internalised and/or offset by an effective monetary aggregate and all necessary private capital is mobilised, we would have achieved a fully decentralised

---

and vulnerable to a credit crunch. A systemic risk buffer funded through a monetary facility seems to be better able to hedge single risks than an isolated transaction tax (Tobin tax) without reducing systemic efficiency.

global market, where all price formations reflect the full cost of each transaction and are equal to the revenue of all parties involved. This near-zero-cost world, which strikes the right balance between public-sector regulation and private-sector allocation, would be totally different from a fully privatised world or a planned economy.

The case of prevention revised: Damage, hazards and lack of order reflect an increase of entropy, which further translates into higher potential costs for the real economy. When we try to avoid damage or a hazard from occurring in the first place, that is a case of *primary prevention*. If we can fully prevent some future damage from occurring, and the expected costs of that damage would exceed the growth rate of our economy, which would in turn negatively impact on our commons, it seems rational to prefer monetary policy measures to fiscal ones. In particular, if R&D or private-sector involvement has the potential to provide new technological solutions or entrepreneurial spirit to cope with the damage, the additional monetary liquidity would act like a non-defaultable loan or a public equity share between regulator and central banks on the one side and the government on the other. This would be the case if, for instance, we started investing in preserving a nature reserve. If we cause damage and have to expect future costs associated with that damage, this is a case of *secondary prevention*. If the associated and expected costs significantly exceed the expected growth trajectory, we need to complement any fiscal measures with monetary ones. This will still be expensive, but less than any BAU scenario where we use fiscal measures only. The same is true at a sectoral level. If one market segment generates additional future costs, in the form of global negative common externalities that exceed the expected growth rate of the economy in general, monetary policy should take precedence over fiscal policy. This is the case with climate change-associated spillovers or the expected costs of a future pandemic. If damage has been caused and will persist over time and our main task is to prevent further damage, which translates into additional costs, we have a case of *tertiary prevention*. In this case, the damage will not disappear any more, and the main task will be to keep the associated costs as low as possible. From a financial and monetary perspective, it seems rational to reduce these additional marginal costs if they significantly exceed the traditional growth trajectory, again by applying an augmented monetary policy rather than fiscal policy. We can see this kind of scenario when climate change mitigation is not sufficient and causes multiple social and ecological externalities. However, we are easily tempted to believe that these hazards are market failures. We should avoid characterising the tendency to generate oligopolies, social and ecological externalities, asymmetric information between buyers and sellers and the exploitation of common goods and governmental externalities, including state failures, corruption, incorrect political decisions, ignorance and denial as mere market failures. Rather, they reflect the lack of a properly functioning market allocation mechanism. If there were a market mechanism in place with adequate regulations and legal containments to prevent any spillovers and externalities, we would live in a much more comfortable and cheaper world.

In the Anthropocene era, these kinds of preventive measures in the financial and monetary domain are becoming very important, as they can promise to potentially reduce costs and risks at the same time. Each time, a subtle interplay between fiscal and monetary measures seems to be the most cost-effective. And each time (primary, secondary or tertiary) prevention measures are applied, they will to some extent act negentropically. That means they will reduce the impact on the overall entropic process, while providing some sort of ordered internal complexity.

The current design of the monetary system, however, tends to have an entropic effect.[293] The ability and resilience to cope with asymmetric shocks has become more relevant than any national sovereignty or the traditional differentiation between Global South and Global North, rich and developing countries. Non-state actors, from Wikipedia to the Wagner Group, each follow their own agenda. From high-net-worth individuals who store their money offshore; to USD supremacy, which sees trillions of dollars being printed to fund sovereign wealth funds extramurally in the Middle East and Asia; to HFT that amplifies pro-cyclical toxic chain reactions; to hedge funds and institutional investors becoming market makers themselves; to countries like Russia, China and India switching to trading in their own currency; to trading platforms and e-cards where decentralised finance enables P2P transactions with cryptocurrencies, cutting out traditional intermediaries like commercial banks. This all adds up to a web without a weaver rather than a top-down hierarchical order. The self-organising system, with functional, alternating hubs and nodes, then gives rise to new formations and features and to ad hoc alliances.

Upgrading the future: Discounted cash flow (DCF) analysis is a standard method in economics. It reflects the fact that we consider the future more uncertain than the present. This myopic view, which attaches less value to future consumption and future generations, is at the heart of disputes about climate change impacts, future pandemics and expected rises in food and energy prices. But discount rates are not a natural law. Rather, they reflect the socioeconomic possibilities we attach to our common shared future, and represent an individual or collective liquidity preference. Instead of consuming today, we postpone spending part of our disposable income and invest in the future with a discount. Take the economists William Nordhaus and Nicholas Stern as two extreme examples. Nordhaus applies a discount rate of 4.3% per annum,[294] while Stern applies one of 1.4%.[295] The difference might not look dramatic, but it leads to very different valuations of the future. The higher the discount, the less weight is given to future income and wealth. Suppose a good or service is worth 100 USD today; that same good or service in 25 years' time, viewed from today's perspective, would be worth 33

293 Khanna 2024.
294 Nordhaus 2007.
295 Stern 2007.

USD for Nordhaus and 70 USD for Stern. Small numbers can make big differences. But regardless of the precise discount rate, the very notion of a monetary discount only makes sense if we regard the future as having less worth and being more uncertain than the present.

Box 40: Discounting the future

$Oc[t2] < Oc[t1]$

Oc: opportunities (costs and revenue)

[t1], [t2]: time 1 and time 2 (with [t2] being later than [t1])

According to this traditional view, the uncertainties and opportunities of the future, Oc [t2], translate into a lower economic value than the uncertainties and opportunities of today, Oc [t1]. However, this is not a given. We could consider this mental exercise from the opposite angle and argue for an inverse discount rate. Instead of diminishing our future by 1–3%, we could create an incentive that allows us to invest in the future, so that it will become less uncertain and worth more than the present. That would involve considering our own present consumption, wealth and opportunities and those of the next generations from the perspective of a better future. If we support a common future where Oc [t2] > Oc [t1], then we should not discount but rather give greater weight to that future. Instead of using a discount rate of 3% per annum, we should reverse that figure. Investors and consumers would then start attaching greater value to our common future instead of discounting it. But this mental exercise requires a shift in our thinking and values and a redesign of our monetary system. Under the current monetary regime, a dead dolphin is worth more than a live one because it can be consumed today. We should instead factor in the value of a dolphin within a complex ecosystem and evaluating the positive externalities of that dolphin for all of us in the future. The figure below (Figure 43) elaborates further on this point and demonstrates why one of the major reasons we discount the future lies in the design of the monetary system itself. Imagine two alternative investments, a pine tree worth 100 euros in ten years or an oak tree worth 1,000 euros in 100 years. If we put this physical reality into our monetary system and apply an interest rate of 5% per annum, the pine tree would have a value of 61.30 euros as of today, and the oak tree one of just 7.60 euros. This is one major reason why we have become myopic and prefer the pine tree to the oak. However, our investment strategy will be fundamentally transformed if we start changing, *ceteris paribus*, the incentives within the existing monetary system. If we applied a demurrage fee[296] to our currency that devaluates the present value relative to the future value at the same rate of 5% annually, the oak tree would suddenly become a preferred object of investment, valued at 168,903.82

---

296 For an introduction to the concept see Lietaer 2001.

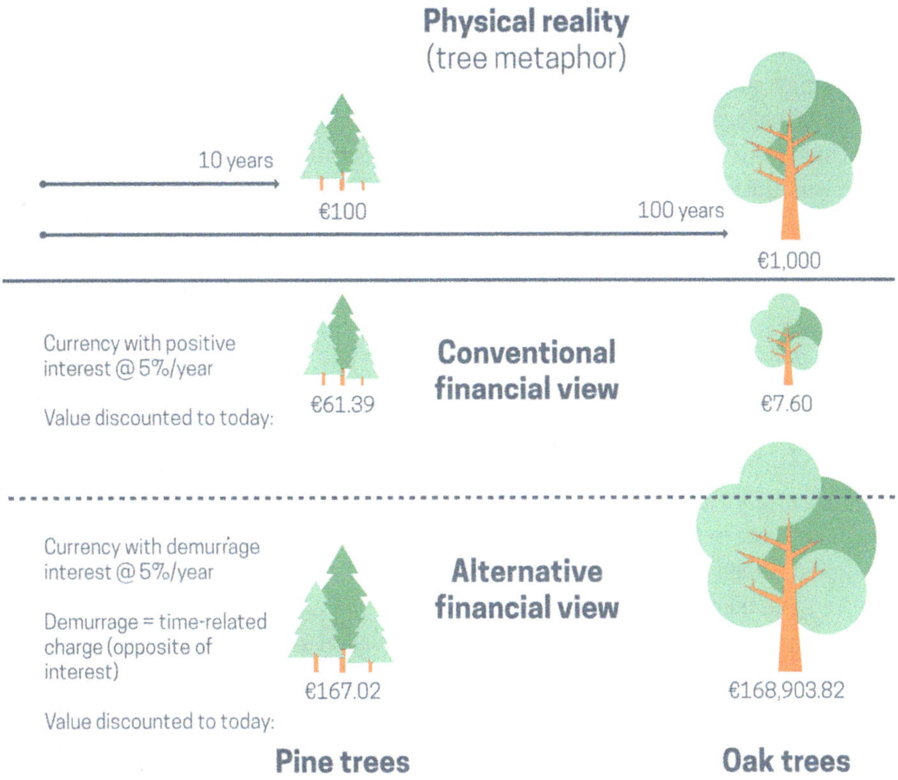

Physical reality
(tree metaphor)

10 years

€100

100 years

€1,000

Currency with positive
interest @ 5%/year

Value discounted to today:

€61.39

**Conventional
financial view**

€7.60

Currency with demurrage
interest @ 5%/year

Demurrage = time-related
charge (opposite of
interest)

€167.02

**Alternative
financial view**

€168,903.82

Value discounted to today:

Pine trees

Oak trees

Figure 43: Short-term thinking: why the future is discounted.

euros, whereas the pine tree would be worth only 167.02 euros, discounted relative to today. This mental exercise supports the idea that DCF analysis is not a natural law but a monetary rule that we can choose to change.

I am not advocating changing our entire monetary system to incorporate a demurrage fee. But simply imagining it serves to demonstrate that the values underlying the monetary incentive determine how we perceive the world. The entire argument of this book is based on the idea that our financial system is one of the most neglected yet powerful tools for achieving a more sustainable common future. At present, we are trapped in the idea that the future is more uncertain and worth less than the present. But if our current basic needs are met through suitable commons and uncertainties are substantially diminished, the entire picture will change. Just imagine finding incentives that enable us to reforest the Sahara, end global plastic waste, restore our entire planetary ecosystem or provide universal healthcare and preschooling for every citizen. The financial engineering required would make our entire future less uncertain and worth more than any present state.

Shedding Light and Going Green: Towards More Transparency

Any formalised economy, measured in terms of global GDP, will find itself confronted with informal-sector and black-market activities. These two categories of activity are interconnected, add up and influence the formal economic sector in one way or another. Any upgrade of the monetary system has to take this into account. Both have always existed in parallel to the formalised sector, but have not always had the same relevance and significance for the stability and functionality of the economy as they do now. Generally speaking, it is seen as a sign of a deficient system if the informal sector and black market are growing to meet people's underserved needs.

The *informal sector* consists of all unregulated activities in our society, including home-based services and excluding illegal activities involving drugs, human trafficking, money laundering and weapons. This sector is sometimes also called system D. D stands for the French term *debroulliard*, which means resourcefulness, the ability to accomplish something successfully in a complex, uncertain and unpredictable environment.[297] The main characteristic of this system is that it is fully unregulated, untaxed and unmonitored. Human activities in this informal sector are ad hoc and self-organised and involve spontaneous decisions with no overarching liabilities. The informal sector has no commitments to basic human rights such as social security, healthcare, trade unions or paid holidays and it runs on a 24/7 basis, 365 days a year.[298] On a global scale, the informal sector accounts for up to ten trillion USD annually, employs almost two billion people or up to 50% of the global labour force and mainly runs in parallel to the official economy – visible but unaccountable. Within the next decade, as millions of young people reach working age, this ratio will most likely increase to two-thirds of the global workforce, representing the second-largest economy in the world in relative terms. In

---

297 Neuwirth 2012.

298 Considered in terms of property rights, the informal sector probably represents one of the largest sleeping giants in the world economy. The Peruvian economist Hernando de Soto estimates the total value of undocumented and untitled property rights to be over 13 trillion USD. That is over 50 times more than any overseas development aid (ODA) or foreign direct investment (FDI) in less developed countries. Only about one-third of the world's population have access to property rights and only up to 10% of African land is registered and formally documented, while the other 90% remains *terra nullius*. This has significant negative consequences for any regional wealth development. Up to three billion people globally live on communal, unregistered land and over one billion people live in fear of being evicted from this land ad hoc because of the lack of clarity about land ownership. Done the right way, land titling can substantially increase the productivity of agricultural activities and create the preconditions for a decent life. Only clear, legally bounded property rights entitle people to trade, subdivide, collateralise, sell, buy and hedge land titles, allowing the poor to participate in the world economy and generate wealth independently and on the spot. See Acemoglu et al. 2001, Galiani and Schargrodsky 2010 and Acemoglu and Robinson 2012.

other words, system D represents the largest field experiment of a fully liberalised, deregulated and singularised marketplace the world has ever seen.[299]

Besides the informal sector, there is also the *black market* or *shadow economy*, which comprises an ever-increasing financial dark pool and unregulated banking sector,[300] fraud, corruption and undocumented offsheet and offshore activities, including a huge number of illicit financial transactions, money laundering, human trafficking, drugs and illegal financial transactions. The black market accounts for at least a third of our world GDP.[301] A commonly used taxonomy for illicit financial transactions distinguishes between theft-type market activities, corruption, illicit tax transactions (including mis-invoicing) and the criminal market of human trafficking, drugs and weapons.[302] Empirical evidence attests to the magnitude of the problem. A growing volume of private wealth, representing up to 10% of global GDP, is managed in unregulated tax havens, causing tax losses of over 200 billion USD every year. Terror financing amounts to almost three trillion USD and almost 10% of total global trading is conducted through illicit financial transactions. This results in a staggering global tax gap of over five trillion USD annually.[303] In this context, we are witnessing a corporate tax race to the bottom. Whereas rich OECD countries have been able to retain their general broad tax base, emerging and developing countries have basically lost it. From a purely administrative perspective, it would require over 650,000 additional tax officers for Africa alone to meet OECD standards. All these informal and illegal transac-

---

299 Societies with a large informal sector have been shown to be more resilient to financial crises, which is evidence that this sector acts like an anti-cyclical buffer in the event of a shock. From a systems perspective, it serves an inclusive, anti-cyclical and reparative function in conventional economies that have just one formal market and one monetary system to allocate goods and services. Any time this monopoly becomes unstable, there is an automatic shift towards the second, parallel system, which is not subject to the same conditions.

300 Investors and firms provide bank-like services through special-purpose vehicles and systematic investment plans, both of which are unregulated and informal. On non-bank financial intermediaries, see Pozsar et al. 2013; Adrian and Ashcraft 2016; Adrian and Jones 2018.

301 Black-market activities only make up one-third of all global financial activities (Shaxson 2018). If we take all offshore and offsheet activities into account, the shadow economy amounts to 240 trillion USD. See Beyond Bretton Woods 2024.

302 Black-market activities are endemic and systemic, especially in the public sector. According to Transparency International (2022), the average corruption index globally is 43 out of 100 across all countries. We therefore require mechanisms that reduce these activities, rather than further increasing them. Any upgrade of the monetary system should take this into account.

303 If we crunch the data further, we can see that over 20% of the tax gap is due to transnational corporations and 80% due to private activities and SMEs, which often trade informally and in cash. Corruption costs the world community 2.6 trillion USD and money laundering up to 1.6 trillion USD. Global revenue losses due to tax losses (base erosion and profit shifting, BEPS) have risen to over 250 billion USD annually. These figures demonstrate the magnitude of the amounts lost to the public sector. It appears next to impossible to regulate such volumes within the existing monetary system. For a review of the vast body of literature, see Cobham and Janský 2018.

tions further increase local inequality, reduce economic growth and social capital and erode tax revenue, reinforcing their own rules over and over again and pulling our entire global economy in the wrong direction.

From a purely economic perspective, illicit financial flows (IFFs) have a different impact on the economy from other black-market activities. Any illicit inflows into a country generate domestic income and jobs, while illicit outflows do not. The losses due to illicit outflows amounted to several trillion USD over the last decade, with a growth rate twice that of formal domestic activities. In the Middle East, for every dollar of formal inflow from ODA, foreign direct investment (FDI), remittance payments and philanthropy, it is estimated that an equivalent illicit outflow of 2.8 USD leaves the country undocumented. Mis-invoicing is the most significant cause. The general equation still holds that the volume of redirected ODA, military-related expenses, external debt payments and IFFs usually outweighs the sum of official ODA, remittance payments and FDI. The current monetary design makes it next to impossible to generate sustainable domestic purchasing power for a decent standard of living. A look at ODA reveals the dilemma: of the 0.7% of world GDP committed to supporting the Global South, up to three-quarters is either indirect subsidies for prestige investments such as the military, is directed to middle-income countries (where the money is less needed) or supports the domestic industry of the donor country. Only one-quarter is considered to be 'real' ODA.

For decades, we have been trying to readjust, prosecute and harmonise regulatory efforts to formalise and legalise the illicit sector. It does not seem to have worked for the last 75 years. But if we were suddenly to succeed and managed to eliminate this complex and toxic basket of activities, the world economy would collapse immediately. The informal sector and black market act as an important stabiliser, interconnected with the formal, conventional financial and real economy, yet pulling our entire society in the wrong direction – resulting in more inequality, less productivity, less wealth creation, less security and less sustainability. Instead of shutting it down, we are better advised to look for financial mechanisms that allow us to incentivise everyone to work towards a better future. And instead of focusing all diplomatic and political efforts on re-regulating and consolidating the existing system, an upgraded IMS should strive to change the rules of the game in order to gradually formalise the informal sector by slowly but surely pulling trade and commerce out of this basket and towards a green, sustainable future without disrupting overall built-in economic capacity, and at the same time systemically driving out illicit transactions. An upgraded IMS that makes the informal sector less and less attractive and provides opportunities to live in a green marketplace will therefore be a key component of any future endeavour. One of the core ideas of this book is the creation of additional, conditioned public liquidity, running through different monetary channels and using a digital format. This would mean that informal and black-market activities would be better documented and trackable. Moreover, investments in a green marketplace would generate better, more resilient, safer and greener jobs and revenue.

The Monetary Inflation Brake: The Bee and the Beekeeper

The traditional way to look at inflation: Inflation is probably one of the most obvious signs of transformation. It reflects, *ceteris paribus*, the relative increase of prices or the relative loss in value of goods and services in an economy. But inflation is not primarily a monetary phenomenon. Rather, it is a product of real economic events, including physical risks leading to output losses, altered consumption patterns and reduced investments due to uncertainty.[304] If we are forced to operate within planetary boundaries, externalities and associated asymmetric shocks can have a devastating impact on macroeconomic stability in general and the stability of price signals in particular. But it is the monetary system that can mitigate, correct and dampen dysfunctional price signals caused by the real economy.[305] Price stability is defined as a monetary environment where relative price increases do not enter into the day-to-day decision-making of households and companies. By contrast, inflation (measured by the Harmonised Index of Consumer Prices (HICP) or by the CPI) is characterised by an environment in which multiple vicious circles reinforce each other in a series of wage–price spirals, leading to changes in households' and businesses' decision-making. There are thus many forms of inflation. One common example is rapid and unexpected increases of imported food and energy prices. This is especially devastating because it affects low-income households and countries first and foremost and destabilises the overall political system. The inflationary pressure from 2021 to 2023 was mainly (> 50%) caused by the increase of energy prices, which indirectly affected the prices of almost all goods and services. Climate-related disasters, like harvest defaults, further contributed to the rising food prices (supply shock), which aggravated overall inequality. The general transition to a greener economy adds an additional layer of potential pressure on the CPI. In short: the lower the dependency on fossil energy, the less volatility and price pressure we can expect.[306] It would appear that managing price inflation, especially food and energy price inflation, is different in the Anthropocene era than it used to be. In the past, if a single price shock hit an economy, like the supply shock of the 1970s oil crisis, we managed this shock and then continued business as usual. However, in the Anthropocene era, single shocks are an exception. The new normal is serial shocks.[307] None of these shocks can be addressed by individuals, single companies or countries alone, but require collective institutional bodies to step in as a safeguard. The financial and monetary sector becomes especially critical if

---

304 Batten et al. 2020; Battiston et al. 2021; King 2023.
305 Isabel Schnabel (2022) has identified three forms of inflationary pressure on the consumer price index (CPI) linked to fossil-driven climate change and efforts to mitigate it: the greening of the economy itself, which requires additional investment; our current dependency on fossil fuels; and serial shocks due to climate change.
306 Beirne et al. 2023; Kotz et al. 2023; Dafermos and Nikolaidi 2021; see also Absolut Research 2024.
307 Bratton 2022.

these shocks affect the relative prices of goods and services in an economy. And in every price we pay (for instance, whenever we buy a cup of coffee), we are paying, directly or indirectly, for all the social and ecological externalities that impact on that cup of coffee: child labour, forced migration, water stress, degenerated soil, to name just a few. This means that inflationary pressure is becoming a systemic not a cyclical issue, heralding the dawn of a backlash from all the externalities we have triggered over the last few decades. We have the incorrigible tendency to think and act in linear, proportional terms when we try to solve complex problems. This becomes particularly obvious in finance and economics. But asymmetric shocks under conditions of uncertainty are complex not complicated, as described in this book, and require a different way of thinking and different kinds of political interventions. For example, the clear-cut correlation between money supply and CPI is weak to non-existent. Again, a systems-thinking approach can help us to attain a new, updated view of pricing, resilience, value creation and the transition to a greener future. I would like to introduce the unorthodox idea of a monetary inflation brake (MIB) to demonstrate the power the monetary system has to overcome price-sensitive shocks to an economy. In order to make the case, let us assume that the price of imported energy soars by 100% in the Eurozone.[308] The EU, with a total GDP of 15 trillion euros, imports between 350 and 400 billion euros' worth of fossil energy per year. A 100% increase would thus increase the price of imported energy to around 700 to 800 billion euros. That figure would be the amount of money the EU has to cover as direct costs only. Assuming that indirect costs (negative social externalities), such as social upheaval, the impact of the increased income gap, bankruptcies and unemployment, add extra costs three times that amount to the bill, that would come to at least another 750 billion × 3 = 2.25 trillion euros. The full amount of energy price inflation due to an external shock would then come to roughly three trillion euros in total.[309] In such scenarios, most, if not all, affected countries traditionally take a linear approach and intervene *downstream and bottom-up* in order to tackle the price inflation. We are confronted with two main, mutually reinforcing cycles. One is between energy supply and food production. As 80% of food production still depends on fossil energy, any sharp increase of energy prices will directly

---

308 This figure is based on Eurostat and IEA data. See European Commission 2020; Eurostat Statistics Explained 2024; Zeniewski et al. 2023; Cambridge Econometrics 2020.
309 Complexity research has shown that there is a non-linear link between food and energy prices on the one hand and social upheavals, wars and state failures on the other. Since 2000, food prices have been deregulated, allowing traders to bet against rising and falling commodities. Up to 80% of any given commodity price has become speculative and does not reflect the real demand for that commodity. This leaves large cohorts in LDCs with unmanageable food prices. At the tipping point, high food and energy prices increase the probability of social unrest by up to 80%. The trend towards urbanisation will probably further exacerbate this development. By 2050, over four billion people across the world will have left rural regions and moved to megacities. Instead of becoming self-sufficient farmers, these four billion people will depend on the international commodity markets to feed themselves. See New England Complex Systems Institute 2024.

translate into rising food prices. To produce wheat, for example, we need tractors, nitrate and phosphate, which are generated using or powered by oil and gas. On top of this, 50% of all global grain is used to produce meat. The more meat we eat, the more grain we need, and the higher the price will be. The second cycle relates to the energy costs themselves. Once these costs hit an economy, they operate like a regressive value-added tax, disproportionately affecting low-income countries and low-income households. For example, households in rich OECD countries spend 15% of their net income on food, whereas least developed countries (LDCs) spend up to 40%. Whenever we purchase anything, the price will be affected by higher energy costs along the entire manufacturing chain. These combined wage–price spirals act like a catalyst that runs through the entire economy, diluting the price signal, decreasing wealth, destabilising governments and destroying our economic systems. As the elasticity of food and energy is low by these goods' very nature, citizens cannot afford to refill their cars or pay their rent, and are forced to spend substantially more on their daily food. The following figure (Figure 44) visualises the vicious wage–price spirals in the event of imported inflation.

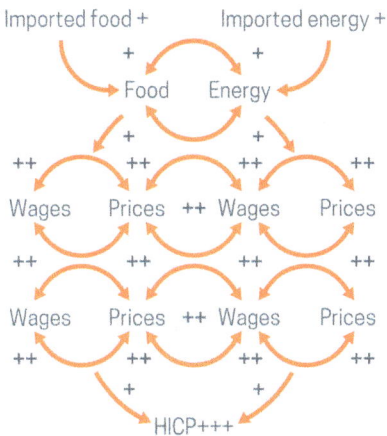

Figure 44: Vicious, positively reinforcing wage–price spirals in the event of imported inflation.
HICP: Harmonised Index of Consumer Prices

Downstream approaches to tackling imported inflation have become very common. Governments provide subsidies for lower-income households or tax breaks for companies, implement a price cap on energy, increase the interest rate to be higher than the inflation rate and/or diversify their supply portfolio to include other, less expensive importers. Finally, they encourage citizens to consume less and invest in new research and technologies to increase energy efficiency. However, these procedures are slow and expensive, and require additional regulatory efforts. There is nothing wrong with any of these traditional measures, but it is questionable how much they can actually achieve and whether they represent the cheapest way to cope with imported inflation. All these downstream approaches amount to simply kicking the can down the road, as the price of the imported energy has already run through the entire economy (via VAT and the wage–price spirals), causing inflation.[310] With these sorts of downstream approaches, we always remain behind the curve. It is like a rubbish dump, where we clean up the mess after it has hit society. Instead, our response should be more like a rescue package. That requires a more upstream approach, which I shall explain in the next section. But before we move on to that discussion, the figure below (Figure 45) illustrates the downstream approach.

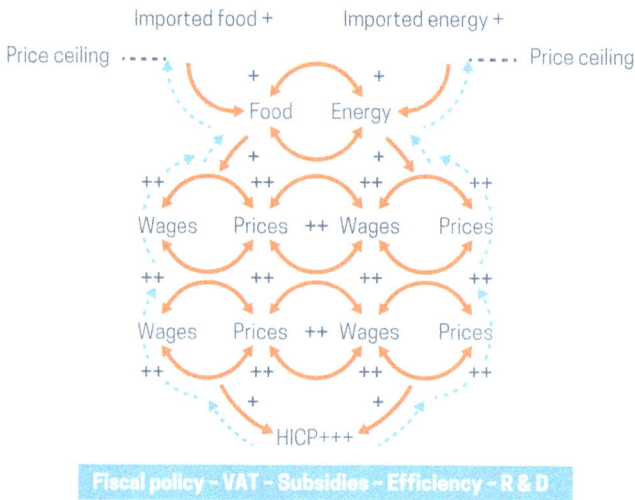

Figure 45: Kicking the can down the road: conventional downstream and bottom-up measures to tackle inflation. (blue dotted lines)

The blue dotted lines represent multiple bottom-up, downstream, ex post measures taken to avoid further damage. The figure above only shows two to three wage–price spirals. But in an open, competitive market, there are hundreds of millions of these relative wage–price equilibriums, and they are constantly changing. They represent a complex, non-linear, open-flow system. Intervening in such a complex system with a simple tax break or a subsidy will create unlimited paradoxes, spillovers and trade-offs.[311] It is like a swarm of bees – and we need a highly skilled beekeeper to manage that swarm.

---

310 It should be noted that due to inflation, public revenue is increasing (nominally). But these additional inflows of money represent a kind of window dressing or cosmetic tweaking of balance sheets. They do not really solve the actual problems we are facing. If public revenue increases by 30 billion euros but the real prices in the economy soar by 45 billion euros, for instance, businesses and households have to cover the difference of 15 billion euros, which decreases their purchasing power. Only credit holders are the winners in this game.

311 The most prominent paradox is the VAT paradox. If a government lowers VAT, households have more money available to spend, which in turn will increase overall inflation even more. The most prominent trade-off is fuel subsidies. In most cases, upper-income households benefit the most and need the support the least. In conclusion, we should not intervene in a complex, non-linear, chaotic

The monetary inflation brake: preventive, targeted, upstream, resilient and indirect: In an alternative approach, monetary regulators, central banks and treasuries come into play. The conventional practice is for central banks to simply print money, which risks worsening the situation.[312] But instead of spending huge amounts of money to counteract ever-increasing wage–price spirals and higher domestic food and energy prices, a significantly smaller amount could be spent in a more targeted, preventive and indirect way to sterilise the estimated 700–800 billion euros (i.e. the total cost of energy imports assuming a 100% price increase) needed by the Eurozone.[313] In this alternative scenario, the European Central Bank would provide the additional money needed through monetary easing.[314] It would further facilitate this amount of money using a central bank currency swap agreement (CBCSA), in which regulators provide additional liquidity for their own currency and swap it into USD in order to cover the additional costs across borders *before* the price rise hits the economy. Given that central banks are already the largest asset managers in the world, they might have to either write off and sterilise this purchase or hold on to it and benefit from potential future revenue via a seigniorage. The balance sheet of the central bank would inflate by that number (nominally), but the domestic HICP of the Eurozone would remain relatively stable.[315] Since all central banks are tasked with keeping inflation under control, such a procedure would remain within their legal mandate. At the same time, the conversion rate of the euro to the USD would slightly depreciate on the international currency markets. This would eventually stimulate the Eurozone's domestic export industry. Prudent and targeted green QE would then operate in an anti-cyclical and anti-inflationary manner. Done in the right way, such a mechanism would act like a *monetary inflation brake* for the domestic economy as a whole. Finally, a domestic public development bank (such as the European Investment Bank) could facilitate these transactions on an executive level, targeting the two dozen companies in the Eurozone that are importing the energy across borders and

---

and dynamic system using a linear tool. Rather, we should learn to 'dance' with the system. See Brunnhuber 2021.

312 As a rule of thumb: a 1% increase (as a proportion of base money) in money creation would increase the CPI by 0.5%.

313 This is substantially less than what the Fed spent in September 2019, when the repo markets crashed overnight. At that time, the Fed injected a series of short-term loans with a total value of 1.5 trillion USD into the system. At its peak, this was equivalent to one million USD per second. See Board of Governors of the Federal Reserve System 2020; Foster 2021.

314 Unlike a credit line or a loan from the capital market, where the money is purchased by a private lender, quantitative easing (QE) is a non-refundable and non-defaultable state loan in base money (M0), created by the central bank itself.

315 It should be noted that the combined balance sheets of the ECB as a public body and its member states remain net zero.

by proxy. This would provide a stable HICP for the EU's citizens downstream for two to three years. The figure below (Figure 46) illustrates this:

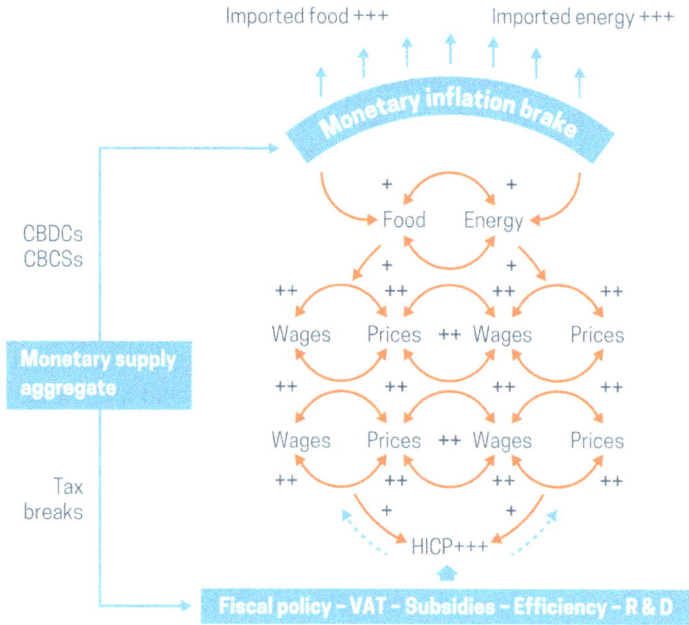

Figure 46: The monetary inflation brake.

Box 41: The Cantillon effect

The Cantillon effect (first described in 1755)[316] refers to how injecting additional money leads to a gradual and non-uniform increase in prices, depending on where the money is injected. Some sectors will benefit, while others will have to bear the consequences of the inflationary pressure. This effect still applies today. Consider a price level p_0 before monetary easing, p_1 after a conditioned monetary intervention and p_2, which represents the natural increase of prices due to asymmetric shocks without the monetary easing. If a monetary intervention is effective, then $p_0 \Rightarrow p_1 < p_2$. This effect still applies. Price levels after monetary easing will be less than they would be under a business-as-usual scenario, as using directly preventive measures will offset the natural increase in prices.

The monetary inflation brake (MIB) is not a panacea but a powerful first-tier emergency monetary tool to protect an economy from speculative or politically motivated imported price inflation and to allow a transition towards a greener future. It acts like a rescue package, not like a rubbish dump. It costs around a tenth as much as a standard approach, functions *pre*- rather than *re*distributively and leaves the current domestic value chains untouched. The mechanism would cushion the HICP and stimulate the domestic

---

316 For an introduction, see Nevin 2013; Mayer 2014.

economy in an anti-cyclical manner. The central bank money facilitates green state bonds and operates like a pass-through and roll-over liability or asset. It would eventually encourage indirect investments within the EU to support a greener future.[317] In numbers: an MIB applied to the Eurozone would prevent the three-trillion-euro bill by providing 350 billion euros of QE, stimulate our export industry and cause a bounce-back effect for the energy exporter, which would now have additional euros with a lower face value that they could use to purchase green goods and services from the Eurozone. It would remain within the CB mandate of inflation-proof measures and provide a strong geopolitical monetary instrument in times of increasing systemic uncertainty.[318] The MIB acts like a conditioned multiplier (*cM*) that generates additional social benefits (*SB*), as explained in previous sections. Instead of remaining a plumber that fixes and repairs damage after it has already happened, we would become beekeepers managing a complex swarm of bees.

Box 42: Turkey as a case study

Turkey as a case study: Turkey has a GDP of about 900 billion USD. It imports around 80 billion USD of energy per year, benefits from domestic tax revenue equal to about 20% of its GDP and receives 13 billion USD of FDI per year. The current official inflation rate is over 50%. An enlightened fiscal and monetary policy to reduce the domestic CPI should follow a supply-driven policy that encourages R&D and renewable energy infrastructure and provides a stimulus for the agriculture sector, with the goal of making the country less dependent on energy and food imports and hence reducing the CPI. A qualified expanded monetary policy can support this approach. A conditioned monetary facility (running through different channels, using CBDCs/CBCSs and including M^{cola}) could be utilised to provide a first-loss tranche for FDI (e.g. 20 billion USD), a tax break for companies (e.g. 40 billion USD), an MIB (e.g. 20 billion USD) to reduce energy import prices and a public stimulus package (e.g. 20 billion USD) for education, agriculture and renewables. These four measures would collectively increase the balance sheet of the Turkish central bank by 100 billion USD equivalent and stabilise the domestic CPI. Domestic and international investors would become more confident, and the imported energy prices and high unemployment rate would decrease over time. Instead of remaining behind the curve, Turkey would generate multiple positive feedback loops that would help it escape the vicious wage–price spirals.

---

317 The volume of currency trading in 2024 exceeded eight trillion USD per day, including all instruments. Adding one billion or so USD per day (out of the 100% increase in the CPI, see above) will not substantially change the face value of the currencies involved. 97% of this volume is speculative and does not relate directly to real economic fundamentals. In contrast, about 18,000 billion USD of goods are exported globally per year, equivalent to 50 billion USD per day. For relevant data, see Statistics. com 2024.

318 The Chinese government implemented price controls and anti-cyclical buffer stocks for specific goods, enabled by an expansive monetary intervention rather than by fiscal measures. It uses organisations such as COFCO (COFCO International 2024) to provide these buffer stocks. We should use similar tools to tackle asymmetric shocks; see Weber 2021 and Parker 2018.

A final note: this calculation is valid not only for imported food and energy prices, but for any sort of external asymmetric shock (climate change, biodiversity loss, pandemics, wars) that hits an economy and is expected to have an impact on the HICP that can be (partly) neutralised. The MIB would not end inflation but would help governments to regain control over imported inflation, and it is cheaper, faster and more resilient than the traditional approach[319] by a factor of 10. An MIB would not operate indefinitely but only for a few years, helping the economy to transition towards a greener, better future. It can help harness the full potential of monetary tools to tackle upcoming asymmetric shocks and minimise direct and indirect costs for our society as a whole, and provide a safe operating space for long-term private investments within an optimum currency area. In other words: an MIB would only address future expected costs and would direct real economic activities towards greater resilience and sustainability. Price signals are not given by nature, but are rather a function of a certain economic narrative. If we change the story and the tools, we will be able to change the relative structure of expected price formation. That is why we should become beekeepers and not plumbers.

Green Transition Financing: How to Shift from Adverse to Beneficial

Transitioning from an adverse state to a more beneficial one will not come for free and it will affect all countries, irrespective of their political agenda. The aim of any financial transition plan is to provide the regulatory framework, liquidity, financial assets and resources necessary to achieve certain targets as efficiently and effectively as possible. The targets themselves are generally set by political and societal consensus. The UN SDGs are examples of such targets. Achieving them will require an additional five to seven trillion USD of liquidity and financial assets per year over the next ten to fifteen years. The five to seven trillion USD annually would be the compound result of additional, conditioned liquidity, assets and measures taken to achieve the UN SDGs within the next two decades. The greater the systemic risks, the greater the role for public bodies and a public monetary aggregate. Moreover, financial transition

---

319 Over the last few decades, the ECB bought up to 80 billion euros of state bonds per month by means of a heterodox, accommodated and expanded monetary policy (QE). The purchasing programmes were mainly run through the national central banks (referred to as 'target accounts'), inflating their balance sheets by a factor of 6 to 8 to almost 4.4 trillion euros. This traditional approach is constrained not by technical limitations of the printing process, but rather by the fact that the money generated runs through a conventional value chain that is 80% dependent on fossil energy and so will further exacerbate the dilemma of ongoing externalities that we wanted to avoid in the first place. In addition, these QE programmes were empirically decoupled from the CPI and the conversion rate to major currencies (USD, yuan, yen, pound sterling). See World Bank 2023.

plans require us to look at the entire process along a timeline and to prioritise the funding accordingly.[320] If we distinguish between immediate support and remedies, medium-term changes and more systemic and institutional reforms,[321] most if not all targets will require frontloading of some sort of additional liquidity. The flowchart below (Figure 47) provides a first model for the transition with some preliminary examples, which are explained in more detail later in this section.

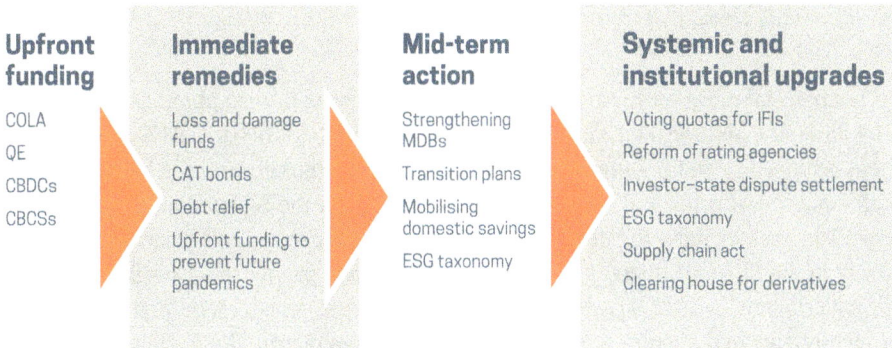

Upfront funding	Immediate remedies	Mid-term action	Systemic and institutional upgrades
COLA	Loss and damage funds	Strengthening MDBs	Voting quotas for IFIs
QE	CAT bonds	Transition plans	Reform of rating agencies
CBDCs	Debt relief	Mobilising domestic savings	Investor–state dispute settlement
CBCSs	Upfront funding to prevent future pandemics	ESG taxonomy	ESG taxonomy
			Supply chain act
			Clearing house for derivatives

Figure 47: The timeline for transition.
COLA: conditioned liquidity assistance; QE: quantitative easing; CBDCs: central bank digital currencies; CBCSs: central bank currency swaps; IFIs: international financial institutions

To make this large number of several trillions more manageable, it needs to be broken down into smaller chunks. That can be done by asking a series of questions. Firstly, how are we to fund and manage planetary commons (like the Amazon rainforest) and domestic and local commons (healthcare, public infrastructure)? Secondly, how are we to mobilise and hedge private capital? Thirdly, how are we to fund, enable and scale up new technologies so as to further increase efficiency and achieve the first two targets? When devising a green transition plan, we should be carefully evaluating existing financial tools that need simple adjustments, while also developing new forms of financial engineering to address new challenges. Let's take the UN SDGs as a case study.

> **Box 43:** Financing the UN SDGs
> The UN SDGs, comprising 17 goals, 169 associated targets and over 240 indicators, were inaugurated by world leaders in New York in September 2015, following the largest UN global review process in history. Based on the five Ps – people, planet, prosperity, peace, partnerships – most of the SDGs focus on common goods, such as clean air, biodiversity and universal healthcare. There is enough scientific evidence, technological expertise and political consensus to achieve each of these goals. But doing so is expensive, requiring a special financial architecture and new forms of financial engineering. At present, we are only on track to meet 16% of the targets, while for 30% of them we have actu-

---

320 See Lomborg 2023.
321 See Prime Minister of Barbados 2023 on the Bridgetown 2.0 Initiative.

ally regressed to pre-2015 levels. Financial costs are increasing due to inflation and rising damage costs (up by 10% during the last year alone), and there is still a financial gap of roughly 12–14 trillion USD annually. That includes base costs (four trillion USD) and the costs of climate transition (over 4.5 trillion USD), inclusive prosperity (e.g. affordable housing, financing of MSMEs and scaling of microfinancing; five trillion USD) and inaction (2.8 trillion USD).[322] Out of the 433 trillion USD in liquid wealth globally, only a small portion is required to meet the financial needs of the UN SDGs. But conventional tools have been little more than homeopathic in effect. For example, impact investment remains at around one trillion USD in 2024. That is why it makes rational sense to think outside the box and come up with bold, unconventional, innovative ideas to finance the UN SDGs.

To further elaborate on these figures: OECD countries will need about 2–4% of their GDP annually, and for the Global South that figure doubles to 4–8%. 85% of all investment required in OECD countries is private and 15% is public, and the ratio between additional investments and replacements is about 2:3. In the Global South, by contrast, there is a greater need for new investments, with the ratio ranging between 5:1 and 10:1.[323] In the EU alone, there is a 40-trillion-euro funding gap for the transition to a low-carbon economy by 2050. 30 trillion of that total comprises replacements and reallocation of investments and about ten trillion is additional investments. These additional investments are equal to about 2.3% of the EU's GDP, or around 50% of the cost of imported fossil energy. That will require a doubling of public spending from 250 to around 500 billion euros per year to unlock private investments and fund public goods equal to 1.6% of the EU's GDP.[324] Three aspects are worthy of particular note here. Firstly, additional fiscal tools to help companies deal with significant depreciation of property, plant and equipment, exemptions from capital gains tax and a loss carry-forward for all asset classes, in order to drive the transition in the private sector. Secondly, new financial tools to mobilise additional private capital to hedge these additional investments. Thirdly, additional liquidity to fund and manage our planetary commons.[325] But this is just half of the story. Transitioning towards a greener and stabler future requires us to admit that we are facing a dual cost curve: the costs of adaptation, mitigation and loss and damage, as discussed above, simply represent an investment in a better future. That investment creates jobs, generates revenue and provides opportunities. The second category of costs relates to managing the costs of the transition itself: disaster management, political instability, additional healthcare costs, welfare losses, food and energy price inflation, harvest defaults and financial losses due to stranded assets. This second cost component is orders of magnitude greater than the first. The dynamic between the two is simple and striking. Both costs add up in the first phase of the transition. The longer we wait, the higher the overall costs will be. Having the costs for adaptation, mitigation and loss and damage

322 Force for Good 2024.
323 Songwe et al. 2022.
324 See Institut Rousseau 2024.
325 Rockström et al. 2024.

properly funded and managed as soon as possible will mean that the costs of managing multiple future disasters will decrease over time. That seems obvious from a clearsighted look at the facts, but actually taking the required action is hard. Again, the structure of the money system is key. From a financial perspective, we can say that *hedging systemic risks, mobilising private capital, buffering unforeseen uncertainties, funding global commons and conditioning all these financial activities will translate into sustainability.*

In the previous sections, I described the role of central banks and regulators in enabling the transition from an adverse to a beneficial economy. That role involves steering and funding components that allow monetary regulators[326] to provide a level playing field and to better adjust and internalise the additional costs. Central banks are never neutral, as each interest rate adjustment and open-market policy affects the distribution and allocation of goods and services. The present monetary regime is heavily biased towards funding the heavy fossil industry.[327] Remaining neutral means augmenting and perpetuating externalities and associated shocks. The table below (Table 13) illustrates some major monetary tools that can be used as an alternative.[328]

Table 13: Monetary tools.

Monetary tools	Characteristics
1. Adjusted interest rate	Different interest rates for brown versus green investment depending on credit institutions' lending practices
2. Equity buffer	Additional equity requirements that act like a counter-cyclical buffer
3. Adjusted collaterals	Eligible collaterals for credit institutions to obtain liquidity from central banks, including a haircut that reflects climate risks
4. Purchasing programmes	Adjusted purchasing programmes for corporate bonds and assets according to ESG ratings
5. Green LTROs	Long-term refinancing operations for companies, with condition that the funds be used for green investments
6. Tiered reserve requirements	Adjusted reserve requirements for the banking sector
7. ESG taxonomy	Disclosure agreements (IFRS, CSDDD, MiFID, ESRS), stress tests, supervision
8. Conditioned liquidity assistance	Green quantitative easing, CBDCs, CBCSs, acts like non-defaultable loans (NDL)

---

326 Basel Committee on Banking Supervision 2022.
327 Cojoianu et al. 2020; Dafermos et al. 2020.
328 Adapted from Kriwoluzky and Volz 2023.

Monetary tools 1–7 are steering measures for the private and public sectors to redirect their investment strategy and policy agendas. Tool 8 is a steering and funding tool, where additional liquidity is directly or indirectly conditioned to finance our transformation. It could utilise different monetary channels, such as CBDCs or CBCSs, and operate in the manner of non-defaultable loans.

Mobilising private capital: Since over 80% of the transition will depend on the private sector, private capital involvement is crucial. But the very nature of private capital is that it is pro-cyclical, short-termist and risk-averse. The regulated international capital market includes the stock and pension markets, with a value of about 110 trillion USD. This money has already been spent and invested, but needs to be substantially redirected. Global liquid assets amount to over 433 trill USD, most of which is privately owned. On the other side, global net savings,[329] factoring in all cash deposits and savings accounts, amount to over 30 trillion USD. Whether we unlock and redirect private capital from the international capital market in a top-down way or mobilise a certain portion of domestic savings[330] from the bottom up, both require additional financial instruments to hedge and manage multiple systemic risks, including currency risks and risks of civil war, corruption, legal prosecution and expropriation, as well as changes in domestic tax schemes to protect these private capital flows. In fact, under the current monetary regime, most savings (84%) flow uphill to the Global North at low interest rates and then re-enter the Global South again with high expected yields and a high hurdle rate (above 8%), including additional regulatory fees. The net effect has been a drain of over 15 trillion USD over the last two decades.[331]

However, the devil is in the detail. The cost of capital represents the return for the investor to compensate for an alternative asset or a perceived loss. The relative cost of capital to invest in a renewable energy site, for example, is determined by two

---

329 See Global Economy 2024.

330 The global savings rate amounts to 23–28% of GDP. China holds about 8.2 trillion USD equivalent, India, Russia and Germany about one trillion each, Africa about 400 billion. Most of these savings are located in domestic cash deposits in the Global North. One way to mobilise this money would be a green citizens' cash deposit, where the state provides a higher interest rate and a public guarantee with a tax-gain exemption over the entire maturity.

331 This capital flow contradicts neoclassical theory, which assumes that factor mobility of labour and capital will under free competitive market conditions lead to a new global equilibrium between the Global North (capital surplus) and the Global South (labour surplus). But the opposite is true. This paradox was described by Kindelberger (1987) and Lucas (1990). In reality, the governance structure, including political instability, imperfect contractions, domestic inflationary pressure, multiple channels for illicit transactions and being forced to hold high foreign exchange reserves, has prevented the Global South from overcoming these toxic, expensive and unhealthy cascades (Buchner et al. 2023). As an alternative, joint capital market programmes (J-caps) are better at utilising and mobilising domestic savings for domestic bonds (Volz et al. 2024).

classes of risks, which both add up. *Macro or systemic risks* (political, currency) are leveraged on a country level, while *micro or project risks* (construction, defaults, domestic regulation) are hedged and managed on the spot. While the costs for micro risks are equal or even lower in most BRICS+ states when compared with the G7, the macro risks are two to three times higher in developing countries, reflecting the significantly lower cost for G7 governments to borrow money.[332] Mobilising private capital to invest in renewables in the Global South therefore requires a public and collective effort to pool and hedge these systemic risks. The longer we wait, the more expensive it will be. If we miss the window of opportunity described in previous chapters during which our ecosystem is still reasonably intact and nation states are still functional, we will eventually loose the capacity and leverage of the financial system to steer us into a better future. And any lost opportunity will ultimately affect everybody. Whether we are poor with no assets at all, have negative savings, run a business, have a bank account, are institutional investors or enjoy the benefits of being a billionaire, each of us has skin in the game and should agree to adjust the rules of that game. Any additional investment will be beneficial for all of us, as we are reducing the costs for future social and ecological externalities (unemployment, adaptation and mitigation costs) and providing opportunities for future generations (education, healthcare and infrastructure). This could involve state guarantees that provide additional liquidity to help cover potential systemic risks for VCPE investments in public goods, following the build–operate–transfer (BOT) agenda that is common in public–private partnerships.[333] In that case, the project risks remain a corporate liability, while the systemic risks are potentially absorbed by a collective monetary facility. Other tools include advance commitment strategies (ACSs), where the public sector guarantees a certain price, amount or volume of a required good (such as an antibiotic or vaccine); direct cash transfers to target populations exposed to poverty, harvest defaults or hunger; or enhanced microcredit lines that support regional businesses.[334] All these measures can be covered and enhanced by an augmented monetary supply aggregate, as explained in this book. Designed in the

---

332 Persaud 2023.

333 Other blended finance strategies include equity shares, credit lines and synthetic-asset-backed securities, outcome bonds, insurance schemes, mezzanine loans and assorted hedging instruments. The current blended finance strategy clearly lacks the necessary speed and scalability. In numbers: 1 USD of public money currently mobilises about 0.75 USD of private capital. Due to a hurdle rate of 8% for the private sector, the money is parked somewhere else. Given that the contraction of state guarantees remains highly underutilised, representing less than 2% of MDBs' portfolios, and that a call-in for public guarantees of only 1:36 is needed, public commitments remain a 'dry powder' that can be used to effectively unleash the trillions of dollars of private liquidity required. See Habbel et al. 2021; Attridge and Engen 2019.

334 Asset-backed securities (ABSs), while still representing less than 1% of the global asset portfolio, can become a relevant asset for institutional investors. If the capital and regulatory requirements are adjusted and public state guarantees collateralise the systemic risks in the first tranche, synthetic ABSs would be able to mobilise a portion of the private capital needed to fund the transition.

form of digital currencies or tokens, this aggregate will be able to generate multiple positive second-round effects that further increase tax revenue and create a non-regret situation for the state and the private sector. Given that over 80% of fossil reserves are public property and should remain in the ground, a fossil-to-commons swap would collateralise the lost revenue using green QE, which would be conditioned to finance public goods in the region. A new CDS (credit default swap) issued by the public sector would provide an interest derivative to cover the systemic risks of private capital costs that come from investing in an adverse environment.[335] A similar contract model would make it possible to cover the additional capital costs for renewable sites in the Global South. The delta is up to ten times higher than in rich OECD countries. Take the untapped private domestic savings accounts holding several trillion USD equivalent. Governments could provide a state guarantee for a fixed interest rate, the principal and tax-free revenue over the next few years.[336] The mobilised money would be conditioned, such that it could only be spent on green communal public goods and adaptive measures. Another option would be a nature reserve conservation fund issued to NGOs to safeguard 30% of protected nature reserves globally. The money would be spent on drones, rangers and software. We could use a similar public contracting model for a pandemic preparedness fund. Fifty billion USD in frontloaded finance for the WHO would save millions of lives, substantially reduce economic output losses and be 100–300 times cheaper than the fix-and-repair approach taken during the Covid-19 pandemic. And as long as the empirical and theoretical correlation between savings on the one side and economic growth on the other still remains unclear, which means we do not know whether initial growth stimulates savings or savings provide the preconditions for additional growth, then we should take a different, better approach that is more targeted and risk-adjusted. This should serve to remind us that finance, as a complex, open-flow system, does not react causally or linearly, but rather follows multiple causal feedback loops.[337]

Instead of directly managing and funding the transition by relying solely on taxpayers' money, philanthropic commitments and private investments, central banks, regulators and public banks should become directly proactive and preventive – rather than being reactive and repairing the damage after the fact. International and domestic public development banks might eventually be able to manage and deliver the necessary financial services. In fact, almost unlimited options and opportunities await. The following table (Table 14) summarises some of the major components of a green

---

335 The CDS market is one of the most liquid markets. It provides tailored solutions for specific projects and customers. In this case the additional risks would be externalised to the CDS market itself and partly covered through an additional monetary facility.

336 Empirically, on average around 1/30th of the value of private portfolio investments is protected by state guarantees (personal communication with Persaud Avinash Divakar, September 2024).

337 See Modigliani's (1986) life-cycle analysis, which distinguishes between the younger generation that prefers to save its income and the older generation that prefers to spend it. Attending to the differences between foreign and domestic savings has the potential to clear up this puzzle; see Volz et al. 2024.

transition plan that would enable us to shift from a brown, adverse economy to a green, beneficial one and provides a preliminary list of principles, tools and financial engineering mechanisms.[338] A combination of the proposals set out below would allow us to cope with most of the challenges we are facing.

Table 14: Outline of a green transition plan.

A	
Common mission	Shared narrative on the purpose of the international monetary system: inclusive, fair, long-term, resilient and anti-cyclical
Prioritisation	Decisions based on ROI, KPIs and empirical evidence
Taxonomy	Multiple disclosure directives (ISSB, ESRS, IFRS, CSDDD, MiFID), ESG accounting, stress tests, supervision
Regulation	Shadow banking and informal sector
Technology	Predictive AI, big data, blockchains, e-governance
Bretton Woods 2.0	Revised voting quotas for IFIs, investor dispute settlement, rating agencies, supply chain act, clearing house for derivatives
B	
Equity buffer	Additional equity buffer that acts like a counter–cyclical stabiliser to enable faster recovery, weighted up to 100% for uncollateralised fossil assets
Adjusted collaterals	Eligible collaterals for credit institutions to obtain liquidity from central banks, including a haircut that reflects climate risks
Bifurcation of interest rate	Risk-adjusted interest rates (adverse versus beneficial), depending on credit institutions' lending practices
Purchasing programmes	Adjusted purchasing programmes for corporate bonds and assets according to ESG ratings
Green LTROs	Long-term refinancing operations for companies, with condition that the funds be used for green investments
Tiered reserve requirements	Adjusted reserve requirements for the banking sector
New monetary supply channels	CBDCs, preventing bank runs, new monetary channels for upfront (direct) loading, funding, hedging and de-risking private-sector involvement, citizens' e-wallet
Institutional swap lines	CBCSs, conditioned currency converter, especially for LICs and MICs, to tackle imported food and energy price inflation and to fund the UN SDGs

---

338 For more concrete examples and best practices see also Brunnhuber 2023, 96 ff.

Table 14 (continued)

B		
COLA	Direct conditioned liquidity assistance for the private and public sector, operating like ELA	
Green quantitative easing	Zero-coupon perpetual facilities acting like a non-defaultable loans (NDLs), can function as a monetary anchor	
C		
Regulation	Encouraged depreciations on property, plant and equipment to enhance replacement investments, capital gains tax exceptions, loss of carry-forwards across all asset classes	
Taxation and subsidies	Earmarked sin tax, emissions trading system (ETS), VAT, corporate, wealth, inheritance and international taxes, offshore sites, expanding the tax base, more efficient tax spending	
Philanthropy	Donor-driven grants, loans and bonds, often conditioned	
Private equity	Impact investment, venture capital, seed money	
Domestic savings	Green savings accounts with guaranteed interest rates	
Credit lines	Mortgage-backed securities (MBSs), on-balance-sheet (bank loans), off-balance-sheet (SPVs)	
Hedging instruments	Commercial swap lines, longevity swap lines, inflation, interest rate and currency swaps, collateral debt securities (CDSs), asset class risk stratification measures	
D		
Debt restructuring	Debt-to-nature swaps, haircuts, adjusted maturity and interest rates	
Blended finance	Advanced commitment strategies (ACSs), asset-backed securities (ABSs), public–private equity shares (PPESs), public endogenous credit creation (PECC)	
Special drawing rights	Providing additional monetary liquidity, especially for LICs and MICs	

Note: A: key principles; B: monetary tools; C: mobilising private capital; D: funding our commons

OneHealth as a case study: Healthcare is the single largest economic sector in most developed economies. Most developing countries, however, spend more on their military or on external debts than on domestic healthcare.[339] This is of particular relevance to an economics of transformation, because the process of change will affect our health in various ways. Moreover, healthcare has the highest priority in most (if not all) countries. The WHO defines health as a state of complete physical, mental and

---

[339] In figures: LICs spend about 40 USD per capita on health, while HICs spend around 3,335 USD, which is nearly 80 times as much. At the same time, the US, representing 4% of the global population, accounts for over 40% of global healthcare spending. See World Bank 2019.

social well-being and not as mere absence of a disease or symptoms. Access to healthcare is a fundamental human right without distinction of race, religion, political belief and economic or social condition. The WHO's main task is to promote global public healthcare. From a financial perspective, the WHO is chronically underfunded, with a balance sheet of five to six billion USD. About 70% of the funding is preconditioned and about 80% comes from private donors. At the same time, the WHO is saddled with a high documentary and regulatory overload that diverts it from its main purpose. We are currently busy stabilising, refunding and repairing the system to maintain its current functionality and have lost sight of the challenges ahead. Traditionally, we finance our healthcare system through private-sector financing, philanthropy and public-sector funding, maintaining a 'sick and alive' bias. That means revenue is generated only as long as the patient is *sick and alive*. If a patient is either dead or healthy, our current healthcare system is not interested in them. The current incentives are insufficient in scale and speed to meet today's pressing challenges and point in completely the wrong direction.[340] The main cost drivers are R&D, ageing, lifestyle, increasing inequality and an expected tripling of the global middle class. Added to this are the costs of hidden indirect subsidies of the fossil industry and the impact of climate change, future pandemics and biodiversity loss. We have to assume that health-related costs will substantially exceed the general growth trajectory of 2–3% annually and so will require new, additional and conditioned upfront funding. The OneHealth[341] or planetary health[342] agenda provides a distinctive approach that will allow us to better cope with these challenges and overcome the healthcare system's traditional biases. Our personal health status is directly or indirectly connected to a healthy planet and the health of all living species on that planet. From a financial perspective it makes next to no sense to treat animal health (veterinary medicine), biodiversity and water and soil quality (farming and agriculture) in isolation from human health (medicine). There are no healthy people without a healthy planet and vice versa. Any attempts to dissect, privatise and sectorise healthcare issues are becoming insur-

---

340 While the world spends almost 1.3 trillion USD annually on climate investments (as of 2023), only about 0.5% is channelled towards protecting or improving human health. But for LICs and MICs twice that amount is necessary to adapt to climate-related impacts on health. If we project this BAU scenario to 2050, we can expect an output loss of over 12 trillion USD, over 500 million people to be at risk of zoonotic disease and vector-borne syndromes, over 15 million additional premature deaths and a loss of over two billion healthy life years (HLYs), which would add another 1.2 trillion USD in extra costs. The paradox is that we have the public health tools and medical knowledge to manage these challenges and prevent the associated costs, but we lack the money to do so. See Forecasting Healthy Futures 2024.
341 Lebov et al. 2017.
342 Myers and Frumkin 2020; Haines and Frumkin 2021.

mountably expensive and inefficient.[343] The OneHealth or planetary health agenda calls for a completely different financial approach. Instead of a 'sick and alive' bias, we need a system that rewards 'restore, include and prevent'. Universal healthcare will then become a public good, an investment in a common future, rather than a cost. Instead of blaming the private sector for maximising its profits and ROI,[344] we should treat universal healthcare as a public good and finance it accordingly. For example, if we as a world community had invested 50 billion USD globally to prevent the Covid pandemic, the benefit for all of us would have been up to nine trillion USD.[345] Instead, the Human Development Index has been set back over ten years and the world economy has suffered an overall output loss of over 15 trillion USD. We could take this argument one step further and apply the idea of the secondary preventive approach and the monetary mechanism explained throughout this book to frontload the WHO with a monetary facility that allows it to meet its main purpose, instead of solely relying on taxpayers' money, member state fees or philanthropic commitments.[346]

Money Is Geopolitics: How to Finance Peace and Security for All

The question of war, peace and security for all in the 21st century will not be settled on the front line between capitalism and communism, between open societies and autocracies, between liberalism and nationalism or between different religious groups. Rather, it will come down to whether or not we are able to identify an institutional configuration of monetary incentives and financial assets that can accommodate all eight billion people on the planet, regardless of their cultural beliefs, their geographic and socioeconomic position and the legal and political system they live under.[347] The

---

343 As long as we permit industrial farming to generate revenue but collectively pay to clean up hyper-nitrified water, or as long as we allow private companies to reap windfall profits from prescribing opioids and have the public sector pay for the negative side effects including rehab, efforts to finance our common future will always remain behind the curve.

344 See WHO Council on the Economics of Health for All 2021.

345 Agarwal and Gopinath 2021.

346 Planetary Health Alliance 2024.

347 Speaking more generally, capitalism promotes profit maximisation (through price signals), private property and competitive market allocation, but earning money has become an end in itself. Communism, on the other hand, emphasises collective goods and planned economies, but has little understanding of free-market allocation of goods and services and its associated liabilities. We need to combine these two mega-trends and give equal emphasis to the commons and market allocation. The monetary system would then become a means to a greater whole. We would end up integrating communism and capitalism and then transcending them as we take the next step in evolution. Or in other words, we would shift from an *egocentric* to an *ethnocentric* to a *world-centric* to an *integral* worldview. See Wilber 2024.

social mechanisms of a risk-adjusted and updated monetary system, as described in this book, represent one critical component of this peace strategy.[348]

War-prone economies[349] have three major characteristics. Firstly, they use military means to secure their resource supply chains, in particular where resources are monopolised (fossil energy, rare materials, information). Secondly, free trade in goods and services is sooner or later replaced by a planned and regulated economy, where strict input–output benchmarking determines the entire value chain, production is channelled towards military assets and consumption is reduced accordingly. Thirdly, war economies exert additional inflationary pressure on the goods and services of daily life, especially in import-dependent countries. They therefore tend to have oligopolistic and over-regulated markets, additional expenditures to ensure access to and control of resources and reduced consumption patterns due to inflationary pressure.[350] A war economy is fundamentally opposed to any sustainability pathway right from the outset. A peace-prone society, meanwhile, encourages exactly the opposite development: a decentralised, free and liberal market economy with multilateral trading partners, non-monopolised energy sources (wind and sun) and significantly lower military and defence spending. Within this sustainable development scenario, the expectations of and preparedness for a belligerent scenario are significantly lower. Costs are consequently also much lower. One major reason is that fossil energy resources are geographically limited, and so countries reliant on them will always require additional financial means to access them, whereas the energy sources in peace-prone economies are decentralised, unlimited and regionalised. There is thus less competition between countries over resources and energy, and more over educational expertise, technological breakthroughs, entrepreneurship and multiple civilian third-sector activities. The choice of peace or war and the choice of energy sources are fundamentally interlinked. Humanity received its first peace dividend in the 1990s at the end of the Cold War, when we had the opportunity to reinvest our mili-

---

348 Amory Lovins (2013) argues that a shift from fossil energy to renewables can make our economy not only more efficient and resilient, but also more peaceful. The fossil industry involves extremely high hidden costs (oil price volatility), blackouts, indirect subsidies (healthcare), direct subsidies and military expenses to secure oil imports. Lovins calculates that for the US economy alone, the benefits of this shift would be up to five trillion USD in savings and a boost to GDP of up to 158% over the next few decades.

349 See also Blum 2011 and Caverley 2018.

350 The direct and indirect costs of war, defence and security measures globally amount to several times the annual spending on the UN SDGs. Military expenses represent the single largest component of the cost of violence, standing at over 2.2 trillion USD globally in 2024, an increase of over 14% compared with 2019, while internal security measures, including police, prison and judicial measures, rank second. Homicide and interpersonal violence represent the third-largest component, with significant indirect economic impacts. From a sustainability perspective we should add all the direct and indirect costs of environmental damage and future output losses to this equation. See Stockholm International Peace Research Institute 2021.

tary budget in a humanitarian peace budget, but this opportunity was squandered. Now we have a second chance. The financial mechanisms explained in this book could operate like a second peace dividend. We should take this opportunity to incorporate financial engineering tools and upgrade our monetary system to generate and support a peace-prone economy, with lower military spending, less centralised energy sources, a more liberal, multilateral competitive market and a fairer trading system.[351] And our investments should operate as preventive measures in parallel to military activities.[352]

> **Box 44:** On war and climate: breaking down the numbers
> Breaking down the numbers: the 2.24 trillion USD spent in 2024 by the military-industrial complex corresponds to 5.5% of global GHG emissions, which is greater than all civilian flights and equal to the entire GHG emissions of Russia. European NATO members' military spending alone has a footprint larger than countries such as Mexico, Australia and South Korea. Achieving the target of 2% of GDP on military spending would increase a country's carbon footprint by up to 50%. The IPCC goal of cutting GHG emissions by 43% by 2030 would become a pipe dream.[353] This figure does not include conflict-related damage to ecosystems (for which no official data is available) or additional collateral costs, such as a rise in energy and food prices, sanctions or output losses.

From an economic perspective, the interplay between military spending and investment in meeting sustainability goals is best described in terms of opportunity costs. As mentioned above, opportunity costs are the relative losses if we choose a more expensive alternative rather than a more effective and efficient way to achieve a certain goal. Military expenditures are opportunity costs relative to sustainability goals. They are often hidden, and pose a fundamental challenge to our current decision-making processes. There is a saying that we must win the peace so as not to lose the war. As long as we spend trillions of USD globally on military and quasi-military security measures, a similar amount of money should be invested in socioecological, humani-

---

351 The cost of forced migration, refugees and internal displacement amounts to several hundred billion USD globally. This crowds out positive investment in peace measures such as education, health, WASH and renewable energy initiatives. The global loss in GDP due to lost opportunities as a result of war and violence is up to 6%, representing a 'prosperity gap' of trillions of USD that would be available under conditions of peaceful development. See Dadush and Niebuhr 2016; IOM 2021.
352 There is a fine line between costs to contain and prevent violence on the one hand and costs to manage violence and its consequences on the other. Prevention costs account for two-thirds of the overall costs arising from violence. Whereas Syria spends up to two-thirds of its GDP on violence-related costs, Switzerland only spends 1%, including direct and indirect costs and prevention. Empirically, a high level of human capital, low levels of corruption, a well-functioning government and an equitable distribution of resources are the four most important factors for preventing violence between people. Any mechanism that can demonstrably reduce the curse of violence is worth considering.
353 Lin et al. 2023; Dill 2023.

tarian and civil projects to achieve the right balance.[354] In other words: the choice between security and sustainability is an illusion and we have to fundamentally redirect the focus of the military-industrial complex.[355]

The Optimum Currency Area Revised

Robert Mundell introduced the idea of an optimum currency area (OCA) not bounded by national borders.[356] He identified several criteria for integrating different economies under a single currency area so as to achieve a social optimum. In most cases the OCA is larger than one country. Assuming countries are faced with external shocks, the major criteria that define an OCA are factor mobility of labour and capital and a transfer mechanism that cuts across national borders. We can adapt Mundell's original concept of an OCA to the specific situation of the Anthropocene era, where multiple shocks have become the new normal and continuous economic transformation has become critical. If OCA 1 is facing serial shocks and backlashes from negative social and ecological spillovers that ultimately affect the economy, enlarging OCA 1 into OCA 2 should make it possible to better mobilise factor mobility (primarily of capital and labour) and provide a monetary transfer mechanism. Let us consider the multiple spillovers faced by the EU, which mainly comprise social externalities due to forced migration from Middle Eastern and North African (MENA) countries and ecological externalities due to climate change. So that the Eurozone can cope with both these externalities, two measures suggest themselves. Firstly, adjusted and qualified migration law that increases labour factor mobility into the Eurozone. Secondly, transfer payments nominated in euros to MENA countries to stimulate the local economy, which would reduce forced migration, and build up a renewable energy infrastructure, which could help reduce negative ecological externalities in the EU. Let us further assume that these two externalities, which cause repetitive external shocks to the Eurozone, amount to 5% of the EU's annual GDP. It would seem to be economically rational to extend the monetary base of the Eurozone by that amount to meet its share of the negative externalities involved and let the MENA countries use this additional liquidity as a medium of payment and as an effective source of tax revenue, both in parallel to their national currency and beyond EU jurisdiction. When it comes

---

354 Public investment in research and development (R&D) is a key indicator. If we look at military spending as a percentage of government budget allocation for R&D (GBARD), data on individual countries shows that Israel, Iran and North Korea spend 65%, Russia, Ukraine, the USA and China 46% and Austria, Switzerland and Belgium between 9% and 13% of their research budget on military-associated research. This means a vast amount of money is being spent contrary to UN SDG 16 (peace). See Dill 2023.
355 See the World Academy of Art and Science's HS4A initiative and Global Security Institute 2024.
356 Mundell 1961 and 1973.

to preparedness for the next symmetric or asymmetric shock to hit the two regions (EU, MENA), the larger the OCA the better. An extended currency union, while imperfect, can act like a shock absorber and risk pooler[357] that is preferable to a flexible currency regime where both regions have to bear the shock alone. In the case of asymmetric shocks that have a greater direct impact on the MENA region than the EU, the EU will still have to bear the indirect impact of additional negative social and ecological externalities, while the MENA currencies will depreciate further. At the same time, adjusted factor mobility of labour and capital for both regions (EU and MENA) would be preferable to conventional monetary policy, as simple interest rate adjustments would be too incremental, slow and granular. That is why the OCA for the EU is larger than the Eurozone alone. I shall now discuss two further examples – the petrodollar system and the Belt and Road Initiative – where an implicit extended currency area follows a similar monetary logic. These examples demonstrate that monetary policy is geopolitics. The OCA becomes a function of internalised externalities and risk-pooling activities, in which the reach of market allocation matches the reach of monetary policy.

The Chinese *Belt and Road Initiative (BRI)*, launched in 2013, involves over 150 countries and dozens of international organisations and has invested almost one trillion USD equivalent.[358] Historically, China has always invested about 1% of its GDP abroad, but it has now become the world's largest creditor – larger than the Paris Club, IMF or World Bank. The main intention of the BRI is to promote international trade and infrastructure development in line with the official agenda of the Communist Party of China (CPC). Most contracts are bilateral agreements that follow the 'Angola protocol': financial contracts for goods, services and infrastructure projects imported to and exported from one country are transferred from one Chinese state bank (e.g. the China Development Bank) to another (e.g. the Export–Import Bank of China). These roll-over procedures have zero effect on the Chinese banking system. In short: China is going on a large-scale, long-term global shopping spree, generating multiple financial liabilities for the countries involved and extending their geopolitical power accordingly.[359]

---

357 The counterbalance for both regions would be to run down foreign exchange reserves (euros) for MENA countries and to have extended institutional euro swap lines with these foreign currencies, which would enable affected countries to recover more quickly, cheaply and effectively.
358 The BRI is the update of the Chinese Silk Road Initiative. See People's Map of Global China 2024. See also Gelpern et al. 2021.
359 In numbers: four-fifths of the banks involved are state banks, over 80% of the contracts remain hidden and there is little published information on the geographic breakdowns. The contracts involve joint ventures, equity funds, FDIs, SPVs and trading loans, mostly running offshore and offsheet. About two-thirds of the contracts are nominated in USD, about 10–15% in renminbi. Central banks mainly use CBCSAs to finance the initiative. Half of the contracts are collateralised through resource-based loans. The published contracts do not involve any Paris clause, which would allow the debtor to seek debt relief, face-value reductions, which allow long-term restructuring only, or cross-default clauses, which involve immediate repayments. See Horn et al. 2019; Desjardins 2018.

The goal of the *US petrodollar system*, meanwhile, was to maintain national energy security while providing military protection for OPEC countries. OPEC countries nominate their oil bills in USD, which are then reinvested in the US economy. The petrodollar system started in June 1974. In October 2019 the US economy became a net energy exporter, and in June 2024 the agreements with OPEC ceased.[360] Future oil exports from OPEC countries will increasingly be nominated in currencies other than the US dollar. In parallel, the overall trend towards renewables and the rise of private cryptocurrencies and CBDCs in different jurisdictions will further weaken the US dollar as a predominant medium of exchange.

The BRI and the petrodollar system may seem like completely different projects, but they share a very similar monetary agenda.[361] The common monetary denominator of both is that the liquidity required to finance energy security on the one hand and promote international trade on the other does not come from domestic savings accounts, taxpayers or international credit lines. It is the political agenda that determines the targets, central banks that generate the money, federal governments and ministries that make public announcements, the public and commercial banking sectors that set up the credit lines to the corporate sector so it can implement the projects and finally the treasury that pays the bill.[362] Each time, the procedure generates additional purchasing power that involves millions of jobs and corporate revenue and benefits America's and China's national sovereign interests and national jurisdiction.

We could take this idea further and apply it to funding the UN SDGs, a Green New Deal agenda or responses to future shocks. What would happen if the EU, representing a third of global currency reserves and one of the largest economic unions globally, were to create a 'peace and wealth belt' in the neighbouring MENA countries, following the same monetary logic as the US and China do for their sovereign interests? Similar to the BRI and the petrodollar system, which generate multiple positive feedback loops for their home countries, the EU could apply this mechanism to generate additional, conditioned liquidity and create a peace and wealth belt within and around its borders. We would end up with a green OCA for Europe. To summarise: monetary policy is geopolitics: we set the targets and create the liquidity necessary to achieve them.[363] The table below (Table 15) summarises the examples discussed in this section.

---

360 See Securing America's Future Energy 2018.

361 There is a third historical example that demonstrates a similar mechanism at work: Britain and its Commonwealth in the colonial (and precolonial) era from 1765 to 1938. During that period, Britain was able to drain a total of ten trillion sterling from India alone, based on a highly complex and opaque trading system of purchasing and taxation using council bills issued by the British Crown. See Patnaik and Patnaik 2016; Chakrabarti and Patnaik 2019. We can do better by having the central banks involved in creating a better, greener and fairer future.

362 See Horn et al. 2019.

363 To be more precise: the limitations of this kind of augmented and risk-adapted monetary policy are determined by four factors: human resources (unemployment and enrolment rate); the availability of natural resources (land, rare materials, energy); external debts in foreign currency; and the

Table 15: The common monetary denominators.

	British Empire/ Commonwealth	Petrodollar system	Belt and Road Initiative	Peace and wealth belt*
Country	UK	USA	China	EU + MENA
Timespan	1765–1938	1974–2024	2013–present	2025 onwards
Currency	Pound sterling	US dollar	Renminbi, yuan	Euro
Goal/ policy	Exploiting the colonies	Energy security and military protection	International trade	Security and sustainability
Financial assets	Council bills issued by the British Crown	Petrodollars that circulate back into the US economy	Foreign reserves, state banking and QE	CBDCs, CBCSs, green QE
Cost	Up to ten trillion USD equivalent over the entire period	2.5 trillion USD annual supply (2023)	About 100 billion USD equivalent annually	Requires an additional 1–1.5 trillion euros annually

Note: *Under the hypothetical assumption of a peace and wealth belt being created in Europe from 2025 onwards.

Towards a Green Bretton Woods 2.0: Resetting the Framework

The Global South is underrepresented in international financial institutions, disproportionately impacted by global externalities and overburdened with debts nominated in foreign currencies. The shadow banking sector, with a total value of 240 trillion USD, is unregulated and exerts uncontrolled pro-cyclical pressure on the real economy. The fossil energy sector, which still provides 80% of the energy required for our global economy, receives massive financial support, with direct and indirect subsidies of over seven trillion USD annually. The existing monetary institutions are currently unable to assess and take into account the risks of future shocks. The four largest central banks alone implemented 26 trillion USD of quantitative easing (QE) over the last few years. This QE lacked any systemic shock risk buffers, failed to factor in physical, transition and political risks and systemically excluded negative externalities such as pollution, emission footprints and soil degradation from credit risk assessments. The entire accounting system is inadequate and underperforming, leaving us with an uncovered financial gap of several trillion USD for loss and dam-

---

monetary channels in which the liquidity is processed. Currently, the additional money supply is driving growth of the asset price index (API) and the stock market, but we could do better: using different monetary channels, tapping into more efficient land, energy and material use and mobilising millions of under- and unemployed people would create space for an augmented and risk-adjusted monetary policy at a time of currency diversification and the decline of USD supremacy.

age, mitigation and adaptation funds. In order to account for biophysical facts and social reality and make a human/nature-centred approach the new standard, we need to realign the entire power structure of the monetary system. Addressing all these challenges requires new institutions and new forms of market allocation.

When delegates from 43 countries met at the Mount Washington Hotel in Bretton Woods, New Hampshire, in July 1944, they embraced a new spirit and mindset, and set new rules that would determine the course of the world economy in the post-war era up until the 1970s. Bretton Woods stands metaphorically for a collective mission involving at least three main aspects.[364] Firstly, *international collaboration*: agreements on common rules were considered to be beneficial for all parties. Even non-binding, 'light-touch' rules were, it was felt, better than taking ad hoc decisions in times of crisis or having nothing in place at all. Secondly, a search for a set of *monetary mechanisms* that would enable the real economy to better adjust for trade imbalances, including (a) *capital controls* that permit governments to insulate and protect domestic markets to some extent and give them scope to meet their own targets; and (b) *pegged but adjustable* currencies to reduce economic instability and the volatility of the currencies involved. Thirdly, the implementation of *new institutional monetary bodies*, in particular the World Bank Group (for financing reconstruction and development projects) and the International Monetary Fund (IMF) (for harmonising international policy and providing assistance to countries that encounter challenges with their balance of payments).[365] With the suspension of gold–dollar convertibility in 1971, this Bretton Woods system broke down. Ever since, under what is known as the Washington Consensus, the new order of the day has been deregulation of capital flows, with uncontrolled capital in- and outflows, lower tariffs and taxes and austerity policies designed to reduce public deficits or public spending. The situation we are facing now 75 years later is similar in many respects to that which preceded the original Bretton Woods meeting.[366] However, the overall political power game has changed dramatically and is affecting the overall financial system, making it more fragile, fractured and fragmented.[367] By contrast with 1944, our current situation is characterised by three major trends. Firstly, serial *ecological crises*. From a purely financial perspective, all these multiple ecological crises represent (opportunity) costs, expressed as prosperity losses and the costs of increasing political instability. And they affect all of us, albeit in an asymmetric manner. Some will be hit harder and sooner, others later. Some will escape more or less unscathed and a few will even benefit in the short term. But none of us know which side of the story we are on. Sec-

---

364 Eichengreen 2019.

365 Attempts were also made to establish an International Trade Organization, but those plans did not come to fruition till the 1990s with the founding of the World Trade Organization (WTO).

366 Dooley et al. 2004.

367 See The Economist 2024.

ondly, a *multipolar moment*,[368] which requires adjustments to our monetary agreements and mechanisms. Simply implementing controls for footloose capital, having pegged and adjustable currencies and allowing the World Bank Group to finance disaster management ex post will not be enough and will clearly be too expensive for all of us. The rise of a multipolar world will go hand in hand with the rise of a multipolar currency system that outpaces the traditional USD supremacy measures and imposes new challenges. Thirdly, the dawn of new *digital technologies*. These technologies, in particular AI and big data, will change the international power game. The country with the first quantum AI computers will set the new rules of the game. New innovations in fintech will alter the money creation process, liabilities, commercial banking and the way financial transactions are carried out. And they will attract investors and ultimately determine future flows of capital. The course of any sustainable future and any multilateral agreement is dependent on them. A Bretton Woods 2.0 agenda therefore needs to provide a comprehensive new monetary architecture that is able to operate within a multipolar world hit by serial ecological crises and adapt to the emerging new technologies in a way that serves the good of humankind. This new design should enable us, first, to mobilise and hedge private capital and, second, to fund and manage our planetary commons. The big takeaway is that we need far more qualified liquidity in the market to help us cope with systemic uncertainties and collective externalities. We should be guided by a narrative that explains why the overall monetary system should act anti-cyclically and preventively rather than on an ad hoc, ex post basis, where we constantly remain in fix-and-repair mode. While all the obvious and traditional measures – in particular green taxonomies, taxation schemes, debt restructuring, green savings accounts, loss and damage funds and philanthropic pledges, ODA and remittance payments – do have value in and of themselves and can help to drive specific political actions, investment strategies or consumption patterns, I shall be making the case for new institutional and systemic incentives.[369] In short: polity needs to take precedence over politics (see figure 48 below). The proposals are grouped around the tandem of *representation* and *money*. Both are necessary. Representation means here new voting quotas that represent a fairer share, give a more equal voice to the stakeholders involved and boost funding in line with vulnerability and risk exposure, while money means the additional, specific funding needed for the transformation. Representation without money will be a

---

368 Entering a multipolar world with five major players – the USA, China, the EU, Russia and India – is changing the playing field. But despite their divergent political agendas, they all operate within the same monetary system. This means that although the IMS is changing, it still remains a common ground or shared framework. See Masala 2022; Münkler 2023; Brunnhuber 2023.

369 To be more precise: a 7/24/365 emissions trading system (ETS); new ways of accounting for welfare and well-being (WAVES; HDI); phasing out fossil subsidies (direct and indirect); accountability and disclosure agreements in line with ESG standards; new regulations for the shadow banking sector, including a 1:1 capital weighting for bank loans for fossil fuel investments.

corpse, inert and ineffective. Money without representation will be a curse, simply prolonging the existing power structures, biases and flaws that we wanted to overcome in the first place. To quote Mahatma Gandhi: 'The difference between what we do and what we are capable of doing would suffice to solve most of the world's problems.'

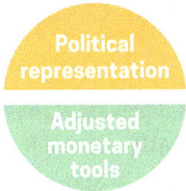

Figure 48: The tandem: additional money and political representation.

Although the list is incomplete, I would propose to take at least the following measures into consideration:

A public central clearing counter-party (PCCP) for derivatives: A clearing house serves as an intermediary between multiple parties, which reduces default risks, enables independent evaluation and monitoring of each party's creditworthiness, reduces the collateral deposits and guarantees funding in the event of a default, without any direct contracts between the parties. Structured as a public central clearing counter-party (PCCP), it would provide an essential mechanism to increase the transparency and stability of the IMS, preventing contagion and domino effects and reducing systemic risk for third parties, especially in the case of collateral debt obligations (CDOs), CDSs, asset-backed securities (ABSs) and unregulated special investment vehicles, multiple conduits and offsheet and offshore transactions. A PCCP would not replace hedging instruments, but rather reduce the costs (including those that would ultimately fall on the public purse) in the event of a chain reaction. It would create a trade-off between decentralised and unregulated over-the-counter transactions and transactions that run through the clearing house. These qualified transactions would be safer and less risky, but subject to the condition that they can only be used to fund and invest in green assets.[370]

Foreign direct investments (FDIs) and a reformed investment court system (ICS): Countries can be sued by private investors if state actions negatively affect private investments, but not the other way round. An international arbitral tribunal pro-

---

370 This demonstrates a more general principle of public-sector involvement. Traditionally, increasing public involvement has driven up interest rates and crowded out private-sector investment. In contrast, a PCCP would reduce systemic risks and private-sector involvement would be crowded in, unlocking the capital formation needed for the green transition.

tects FDIs through several thousand bilateral investment treaties, assorted multilateral agreements and the Transatlantic Trade and Investment Partnership (TTIP). It provides security, 'free transfer of means' and legal protection for foreign investors against expropriation. The current set of rules, however, is inconsistent and unfair, and lacks transparency and integrity.[371] Private investors should be protected against expropriation, but should also respect democratic decisions. At its core, the existing regulatory framework prevents both states and investors from achieving a sustainable future. Instead, it creates a 'regulatory chill', so that smoking bans, minimum wages and ESG standards are not implemented because of the potential private claims that are anticipated.[372] We could either continue 'business as usual' (BAU), exit the ICS or implement rules that on the one hand subject international investors to approved ESG standards that have long-term applicability and do not entitle them to claim for damages, and on the other provide public bodies with upfront funding to hedge potential systemic risks associated with these investments.[373]

A reformed supply chain act: The numerous global supply chains that exist today reflect the general assumption that labour specialisation is a fundamental component of any free-market economy, crucial to development efforts and to capital and wealth formation. Currently, several regulatory efforts are underway to implement environmental and human rights standards along these global supply chains.[374] We are currently trying to solve these challenges by increasing documentation, regulation and sanctions, which risks making the entire network of supply chains ineffective, inefficient and expensive and has resulted in a legal framework that is anything but fit for purpose. Seen from a systemic angle, the collective externalities we are facing along multiple supply chains globally do not necessarily reflect a genuine single market failure, but rather a lack of a proper, functioning market, in which liabilities, ownership rights, corporate laws and symmetric information would provide a more adequate price signal. These multiple negative externalities in most cases represent a collective failing by all of us, rather than a misstep by a single company. If we aim to adjust global supply chains so that they respect private investments, harness the benefits of international labour specialisation, prevent misuse and make it possible to better hedge and manage the associated collective externalities, then, instead of further reg-

---

371 Anderson and Beaumont 2020.

372 Historically, the first investor protection act dates back to the 1959 agreement between Germany and Pakistan. The goal was to increase FDI in regions where there was a lack of private investment. Sixty-five years later, the empirical evidence on its economic impact is inconclusive. About one-third of related lawsuits are settled, one-third are won by the private sector and one-third by the public sector. See also Dotzauer 2023.

373 Johnson et al. 2019; Kyla et al. 2022.

374 In May 2024, the EU adopted the Corporate Sustainability Due Diligence Directive; similar legislation is in effect and/or has been proposed in other countries, including Australia, Canada, China, Brazil, the USA and India. See LRQA 2024.

ulating the supply chain, which encourages companies to withdraw, we should keep the initial supply chain in place, guaranteeing human rights standards, while (partially) covering the associated negative social externalities with a green monetary facility provided by the European Investment Bank, with the domestic multilateral development bank (MDB) operating as an intermediary to transfer the money. Again, this monetary facility would not come from a fiscal squeeze, nor from a public credit line provided to the international capital market, but rather from the monetary creation process that any public central bank is entitled to carry out, as explained in the previous section.

Reforms to rating agencies: Rating agencies are meant to reduce the information asymmetry and provide reliable, objective and independent data so that borrowers can take a preventive, anti-cyclical, foresighted approach. However, the results from providing robust information on systemic risks, future shocks and externalities are uninspiring. There are several systemic flaws built in. Rating agencies are operating within an oligopoly, where a handful of private firms have a market share of over 95%. The current contracting model creates a systemic conflict of interest, where the borrower is paying the agency and not the lender. This further leads to a pro-cyclical tendency, where potential risks are not buffered but amplified. Once a shock or a default occurs, rating agencies provide little transparency about their evaluation process, nor do they assume any expert liability. We should either re-regulate each of these flaws of the rating process (reverse billing) or introduce a public entity that is able to provide competitive data. An intermediary step would include a public–private partnership that pools the expertise of both sides.

Reforming voting powers at international monetary institutions: International monetary institutions are supposed to collaborate and keep the entire global monetary web alive and interconnected. But they are increasingly fracturing and fragmenting. This has resulted in the rise of regional financial security measures,[375] an increase in central bank swap lines and repurchasing agreements (repos)[376] and the accumulation of foreign currency reserves with a total value of over 12 trillion USD (2024), of which over 50% (7.5 trillion USD) are held by emerging and developing countries. These trends reflect further regional decoupling and resilience strategies in the face of increasing volatility, shocks and potential contagion effects, instead of an effort to further integrate, pool and collectively manage common tasks. Reforms to the three traditional Bretton Woods institutions – the World Bank, the IMF and the WTO – should take this into account.

---

375 Such as the European Stability Mechanism (over 550 billion USD), the Chiang Mai Initiative (250 billion USD) and the new BRICS Group swap lines (100 billion USD), which will be expanded in the medium term to include the UAE and Saudi Arabia. See Green 2023 and Hoffner 2023.
376 China alone settled over 550 billion USD using currency swap lines with over 40 countries over the last few years. See Horn et al. 2023 and Jung 2024.

The *World Bank* was established to eliminate poverty globally and to promote sustainable development. It comprises five institutions with different agendas. The bank primarily raises the money it lends from the capital market and through fees, shares and interest payments. Recent reforms[377] are intended to streamline the lending process and make it more transparent. The goals are to triple the annual guarantee issuance from 6.8 billion USD to 20 billion USD by 2030 and to consolidate the 20 different forms of public guarantees into a single 'menu'.[378] Another proposed measure is to mobilise private investments and domestic savings and frontload MDBs to provide security against systemic risk through multiple hedging or equity instruments.

The main task of the *IMF* is to increase international monetary cooperation and financial stability and to encourage global trade, economic growth, employment and prosperity. The IMF's unique monetary tool is its 982 billion special drawing rights (SDRs), equivalent to about the same number of USD, which come from member quotas and multi- or bilateral borrowing agreements. The entire process is currently under negotiation and illustrates the dilemma of *representation* and *money*. If GDP were measured in terms of purchasing power parity (PPP), that would upgrade the Global South to almost 60% of quota power, but it would not take into account the relative weight of these countries in real international economic transactions[379] and would undermine the capacity of the Global South to contribute to the stability of the financial system. If we take the ecological crisis seriously, the whole process should be re-evaluated based on cumulative carbon emissions[380] and weighted by population as a fair measure.

The *WTO* is underpinned by the belief that free trade flows stimulate domestic growth and prosperity for all. The WTO is a legally binding mediator that deals with matters of unfair subsidies, trade barriers, violations of intellectual property and disputes among trading partners and is supposed to adapt national trade policy to international requirements. However, the trading environment has changed fundamentally since the WTO was founded. The rise of e-commerce and cybercrime, the digital divide, serial ecological shocks that threaten the global value chain, the disconnect between the financial system and real trading activities and the need to fairly integrate emerging and developing markets into the global trading system are all challenging the free trade principle.[381]

---

377 See World Bank 2024a.

378 At present, these guarantees represent not even 5% of exposed lending. See IMF Datamapper 2023; World Bank 2024.

379 This is because PPP reflects the prices of domestic non-tradable goods and services. See Krugman et al. 2009, 386 ff.

380 Hickel 2020; Hickel et al. 2022.

381 A second-best step would be an *open plurilateralism*, which would allow binding agreements for subgroups with potential benefits for non-signatories. The General Agreement on Tariffs and Trade (GATT) was designed with a plurilateral structure. See Schmucker and Mildner 2023.

In short, the current Bretton Woods system is simply too narrow in scope to tackle the challenges of the 21st century. Facing all the calamities, challenges and conflicting agendas, respecting what we have already achieved, acknowledging both our institutional and intellectual constraints and our planetary boundaries, criticising oversights or deficiencies within the current system and then moving beyond the status quo towards a better common future seems to be a reasonable, modest first step that we can take together.

Extending the role of regulators: The main task of any new, upgraded, green Bretton Woods 2.0 agenda should focus not on regulating the market or intervening in sovereign states' laws and self-determination, but rather on identifying and introducing the most appropriate regulatory framework for the regulators themselves. The primary goal would then not be to constrain private and corporate initiatives, but rather to correct inefficient, irresponsible, unfair and misdirected financial incentives. The final result would not be a reduced role for the private sector, but rather expanded, better and more efficient market solutions. And nor would it entail a reduced role for the public sector, but would rather encourage more preventive and proactive government initiatives. In this sense, the rules for the regulators would serve as a global public good, providing a comprehensive, collectively shared and approved framework, rather than a casino where outcomes are determined by risky bets and (good or bad) luck and where systemic risks and externalities have to be blamed on 'someone' who cannot be identified or held accountable. In short, we need more competitive markets and more government action, but they need to be implemented differently or take a different form.

Box 45: The 'bancor' and beyond

In the 1940s, J. M. Keynes[382] proposed a monetary regime that was intended to avoid the future misalignments, asymmetries and instabilities of the financial system that we are facing now. His 'bancor' is a supranational virtual currency that operates like a multilateral clearing house. It functions solely as a unit of account and is not backed by any collateral. The beauty of this proposal is that it affects surplus and deficit countries and their international trade in a reciprocal manner: surplus countries' currencies appreciate and deficit countries' currencies depreciate automatically. If we had decided to implement the 'bancor', development would have accelerated in all countries involved. Instead, we opted for a USD system that operates as the world's reserve currency, leaving the US economy with a high deficit and further destabilising the global financial system in the periphery. The green digital parallel system proposed in this book differs from the bancor in several respects. Although theoretically the bancor regime would be a very elegant way to balance out the world economy, no supranational currency and clearing system is politically likely to emerge within the next decade. I am proposing the most feasible best next step instead. Moreover, the bancor regime is not sensitive to sustainability issues and has no built-in mechanism to steer our society towards a green marketplace. Meaning that even if we had followed Keynes's advice, the world economy would have been left alone to hedge, fund, manage and finance our commons in the Anthropocene era.

---

382 Schumacher 1943; Keynes 1980.

One of the core ideas of this book is that we are in need of additional, conditioned liquidity that operates on different monetary channels than those we are used to and is linked to digital technologies. CBDCs, CBCSs and green QE, direct emergency facilities or conditioned SDRs could serve these purposes. We would then be able to install a green monetary ecosystem, built upon the existing USD supremacy but adding additional, conditioned liquidity and incentives to the market, which could potentially transform our economy in the direction of less harm and more good. And unlike Bretton Woods 1.0, where capital controls provided some sort of stability, a green Bretton Woods 2.0 should favour *conditioning over controlling*. Meaning that deregulated capital would remain untouched, but would not benefit from any bailouts in the event of a systemic default. If private capital becomes vested in domestic markets and requires public agencies to hedge associated systemic risks and uncertainties, the liquidity provided by the public sector would then come with a condition attached: it can only be invested in certified green assets.[383] I call this monetary facility M^{cola}: *conditioned liquidity assistance* issued by public regulators to provide additional money in the form of swaps, direct funds, grants, credit lines or public guarantees. M^{cola} could take the form of 'net-zero-coupon perpetual facilities' or 'non-defaultable loans', where one public body (the regulator) provides liquidity assistance for another (the government or an IGO) to manage public goods. The public balance sheet would be net zero. These facilities would be wholly digital and would utilise distributed ledger technologies and, potentially, digital smart contracts. They should be able to decrease fraud and corruption, bank runs and excessive boom-and-bust volatility, increase traceability and help investors meet their targets more reliably. MDBs would become key players, since they have the expertise and knowledge but, at present, often lack adequate funding to finalise the deals.[384] These new forms of monetary supply aggregate would be proof that regulators are moving from a climate-agnostic to a climate-informed policy agenda and would better equip them to track and price in the expected inflationary pressure we have already triggered. The following figure (Figure 49) summarises these examples for a new Bretton Woods 2.0 moment.

---

[383] If we took this argument one step further, we would end up with a dual currency system, where a green euro, dollar or pound complements the conventional currency and pulls our society towards a greener, more inclusive future. See Brunnhuber 2021 and 2023.
[384] Marois et al. 2024.

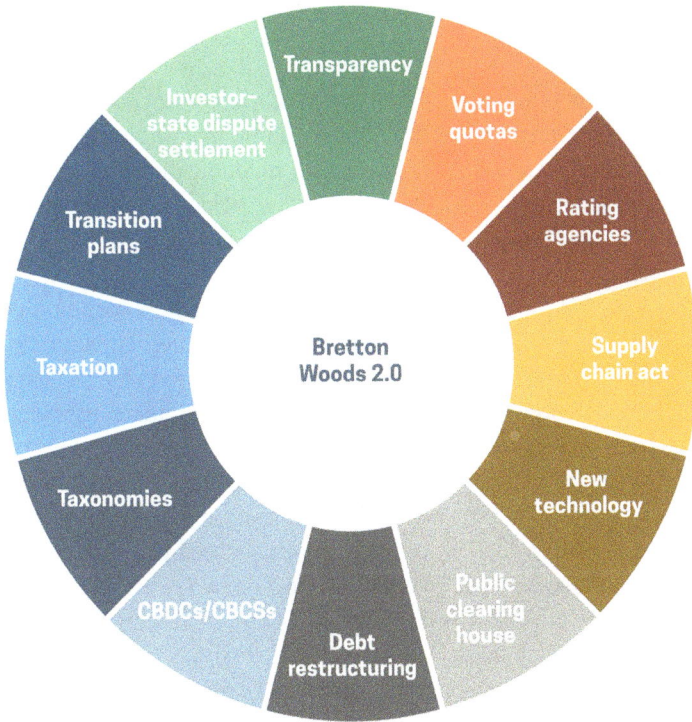

Figure 49: Components of a Bretton Woods 2.0 agenda.

E: Conclusion

The core argument of this book is simple, but non-trivial. It has far-reaching implications for the financing of our transformation. Providing additional and conditioned liquidity in the way described throughout this book will fundamentally change the playing field for everyone involved. Investor and consumer behaviour, risk assessments and political and corporate decisions will be fundamentally different with these new monetary mechanisms.

Keynes argued that markets are unstable, provide imperfect information and tend towards a suboptimal equilibrium with high unemployment rates. Capital owners' liquidity preferences can drive deflation and so, according to Keynes, the state should provide additional liquidity in an anti-cyclical manner to stimulate aggregate demand (net income minus savings rate), which will ultimately determine the multiple price signals that exist in our economy. Keynes's famous metaphor of an 'animal spirit'[385] describes how savers and investors will withdraw their money in the face of uncertainty. That still holds true in the 21st century, but in a closed planetary economy the impact of uncertainties does not go away. Keynes's analogy comparing investors' behaviour to a 'beauty contest'[386] still holds too. Investors do not choose the most beautiful face, but the one they think the majority will choose. That means they will pro-cyclically amplify shocks, rather than acting rationally and countering them. This is an innate flaw of the financial sector. However, both notions – the 'animal spirit' and the 'beauty contest' – need to be updated for the 21st century.

Keynesianism 2.0 makes reference to Keynes's original theory, but modifies and improves upon it. In both cases (Keynes 1.0 and 2.0), there is a general steering measure that responds to volatile, pro-cyclical and risk-averse market participants. But the Keynes 2.0 moment reflects the fact that we are confronted with serial compound shocks and systemic externalities that feed back into market activities. And the required interventions are no longer merely anti-cyclical, but far more fundamental. Rather than an aggregate demand stimulus, we need a *qualified monetary supply aggregate* that sterilises and hedges a non-cyclical disruptive process. In this Keynes 2.0 world, governments do not just need taxation and conventional credit lines to fund our common future, but also adjusted monetary governance to provide the adequate liquidity to make it happen. Taxation then becomes a steering tool rather than a funding one. A qualified, conditioned monetary aggregate can generate almost unlimited positive second-round effects that will benefit all humanity.

In the first chapter, I introduced the notions of return on capital (r) and the economic growth rate (g). In modern, integrated economies $r > g$. Under the current

---

385 Keynes 1936, 144.
386 Keynes 1936, chapter 12.

https://doi.org/10.1515/9783111421520-006

conditions of serial shocks, increasing impact from negative externalities and under-funded planetary commons, we can expect the gap between r and g to further in-crease, due to the combined effect of widening wealth and income spreads, higher risk premiums for insurance, a growing disconnect between the financial sector and real economy, green taxonomies and higher fiscal burdens. In this book, I have ar-gued that an additional, conditioned monetary aggregate will be crucial for any eco-nomics of transformation in the 21st century. If my recommendations are followed, we will end up in a situation such that $r + M^{cola} \geq g^*$, where g^* represents a qualified green growth trajectory towards a more sustainable future. This new monetary sup-ply aggregate (M^{cola}) will decrease over time, since planetary commons and negative externalities will be funded and private capital unlocked, and so r will further de-cline. Systemic risks, volatility and instability will decrease, covered by M^{cola}. In con-sequence, we can expect that the CPI will decrease in the long run, as negative exter-nalities decline. Ultimately, governments will be able to lower taxes as the costs of public goods are ultimately met and systemic hazards decrease, which will further increase incentives for g^*. As g^* increases, public interest rates, debt payments and income inequality will decline and we will finally end up in a new state of economic equilibrium, where $r = g^*$. In that ideal-typical case, capital gains will be equal to eco-nomic costs, wages and expenditures, savings will match investments, supply will match demand. We will have finally replaced the toxic downwards spiral with a healthy upwards one. This means that return on capital will eventually reflect the an-nual green growth rate – precisely the outcome this book's arguments are geared to-wards achieving. What Keynes called the 'beauty contest' of the financial sector would be replaced by a 'science slam' where the winner is whoever can best sell their empirical findings. Moreover, the well-documented 'liquidity trap', where investors withdraw their savings because risk premiums are too low, will ultimately give way to a bonanza for savvy investors – laying the foundations for a brighter future.

One common objection is the supply shock argument. Any economy exposed to a supply shock – meaning a lack of skilled workers (human capital), rare materials, en-ergy and soil (natural capital) and/or technology and tangible assets (produced capi-tal) – will end up in an inflationary state if additional money is merely injected into the existing value chain. This objection is not entirely without merit, but the argument for M^{cola} still holds if we note that M^{cola} is redirected into education and controlled migration to increase the skilled workforce, into R&D to increase efficiency and into restoring nature reserves and soil to increase the productivity of our natural capital. M^{cola} is therefore not a subsidy, a public tool to protect the domestic economy or an industry-specific policy, but a market-like hedging instrument to reduce systemic risks, a funding instrument for planetary commons and a tool to tackle global negative externalities and spillovers, thus enabling an economy to transform for the better.[387] The box below (Box 46) summarises the argument.

Box 46: Reconciling r and g^*

In modern economies with a mature financial sector $r > g$. But that does not reflect the costs of externalities and systemic shocks within a planetary closed economy. If we are prepared to add M^{cola}, we get $r + M^{cola} \geq g^*$ and the cost of financial capital will consequently decrease. Since $M^{cola} \approx Co + Ex + mPC$, which reflects the additional costs for any economics of transformation, M^{cola} will tend to zero as the costs to fund planetary commons and negative externalities and mobilise private capital decrease over time. Singular conventional measures alone (TTRAPP) will instead cause a 'green paradox': withdrawing purchasing power from the existing value chain and preventing the economy from transforming. On the assumption that secondary prevention is cheaper than business as usual, any expected future CPI with M^{cola} will be lower than any CPI without M^{cola}; in the long run we will end up with $r \cong g^*$, which means that return on capital will be precisely matched to a green, sustainable growth trajectory, in which costs, benefits and wages will form a new Pareto-superior equilibrium. This will ultimately have a positive impact on the distribution of income and wealth and reconnect the financial sector to the real economy.

The table below (Table 16) summarises the comparison between Keynes 1.0 and 2.0.

Table 16: Keynes 1.0 versus Keynes 2.0.

Keynes 1.0	Keynes 2.0
Instability and imperfection of markets	Externalities and serial compound shocks; managing planetary commons
Liquidity trap	Bonanza for savvy investors
Beauty contest	Science slam
Aggregate demand multiplier	A qualified monetary supply aggregate
Main role played by the state	Main role played by the regulators/central banks; a secondary preventive approach in finance
Anti-cyclical stabiliser	Transformation and development; not a cyclical process
National fiscal measures	International monetary system; shadow markets and speculation; role of new technologies

No nation, no single academic discipline, no individual or group and no technology alone is able to master this transformation. Given their scope and complexity, the global challenges can only be addressed by radically changing our institutions and ways of thinking. Periods of radical and rapid transformation involve conflicts be-

---

387 In absolute terms, M^{cola} should be equal to all TTRAPP measures minus the reduced consumption and welfare over time plus the increased productivity due to R&D and education.

tween established institutions, mindsets and social power structures and new, emerging ones. The Renaissance, the Reformation, the Enlightenment and the French Revolution are notable historical examples. There has always been a need for new knowledge and wisdom, for new skills and practices, that outstrips our personal and institutional capacities to acquire them. I started the book by claiming that finance as an academic discipline has a single crucial *differentia specifica* that sets it apart from any other academic discipline. Neither neoclassical nor institutional economics nor behavioural finance, neither Marxism nor the Austrian School can do full justice to the complexity, interdependencies and boundaries of any economic system and integrate their theories with interdisciplinary findings. Only a systems-thinking approach can do that. And it is not macroeconomic modelling, studies of statistical correlations or theoretical mathematics that can reveal the specific contribution of finance to this overall process of transformation. Financial economics can provide unique arguments, instruments and insights no other discipline is capable of, and thus show us how to live in the *cheapest of all possible worlds.* I strongly believe that it is the unique task of the academic world to reveal options and possibilities that go beyond the obvious and transcend traditional ways of thinking. Systems thinking can provide the most promising results – with fuzzy logic rather than clear-cut data, complementary pairs rather than simple causal links, emergence rather than historical analysis, fractals rather than micro–macro dichotomies offering us a glimpse into the future.

Societal transformation has not previously been a major topic of discussion within economics and finance. Rather, it has been external factors such as education, R&D and technological breakthroughs that have driven change. But now, in the 2020s, things are different. Transformation has become a property of economics and finance in its own right. In a general sense, any economic transformation is an intentional and conscious shift from one state to another. Around 100 years ago, Keynes provided us with new means and measures to overcome the economic challenges that existed at that time. The present book has attempted to translate some of his foundational insights for the 21st century, and to upgrade and adapt them for the Anthropocene era. One major difference from the situation some 100 years ago is that we are living in a closed planetary economy, where everything is interconnected, and we are operating within biophysical boundaries. Meaning that any negative social or ecological externality we create in one part of the planet will directly or indirectly affect investor assessments, consumer and business behaviour and political decisions in one way or another, as each of these negative externalities has a direct or indirect impact on costs, expenditures, revenue and profits. There is simply no 'free lunch' any more: costs are equal to damage, losses or risks and vice versa. I have outlined some preliminary elements of a *general theory of economic transformation* and identified the IMS and its intrinsic architecture as the main leverage point. *Money* is not a natural law, but rather a social contract, a public good, a planetary institutional commons that everybody should have access to and can potentially benefit equally from. The current monetary design is not a neutral veil. Rather, its built-in myopic view, pro-cyclical tendency, inherent instability and systemic imbalances have a negative impact on the process of transformation. The money system acts like a funnel or an attractor that pulls the entire economy in either the right or the wrong direction. So alongside the traditional three forms of capital – natural, produced and human – I added a fourth: monetary capital. This fourth kind of capital affects the three others and vice versa. Any economic transformation that qualifies as *sustainable development* needs to take an intergenerational perspective and provide a solution to the problem of funding and managing our planetary commons, hedging systemic risks and managing the impact of our negative collective social and ecological externalities on any price formation. That will ultimately involve a qualified growth trajectory. The core of my argument is based on the relevance of our *planetary commons*. The very nature of such commons is that they predetermine all private business activities. The main takeaway is that the real tragedy of the commons is not their overuse or moral hazard, since commons – such as fresh water, universal healthcare or intact nature reserves – will remain the same over time. The real tragedy of the commons is that the current architecture of the IMS prevents us from harnessing their full potential. If a product, asset or service cannot be reduced, reused, repaired, rebuilt, remanufactured, resold or recycled and is meant to be a public good, service or asset, we should redesign our monetary system to reflect that fact. Kuhn's notion of 'paradigm shifts' helps us to understand these processes. Instead of optimising the existing rules of the game, we need to change them. The traditional ways of financing our future, namely taxation schemes, taxonomies, loan restructuring, austerity policies, privatisation and philanthropy (TTRAPP for short), are insufficient in scale, speed and volume to provide the means for our transformation. They are redistributive, end-of-pipe interventions with a poor evidential basis and disappointing results. All redistributive measures follow the logic of Laffer curves. There is currently no comprehensive taxation scheme available that is able to fund, manage and hedge our common future. The paradox is that all conventional tools fundamentally rely on the functionality of the existing system, which is flawed, imbalanced and unstable.

I have argued that humans' selection advantage consists in the narratives we use to explain the world. This is particularly relevant for finance and economics. Multiple price formation, indicating the scarcity of goods and services, is a function of the narrative we apply, not the other way round. Meaning that if we change the story, we change the relative formation of prices. I used the metaphor of a spiral staircase to describe the overall narrative of an economics of transformation. Transformation is not a line, a square or a circle, but rather proceeds up a series of steps and levels that we can either successfully ascend – or else fall back down. In the face of multiple unknowns, risks and uncertainties, which turn economic activities into physical, political and transitional risks, all reflecting potential costs, losses, benefits and revenue, efficiency measures need to be complemented by resilience measures that bring us to an 'anti-fragile zone' where we achieve the optimum level of sustainable development. Our native mind is prone to short-termism, geared towards proportional and linear relations and generally risk-averse. It operates within the 'middle dimension' of metres and minutes, using incomplete and (partly) false information. All these features make it impossible for us to fully grasp and manage long-term decisions and increasing complexity. We humans, never fully adapted to our environment, need a crutch to help us bridge the gap. In particular, we need cultural achievements, new technologies (such as AI) and an upgraded monetary system that allow us to cope with ever-increasing complexity and adapt to an ever-changing environment.

My discussion of the *conversion rate* provided some preliminary insights into how high the annual rate of transformation should be, considering all incomes and wages along the entire value chain. A figure substantially higher than the current annual growth rate is needed to ensure a shift from a fossil to a green marketplace. The concept of a *conditioned multiplier* can help us to better grasp this process: additional, conditioned liquidity injected into the economy will provide numerous positive and desirable second-round effects that promote a greener future. The *20:80 Pareto ratio* offers a practical rule of thumb for how the fiscal and monetary components, both of which are necessary for any investment, should be balanced out. This leads us to a *monetary triangulation* that is able to overcome the opposition between economic activities and ecological boundaries. It can also provide a means to mitigate if not overcome the well-known *open economy trilemma*, where national sovereignty, democratic politics and global integration stand in opposition to each other. CBDCs and CBCSs seem to be perfect candidates for providing a new monetary supply aggregate and monetary channels. That would in turn make it possible to offer conditioned liquidity assistance (M^{cola}), which could act like grease, a buffer or an enabler for an economics of transformation in the 21st century. There is no regulatory incentive that can completely eliminate moral hazards and irrational pro-cyclical herd behaviours, but we can keep them to a minimum. An ad hoc, automatic, predetermined and conditioned monetary supply aggregate would make a substantial contribution to that aim, reducing pro-cyclical herd behaviours and the destabilising effect of currency carry traders and HFT, while also helping to address the systemic monetary asymmetry we are faced with: countries with a strong convertible currency that have the sovereign right to print money can act anti-cyclically in the event of a shock, but other countries cannot. Whenever the Global South is hit by a shock, increasing debt loads and risk premiums, capital outflows and investor freezes pro-cyclically exacerbate the crisis. Take sovereign bonds, for instance: if risks are perceived as higher, interest rates will go up and decrease the face value of the bonds, which further decreases the value of the assets held by banks, which in turn reduces those banks' lending capacity and causes recession in the domestic economy, further reducing the government's tax revenue and increasing the initial risks. These toxic feedback loops require an upfront buffer and an ad hoc, automatic monetary response within a predetermined corridor and set of benchmarks. This is universally true for all unforeseen events. As soon as the WHO declares a pandemic, or the FAO declares a harvest default, or a residential area is flooded, the necessary liquidity would be released – with the condition that it be used to mitigate and/or improve adaptation to the next shock. Only if we have a mechanism in place that acts quickly, upfront and early enough to avoid additional damage can we reasonably assume that we are on track for successful transformation. That would usher in a new monetary ecosystem. Parallelising our currency regime appears counterintuitive at first glance, since it seems to increase the regulatory load and decrease the efficiency of financial transactions. But in fact the opposite is true, and the process has already begun. It started with a bifurcation of interest rates, differentiating between green and brown investments. We could extend this to the entire bond purchasing programmes, introduce green CBDCs and CBCSs with conditioned digital contracts and finally end up with a parallel green marketplace where additional green taxation schemes and multiple positive feedback loops would help us to shift from an adverse state to a more beneficial one. In the resulting monetary ecosystem, green dollars, euros and yen would be gradually introduced alongside the current currency regime – complementing rather than competing with it. These new currencies would operate on different channels and serve different purposes, reflecting the reality of the multipolar world of the 21st century. This is what the entire transformation process is about, and is where the role of the monetary system becomes obvious. That has far-reaching implications for our economic activities. I conclude that there is a trade-off between the law of entropy, which asserts that chaos and disorder will increase, on the one side and the law of evolution, which posits an increase of ordered complexity in the biological and social realms, on the other. As long as the marginal increase of entropy (expressed as waste and negative externalities) remains lower than the marginal increase of ordered complexity, the second law of thermodynamics and the law of evolution will not be violated. Instead, a viable path will be created for human societies and their economic activities. This has further consequences for the traditional production function, which completely leaves out *energy* and *money* as relevant variables for explaining economic output. An *adjusted monetary production function* can remedy that flaw.

Taking this point to the next level, we could postulate that if we fully factored in the power of money, we could live in a *near-zero-cost world*. A world where commons and externalities are funded, and the only additional costs are the costs of preventing the next shock. All other private economic activities will remain within an equilibrium of supply and demand, losses and gains, jobs and profits – simply reflecting the *creative destruction* of fair market competition. This has further consequences. We could speculate about the traditional DCF analysis that prioritises short-term thinking. A mental exercise that invites us to change perspective and imagine introducing a negative interest rate provides a strong, though theoretical, argument for the idea that money is a social contract and not a natural law. Adopting this idea would help us to think and act with a view to the long term. Further examples demonstrate the power of an adjusted monetary system that can open up almost unlimited options and possibilities for the financial sector, such as green transition plans to mobilise private capital or smart digital contracts for currencies that provide more transparency, lower the costs of transactions and address black and shadow-market activities and their negative impact on the economy. I also introduced the notion of a *monetary inflation brake*, which would allow us to better cope with increasing energy and food price inflation. Finally, the monetary system itself has become a geopolitical tool. We could adopt an improved version of the model that was historically used to fund the British Empire during the Commonwealth era, and was later used in the US petrodollar system and China's Belt and Road Initiative; in all these cases, a country uses its monetary supremacy so that it can print money and fund its political agenda. Based on the idea of an *optimum currency area (OCA)*, the EU could use its geopolitical and monetary power to implement a *peace and wealth belt*. I applied these ideas to the new, green Bretton Woods moment, all in line with the general assumption that we must upgrade the rules of the monetary game so that we can adapt the IMF, World Bank and WTO to meet the challenges of the 21st century. We could conclude that transformation does not come for free. It involves the economic costs of welfare losses and the political costs of instability and polarisation. Both add up. But any *business-as-usual (BAU)* or *wait-and-see (WAS)* scenario will be even more expensive. The required *business-under-transformation (BUT)* approach will be costly too, but less so than any other scenario. A BUT approach highlights two cost components: the costs of future shocks, backlashes and feedback loops, and the costs to adapt to and mitigate these shocks. Both these components add up, too. From a purely financial perspective, a BUT scenario reflects the costs of multiple trade-offs. That includes trade-offs between regions, between generations, between the private and public sectors, between rich and poor households and rich and poor countries, between economic activities and ecological externalities and finally between economics as a whole and its political agendas. In short: trade-offs of opposites, like state versus market, ecology versus economy, private versus public goods, are the most important and significant indicators of the need for an economic transition. If there were no trade-offs at all, there would be no need for transformation. Identifying, rebalancing, managing, funding and finally reconciling such trade-offs is a major challenge for any economics of transformation. And financing these trade-offs will not come for free, but will require additional liquidity and specific, qualified financial engineering tools. If the expected costs of an incident of loss or damage, a disaster, identified risk factors or adverse conditions significantly exceed the traditional growth corridor, then traditional measures, including fees and taxation schemes, will be insufficient and ineffective. The response to such events can then best be described as a case of secondary prevention. We have already triggered the loss or disaster, the risk or the adverse condition and must expect (exponentially) rising costs in the near future. In such cases, an augmented, risk-adjusted monetary policy can act like a secondary preventive measure that can help to mitigate and reduce the expected costs. So that instead of finance driving sustainability, sustainability drives finance – opening up almost unlimited new financial engineering tools for our economics of transformation. In other words: finance should remain agnostic about whether we invest in solar fusion, synthetic biology, robotics or AI, but once a society settles on one of those alternatives, the financial sector should be able to provide the specific financial means to invest in it. And finance should remain agnostic about the level of a minimum wage, the desirability of universal healthcare and whether or not we should fund restoration of our nature reserves, but once a certain course of action has been decided upon it should provide the most efficient monetary and fiscal means to pursue it. To summarise: answering the questions '*What* should we finance?' or 'in which society we would like to live in?' is a task for the whole of society, whereas answering the distinct question '*How* can we finance the decisions we have made?' is a task for the financial sector. If we recognise this distinction, we will be able to usher in a phase of transformation, where we might not get much richer and wealthier, as we will have to reallocate resources to adapt to, mitigate, compensate for and hedge all the externalities we created in the first place, but if this shift towards a new equilibrium is successful we will ultimately become less poor, less sick, less vulnerable and richer in experience than if we embarked on the journey without all the financial tools described in this book.

As a final note: I believe that the monetary mechanisms described in this book would provide a competitive geopolitical advantage for any country that is prepared to implement them before others do, irrespective of that country's political agenda, since these mechanisms will enable the first mover to manage the future better than its political opponents. However, I am aware that this is a far-reaching claim that goes well beyond financial economics.

F: Appendices

Excursus 1: The Grammar of Social Development

Evolution is an indisputable process, stretched between the second law of thermodynamics and a path of ever-increasing consciousness (see excursus 2). I would like to take a closer look at the evolutionary process in general and the grammar of social development in particular, in order to more precisely define the role of economics and finance in this interplay. The most prominent features, as discussed earlier in the book, are the key role played by the monetary system in relation to planetary commons and the impact of negative externalities on our welfare, well-being and wealth. The development of consciousness – the inner part of the overall process of evolution – is characterised by a series of stages and levels. This is true for cognitive, emotional, behavioural, sensorimotor, moral, spiritual and motivational development. It also holds true for the ontogenetic development of individuals and the phylogenetic development of societies as a whole. Despite different authors exploring different sectors of development and applying different scales and levels of granularity to explain and characterise this evolution, one common thread is that humans evolve along a series of stages and levels.[388] Despite different research agendas, these works and studies also share a common understanding of human development as characterised by increasing complexity and increasing consciousness, which enables individuals and societies to potentially 'see more and do better'. This means that intermediary results are always 'true but incomplete', so that 'nobody is 100% wrong'. Rather, each person's perspective represents a relevant and significant, but fractured and fragmented part of the whole. And each level or stage provides a unique way to interpret the world that respects previous interpretations while criticising their limitations and moving beyond them to the next level. If successful development fails, we will end up either regressing, denying upcoming challenges or fuelling various forms of dissociation, so that elements of any future development remain fractured and split apart.[389] Either way is associated with additional costs and risks, which have to be factored in. Empirical studies have shown that around 75% of people across the world hold an *ego- or ethnocentric worldview*: that is to say, one dominated by basic needs, a 'sur-

---

388 Wilber 2024.
389 The extreme fragmentation we have witnessed in modernity is one of the most prominent historical examples. In modern times, we began separating different spheres of value. Politics, economics, science and religion each lay claim to their own areas of responsibility and follow their own unique agendas and forms of rationality. But the separation went too far, so that these spheres became disconnected and their interior aspect (consciousness and culture) was reduced to the exterior one (matter and technology). This subtle reductionism, whether mechanistic, atomistic or materialistic in form, ultimately denied the entire interior realm as an independent part of our reality. See Habermas 1988; Taylor 2024; Wilber 2024.

https://doi.org/10.1515/9783111421520-007

vival mode', primary emotions and mythological and magical ways of thinking, in which group identity, conformism and fundamentalism determine the way the inner and outer worlds are interpreted. Rationality and critical thinking, as expressed in research and development, follow the rules of different value spheres and remain within the bounds of academic disciplines and silos. A *world-centric view* further integrates the ethnocentric perspective and applies universal standards such as human rights, advocates principles such as a basic income and planetary commons and takes a systems-thinking approach that factors in the impact of new general-purpose technologies.[390] An *integral approach*, finally, can acknowledge both the accomplishments and the limitations of previous stages, and provide a framework to position and evaluate all the different levels. This means that an integral worldview will integrate group identity *and* universal rights, basic needs *and* different value spheres, technological and scientific progress *and* the overall connectedness to nature. The table below (Table 17) summarises these different levels of social development.

Table 17: The grammar of social development.

Worldview	% of population	Characteristics
Integral	5%	Holistic view
World-centric	20%	Universal rights
Ethnocentric	40%	Group identity
Egocentric	35%	Basic needs

This has significant implications for social innovations and financial architecture. If the vast majority of the world population is not ready to adopt a world-centric or integral worldview, any social push for global governance will remain a pipe dream. The proposals made in this book are at the borderline between an ethnocentric and a world-centric view. The underlying principle is that we should aim for an IMS that respects the level of consciousness of the majority of the world population, which tends to be nationalistic and group-centred, while trying to provide the means for the best next step, where planetary visions become a reasonable choice. Therefore, instead of calling for global governance, I instead advocate updating and adjusting existing financial institutions, in particular central banks and the Bretton Woods institutions. The proposals in this book do not outline an ideal, hypothetical financial market, a greenfield experiment or a theory of the best of all possible worlds, but rather a politically feasible, logical next step in the evolution of the monetary system and its impact on our common future. A more detailed description is provided in the table below (Table 18), based on a distinction between pre-conventional, conventional and post-conventional stages or levels of our social development. Whereas the world-

---

390 Keagan 1982; World Values Survey Association 2023; Wilber 2024.

views and social developments at a pre-conventional level are grouped around *concretism*, the conventional worldview favours *causalities* and the post-conventional level then identifies *complementary pairs* to describe the world. Each time, the inner and outer worlds are interpreted differently, and each time the understanding of money and finance will differ. The pre-conventional levels of development are similar to the post-conventional ones inasmuch as they both emphasise collaborative and collective reality. But they differ in that at a pre-conventional level, ego functions, personality traits and individuality have not yet been differentiated. We should therefore speak of a first-tier collectivism, where individual choices are not yet possible, and a second-tier collectivism, where individual rights are adequately acknowledged.

Table 18: The developmental logic of social evolution.

Developmental level	Emotional/cognitive characteristics	Form of consciousness	Relationships with collective/social
Post-conventional	Integrative, embracing all perspectives, reciprocal tolerance, cooperative, altruistic, solidarity, sustainability, long-term priorities, humility, grace, bliss	Transpersonal, multiple roles and perspectives, inclusive, complementarities, universal and pluralistic, empathic, multiple time framework, synchronicities, collectivism	Self-transcendence, multicultural human rights, universal fairness, openness, assimilation, integral praxis, global relationships
Conventional	Concrete, operational, linear, rational, competitive, short-term priorities, self-development	Ego-based/individualistic, socio- and ethnocentric, causal/analytical, linear timeframe, historical perspectives, self-authorship	Differentiation of value spheres, science, legal systems, nation states, functional specialisation, imperialism, technocratic development, experimental praxis
Pre-conventional	Fusion of object and idea, instinctive, unsocialised, psycho-biologically determined (needs, emotions, motivations), here/now priorities, survival mode	Autism, primary narcissism, pre-personal, symbiotic, archaic, collectively determined role identity, cyclical timeframe, first-tier collectivism	Belonging, security, connectedness to nature, magical/mythological worldview, magical/mythological determinism, ritualised praxis

Excursus 2: Eternity, Entropy, Evolution and Economics

There seems to be an obvious contradiction between the second law of thermodynamics, which refers to the law of entropy, and the increasing complexity, order and consciousness that has evolved throughout our planet's history. Whereas the law of entropy claims there will be ongoing decay, disorder and disarray along an irreversible linear time axis, with waste, chaos and unavailable energy determining the course of history, the trajectory of evolution suggests the opposite, with development characterised by increasing complexity, consciousness and order, and the time axis leading to greater wholeness and completeness; instead of finite disarray, evolution progresses towards infinite permutations and possibilities.[391] It seems that evolution is stretched between entropy and eternity. Whereas the law of entropy represents the external part that we can put our finger on, that we can touch and measure, the path to eternity reflects the internal aspect of subjective experiences and perceptions of, and collective beliefs about, that evolution. This seems to be true not only in the biological realm, with regard to the evolution of species and the selection advantage of the fittest and best adapted, but also with regard to the social and cultural evolution of humankind.[392] Focusing solely on the external part of evolution subtly perpetuates a mechanistic, materialistic and atomistic reductionism. And vice versa: referring solely to the ever-increasing complexity and consciousness ignores the biophysical laws of limits, boundaries and finite resources.[393] Evolution, then, is characterised by stages and levels, lines and frames, that help us to translate and transform, to progress and regress, so that transitory order is generated out of chaos and self-organising, emergent and autopoetic phenomena preordain a 'creative advance into novelty'.[394] This means that development and evolution become an indisputable given, following the path of a spiral staircase.[395] There are three major catalysts that have furnished us

---

391 I refer to eternity in the sense of a state in the development of our consciousness that transcends time and space and enables a timeless and spaceless state of being. In the vast literature of perennial philosophy, this is referred to as the 'timeless now'. Other traditions call it *samadhi, sunyata, satori,* one taste, *ananda* or ultimate bliss. See Wilber 2024; Spencer 2012.

392 One cornerstone of social evolution is the 'cognitive revolution' that occurred some 50,000 years ago, which led to humans developing the capacity for storytelling, music, art and visionary thinking. That increased the inner mental space between stimulus and response, and greatly influenced the future development of humankind.

393 Ilya Prigogine and Isabelle Stengers (1984) introduced the concept of 'dissipative structures'. These structures occur when a high energy jump, defined as higher output per input (or energy return on investment, EROI), enables a higher order to emerge out of chaos, complexity and new and multiple equilibriums. Energy jumps have been key determinants of human evolution, which have allowed us to attain higher levels of wealth and well-being. I am grateful to Ugo Bardi (July 2024) for bringing this point to my attention.

394 Whitehead 1929.

395 This requires us to distinguish between two fundamental questions: firstly, why is there evolution and, secondly, what is evolving? The first question is the harder one and has yet to be answered. The

with the means to ascend that staircase: firstly, shifts in our mindset;[396] secondly, new technologies;[397] and thirdly, the financial sector. This book applies these general ideas to the field of economics and finance. Financial economics finds itself exposed to, and has to respect, both the biophysical laws of nature and the ever-increasing complexity of our consciousness. In this book, I have identified finance as one of the crucial but overlooked factors that either enables or hinders that development. The design of the monetary system appears to be an important determinant of whether we successfully progress up the staircase or tumble down it. And it is the financial sector that provides the institutional incentives to leverage, hedge, rebalance, fund and manage this development. Assuming a situation where there is no financial system in place at all, where we have to rely solely on human ingenuity and charity, we would end up in the endless zero-sum Malthusian cycles that humans were trapped in for centuries before the modern financial system was established. Meaning that if the monetary system is not updated to meet the challenges we are facing and does not align with biophysical reality on the one side and increasing complexity and consciousness on the other, we risk going down the staircase rather than up it. This point is illustrated in the figure below (Figure 50).

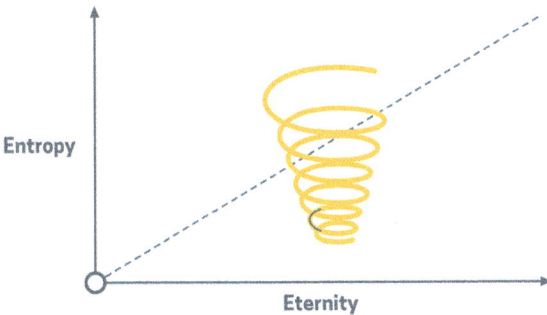

Figure 50: The law of entropy – eternity and evolution.

---

answer to the second is that it is complexity, completeness and consciousness itself that are evolving. We literally start from soil and end up with soul.

396 The process of changing our mental frames and mindsets involves education, contemplative practices and the use of psychedelic drugs. All three methods can bring about a shift in our individual and collective consciousness, allowing us to perceive inner and outer reality in a different way. But we are then caught in an 'individuality trap' that makes individuals responsible for the entire development process and neglects the institutional framework within which it occurs.

397 This refers mainly to general-purpose technologies and inventions, such as the wheel, the printing press, the steam engine, electricity and AI. If they are unregulated, general-purpose technologies tend to create oligopolies and drive inequality and disempowerment. But there is no natural law or 'destiny' that binds technologies to a certain outcome; rather, how they are used is a social and political choice. See Acemoglu and Johnson 2023.

> **Box 47:** Entropy, evolution and eternity
> First, entropy (*En*) increases over time:
>
> $En[t2] > En[t1]$
>
> Eternity (*Et*) is defined as a path along a time axis (*t+*) of ever-increasing consciousness (*con*), ordered complexity (*cx*) and completeness (*com*):
>
> $En[t2](con, cx, com) > En[t1](con, cx, com)$
>
> Entropy and eternity are the two vectors within which any successful evolution occurs. At any given time, successful evolution will result if the marginal increase of entropy is smaller than the marginal increase of consciousness, ordered complexity and completeness or wholeness.

In other words: the flatter the gradient, the greater the complexity and consciousness and the less the entropic factor per unit of time will be. Evolution in general and economic progress in particular then become a path from meaningless noise to meaningful narratives, from chaos to complexity, from unconsciousness to consciousness. The monetary system can make a substantial contribution to this gradient.

Appendix 1: Abbreviations

ABS	Asset-backed security	**IGO**	Intergovernmental organisation
ACS	Advance commitment strategy	**ILO**	International Labour Organization
AFZ	Anti-fragile zone	**IMF**	International Monetary Fund
AuM	Assets under management	**IoT**	Internet of Things
B2B	Business to business	**LIC**	Low-income country
B2P	Business to private	**MDB**	Multilateral development bank
BEPS	Base erosion and profit shifting	**MENA**	Middle East and North Africa
BRI	Belt and Road Initiative	**MIC**	Middle-income country
BRICS+	Brazil, Russia, India, China, South Africa and others	**MSMEs**	Micro-, small and medium-sized enterprises
		NFC	Near-field communication
CBCS	Central bank currency swap	**OCA**	Optimum currency area
CBDC	Central bank digital currency	**ODA**	Official development aid
CCUS	Carbon capture, utilisation and storage	**OECD**	Organization for Economic Cooperation and Development
CDS	Credit default swap		
CFC	Chlorofluorocarbon	**P3S**	Public to third sector
COLA	Conditioned liquidity assistance	**PCCP**	Public central clearing counter-party
CPC	Communist Party of China	**PPP**	Purchasing power parity
CPI	Consumer price index	**ROI**	Return on investment
DCF	Discounted cash flow	**SDR**	Special drawing right
EBITA	Earnings before income and tax	**TCA**	Total cost analysis
ETI	Elasticity of taxable income	**UN-SDGs**	United Nations Sustainable Development Goals
FAO	Food and Agriculture Organization		
FDI	Foreign direct investment	**VAT**	Value-added tax
GDP	Gross domestic product	**VCPE**	Venture capital private equity
HFT	High-frequency trading	**WB**	World Bank
HICP	Harmonised Index of Consumer Prices	**WHO**	World Health Organization
ICS	Investment court system	**WTO**	World Trade Organization
IDA	International development assistance	**WWF**	Worldwide Fund for Nature
IFF	Illicit financial flow		

Appendix 2: Formalising the Economics of Transformation

Business under transformation (BUT) is different from business as usual (BAU). Unlike conventional business cycles, in a BUT scenario the entire value chain is under construction. BUT requires substantially more liquidity than BAU to fund transformative measures. Modern domestic economies with an integrated global financial sector are characterised by a systemic asymmetry between return on capital (r) and the growth rate of the real economy (g).

[1]
$$r > g$$

This asymmetry increases volatility, instability, inequality and resource depletion, and impacts on real estate prices and consumption patterns. In a closed planetary economy, we are exposed to additional expenditures (e) resulting from negative externalities (Ex), underfunded commons (Co) and the mobilisation of risk-averse private capital (mpC), which will further increase this asymmetry.

[2]
$$r >> g - e$$
[3]
$$e = Ex + Co + mpC$$

If we start redistributing (re) liquidity through taxation or credit lines only $r^{re} >> g^{re} - e$, we can expect this to further aggravate the asymmetry. Taxation will withdraw and redirect purchasing power and credit lines will amplify the debt trap, causing toxic cascades and drain-out effects for the entire economy. A *liquidity trap*, where money is withdrawn from the value chain, and the *tragedy of the horizon*, where shocks affect the economy along a different timeline, will further prevent any adequate resource allocation and the required transformation. The equilibrium will remain Pareto-inferior.

[4]
$$r^{re} >> g^{re} - e$$

By introducing a qualified monetary aggregate (M^*), comprising an additional monetary supply aggregate (M^{cola}) plus fiscal measures (Fm) in line with an 80:20 Pareto ratio, we can provide any economy with the means for transformation.

[5]
$$M^* = (M^{cola} + Fm)$$

If we then add this qualified monetary aggregate to the initial equation, the playing field for transformation will change fundamentally.

[6]
$$r + M^* > g$$

We therefore have to claim, that financing the expected additional expenses (e) through redistributing liquidity only, creates a larger negative net welfare effect, then considering M^*. Since M^* is conditioned to finance externalities and underfunded planetary commons and to mobilise private capital, M^*, Ex, Co and mpC will all tend to zero.

[7] $$M^* \Rightarrow 0$$
[8] $$e \Rightarrow 0$$
[9] $$Ex + Co + mpC \Rightarrow 0$$

If we take a secondary preventive approach in finance, assuming that the damage to planet and people has already been done, any regime under M^* will be superior to any BAU, measured by consumer prices (CPI) at any given time (t^n).

[10] $$CPI(t^n)^{BAU} > CPI(t^n)^{BUT}.$$

We will then ultimately end up with a new equilibrium, where qualified green capital gains (r^*) are almost equal to a qualified green growth rate (g^*). Over time, this will give rise to a new Pareto-superior equilibrium.

[11] $$r^* \geqq g^*$$

That would bring about a next-to-zero-cost world, as each capital gain on the one side would match the income, profits and shares on the other. We would have an economy with reduced instability, volatility and income inequality and higher wealth and well-being. Some scholars characterise this new equilibrium as an ecological, regenerative, steady-state or circular economy, or what the Swedish call a 'lagom' economy: a 'just enough' economy that reconciles individual freedom and common goods.

G: Summary (short)

This book attempts to upgrade J. M. Keynes's 'general theory' to meet the needs of the 21st century. It provides the foundations for a new general theory and proposes innovative financial engineering tools to manage negative collective externalities and planetary commons and unlock the private capital needed to fund, hedge and manage our common future. Instead of operating within the existing rules, Brunnhuber argues that we need to introduce new rules of the game, so that monetary instruments are given priority over fiscal ones, regulators and central banks become key players and a new monetary supply aggregate equips us to deal with serial asymmetric shocks, rising costs and risks. *The Economics of Transformation* sparks a debate on how to finance our transition to a better economic system.

https://doi.org/10.1515/9783111421520-008

H: Summary (long)

J. M. Keynes is considered one of the most influential economists of the 20th century. This book outlines some foundations for a new general theory of money, ways of funding our planetary commons and sustainable development for the 21st century. Living in the Anthropocene era, we are confronted with serial asymmetric shocks, unfettered negative externalities, underfunded planetary commons and a risk-averse, pro-cyclical, short-termist private sector. These factors require an update to Keynes's foundational ideas. Instead of nation states providing an anti-cyclical demand stabiliser to rebalance imperfect market allocation, Brunnhuber argues that regulators and central banks should provide additional, conditioned liquidity in the form of a digital supply aggregate to master these challenges. The major game changers that will facilitate an economics of transformation include new, unconventional monetary channels, new technologies (e.g. blockchains), new forms of money (e.g. central bank digital currencies, central bank currency swaps, adapted green monetary easing and conditioned special drawing rights). By contrast with a cyclical process of booms and busts, transformational processes are best described by the metaphor of a staircase that economic actors can climb up and down. That requires us to introduce new rules of the game, instead of optimising the existing ones. *The Economics of Transformation* describes the crucial role of the international monetary system and its intrinsic architecture, offering a systems view that goes beyond traditional economic schools. If planetary commons and negative externalities are properly funded and managed and the necessary private capital unlocked, we will find ourselves in a next-to-zero-cost world. That would also have implications for the role of black and informal-market activities, and would help to curb rising imported food and energy costs. Brunnhuber also sets out elements of a preliminary green transition plan and explains the foundational role of money as a geopolitical tool to promote peace and security. Implementing the additional monetary supply aggregate recommended in this book would require an approach that goes beyond conventional measures (taxation, taxonomies, restructuring loans and debts, austerity, privatisation, philanthropy). This approach would create a new optimum currency area and usher in a Bretton Woods 2.0 moment, ultimately reconciling profits and return on capital with a green, sustainable future. The book concludes with some critical remarks on the relation between entropy and economics and the grammar of social development.

https://doi.org/10.1515/9783111421520-009

References

Absolut Research (2024): Einfluss des Klimawandels auf die Inflation, https://www.absolut-research.de/detail/n/einfluss-des-klimawandels-auf-die-inflation/.

Acemoglu, Daron; Johnson, Simon; Robinson, James (2001): "The Colonial Origins of Comparative Development: An Empirical Investigation", American Economic Review, 91, 1369–1401.

Acemoglu, Daron; Robinson, James (2012): Why Nations Fail, New York: Crown Business.

Acemoglu; Daron, Johnson, Simon (2023): Power and Progress: Our Thousand-Year Struggle over Technology and Prosperity, London: Basic Books.

Adger, W. Neil et al. (2022): "Climate Change Affects Multiple Dimensions of Well-Being through Impacts, Information and Policy Responses", in: Nature Human Behaviour 6, 1465–1473, https://doi.org/10.1038/s41562-022-01467-8.

Adrian, Tobias; Ashcraft, Adrian (2016): "Shadow Banking: A Review of the Literature", in: Banking Crises: Perspectives from The New Palgrave Dictionary, London: Palgrave, 282–315, https://doi.org/10.1057/9781137553799_29.

Adrian, Tobias; Jones, Bradley (2018): Shadow Banking and Market-Based Finance, IMF Monetary and Capital Markets Department No. 18/14, https://doi.org/10.5089/9781484343883.087.

African Development Bank Group (2022): Annual Report 2021, https://www.afdb.org/en/documents/annual-report-2021.

Agarwal, Ruchir; Gopinath, Gita (2021): A Proposal to End the COVID-19 Pandemic, Staff Discussion Notes, International Monetary Fund, https://www.imf.org/en/Publications/Staff-Discussion-Notes/Issues/2021/05/19/A-Proposal-to-End-the-COVID-19-Pandemic-460263.

Aguiar, Mark et al. (2019): "Take the Short Route: Equilibrium Default and Debt Maturity", in: Econometrica, 87/2, 423–462, https://doi.org/10.3982/ECTA14806.

Aigner, John (2019): „The Unstoppable Surge in Negative Yields Reaches $17 Trillion", in: Broadcast by Bloomberg, 23 December 2019, https://www.bloomberg.com/graphics/negative-yield-bonds/.

Akgiray, Vedat (2019): Gold Finance, Why we need a new concept pf finance, Bristol: Bristol University Press

Alberti, Caroline (2024): The Cost of Inaction, Climate Policy Initiative, https://www.climatepolicyinitiative.org/the-cost-of-inaction/.

Alfonso, António; Schuknecht, Ludger; Tanzi, Vito (2006): Public Sector Efficiency: Evidence for New EU Member States and Emerging Markets, European Central Bank Working Paper No. 571, https://www.ecb.europa.eu/pub/pdf/scpwps/ecbwp581.pdf.

Anderson, Alan M.; Beaumont, Ben (Eds.) (2020): The Investor State Dispute Settlement System, Alphen aan den Rijn: Kluwer Law International.

Armanious, Amir (2024): "Too-Systemic-to-Fail: Empirical Comparison of Systemic Risk Measures in the Eurozone Financial System", in: Journal of Financial Stability, 73, 101273, https://doi.org/10.1016/j.jfs.2024.101273.

Atlantic Council (2024): Central Bank Digital Currency Tracker, https://www.atlanticcouncil.org/cbdctracker/.

Attridge, Samantha; Engen, Lars (2019): Blended Finance in the Poorest Countries. The Need for a Better Approach, London: ODI.

Aurobindo, Ghose (1997): Complete Works of Sri Aurobindo, 36 Volumes, Puducherry: Sri Aurobindo Ashram Publication Department.

Axelrod, Robert (2006): The Evolution of Cooperation, Revised Edition, New York: Basic Books.

Ayers, Robert (2016): Energy, Complexity and Wealth Maximization, The Frontiers Collection, Switzerland: Springer.

https://doi.org/10.1515/9783111421520-010

Bachmann, Rüdiger et al. (2022): Was wäre, wenn . . .? Die wirtschaftlichen Auswirkungen eines Importstopps russischer Energie auf Deutschland, ifo Schnelldienst, 75, https://www.ifo.de/publikatio nen/2022/aufsatz-zeitschrift/was-waere-wenn-die-wirtschaftlichen-auswirkungen-eines#:~:text=Die% 20wirtschaftlichen%20Auswirkungen%20eines%20möglichen,5%25%20und%203%25%20führen.

Bainbridge, David A. (2023): Accountability: Why We Need to Count Social and Environmental Cost for A Livable Future, New York: Rio Redondo Press.

Banerjee, Onil et al. (2022): "Can we avert an Amazon tipping point? The economic and environmental costs", in: Environ. Res. Lett., 17, 1250005, https://iopscience.iop.org/article/10.1088/1748-9326/aca3b8.

Banuri, Sheheryar; Ha, Nguyen (2020): Borrowing to Keep Up (With the Joneses): Inequality, Debt, and Conspicuous Consumption, http://dx.doi.org/10.2139/ssrn.3721084.

Barman, Emily (2018): "Doing Well by Doing Good: A Comparative Analysis of ESG Standards for Responsible Investment", in: Sustainability, Stakeholder Governance, and Corporate Social Responsibility (Advances in Strategic Management, Vol. 38), Leeds: Emerald Publishing Limited, 289–311, https://doi.org/10.1108/S0742-332220180000038016.

Barro, Robert J. (1996): Determinants of Economic Growth: A Cross-Country Empirical Study, NBER Working Paper 5698, National Bureau of Economic Research, Cambridge, Massachusetts.

Bartlett, Bruce (2012): The Benefit and The Burden: Tax Reform-Why We Need It and What It Will Take by Bruce Bartlett, New York et al.: Simon & Schuster.

Basel Committee on Banking Supervision (2022): Principles for the Effective Management and Supervision of Climate Rated Financial Risks, BIS, https://www.bis.org/bcbs/publ/d532.htm.

Bateson, Gregory (1972): Steps to an Ecology of Mind: Collected Essay in Anthropology, Psychiatry, Evolution, and Episemology, London, Nothvale, NJ.: Jason Aronson Inc.

Bateson, Nora (2016): Small Arcs of Larger Circles: Framing Through Other Patterns, Station Offices, Axminster, England: Triarchy Press.

Batten, Sandra; Sowerbitts, Rhihannon; Tanaka, Misa (2020): "Climate Change. Macroeconomic Impact and Implications for Monetary Policy", in: Walker, Thomas et al. (Eds). Ecological, Societal and Technological Risks and the Financial Sector, London, Palgrave Macmillan, 13–38;

Battiston, Stefano et al. (2012): "DebtRank: Too Central to Fail? Financial Networks, the FED and Systemic Risk", in: Scientific Report 2/54, https://doi.org/10.1038/srep00541.

Battiston, Stefano et al. (2021): "Climate risks and financial stability", in: Journal for Financial Stability 54, 100867, https://doi.org/10.1016/j.jfs.2021.100867.

Baum, Seth; Handoh, Itsuki C. (2014): "Integrating the planetary boundaries and global catastrophic risk paradigms", in: Ecological Economics 107, 13–21,

Beirne, John et al. (2022): Natural Disasters and Inflation in the Euro Area, Beiträge zur Jahrestagung des Vereins für Socialpolitik 2022: Big Data in Economics, ZBW – Leibniz Information Centre for Economics, Kiel, Hamburg, https://www.econstor.eu/bitstream/10419/264132/1/vfs-2022-pid-70653.pdf.

Beirne, J. et al. (2023). "Natural Disasters and Inflation in the Euro Area", Revised Working Paperk, https:// www.econstor.eu/bitstream/10419/264132/1/vfs-2022-pid-70653.pdf.

Bénassy-Quéré, Agnes et al. (2018): Economic Policy: Theory and Practice, Oxford: Oxford University Press.

Berg, Florian; Kölbel, Julian F., Rigobon, Roberto (2022): "Aggregate Confusion: The Divergence of ESG Ratings", in: Review of Finance 26/6, 1315–1344, https://doi.org/10.1093/rof/rfac033

Bernanke, Ben. 1982. "The Real Effects of Financial Crises: Theory and Evidence", in Federal Reserve Bank of San Francisco, Proceedings of Sixth Fall Academic Conference, November, pp. 134–162.

Bernholz, Peter; Gersbach, Hans (1992): "The Present Monetary Theory of Advanced Inflation: A Failure?", in: Journal of Institutional and Theoretical Economics (JITE) 148/4, 705–19, http://www.jstor.org/sta ble/40751559.

Beirne, J. et al. (2023). "Natural Disasters and Inflation in the Euro Area", Revised Working Paperk, https:// www.econstor.eu/bitstream/10419/264132/1/vfs-2022-pid-70653.pdf.

Beyond Bretton Woods (2024): Website: Home, https://www.beyondbrettonwoods.org.

Bilal, Adrien; Känzig, Diego R. (2024): „The Macroeconomic Impact of Climate Change: Global vs. Local Temperature", in: NBER Working Paper No. w32450, https://papers.ssrn.com/sol3/papers.cfm?abstract_id=4826056.

Blanchard, Olivier (2019): "Public Debt and Low Interest Rates", in: American Economic Review, 109/4, 1197–1229, https://www.aeaweb.org/articles?id=10.1257/aer.109.4.1197.

Blum, Matthias (2011): "Government Decisions before and during the First World War and the Living Standards in Germany during a Drastic Natural Experiment", in: Explorations in Economic History, 48/4: 556–567, https://doi.org/10.1016/j.eeh.2011.07.003.

Blum, Ulrich (2004): Volkswirtschaftslehre: Studienhandbuch, München, Wien: Oldenbourg.

Blumenberg, Hans (2014): Beschreibung des Menschen, Frankfurt: Suhrkamp.

Board of Governors of the Federal Reserve System (2020): What Happened in Money Markets in September 2019?, FEDS Notes, https://www.federalreserve.gov/econres/notes/feds-notes/what-happened-in-money-markets-in-september-2019-20200227.html.

Bohr, Niels (2008): Collected works, vol 10: Complementarity beyond physics (1928–1962). Amsterdam: Elsevier.

Böick, Marcus; Lorke, Christoph (2019): „Aufschwung, Abbau, Anpassung? Eine kleine Geschichte des ‚Aufbau Ost'", in: APuZ, 46, 32–40, https://www.bpb.de/shop/zeitschriften/apuz/300059/aufschwung-abbau-anpassung/.

Bolton, Patrick et al. (2020): The Green Swan – Central Banking and Financial Stability in the Age of Climate Change, Bank for International Settlements.

Boltzmann, Ludwig (1974): The second law of thermodynamics, Populare Schriften, Essay 3, address to a formal meeting of the Imperial Academy of Science, 29 May 1886.

Bossu, Wouter; Weenink, Hans (2021): Central Bank Exceptional Measures in the COVID-19 Crisis: Key Legal Design Issues, International Monetary Fund, Special Series on Central Bank Law Design Issues to Respond to COVID-19, Washington, DC.

Bostrom, Nick (2008): Global Catastrophic Risks, Oxford: Oxford University Press.

Boulding, Kenneth E. (1966): "The economics of the coming spaceship earth", in: Jarrett, H. (Ed.): Environmental Quality Issues in a Growing Economy, Baltimore: Johns Hopkins University Press, pp. 3–14.

Bowlby (1995) [1950]: Elternbindung und Persönlichkeitsentwicklung, Heidelberg: Dexter.

Bratton, Benjamin (2022): Die Realität schlägt zurück: Politik für eine postpandemische Welt, Berlin: Matthes & Seitz.

Braxton, John M.; Hargens, Lowell L. (1996): "Variation Among Academic Disciplines: Analytical Frameworks and Research", in: Smart, John C. (Ed): Higher Education: Handbook of Theory and Research, Volume XI, 1–46, New York: Agathon Press.

Brink, Ebba et al. (2016): "Cascades of green: A review of ecosystem-based adaptation in urban areas", in: Global Environmental Change, 36, 111–123, https://doi.org/10.1016/j.gloenvcha.2015.11.003.

Bromley, Hugh (2023): Ten Case Studies Highlight the Financial Costs of Nature Related Risk, Bloomberg, https://about.bnef.com/blog/ten-case-studies-highlight-the-financial-costs-of-nature-related-risk/.

Brouwer, Roy et al. (2022): "The economic value of the Brazilian Amazon rainforest ecosystem services: A meta-analysis of the Brazilian literature", in: PLoS One, 17/5, e0268425, https://doi.org/10.1371%2Fjournal.pone.0268425.

Brunnermeier, Markus K.; Landau, James; Landau, Jean-Pierre (2019): The Digitization of Money, Working paper 26300 NBER, http://www.nber.org/papers/w26300.

Brunnhuber, Stefan (2019): Die Offene Gesellschaft – Ein Plädoyer für Freiheit und Ordnung, München: OEKOM Verlag, München.

Brunnhuber, Stefan (2020): The Tao of Finance: The Future Wealth of Nations, München: Oekom-Verlag.

Brunnhuber, Stefan (2021): Financing Our Future: Unveiling a Parallel Digital Currency System to Fund the SDGs and the Common Good, London: Palgrave Macmillan.

Brunnhuber, Stefan (2023): Financing our Anthropocene: How Wall Street, Main Street and Central Banks Can Manage, Fund and Hedge Our Global Commons, Berlin, Heidelberg: Springer.

Brunnhuber, Stefan (2023a): Freiheit oder Zwang: Wer kann Nachhaltigkeit besser – offene Gesellschaften oder Autokratien?, München: Oekom-Verlag.

Brunnhuber, Stefan (2024): Die Kunst der Transformation, 2. Edition, München: Oekom.

Brunnhuber, Stefan (2024a): The Third Culture: The Impact of AI on Knowledge, Society and Consciousness in the 21st Century, Berlin, Heidelberg: Springer.

Brunnhuber, Stefan; Lietaer Bernhard (2005): "Economics as an Evolutionary System – Psychological Development and Economic Behaviour", in: Evolutionary and Institutional Economics Review 2, 113–139.

Buchanan, James M. (1965): "An Economic Theory of Clubs", in: Economica, 32/125, 1–14, https://doi.org/10.2307/2552442.

Buchanan, James M. (2008). "Opportunity Cost", in: Durlauf, Steven N.; Blume, Lawrence E. (Ed.), The New Palgrave Dictionary of Economics, New York: Palgrave Macmillan, http://www.dictionaryofeconomics.com.

Buchanan, Mark (2013): Forecast: What Physics, Meteorology, and the Natural Sciences Can Teach Us About Economics, London et al.: Bloomsbury.

Buchner, Barbara et al. (2023): Global Landscape of Climate Finance 2023, San Francisco et al.: Climate Policy Initiative.

Buckminster Fuller, Richard (2010): Bedienungsanleitung für das Raumschiff Erde und andere Schriften, Hamburg: FUNDUS.

Buckminster Fuller, RIchard, 2022, operating manual for spaceship earth, 11 edition, Lars müller publisher Hamburg

Bunge, Mario (2003): Emergence and Convergence: Qualitative Novelty and the Unity of Knowledge. Toronto, ON: University of Toronto Press

Byers, William (2014): Deep thinking: what mathematics can tell us about the mind, New Jersey at al.: World Scientific Publishing.

Byrne, David; Callaghan, Gillian (2023): Complexity Theory and the Social Sciences: The State of the Art, London, New York: Routledge.

Cambridge Econometrics (2020): Oil Dependency in the EU, https://te-cdn.ams3.cdn.digitaloceanspaces.com/files/2020_CE_Oil_Dependency_in_EU_report.pdf.

Capitals Force for Good (2024): Shifting the Global Order through the Mass Mobilization of Solutions, https://www.forcegood.org/cf4greport-2024.

Caverley, Jonathan D. (2018): "The economics of war and peace", in: Gheciu, Alexandra; Wohlforth, William C. (Ed.): The Oxford Handbook of International Security, 304–318 https://doi.org/10.1093/oxfordhb/9780198777854.013.20

CDP (2023): Scoping Out: Tracking Nature Across the Supply Chain, https://cdn.cdp.net/cdp-production/cms/reports/documents/000/006/918/original/CDP-Supply-Chain-Report-2022.pdf?1678870769

Centre for Thriving Places (2024): The Thriving Places Index, https://www.thrivingplacesindex.org.

Chakrabarti, Shubhra; Patnaik, Utsa (2019): Agrarian and Other Histories: Essays for Binay Bhushan Chaudhuri. New Delhi: Tulika Books.

Clausius, Rudolf (1865): Ueber verschiedene für die Anwendung bequeme Formen der Hauptgleichungen der mechanischen Wärmetheorie, Vorgetragen in der naturforsch. Gesellschaft zu Zürich den 24. April 1865, Leipzig: Johann Ambrosius Barth Verlag.

Climate Policy Initiative (2023): Global Landscape of Climate Finance 2023, https://www.climatepolicyinitiative.org/wp-content/uploads/2023/11/Global-Landscape-of-Climate-Finance-2023.pdf.

Club of Rome (2024): Rethinking Finance Impact Hub, https://www.clubofrome.org/impact-hubs/rethinking-finance/.

Coase, Ronald (1960): "The Problem of Social Cost", in: Journal of Law and Economics. 3, 1–44.

Cobb, Charles W.; Douglas. Paul H. (1928): "A Theory of Production", in: The American Economic Review 18/1, 139–165, https://www.jstor.org/stable/1811556.

Cobham, Alex; Janský, Petr (2018): "Global Distribution of Revenue Loss from Corporate Tax Avoidance: Re-Estimation and Country Results", in: Journal of International Development, 30/2, 206–232, https://doi.org/10.1002/jid.3348.

Cofco International (2024): Website: Home, https://www.cofcointernational.com.

Cojoianu, Theodor F. et al. (2020): "Entrepreneurs for a Low Carbon World: How Environmental Knowledge and Policy Shape the Creation and Financing of Green Start-ups", in: Research Policy, 49 6, https://doi.org/10.1016/j.respol.2020.103988.

Cort, T., & Esty, D. (2020): ESG Standards: Looming Challenges and Pathways Forward. Organization & Environment, 33/4, 491–510, https://doi.org/10.1177/1086026620945342.

Costanza, Robert (1980): "Embodied Energy and Economic Valuation", in: Science 210/4475, 1219–1224.

Costanza, Robert et al. (1997): The value of the world's ecosystem services and natural capital, Nature 387, 253–260, https://doi.org/10.1038/387253a0.

Credit Suisse (2021): Global Wealth Report 2021, https://www.credit-suisse.com/about-us/en/reports-research/global-wealth-report.html.

Crutzen, Paul J. (2002): "Geology of mankind", in: Nature 415, 23 (2002), https://doi.org/10.1038/415023a.

Crutzen, Paul J.; Stoermer, Eugene F. (2000): "The Anthropocene", in: IGBP Global Change Newsletter, Nr. 41, May 2000, 17–18.

Dadush, Uri; Niebuhr, Mona (2016): The Economic Impact of Forced Migration, OCP Policy Center, Research Paper April 2016, https://www.shram.org/uploadFiles/20171228014704.pdf.

Dafemos, Yannis; Nikolaidi, Maria et al. (2021): How Can Green Differentiated Captain Requirements Affects Climate Risks? A Dynamic Macrofinancial Analysis, in: Journal of Financial stability 4, 100871, https://dx.doi.org/10.2139/ssrn.3658088.

Dafermos, Yannis et al. (2020): Decarbonising is easy: Beyond market neutrality in the ECB's QE, New Economics Foundation, October.

Dahrendorf, Ralf (1973): Homo Sociologicus, Opladen, Leverkusen: Westdeutscher Verlag.

Daly, Herman (1977): Steady-State Economics, Washington, D.C.: Island Press.

Damgaard, Jannick; Elkjaer, Thomas; Johannesen, Niels (2019): The Rise of Phantom Investments. Finance & Development, 56/3, 11–13, https://www.imf.org/external/pubs/ft/fandd/2019/09/ the-rise-of-phantom-FDI-in-tax-havens-damgaard.htm.

Damodaran, Aswath (2019): Annual returns on stock, T. Bonds and T. Bills: 1928–current., Federal Reserve Database, https://pages.stern.nyu.edu/~adamodar/New_Home_Page/datale/histretSPX.html.

Danielsson, Jon (2022): The Illusion of Control: Why Financial Crises Happen, and What We Can (and Can't) Do About It, New Haven: Yale University Press, https://doi.org/10.12987/9780300265095-012.

Dasgupta, Partha (2021): The Economics of Biodiversity: The Dasgupta Review, London: HM Treasury, https://assets.publishing.service.gov.uk/media/602e92b2e90e07660f807b47/The_Economics_of_Biodiversity_The_Dasgupta_Review_Full_Report.pdf.

Debelle, Guy; Fischer, Stanley (1994): "How Independent Should a Central Bank Be?", in: Federal Reserve Bank of Boston: Conference Series 38, Boston: Federal Reserve Bank of Boston, 195–225.

Desan, Christine A. (2022): "The Key to Value (2.0): The Debate Over Commensurability in Neoclassical and Credit Approaches to Money", in: Feichtner, I. and Gordon, G. (Eds.): Constitutions of Value: Law, Governance and Political Ecology; London: Routledge.

Desjardins, Jeff (2018): "Mapped: China's Most Ambitious Megaproject – the New Silk Road", in: Business Insider, 19 March 2018, https://www.businessinsider.com/chinas-most-ambitious-megaproject-the-new-silk-road-mapped-2018-3?r=US&IR=T.

Deutz, Andrew et al. (2020): Financing Nature: Closing the Global Biodiversity Financing Gap, Chicago: Paulson Institute, https://www.paulsoninstitute.org/conservation/financing-nature-report/.

Diamon, Jared (1991): The Third Chimpanzee: The Evolution and Future of the Human Animal, London: Hutchinson.

Diem, Christian et al. (2022): "Quantifying Firm-Level Economic Systemic Risk from Nation-Wide Supply Networks", in: Scientific Reports 12/1, 7719, https://doi.org/10.1038/s41598-022-11522-z.

Diem, Christian; Pichler, Anton; Thurner, Stefan (2020): "What Is the Minimal Systemic Risk in Financial Exposure Networks?", in: Journal of Economic Dynamics and Control, 116, 103900, https://doi.org/10.1016/j.jedc.2020.103900.

Dilip, A and Kundu, S. (2020): Climate Change: Macroeconomic Impact and Policy Options for Mitigating Risks. RBI Bulletin, Reserve Bank of India.

Dill, Alexander (2023): Science shift to supporting SDGs, https://sdgs.un.org/sites/default/files/2023-05/B22%20-%20Dill%20-%20Science%20shift%20to%20supporting%20the%20SDGs.pdf

Dobson, Andrew P. et al. (2020): "Ecology and Economics for Pandemic Prevention: Investments to Prevent Tropical Deforestation and to Limit Wildlife Trade Will Protect against Future Zoonosis Outbreaks", in: Science, 369/6502, 379–381, https://doi.org/10.1126/science.abc3189.

Dooley, Michael; Folkert-Landau, David; Garber, Peter (2004): "The Revived Bretton Woods System", in: International Journal of Finance & Economics, 9/4, 307–313, https://doi.org/10.1002/ijfe.250.

Dotzauer, Marius (2023): The Popular Legitimacy of Investor State: Contestation, Crisis, and Reform, London: Routledge.

Douglas, Peter H. (1976): "The Cobb-Douglas Production Function Once Again: Its History, Its Testing, and Some New Empirical Values", in: Journal of Political Economy 84/5, 903–916, https://doi.org/10.1086/260489.

Dynamic Math (2024): Aizawa Attractor, https://www.dynamicmath.xyz/calculus/velfields/Aizawa/.

EFRAG (2024): The First set of ESRS, https://www.efrag.org/lab6.

Egmond, Klaas van; Vries, Bert de (2024): "Reforming the Eurozone Financial System: A System-Dynamics Approach", in: International Review of Financial Analysis, 93, 103192, https://doi.org/10.1016/j.irfa.2024.103192.

Ehrlich, Paul; Holdren, John P. (1971): "Impact of Population Growth: Complacency Concerning this Component of Man's Predicament is Unjustified and Counterproductive", in: Science, 171/3977, 1212–1217, https://doi.org/10.1126/science.171.3977.1212.

Eichengreen, Barry (2019): Globalizing Capital: A History of the International Monetary System, 3rd Edition, Princeton, New Jersey: Princeton University Press.

Eigen, Manfred (1987): Stufen zum Leben. Die frühe Evolution im Visier der Molekularbiologie, München: Piper.

Elderson, Frank (2022): Keynote speech by Frank Elderson, Member of Executive Board of the ECB and Vice-Chair of the Supervisory Board of the ECB, Lustrum Symposium organized by Dutch Financial Law Association, Amsterdam.

Ellis, Brian (2020): The New Enlightenment: On Steven Pinker & Beyond, Melbourne: Australian Scholarly Publishing.

European Commission (2019): Guidelines On Reporting Climate-Related Information, European Union, https://ec.europa.eu/finance/docs/policy/190618-climate-related-information-reporting-guidelines_en.pdf.

European Commission (2020): Energy Prices and Costs in Europe, Brussels, https://eur-lex.europa.eu/legal-content/EN/TXT/?qid=1602774170631&uri=CELEX:52020DC0951.

European Environment Agency (2024): European Climate Risk Assessment, EEA Report 01/2024, European Environment Agency, https://www.eea.europa.eu/publications/european-climate-risk-assessment.

Eurostat Statistics Explained (2024): EU Imports of Energy Products – Latest Developments, Brussels, https://ec.europa.eu/eurostat/statistics-explained/index.php?title=EU_imports_of_energy_products_-_latest_developments#Overview.

Falk, Armin et al. (2018): "Global Evidence on Economic Preferences", in: The Quarterly Journal of Economics 133/4, 1645–1692, https://doi.org/10.1093/qje/qjy013.

Fama, Eugene F.; MacBeth, James D. (1973): "Risk, Return, and Equilibrium: Empirical Tests", in: Journal of Political Economy, 81/3, 607–636, https://doi.org/10.1086/260061.

Farmer, J. Doyne. (2024) making sense of Chaos, a better Economics for a better world, London: Allen Lane, Penguin books

Fassnacht, Martin; Dahm, Jil-Marie (2018): „The Veblen effect and (in)conspicuous consumption – a state of the art article", in: Luxury Research Jounral, 1/4, 343–371, https://doi.org/10.1504/LRJ.2018.090989.

Feinig, Jakob (2022): Moral Economies of Money: Politics and the Monetary Constitution of Society, Stanford, CA: Stanford University Press.

Finance Watch (2024): Policy Portal, https://www.finance-watch.org/policy-portal/.

Flyvbjerg, Bent et al. (2018): "Five Things You Should Know about Cost Overrun", in: Transportation Research, Part A 118, 174–190, https://doi.org/10.1016/j.tra.2018.07.013.

Food and Agriculture Organization of the United Nations (2019): The State of Food and Agriculture: Movin Forward on Food Loss and Waste Reduction, Food and Agriculture Organization of the United Nations, https://openknowledge.fao.org/server/api/core/bitstreams/11f9288f-dc78-4171-8d02-92235b8d7dc7/content.

Force for Good (2022): Capital as a Force for Good: Capitalism for a Secure and Sustainable Future, https://www.forcegood.org/frontend/img/2022-report/pdf/2022_full_report.pdf.

Force for Good (2024): Technology as a Force for Good Technology Driving the Transition to a Superior Future, https://www.forcegood.org/frontend/img/2024-report/pdf/2024_Technology_as_a_Force_for_Good_Report_v.1.2_09-01.pdf.

Forecasting Healthy Futures (2024): Website: Home, https://forecastinghealthyfutures.org.

Foster, Sarah (2021): The repo market, explained — and why the Fed has pumped hundreds of billions into it, Bankrate, https://www.bankrate.com/banking/federal-reserve/why-the-fed-pumps-billions-into-repo-market/.

Freeman III, A. Myrick; Herriges, Joseph A.; Kling, Catherine L. (2014): The Measurement of Environmental and Resource Values: Theory and Methods, New York: Routledge. https://doi.org/10.4324/9781315780917.

Friedman, Milton (1969): The Optimum Quantity of Money, London: Macmillan.

Gaffney, Owen et al. (2021): Global Commons Survey: Attitudes to planetary stewardship and transformation among G20 countries, Global Commons Alliance, https://globalcommonsalliance.org/wp-content/uploads/2024/01/Global-Commons-G20-Survey-full-report.pdf.

Gahvari, Firouz (1989): "The Nature of Government Expenditures and the Shape of the Laffer Curve", in: Journal of Public Economics, 40/2, 251–260, https://doi.org/10.1016/0047-2727(89)90006-6.

Gal, David (2006): "A Psychological Law of Inertia and the Illusion of Loss Aversion", in: Judgment and Decision Making, 1/1: 23–32, https://doi.org/10.1017/S1930297500000322.

Galiani, Sebastian; Schargrodsky, Ernesto (2010): Property Rights for the Poor: Effects of Land Titling, ocumento de Trabajo, No. 103, Universidad Nacional de La Plata, Centro de Estudios Distributivos, Laborales y Sociales (CEDLAS), La Plata.

Gallagher, Kevin P.; Kozul-Wright, Richard (2022): The Case for A New Bretton Woods, New York: Wiley.

Gehlen (2014) [1940]: Der Mensch: Seine Natur und seine Stellung in der Welt, Wiebelsheim: AULA-Verlag.

Gelpern, Anna et al. (2021). How China Lends, https://docs.aiddata.org/reports/how-china-lends.html.

Georgescu-Roegen, Nicholas (1971): The Entropy Law and the Economic Process. Cambridge: Harvard University Press.

Georgescu-Roegen, Nicholas (1979): "Energy analysis and economic valuation", in: Southern Economic Journal, 45 (4), 1023–1058, https://doi.org/10.2307/1056953.

Georgescu-Roegen, Nicholas (1993): "Thermodynamics and We, the Humans", in: J. C. Dragan, E. K. Seifert and M. C. Demetrescu (eds.): Entropy and Bioeconomics: Proceedings of the First International Conference of the European Association for Bioeconomic Studies, Rome 28–30, Milan: Nagard.

German Marshall Plan (2024): The Spirit of the Marshall Plan, https://www.gmfus.org/spirit-marshall-plan.

Global Security Institute (2024): Website: Home, https://gsinstitute.org.

Green, Robert (2023): The Difficult Realities of the BRICS' Dedollarization Efforts—and the Renminbi's Role, Carnegie Endowment for International Peace, https://carnegieendowment.org/research/2023/12/the-difficult-realities-of-the-brics-dedollarization-effortsand-the-renminbis-role?lang=en.

Gribbin, John R. (2005): Deep Simplicity: Bringing Order To Chaos And Complexity, London: Random House.

Griffith-Jones, Stephany; Gallagher, Kevin; Volz, Ulrich (2021): Debt Relief by Private Creditors: Lessons from the Brady Plan, Background Paper #7, Heinrich Böll Stiftung et al., https://www.boell.de/sites/default/files/2021-10/Background%20Paper%20_7%20Endf.pdf.

Habbel, Valerie et al. (2021): Evaluating Blended Finance Instruments and Mechanisms: Approaches and Methods, OECD Development Co-operation Working Paper No. 101, Paris: Organisation for Economic Co-operation andDevelopment.

Habermas, Jürgen (1988): Der philosophische Diskurs der Moderne, Frankfurt: Suhrkamp.

Haines, A., Frumkin, H., (2021): Planetary health: Safeguarding human health and the environment in the Anthropocene. Cambridge University Press.

Harari, Yuval Noah (2014): Sapiens: A Brief History of Humankind, New York: Random House.

Harari, Yuval Noah (2018): 21 Lessons for the 21st century, London: Jonathan Cape.

Harari, Yuval Noah (2024): Nexus: A Brief History of Information Networks from the Stone Age to AI, New York, Penguin.

Hardin, Garrett (1968): "The Tragedy of the Commons: The population problem has no technical solution; it requires a fundamental extension in morality", in: Science, 162/3859, 1243–1248, https://doi.org/10.1126/science.162.3859.1243.

Hare, Brian; Woods, Vanessa (2020): Survival of the Friendliest: Understanding Our Origins and Rediscovering Our Common Humanity, New York, London: Random House.

Heinsohn, Gunnar (2019): Wettkampf um die Klugen: Kompetenz, Bildung und die Wohlfahrt der Nationen, Zürich: Orell Füssli Verlag.

Hickel, Jason (2020): "Quantifying National Responsibility for Climate Breakdown: An Equality-Based Attribution Approach for Carbon Dioxide Emissions in Excess of the Planetary Boundary", in: Lancet Planet Health, 4, e399–404, https://doi.org/10.1016/S2542-5196(20)30196-0.

Hickel, Jason et al. (2022): "Imperialist Appropriation in the World Economy: Drain from the Global South through Unequal Exchange, 1990–2015", in: Global Environmental Change, 73, 102467, https://doi.org/10.1016/j.gloenvcha.2022.102467.

Hiebert, Paul; Monnin, Pierre (2023): „Climate-related systemic risks and macroprudential policy", in: Inspire Sustainability Central Banking Toolbox, Policy Briefing Paper 14, https://www.inspiregreenfinance.org/wp-content/uploads/2023/08/INSPIRE-Sustainable-Central-Banking-Toolbox-Paper-14.pdf,

Hoffner, Benjamin (2023): United States: Central Bank Swaps to 14 Countries, 2020 (June 2023), Yale Program on Financial Stability Case Study, https://ssrn.com/abstract=4509325.

Holcombe, Rendall G. (2001): "James M. Buchanan and Richard A. Musgrave, Public Finance and Public Choice: Two Contrasting Visions of the State", in: Public Choice, 106, 196–199, https://doi.org/10.1023/A:1005271812684.

Holston, Kathryn; Laubach, Thomas; Williams, John C. (2017): "Measuring the Natural Rate of Interest: International Trends and Determinants", in: Journal of International Economics, 108, 59–75.

Horn, Sebastian; Reinhart, Carmen M.; Trebesch, Christoph (2019): China's Overseas Lending, National Bureau of Economic Research Working Paper 26050. https://www.nber.org/papers/w31105.

Horn, Sebastian; Reinhart, Carmen M.; Trebesch, Christoph (2023): China as an International Lender of Last Resort, National Bureau of Economic Research Working Paper 26050. https://www.nber.org/papers/w26050.

Hsu, Po-Hsuan et al. (2024): "The Out-Of-Sample Performance of Carry Trades", in: Journal of International Money and Finance, 143, 103042, https://doi.org/10.1016/j.jimonfin.2024.103042.https://doi.org/10.1016/j.ecolecon.2014.07.024.

Hu, Wangjie et al. (2023): "Genomic inference of a severe human bottleneck during the Early to Middle Pleistocene transition", in: Science, 381/6661, 979–984.

Huber, Joseph (2024): The Monetary Turning Point: From Bank Money to Central Bang Digital Currency (CBDC), London: Palgrave Macmillan.

Human Security for All (2024): HS4A – Human Security for ALL, https://humansecurity.world.

IMF Datamapper (2023): General government gross debt: Percent of GDP, https://www.imf.org/external/datamapper/GGXWDG_NGDP@WEO/OEMDC/ADVEC/WEOWORLD/CHN.

Institut Rosseau (2024): Road to Net Zero: Bridging the Green Investment Gap, https://institut-rousseau.fr/road-2-net-zero-en/.

IOM (2021): World Migration Report 2022, https://reliefweb.int/sites/reliefweb.int/files/resources/WMR-2022-EN.pdf.

Jackson, Andrew; Dyson, Ben (2012): Modernising Money: Why Our Montary System is Broken and How it Can be Fixed, London: Positive Money.

Johnson, Emma (2017): Health and social care spending cuts linked to 120,000 excess deaths in England, BMJ, https://www.sciencedaily.com/releases/2017/11/171115195300.htm.

Johnson, Lise; Sachs, Lisa; Lobel, Nathan (2019): "Aligning International Investment Agreements with the Sustainable Development Goals", in: Columbia Journal of Transnational Law 58/1, 58–120, https://ccsi.columbia.edu/sites/default/files/content/docs/publications/Briefing-Aligning-International-Investment-Agreements-with-the-Sustainable-Development-Goals.pdf-.

Johnson, Neil (2010): Simply Complexity: A Clear Guide To Complexity Theory, Oxford: Oneworld.

Jung, Carl Gustav (1968): The Collected Works of C. G. Jung Vol. 9/I: The Archetypes and the Collective Unconscious, 2nd Edition, Princeton: Princeton University Press.

Jung, Suehyun (2024): "Evolution of China's Bilateral Swap Lines: exploring the case of East Asia", in: Australian Journal of International Affairs, 78/1, 79–101, https://doi.org/10.1080/10357718.2024.2309327.

Kahneman, Daniel; Tversky, Amos (1979): "Prospect Theory: An Analysis under Risk", in: Econometric Society, 47/2, 263–292, https://doi.org/10.2307/1914185.

Kanigel, Robert (2000): The one best way: Frederick Winslow Taylor and the enigma of efficiency, Cambridge, Massachusetts: MIT Press.

Kanigel, Robert (2005): The One Best Way: Frederick Winslow Taylor and the Enigma of Efficiency, Cambridge, MA.: The MIT Press.

Karlqvist, Anders (1999): "Going beyond Disciplines: The Meanings of Interdisciplinarity", in: Policy Sciences, 32/4, 379–83, http://www.jstor.org/stable/4532477.

Keagan, Robert (1982): The Evolving Self: Problem and Process in Human Development, Bostong: Harvard University Press.

Keen, Steven (2021): The New Economics. A Manifesto, Londong: John Wiley & Sons, Hoboken.

Keen, Steven; Ayres, Robert U.; Standish, Russell (2019): "A Note on the Role of Energy in Production", in: Ecological Economics, 157, 40–46, https://doi.org/10.1016/j.ecolecon.2018.11.002.

Keynes, John M. (1936): The General Theory Of Employment Interest And Money, Whitefish, MO.: Kessinger Publishing.

Keynes, John M. (1980): Collected Writings. Vol. XXV: Activities, 1940–1944: Shaping the Post-War World: The Clearing Union. Basingstoke: Macmillan.

Keynes, John Meynard (2012) [1942]: Collected Writings Volume 27, Cambride: Cambridge University Press.

Khanna, Parag (2024): "The Coming Entropy Of Our World Order. How do we reconcile an increasingly fractured order with an increasingly planetary reality?", in: Noéma, https://www.noemamag.com/the-coming-entropy-of-our-world-order/.

Kindleberger, Charles P. 1978. Manias, Panics, and Crashes: A History of Financial Crises, first edition, New York, Basic Books.

Kindleberger, Charles P. (1987): "Capital Flight – A Historical Perspective", in: Lessard, Donald R., Williamson, John (eds.), Capital Flight: The Problem and Policy Responses, Washington: Institute for International Economics, 326–346.

King, Stephen D. (2023). We Need to Talk About Inflation: 4 Urgent Lessons from the Last 2,000 Years, New Haven: Yale University Press.

Kisling, Lisa A., Das, Joe M. (2023): Prevention strategies, StatPearls Publishing, https://www.ncbi.nlm.nih.gov/books/NBK537222/.

Koch, Richard (2022): The 80/20 Principle: Achieve More with Less, London: Nicholas Brealey Publishing.

Kolb, Gerhard (2017): Ökonomische Ideengeschichte: Volks- und betriebswirtschaftliche Entwicklungslinien von der Antike bis zum Neoliberalismus, München: De Gruyter.

Kotz, Maximilian et al. (2023): The Impact of Global Warming on Inflation: Averages, Seasonsality and Extremes, ECB Working paper 2821, Frankfurt ECB, https://www.ecb.europa.eu/pub/pdf/scpwps/ecb.wp2821~f008e5cb9c.en.pdf.

Kriwoluzky, Alexander; Volz, Ulrich (2023): Monetary Policy at the Crossroads – How to Respond to the Climate Crisis, focus paper 9, Bertelsmann Stiftung.

Krugman, Paul; Obstfeld, Maurice; Melitz, Marc J. (2009): International Economics: Theory & Policy, 9th Edition, Boston et al.: Addison-Wesley, 386–388.

Kubiszewski, Ida et al. (2013): "Beyond GDP: Measuring and achieving global genuine progress", in: Ecological Economics, 93, 57–68, https://doi.org/10.1016/j.ecolecon.2013.04.019.

Kuhn, Thomas (1962): The Structure of Scientific Revolutions, Chicago: University of Chicago Press.

Kumhof, Michael; Noone, Clare (2021): "Central bank digital currencies – Design principles for financial stability", in: Economic Analysis and Policy. 71/C, 553–572, https://doi.org/10.1016/j.eap.2021.06.012.

Kümmel, Reiner (2013): "Why energy's economic weight is much larger than its cost share", in: Environmental Innovation and Societal Transitions 9/Dezember 2013, 33–37, https://doi.org/10.1016/j.eist.2013.09.003.

Kyla, Tienhaara et al. (2022): "Investor-State Disputes Threaten the Global Green Energy Transition", in: Science 376: 701–3, https://doi.org/10.1126/science.abo4637.

Larsen, Lotta Björkland (2018): A Fair Share of Tax: A Fiscal Anthropology of Contemporary Sweden, London: Palgrave Macmillan.

Laszlo, Alexander (2001): "The epistemological foundations of evolutionary systems design", in: Special Issue: Designing Educational Systems for the Twenty-First Century July/August 2001, 307–321, https://doi.org/10.1002/sres.426.

Laszlo, Alexander (2009): "The Nature of Evolution", in: World Futures, 65/3, 204–221. https://doi.org/10.1080/02604020802392112.

Laszlo, Ervin (2016): What Is Reality? The New Map of Cosmos and Consciousness. New York, NY: SelectBooks.

Laszlo, Ervin (2016): What Is Reality? The New Map of Cosmos and Consciousness. New York, NY: SelectBooks.

Lazard (2022): How to Make Sovereign Debt Restructuring More Effective: How Warring Parties to a Better Standard of „Comparability", Policy Brief, https://www.lazard.com/media/c5bb0n11/lazard-policy-brief-on-comparability-of-treatment-may-2022.pdf.

Leaven, Luc; Valencia, Fabián (2012): Systemic Banking Crises Database: An Update, IMF Working Paper 12/163, https://www.imf.org/external/pubs/ft/wp/2012/wp12163.pdf.

Lebov, J. et al. (2017): „A Framework for One Health Research", in: One Health, 24:3, 44–50, https://doi. org/10.1016/j.onehlt.2017.03.004.

Lebov, J. et al. (2024): "A Framework for One Health Research", in: One Health, 24/3, 44–50, https://www. sciencedirect.com/science/article/pii/S2352771416300696.

Leibnitz, Gottfried Wilhelm (1710): Essais de Théodicée, Amsterdam.

Levermann, Anders (2023): Die Faltung der Welt: Wie die Wissenschaft helfen kann, dem Wachstumsdilemma und der Klimakrise zu entkommen, München: Beck.

Lietaer, Bernard (2000): Mysterium Geld: Emotionale Bedeutung und Wirkungsweise eines Tabus, München: Riemann Verlag.

Lietaer, Bernard et al. (2012): Money and Sustainability: The Missing Link, Charmouth Dorset: Triarchy Press Ltd.

Lietaer, Bernhard (2001): The Future of Money: A New Way to Create Wealth, Work, and a Wiser World, London: Century.

Lin, Ho-Chih et al. (2023): Climate Crossfire: How NATO's 2% military spending targets contribute to climate breakdown, https://www.researchgate.net/publication/374756619_Climate_Crossfire_How_ NATO's_2_military_spending_targets_contribute_to_climate_breakdown.

Lomborg, Bjørn (2023): Best Things First: The 12 Most Efficient Solutions for the World's Poorest and our Global SDG Promises, Copenhagen: Copenhagen Consensus Center.

Lorenzoni, Guido; Werning, Iván (2019): "Slow Moving Debt Crises", in: American Economic Review, 109/9, 3229–63, https://www.aeaweb.org/articles?id=10.1257/aer.20141766.

Lovins, Avory (2013): Reinventing Fire: Solutions for the New Energy Era, White River Junction: Chelsea Green Publishing.

LRQA (2024): Supply Chain Due Diligence Legislation Map, https://www.lrqa.com/en/supply-chain-due-diligence-legislation-map/.

Lucas, Robert E. (1976): "Econometric Policy Evaluation: A Critique", in: Carnegie-Rochester Conference Series on Public Policy, 1, 19–46, https://doi.org/10.1016/S0167-2231(76)80003-6.

Lucas, Robert E. (1990): "Why Doesn't Capital Flow from Rich to Poor Countries?", American Economic Review, 80/2, 92–96, https://www.jstor.org/stable/2006549.

MacAskill, Williamn (2017): "Effective altruism: introduction", in: Essays in Philosophy, 18/1, 1–5, http://dx. doi.org/10.7710/1526-0569.1580.

Mainzer, Klaus (1997): Thinking in Complexity: The Complexity Dynamics of Matter, Mind, and Mankind, Berlin, Heidelberg: Springer.

Mancuso, Stefano (2022): The Nation of Plants, London: Profile Books.

Mandelbrot, Benoît (1977): Fractals: Form, Chance, and Dimension. San Francisco: W. H. Freeman.

Mandelbrot, Benoît; Hudson, Richard L. (2004): The (Mis)Behaviour of Markets: A Fractal View of Risk, Ruin and Reward, London: Profile Books.

Markowitz, Harry M. (1959): "Portfolio Selection: Efficient Diversification of Investments.", in: New Haven: Yale University Press.

Marois, Thomas; Stewart, Jacob; Marodon, Régis (2024): From Multi- to National-and Back Again: Realizing the SDG Potential of Public Development Banks. Éditions AFD: Research Papers, https://www.cairn-int.info/revue-afd-research-papers-2023-267-page-1.htm.

Marouani, Albert (2018): "The limits of the quantitative easing monetary policies: How to overcome them", https://www.academia.edu/40585139/The_limits_of_the_Quantitative_Easing_Monetary_Policies_ how_to_overcome_them?email_work_card=view-paper.

Masala, Carlo (2022): Weltunordnung: Die globalen Krisen und die Illusionen des Westens, München: C.H. Beck.

Maslow, Abraham H. (1943): "A Theory of Human Motivation", in: Psychological Review, 50/4, 370–396.

Maturana, Humberto R.; Varela, Francisco J. (1987): Der Baum der Erkenntnis. Die biologischen Wurzeln menschlichen Erkennens, Frankfurt a. M.: Suhrkamp.

Maurice,Obstfeld; Taylor, Alan M. (1998): "The Great Depression as a Watershed: International Capital Mobility over the Long Run", in: The Defining Moment: The Great Depression and the American Economy in the Twentieth Century, 353–402, Washington, D.C.: National Bureau of Economic Research.

Mayer, Colin (2024): Capitalism and Crises: How to Fix Them, Oxford: Oxford University Press.

Mayer, Thomas (2014): „Die wahre Ursache der Ungleichheit", in: faz.net, 27. September 2014 https://www.faz.net/aktuell/wirtschaft/mayers-weltwirtschaft/mayers-weltwirtschaft-die-wahre-ursache-der-ungleichheit-13177381.html.

Mazzucato, Mariana (2023): The Entrepreneurial State: Debunking public vs. private sector myths, New York: Penguin.

McDermott, Rose; Fowler, James H.; Smirnov, Oleg (2008): "On the Evolutionary Origin of Prospect Theory Preferences", in: Journal of Politics 70/2, 335–350, https://ssrn.com/abstract=1008034.

Megliani, Mauro (2021): "Single-Limb Collective Action Clauses and the European Stability Mechanism Reform", in: European Business Law Review, 32/1, 77–92, https://doi.org/10.54648/eulr2021004.

Mehrling, Perry . 2022, Money and Empire, Charles P. Kindleberger and the Dollar System (Studies in New Economic Thinking), Cambridge University Press

Meyer-Abich, Klaus Michael (1965): Korrespondenz, Individualität und Komplementarität. Wiesbaden: Franz Steiner Verlag.

Meyer, Eva; Welpe, Isabell M.; Sander, Philipp G. (2022): Decentralized Finance—A Systematic Literature Review and Research Directions, ECIS 2022 Research Papers 25 https://aisel.aisnet.org/ecis2022_rp/25.

Millennium Ecosystem Assessment (2005): Ecosystems and Human Well-being: Current State and Trends: Findings of the Condition and Trends Working Group (Volume 1), Washington, D.C.: Island Press.

Minsky, Hyman (1986): Stabilizing an Unstable Economy. McGraw-Hill Professional, New York.

Minsky, Hyman P. (1986): Stabilizing an Unstable Economy, New York: McGraw-Hill Professional.

Mises, Ludwig von (1949): Human Action: A Treatise On Economics, Whitefish, Montana: Kessinger Publishing.

Modigliani, Franco (1986): "Life Cycle, Individual Thrift, and the Wealth of Nations", in: The American Economic Review, 76/3, 297-313, https://www.jstor.org/stable/1813352

Montesi, Cristina (2023): "The Promethean Fate of Economy: Will Hydrogen Really Be Prometheus III's New Gift to Humanity?", in: Pellat, G., Zafiroski, J., Šuplata, M. (Eds.): Cooperation and Enlargement: Two Challenges to be Addressed in the European Projects-2022, Studies in Systems, Decision and Control, vol 500. Springer, Cham. https://doi.org/10.1007/978-3-031-42253-9_16.

Mundell, Robert (1973): "A Plan for a European Currency", in: Johnson, Harry; Swoboda, Alexander (Eds.): The Economics of Common Currencies, London: Routledge, 147 and 150.

Mundell, Robert A. (1961): "A Theory of Optimum Currency Areas", in: American Economic Review, 51/4, 657–665, JSTOR 1812792.

Münkler, Herfried (2023): Welt in Aufruhr: Die Ordnung der Mächte im 21. Jahrhundert, Berlin: Rowohlt.

Myers, S., Frumkin, H., (2020): Planetary health: protecting nature to protect ourselves, Washington, D.C.: Island Press.

Nagan, Winston P. (2016): "The Concept, Basis and Implications of Human-Centered Development", in: Cadmus, 3/1, 28–35, https://www.cadmusjournal.org/files/pdfreprints/vol3issue1/cadmus-v3-i1-human-centered-development-wnagan-reprint.pdf.

Nash, John Forbes (1950): Non-cooperative games, Dissertation, Princeton: Princeton University 1950.

Neuwirth, Robert (2012): Stealth of Nations: The Global Rise of the Informal Economy, New York: Knopf Doubleday Publishing Group.

Nevin, Seamus (2013): "Richard Cantillon: The Father of Economics", in: History Ireland, 21/2, 20–23.

New England Complex Systems Institute (2024): Online Certificate Programs, https://necsi.edu.

NGFS (2020): Guide for Supervisors: Integrating Climate-Related and Environmental Risks into Prudential Supervision, https://www.ngfs.net/sites/default/files/medias/documents/ngfs_guide_for_supervi sors.pdf.

Nguyen, D. D. et al. (2022): "Climate Change Risk and the Cost of Mortgage Credit", in: Review of Finance, 26/6, 1509–1549, https://doi.org/10.1093/rof/rfac013.

Norberg, Johan (2016): Progress: Ten Reasons to Look Forward to the Future, London: Oneworld Publications.

Nordhaus, William (2007): „A Review of the Stern Review on the Economics of Climate Change", in: Journal of Economic Literature 45, 686–702, https://www.aeaweb.org/articles?id=10.1257/jel.45.3.686.

OECD (2020): A Comprehensive Overview of Global Biodiversity Finance, OECD, http://www.oecd.org/envi ronment/resources/biodiversity/report-a-comprehensive-overview-of-global-biodiversity-finance.pdf.

Oexelheim, Lars (1990): International Financial Integration, Berlin, Heidelberg: Springer.

Olson, Mancur (1971): The Logic of Collective Action, Cambridge: Harvard University Press.

Oman, William; Svartzman Romain (2021): What Justifies Sustainable Finance Measures?, CESifo From, 22/ 3, 3–11, https://www.econstor.eu/bitstream/10419/250915/1/CESifo-Forum-2021-03-p03-11.pdf.

Ormerod, Paul (2005): Why Most Things Fail: Evolution, Extinction and Economics. London: Faber and Faber Limited.

Ostrom, Elinor (1990): Governing the commons: The evolution of institutions for collective action, Cambridge: Cambridge University Press.

Oxelheim, Lars (1990): International Financial Integration, Heidelberg: Springer.

Paduano, Stephen (2024): A State of Play on SDRs: What To Make of 2023, What to Watch in 2024, FDL Short Notes, FDL Finance for Development Lab, https://findevlab.org/wp-content/uploads/2024/01/ FDL_ShortNote_SDR_State_of_Play_Paduano_Jan24.pdf.

Paduano, Stephen; Setser, Brad (2023): The Magic Of An SDR-denominated Bond, in: Financial Times, https://elischolar.library.yale.edu/cgi/viewcontent.cgi?article=1674&context=ypfs-documents2.

Pareto, Vilfredo (1906): Manuale d'economia politica, Milano: Societa Editrice Libraria.

Parisi, Giorgio (1999): "Complex systems: a physicist's viewpoint", in: Physica A: Statistical Mechanics and its Applications 263/1–4, 557–564, https://doi.org/10.1016/S0378-4371(98)00524-X.

Parker, Miles (2018): "The Impact of Disasters on Inflation", in: Economics of Disasters and Climate Change, Springer, vol. 2/1, pages 21–48.

Patnaik, Utse; Patnaik, Prabhat (2016): A Theory of Imperialism. New York: Columbia University Press.

People-Centered Internet (2023): People Centered Internet, https://peoplecentered.net.

Perks, Michael et al. (2021): Evolution of Bilateral Swap Lines, IMF Working Paper, IMF, https://www.imf. org/-/media/Files/Publications/WP/2021/English/wpiea2021210-print-pdf.ashx.

Persaud, Avinash (2023): Unblocking the green transformation in developing countries with a partial foreign exchange guarantee, Climate Policy Initiative, https://www.climatepolicyinitiative.org/wp-content/uploads/2023/06/An-FX-Guarantee-Mechanism-for-the-Green-Transformation-in-Developing-Countries.pdf.

Pichler, Anton et al. (2021): "Systemic risk-efficient asset allocations: Minimization of systemic risk as a network optimization problem", in: Journal of Financial Stability, 52, 100809, https://www.sciencedir ect.com/science/article/abs/pii/S1572308920301121.

Pigou, Arthur Cecil (1932): The Economics of Welfare, Fourth Edition, London: Macmillan.

Piketty, Thomas (2014): Capital in the 21st Century, Cambridge, MA: Belknap.

Piketty, Thomas (2015): "Putting Distribution Back at the Center of Economics: Reflections on Capital in the Twenty-First Century", in: Journal of Economic Perspectives 29, 67–88.

Piketty, Thomas; Saez, Emmanuel (2013): "A Theory of Optimal Inheritance Taxation", in: Econometrica 81, 1851–1886, https://www.jstor.org/stable/23524306.

Pinker, Steven (2018): Enlightenment Now: The Case for Reason, Science, Humanism, and Progress, London: Penguin Books/Viking.

Pistor, Katharina (2019): The code of capital, Princeton University Press.

Planetary Health Alliance (2024): Website: Home, https://www.planetaryhealthalliance.org.

Plessner, Helmut (1975): Die Stufen des Organischen und der Mensch: Einleitung in die philosophische Anthropologie, Berlin: De Gruyter.

Plessner, Helmut (1983): „Die Frage nach der Condition humana", in: Plessner, Helmut (Ed.): Gesammelte Werke, Band 8, Frankfurt/Main: Suhrkamp.

Pollman, Elizabeth (2022): The Making and Meaning of ESG, University of Penn, Institute for Law & Econ Research Paper No. 22–23, https://papers.ssrn.com/sol3/papers.cfm?abstract_id=4219857.

Pozsar, Zoltan et al. (2013): Shadow Banking, FRBNY Economic Policy Review.

Prigogine, Ilya; Stengers, Isabelle (1984): Order out of Chaos: Man's New Dialogue with Nature, London: Flamingo Edition.

Prime Minister of Barbados (2023): Bridgetown 2.0 Initiative, https://pmo.gov.bb/bridgetown2-0-2pager-3/.

Pyle, Robert Michael (2003): "Nature matrix: reconnecting people and nature", in: Oryx, 37/2: 206–214, https://doi.org/10.1017/S0030605303000383.

Radermacher, Franz Josef; Beyers, Bert (2024): All in! Energie und Wohlstand für eine wachsende Welt. Hamburg: Murmann.

Ragin, Charles C. (2000): Fuzzy-Set Social Science, Chigago: Chigago University Press.

Rawls, John (1971): A Theory of Justice, Cambridge, Massachusetts: Belknap Press.

Reheis, Fritz (2022): Erhalten und Erneuern: Nur Kreisläufe sind nachhaltig, Durchläufe nicht, Hamburg: VSA Verlag.

Reinhart, Carmen M.; Reinhart, Vincent; Trebesch, Christoph (2016): "Global Cycles: Capital Flows, Commodities, and Sovereign Defaults, 1815–2015", in: American Economic Review,106/5, 574–80. http://www.jstor.org/stable/43861085.

Reinhart, Carmen M.; Rogoff, Kenneth S. (2013): Opinion | Debt, Growth and the Austerity Debate", in: The New York Times, https://www.nytimes.com/2013/04/26/opinion/debt-growth-and-the-austerity-debate.html.

Peters, Glen.(2008): ‚From productions-based on consumption-based national emission inventories', Ecological economics 65, 13–23

Peters, Glen, Davis SJ. & Andrews R. (2012): A synthesis of carbon in international trade, Biogeosciences, 9, 3247–76

Richardson, Katherine et al. (2023): "Earth beyond six of nine planetary boundaries", in: Science Advances 9, eadh2458, https://www.science.org/doi/10.1126/sciadv.adh2458.

Rifkin, Jeremy (2022): The Age of Resilience: Reimagining Existence on a Rewilding Earth, London: Maxmillan.

Rindermann, Heiner (2018): Cognitive Capitalism: Human Capital and the Wellbeing of Nations, Cambridge: Cambridge University Press.

Robbins, Lionel (1935): An Essay on the Nature and Significance of Economic Science, London: Macmillan.

Rockström, Johan et al. (2024): "The planetary commons: A new paradigm for safeguarding Earth-regulating systems in the Anthropocene", in: PNAS 121/5, e2301531121, https://doi.org/10.1073/pnas.2301531121.

Rockström, Johan; Klum, Mattias (2016): Big World Small Planet: Wie wir die Zukunft unseres Planeten gestalten, Berlin: Ullstein.

Rodrik, Dani (2011): The Globalization Paradox: Democracy and the Future of the World Economy, New York, London: W.W. Norton.

Rolnick, Arthur J.; Weber, Warren (1986): "Gresham's Law or Gresham's Fallacy?", in: Journal of Political Economy, 94/1, 185–99, https://www.jstor.org/stable/1831965.

Roser, Max. (2021): How much economic growth is necessary to reduce global poverty substantially? Our world in Data.

Rössner, Philipp R. (2018): Monetary Theory and Cameralistic Economic Management, 500–1900 AD, in: Journal of the history of economic thought, 40/1, 99–134, https://doi.org/10.1017/S1053837216001152.

Rueffler, Claus; Hermisson, Joachin; Wagner, Günter P. (2012): „Evolution of functional specialization and division of labor", in: PNAS 109/6, E326–E335, https://doi.org/10.1073/pnas.1110521109.

Santarius, Tilman (2015): Der Rebound-Effekt: Ökonomische, psychische und soziale Herausforderungen für die Entkopplung von Wirtschaftswachstum und Energieverbrauch , Berlin: Metropolis.

Sattari, Reza et al. (2022): "The ripple effects of funding on researchers and output", in: Science Advances 8, eabb7348, https://doi.org/10.1126/sciadv.abb7348.

Scheler, Max (2007): Die Stellung des Menschen im Kosmos, 16th Edition, Bonn: Bouvier.

Schmidt, Ulrich; Zank, Horst (2005): "What is Loss Aversion?", in: Journal of Risk and Uncertainty, 30/2, 157–167, https://doi.org/10.1007/s11166-005-6564-6.

Schmucker, Claudia; Mildner, Stormy-Annika (2023): "Reforming the WTO Through Inclusive and Development-friendly Approaches: How to Make Plurilateral Initiatives Work for All", in Berling: Forschungsinstitut der Deutschen Gesellschaft für Auswärtige Politik e.V., https://www.ssoar.info/ssoar/handle/document/89986.

Schnabel, Isabel (2022): A New Age of Energy Inflation: Climateflation, Fossileflation and Greenflation, Remarks at a Panel on ‚Monetary Policy and Climate Exchange at the ECB and Its Watchers, XXII Conference, Frankfurt 17. March 2022, https://www.ecb.europa.eu/press/key/date/2022/html/ecb.sp220317_2~dbb3582f0a.en.html.

Schneider, Michael (2007): "The nature, history and signi cance of the concept of positional goods", in: History of Economics Review, 45/1, 60–81.

Schrödinger, Erwin (1944): What Is Life? and Other Scientific Essays. Based on lectures delivered under the auspices of the Dublin Institute for Advanced Studies at Trinity College, Dublin, in February 1943, London: Doubleday Anchor.

Schroeder, Frank (2006): Innovative Sources of Finance after the Paris Conference: The Concept Is Gaining Currency but Major Challenges Remain, Friedrich-Ebert-Stiftung Briefing Paper, https://library.fes.de/pdf-files/iez/global/50423.pdf.

Schubert, Christian (2023): Geometrie der Seele: Wie unbewusste Muster das Drehbuch unseres Lebens bestimmen, 3rd Edition, München: Gräfe und Unzer Verlag.

Schularick, Moritz (2022): The New Economics of Debt and Financial Fragility, Chicago: University of Chicago Press.

Schumacher, Ernst Friedrich (1943): „Multilateral Clearing", in: Economica 10/38, pp. 150–165.

Schumacher, Ernst Friedrich (1973): Small is Beautiful: A Study of Economics as if People Mattered, London: Blond & Briggs.

Securing America's Future Energy (2018): The Military Cost of Defending the Global Oil Supply, http://secureenergy.org/wp-content/uploads/2020/03/Military-Cost-of-Defending-the-Global-Oil-Supply.-Sep.-18.-2018.pdf.

Seery, Emma (2020): 50 Years of Broken Promises, Oxfam International, https://oxfamilibrary.openrepository.com/bitstream/handle/10546/621080/bn-50-years-broken-promises-aid-231020-en.pdf.

Setser, Brad W.; Paduano, Stephen (2022): How an SDR Denominated Bond Could Work, Council on Foreign Relations, https://www.cfr.org/blog/how-sdr-denominated-bond-could-work#:~:text=The%20World%20Bank%20can%20issue,usable%20currencies%20through%20the%20IMF.

Shannon, Claude E. (1948): "A Mathematical Theory of Communication", in: Bell System Technical Journal, 27 /4, 623–656, https://doi.org/10.1002/j.1538-7305.1948.tb00917.x.

Shaxson, Nicholas (2018): The Finance Curse: How Global Finance is Making Us All Poorer, London: Beadley Head.

Shiller, Robert J. (2019): Narrative Economics: How Stories Go Viral and Drive Major Economic Events, New Jersey: Princeton University Press.

Simmel, Georg (2004) [1900]: Philosophy of Money, London: Routledge.

Singhania, Monica; Saini, Neha (2021): "Institutional framework of ESG disclosures: comparative analysis of developed and developing countries", in: Journal of Sustainable Finance & Investment, 13/1), 516–559. https://doi.org/10.1080/20430795.2021.1964810

Singhania, Monica; Saini, Neha (2022): "Quantification of ESG Regulations: A Cross-Country Benchmarking Analysis", in: Vision, 26/2, 163–171. https://doi.org/10.1177/09722629211054173

Sinn, Hans-Werner (2009): Kasino-Kapitalismus: Wie es zur Finanzkrise kam, und was jetzt zu tun ist, Berlin: Econ Verlag.

Sinn, Hans-Werner (2012): The Green Paradox. A Supply-Side Approach to Global Warming, Cambridge, Massachusetts: MIT Press.

Singhania, Monica; Saini, Neha (2021): "Institutional framework of ESG disclosures: comparative analysis of developed and developing countries", in: Journal of Sustainable Finance & Investment, 13/1), 516–559. https://doi.org/10.1080/20430795.2021.1964810

Šlaus, Ivo (2020): Transforming Our World: Necessary, Urgent, and Still Possible, Cambridge: Cambridge Scholars Publishing.

Smith, Adam (1986): The Wealth of Nations, Books I–III, New York: Penguin Classics.

Smith, R. Todd (1998): "The Friedman Rule and Optimal Monetary Policy", in: The Canadian Journal of Economics / Revue canadienne d'Economique, 31/2, 295–302, https://doi.org/10.2307/136324.

Smitsman, Anneloes, Currivan, Jude (2019): "Systemic Transformation into the Birth Canal", in: Systems Research and Behavioral Science, 36/4: 604–613, https://doi.org/10.1002/sres.2573.

Solow, Robert (1957): "Technical Change and the Aggregate Production Function", in: Review of Economics and Statistics 39, 312–320.

Songwe, Vera; Stern, Nicholas; Bhattacharya, Amar (2022): Finance for Climate Action: Scaling up Investment for Climate and Development, Report of the Independent High-Level Expert Group on Climate Finance, Grantham Institute, https://www.lse.ac.uk/granthaminstitute/wp-content/uploads/2022/11/IHLEG-Finance-for-Climate-Action-1.pdf.

Spencer, Maya (2012): What is spirituality? A personal exploration, https://www.rcpsych.ac.uk/docs/default-source/members/sigs/spirituality-spsig/what-is-spirituality-maya-spencer-x.pdf?sfvrsn=f28df052_2.

Standing, Guy (2019): Plunder of the Commons: A Manifesto for Sharing Public Wealth, New York: Pelican.

Statistics.com (2024): Website: Home, https://www.statistics.com.

Steil, Benn et al. (2024): "Central Bank Currency Tracker", in: Council on Foreign Relations, https://www.cfr.org/article/central-bank-currency-swaps-tracker.

Stern, Nicholas (2007): The Economics of Climate Change: The Stern Review. Cambridge, UK, and New York: Cambridge University Press.

Steven Keen (forthcoming): Rebuilding Economics from the Top Down, London: Pallas Athene.

Stockholm International Peace Research Institute (2021): SIPRI Yearbook 2021, https://www.sipri.org/yearbook/2021.

Strom, Stephanie (2007): "2 Young Hedge-Fund Veterans Stir Up the World of Philanthropy", in: The New York Times, https://www.nytimes.com/2007/12/20/us/20charity.html.

Sukhdev, Pavan (2012): Corporation 2020: Transforming Business for Tomorrow's World, Washington, D.C.: Island Press.

Suleyman, Mustafa (2023): The Next Wave: A.I., Power and the Twenty-First Century's Greatest Dilemma, London: The Bodley Head.

Tabachov'a, Zlata et. al. (2023): "Estimating the Impact of Supply Chain Network Contagion on Financial Stability", Papers 2305.04865, https://ideas.repec.org/p/arx/papers/2305.04865.html.

Tabachová, Zlata et al. (2023): Estimating the Impact of Supply Chain Contagion on Financial Stability, Research Paper, https://arxiv.org/abs/2305.04865.

Taleb, Nassim (2007): The Black Swan: The Impact of the Highly Improbable, New York: Random House.

Taleb, Nassim (2012): Antifragile: Things That Gain from Disorder. New York: Random House.

Tamez, Mario; Weenink, Hans; Yoshinaga, Akihiro (2024): Central Banks and Climate Change: Key Legal Issues, IMF Working Paper No. 24/192, International Monetary Fund, Washington, DC.

TEEB (2010): The Economics of Ecosystems and Biodiversity Ecological and Economic Foundations. Edited by Pushpam Kumar. Earthscan: London and Washington.

Tegmark, Max (2019): Leben 3.0: Mensch sein im Zeitalter Künstlicher Intelligenz, Berlin: Ullstein.

The Club of Rome (2018): The Climate Emergency Plan, https://www.clubofrome.org/publication/the-climate-emergency-plan/.

The Economist (2024): Special report: Deglobalization and Finance, https://www.economist.com/briefing/2024/05/09/the-worlds-economic-order-is-breaking-down.

The European Central Bank (2024): Digital Euro, https://www.ecb.europa.eu/euro/digital_euro/html/index.en.html.

The Global Economy (2024): Savings, in dollars – Country rankings, https://www.theglobaleconomy.com/rankings/savings_dollars/.

The Guardian (2023): "$700m Pledged to Loss and Damage Fund at Cop28 Covers Less than 0.2% Needed", in: The Guardian 6 Dec 2023, https://www.theguardian.com/environment/2023/dec/06/700m-pledged-to-loss-and-damage-fund-cop28-covers-less-than-02-percent-needed.

The People's Map of Global China (2024): Project Database, https://thepeoplesmap.net/project-database/.

The United Nations (2024): Sustainable Development Goals, https://www.un.org/sustainabledevelopment/sustainable-development-goals/.

The WHO Council on the Economics of Health for All (2021): Financing Health for All: Increase, transform and redirect, Council Brief No. 2, https://cdn.who.int/media/docs/default-source/council-on-the-economics-of-health-for-all/who_councileh4a_councilbrieffinal-no2.pdf?sfvrsn=bd61dcfe_5&download=true.

The World Bank (2019): High-Performance Health Financing for Universal Health Coverage (Vol. 2): Driving Sustainable, Inclusive Growth in the 21st Century (English), https://documents.worldbank.org/en/publication/documents-reports/documentdetail/641451561043585615/driving-sustainable-inclusive-growth-in-the-21st-century.

The World Bank (2021): From Accounts to Policy: WAVES closeout report Wealth Accounting and Valuation of Ecosystem Services (WAVES) Global Partnership: 2012–2019, https://documents1.worldbank.org/curated/en/779351636579119839/pdf/From-Accounts-to-Policy-WAVES-Closeout-Report-Wealth-Accounting-and-Valuation-of-Ecosystem-Services-Global-Partnership-2012-2019.pdf.

The World Bank (2023): World Development Indicators, https://databank.worldbank.org/home.

The World Bank (2024): Private Sector Investment Lab, https://www.worldbank.org/en/about/unit/brief/private-sector-investment-lab.

The World Bank (2024a): World Bank Group Prepares Major Overhaul to Guarantee Business, Press Release, https://www.worldbank.org/en/news/press-release/2024/02/27/world-bank-group-prepares-major-overhaul-to-guarantee-business.

The World Economic Forum (2024): Global Risks Report 2024, https://www.weforum.org/publications/global-risks-report-2024/.

The World Economic Forum (2024a): Centre for Financial and Monetary Systems, https://centres.weforum.org/centre-for-financial-and-monetary-systems/home.

Thelwall, Mike et al. (2023): "What is research funding, how does it influence research, and how is it recorded? Key dimensions of variation", in: Scientometrics 128, 6085–6106, https://doi.org/10.1007/s11192-023-04836-w.

Tietenberg, Tom; Lewis, Lynn (2018). Environmental and Natural Resource Economics, 11th Edition, New York: Routledge, https://doi.org/10.4324/9781315208343.

Tobin, James (1989): "Reviewed Work: Stabilizing an Unstable Economy. Hyman P. Minsky", in: Journal of Economic Literature, 27/1, 105–108, https://www.jstor.org/stable/2726964.

Tomasello, Michael (2019): Becoming Human: A Theory of Ontogeny, Cambridge, MA: Belknap.

Tran, Hung (2024): Is the End of Petrodollar Near?, Atlantic Council, https://www.atlanticcouncil.org/blogs/econographics/is-the-end-of-the-petrodollar-near/.

Transparency International (2022): Corruptions Perceptions Index 2022, https://www.transparency.org/en/cpi/2022.

Tsoukalas, Lefteri H. (2023): Fuzzy Logic: Applications in Artificial Intelligence, Big Data, and Machine Learning, New York: McGraw-Hill Education.

Tylor, Charles (2024): Cosmic Connections: Poetry in the Age of Disenchantment, Cambridge: Bleknap Press.

Uexküll, Jakob Johann von (1949): Nie geschaute Welten: Die Umwelten meiner Freunde, Frankfurt, Suhrkamp Verlag.

Ulgiati, S., Raugei M., Bargigli S. (2004): Dotting the I's and Crossing the T's of Emergy Synthesis: Material Flows, Information and Memory Aspects, and Performance Indicators, Proceedings from the Third Biennial Emergy Evaluation Research Conference, Gainesville, Florida.

UN Environment Programme (1987): The Montreal Protocol on Substances the Deplete the Ozone Layer, https://web.archive.org/web/20130602153542/http://ozone.unep.org/new_site/en/montreal_protocol.php.

UN Environment Programme (2024): International Resource Panel: Global Resources Outlook 2024, United Nations, https://www.resourcepanel.org/sites/default/files/documents/document/media/gro24_full_report_29feb_final_for_web.pdf.

UN Global Crisis Response Group (2023): A world of dept: A growing burden to global prosperity, New York: United Nations, https://unctad.org/system/files/official-document/osgmisc_2023d4_en.pdf.

United Nations (2014): System of Environmental-Economic Accounting 2012, Central Framework, New York: United Nations, https://unstats.un.org/unsd/envaccounting/seeaRev/SEEA_CF_Final_en.pdf.

United Nations (2024): Human Development Report 2023–24, United Nations, https://hdr.undp.org/content/human-development-report-2023-24.

US Security and Exchange Committee (2024): Security-Based Swap Markets, https://www.sec.gov/about/divisions-offices/division-trading-markets/security-based-swap-markets.

Vasic-Lalovic, Ivana; Merling, Lara; Wu, Aileen (2023): The Growing Debt Burdens of Global South Countries: Standing in the Way of Climate and Development Goals, Center of Economic Policy Research (CEPR), https://www.cepr.net/wp-content/uploads/2023/10/The-Growing-Debt-Burdens-of-Global-South-Countries_Standing-in-the-Way-of-Climate-and-Development-Goals-Lalovic_-Merling_-Wu.pdf.

Veblen, Thorstein (1899): Theory of the Leisure Class, London: Macmillan.

Verbaanderd, Ciska; Rooman, Ilse; Huys, Isabelle (2021): "Exploring New Uses for Existing Drugs: Innovative Mechanisms to Fund Independent Clinical Research", in: Trials 22/322, https://doi.org/10.1186/s13063-021-05273-x.

Volz, Ulrich; Lo, Yuen C.; Mishra, Vaibhav (2024): Scaling Up Green Investment in Global South, Strengthening Domestic Financial Resource Mobilisation, and Attracting Patient International Capital, London: SOAS Centre for Sustainable Finance, https://doi.org/10.25501/SOAS.00041078.

Volz, Urlich et al. (2020): Debt Relief for a Green and Inclusive Recovery: A Proposal. Berlin, London, and Boston, MA: Heinrich-Böll-Stiftung; SOAS, University of London; and Boston University, https://www.boell.de/sites/default/files/2021-01/Endf%20DRGR%20Hauptreport%20%28klein%29.pdf.

Voshgmir, Shermin (2023): Token Economy: Money, NFTs & DeFi, Elvas: Token Kitchen.

Voshgmir, Shermin (2024): Token Economy: DAOs & Purpose-Driven Tokens, Elvas: Token Kitchen

Voshgmir, Shermin (2024): Web 3 Infrastructure, Elvas: Token Kitchen.

Vulnerable Club of the 20 (2024): About, V20 Website, https://www.v-20.org/about.

Walach, Harald (2010): Complementary? Alternative? Integrative? Forsch Komplementmed, 17/4, 215–6, https://doi.org/10.1159/000317639.

Waller, Christopher J. (2024): "Some thought on R*: Why did it fall and will it rise? Remarks by Christopher Waller Member Board of Governors of the DED at the Reykjavik Economic Conference: Reykjavik, Iceland, 24 May 2024.

Weber, Isabella M. (2021): How China Escaped Shock Therapy: The Market Reform Debate, London, New York: Routledge.

Weizsäcker, Carl Friedrich Freiherr v. (1974): „Evolution und Entropiewachstum", in: Ernst von Weizsäcker (Hrsg.): Offene Systeme 1: Beiträge zur Zeitstruktur von Information, Entropie und Evolution. Stuttgart: Klett, 200–221.

Weizsäcker, Ernst Ulrich von; Wijkman, Anders (2017): Wir sind dran. Club of Rome: Der große Bericht, Gütersloh: Guetersloher Verlagshaus.

Whitehead, Alfred N. (1929): Process and Reality: An Essay in Cosmology, Gifford Lectures Delivered in the University of Edinburgh During the Session 1927–1928, Macmillan, New York, Cambridge University Press, Cambridge UK.

Wilber, Ken (1998): The Marriage of Sense and Soul: Integrating Science and Religion. New York: Random House.

Wilber, Ken (2000): Integral psychology: Consciousness, Spirit, Psychology, Therapy, Boston: Shambhala.

Wilber, Ken (2024): Finding Radical Wholeness, The Integral Path to Unity, Growth, and Delight, Coulder, CO: Shambhala.

Williams, B.A. et al. (2023): "Outlook of Pandemic Preparedness in a post-COVID-19 World", in: Vaccines 8, 178, https://doi.org/10.1038/s41541-023-00773-0.

Williamson, John (1990): What Washington Means by Policy Reform, in: Williamson, John (ed.): Latin American Readjustment: How Much has Happened, Washington: Institute for International Economics.

Williamson, John (2008): "A Short History of the Washington Consensus", in: Serra, Narcís; Stiglitz, Joseph E. (eds.): The Washington Consensus Reconsidered (1 ed.), Oxford: Oxford University Press, 14–30.

Winthrop, Rebecca; McGivney, Eileen (2015): "Why Wait 100 Years? Bridging the Gap in Global Education", Brookings Institution, https://www.brookings.edu/wp-Zontent/uploads/2015/06/global_20161128_100-year-gap.pdf.

Woodward, David (2015): "Incrementum ad Absurdum: Global growth, inequality and poverty eradication in a carbon-constrained world", in: World Economic Review, 4, 43–62, http://wer.worldeconomicsasso ciation.org/files/WEA-WER-4-Woodward.pdf.

World Bank (2023): World Development Indicators: Tax revenue (% of GDP), https://databank.worldbank. org/home.

World Values Survey Association (2023): Findings and Insights, https://www.worldvaluessurvey.org/ WVSContents.jsp?CMSID=findings&CMSID=findings.

Wullweber, Joscha (2020): "Embedded Finance: The Shadow Banking System, Sovereign Power, and a New State-Market Hybridity", in: Journal of Cultural Economy, https://doi.org/10.1080/17530350.2020. 1741015.

WWF (2020): NATURE HIRES: How Nature-based Solutions can power a green jobs recovery, https://www. ilo.org/sites/default/files/wcmsp5/groups/public/@ed_emp/documents/publication/wcms_ 757823.pdf.

WWF (2023): Nature Restoration Fact Sheet 2, https://wwfeu.awsassets.panda.org/downloads/wwf_fact sheet_nature_restoration_soc_economic_web.pdf.

Yan, Wang; Qian, Ying (2022): In Debt Restructuring, is a 'Haircut' Better than 'Rescheduling?' New Research Shows They are Comparable Approaches, Boston University Global Development Policy Center, https://www.bu.edu/gdp/2022/09/21/in-debt-restructuring-is-a-haircut-better-than-rescheduling-new-research-shows-they-are-comparable-approaches/.

Yong, Ed (2023): An Immense World: How Animal Senses Reveal the Hidden Realms Around Us, New York: Vintage.

Zadeh, Lotfi A. (1965): "Fuzzy sets", in: Information and Control, 8/3, 338–353, https://doi.org/10.1016/S0019-9958(65)90241-X.

Zalasiewicz, Jan et al. (2010): "The New World of the Anthropocene", in: Environmental Science & Technology, 44 (7): 2228–2231, https://pubs.acs.org/doi/10.1021/es903118j.

Zeniewski, Peter; Molnar, Gergely; Hugues, Paul (2023): Europe's energy crisis: What factors drove the record fall in natural gas demand in 2022, International Energy Agency, https://www.iea.org/commentaries/europe-s-energy-crisis-what-factors-drove-the-record-fall-in-natural-gas-demand-in-2022.

Žižek, Slavoj (2022): Surplus-Enjoyment: A Guide For The Non-Perplexed, London: Bloomsbury Academic.

Zucker-Marques, Marina et al. (2023): Debt Relief by Multilateral Lenders: Why, How and How Much?, Debt Relief for a Green & Inclusive Recover, https://www.boell.de/sites/default/files/2023-09/drgr-report-2023-digitalversion-final.pdf.

Boxes

https://doi.org/10.1515/9783111421520-011

Tables

https://doi.org/10.1515/9783111421520-012

Figures

https://doi.org/10.1515/9783111421520-013

About the Author

Professor **Stefan Brunnhuber** is Chair of Psychology and Sustainability at Mittweida University of Applied Sciences. His research focuses on intersections between the life sciences and sustainability, in particular the psychology of the Anthropocene, behavioural finance, risk analysis and new forms of financial engineering. He has doctorates in both medicine and socioeconomics and holds more than a dozen international visiting professorships in the fields of medicine, finance and sustainability. Since 2010, he has served as medical director and chief medical officer at a German teaching hospital. He is board-certified in two medical specialisms (psychiatry, psychosomatics) and multiple sub-specialisms (pain management, addiction, naturopathy ao.). Alongside his work in academia and medicine, he also works as a political and corporate consultant. His positions and memberships (past and present) include: Vice Chair of the European Institute of Medicine; Senator of the European Academy of Sciences and Arts (EASA) (2015–2020); member of several international working groups for the EASA and EU Commission; founding member of Alma Mater Europaea; trustee of the World Academy of Art and Science (2015–present); full international member of the Club of Rome (2018–present); member of Friends of the Earth; member of the German Free Democratic Party (FDP) and its national economic forum (2020–present); member of the Lancet Commission (2021–2022); member of the German federal government's Sustainable Finance committee (2022–present). Professor Brunnhuber has over 500 publications and lectures to his name – including *Money and Sustainability* (2014), a co-authored report to the Club of Rome; *The Art of Transformation* (2nd ed. 2024); 'The Open Society – A Pledge for Freedom and Order' (2019, only available in German); *Financing Our Future* (2021); *Financing Our Anthropocene* (2023); 'Freedom and Coercion' (2023, only available in German); and *The Third Culture* (2024) – and has delivered several international lecture series on these topics.

He lives in Dresden, Germany, with his wife and two children. He enjoys yoga, Zen meditation, fasting, sports and gardening.

Contact: www.stefan-brunnhuber.de

https://doi.org/10.1515/9783111421520-014

Subject Index

https://doi.org/10.1515/9783111421520-015

Name Index

https://doi.org/10.1515/9783111421520-016

www.ingramcontent.com/pod-product-compliance
Lightning Source LLC
Chambersburg PA
CBHW080131270326
41926CB00021B/4429